Applied
Transport
Economics

Applied
Transport
Economics

Policy, Management & Decision Making

THIRD EDITION

STUART COLE

The Chartered Institute of
Logistics and Transport (UK)

**KOGAN
PAGE**

London and Sterling, VA

First published in Great Britain by Kogan Page Limited, 1987
Second edition 1998
Third edition 2005

Kogan Page Limited
120 Pentonville Road
London N1 9JN
United Kingdom
www.kogan-page.co.uk

Kogan Page US
22883 Quicksilver Drive
Sterling VA 20166-2012
USA

© Stuart Cole 1987, 1998, 2005

ISBN 0 7494 3964 5 (paperback)
    0 7494 4102 X (hardback)

British Library Cataloguing in Publication Data

A CIP record for this book is available from the British Library.

Library of Congress Cataloging-in-Publication Data

Cole, Stuart.
  Applied transport economics : policy, management and decision making / Stuart Cole.-- 3rd ed.
    p. cm.
  Includes bibliographical references and index.
  ISBN 0-7494-3964-5 (pbk.) -- ISBN 0-7494-4102-X (hardcover)
  1. Transporation. 2. Transportation and state. I. Title.
HE151.C7 2005
388--dc22   2005004336

Typeset by Saxon Graphics Ltd, Derby
Printed and bound in Great Britain by Creative Print and Design (Wales), Ebbw Vale

Contents

Contents

About the Author

Professor Stuart Cole has been Professor of Transport and Director of the Wales Transport Research Centre at the University of Glamorgan since March 2001. He was invited to be the first Director following three years as Visiting Professor of Transport.

He has been a Specialist Adviser on Transport at the House of Commons for 20 years, having advised at his first inquiry in 1984. Advising the Select Committee on Welsh Affairs has involved him in 12 inquiries since then. He was the adviser for 'Transport in Wales', published in December 2002, and is currently advising the Committee on its 'Railway Services in Wales' inquiry (2003–04).

Professor Cole is Cadeirydd (Chairman) of the Chartered Institute of Logistics and Transport Cymru/Wales (2002–04) and a member of the Institute's UK national council. His involvement with the Institute began as a member of the Chester and North Wales branch; he was a committee member of the Metropolitan (London) Section, and Chairman (1990–92), as well as a member of the UK Council. He is a past Chairman of the Institute of Highways and Transportation South Wales branch (2002–03); Chairman, PTI Cymru Steering Group, Welsh Assembly Government (2002–04); Chairman, Wales Transport Strategy Group (1999–) and a member of the Assembly Government's Welsh Transport Forum, chaired by the Minister of Economic Development and Transport (2001–).

He was recently asked to join the First Great Western Stakeholders Advisory Group representing travellers, business and academia. Its role is to provide a forum to discuss FGW plans and operations in South Wales and the West of England.

His recent research has included the 'Information needs of the independent traveller' report (published in May 2003 by the Welsh Assembly Government); he is the joint author of *Capitals United*, a report on rail services between the south of Wales and London (2003), published by the Institute of Welsh Affairs; creator of the 4 I's concept of information, interchange and investment as a basis for integration (a report for the British Tourist Authority); and has worked on the changes in the governance of transport post devolution and new approaches to public transport in rural areas. He prepared the Transport Appendix for the Cardiff 2008 European City of Culture bid. Professor Cole has also advised the Bwrdd Croeso

(Wales Tourist Board), and provided input into the National Assembly's inquiry into its 'Policy review of public transport'.

He has recently been involved in the use of GPS and demand responsive transport as a means of improving rural accessibility; an international project, funded by the EU and the NAfW, on ports and hinterlands – the economic impact, the modal shift and the infrastructure requirements; and the provision of yellow school buses. All have involved the use of economic appraisal techniques.

Professor Cole is a regular broadcaster on BBC radio and television and on S4C in both Welsh and English.

He was previously Director of Transport Research and Consultancy (TRaC) at the University of North London (now London Metropolitan University) with a personal professorial chair (1979–2001) and Transport Adviser to the English Tourist Board (1998–2000).

Professor Cole is the author of numerous articles and conference papers at a national and international level on transport economics and policy and was editor of the *Transport Economist* journal for eight years. His transport economics and policy research has covered public transport, rail and road economics, including rail and bus privatisation, the Channel Tunnel rail link, the policy structure of public transport operations, integrated transport policy and the transport issues facing the European Union. His research has been carried out in the European Union, Eastern Europe, North America, South America and Southern Africa in addition to Great Britain. He has been the director of several European Commission research projects into transport issues and policy both within the European Union and in central and eastern European states.

His experience in these fields extends over 30 years, from joining Cheshire County Council's Transportation Unit as economic adviser in 1974 following a career as an economist in the City, with an electricity board and with a major hotel and leisure company.

Acknowledgements

Opportunities to carry out transport research have taken me to Cymru/ Wales, England and Scotland, to most European Union member states (Ireland, Sweden, Netherlands, Germany, France, Italy, Portugal, Spain, Finland, Denmark) to central and eastern Europe (eg Lithuania, where a major project was undertaken); Estonia, Poland, Ukraine, Georgia, Czech Republic, Russia to the United States and Canada, to South America (Peru, Bolivia, Venezuela) and to southern Africa (South Africa, Zimbabwe, Zambia, Botswana, Swaziland). Funding has been awarded by the European Commission Interreg 3 and DG-TREN research programmes, Temps-Phare, the British Academy, the Chartered Institute of Logistics and Transport and commercial clients. Roles in government and parliamentary environments and for commercial groups enabled me to work directly in public policy. To all of these I am grateful for the research opportunities afforded to me.

The author is also grateful for the advice of and discussions with previous students, current students (upon whom some of the material has been 'tested') and colleagues in the transport industry on the content of the book – all were valuable. The responsibility for the final version however rests entirely with the author.

Many of my previous students on courses at North London and at Glamorgan have achieved senior positions in the industry or in government all over the world and have of course been presumed upon in many ways since then. Few professors see the world otherwise. I am most grateful to them and proud of their achievements; much satisfaction in polytechnic and university teaching derives from this.

There have been many fellow workers in the transport industry who kindly allowed me to draw on their material and in particular those who gave me their time to interview them and permission to copy graphs or illustrations used in this book, which enabled the material to be current and hopefully correct. However, any errors and omissions are entirely mine, due to not heeding advice given or misinterpreting the information.

I should like to thank the following organisations, companies and individuals, many in areas where increased competition has made information even more difficult to obtain than for the previous editions because of its commercially valuable nature; however, the information given was used directly or through a circumspect analysis of several sources to derive the data. Some people wished to remain anonymous (I don't believe they gave me too many secrets) but the others are:

Air Cardiff (Martin Evans, MD); ARUP (Stuart Watkins); British Tourist Authority (Dr David Quarmby); Cardiff Bus (David Brown, Peter Heath, Alan Kreppel); Cardiff International Airport (Jon Horne); Phil Goodwin; Institute of Welsh Affairs (Jon Osmond, Rhys David); Institution of Civil Engineers – Cymru Wales (Denys Morgan); National Assembly for Wales (Robin Shaw, Denzil Jones, Tony Parker); PROFIT European Commission project team; SONERAIL European Commission project team (Torben Holvad, Michael Hommers, Andrea Soehnchen); Strategic Rail Authority (Chris Austin); Tempus Phare European Commission projects (Arne Kullbjer, Ingrid Nyman); Transport for London (Peter Hendy, Elaine Seagriff); Arne Kullbjer; Arriva (Keith Weightman); BAA; British Airways plc; Bromley Borough Council (Gordon Hayward, Roger Perry); CBI; Clayton Jones; Commissariat Général du Plan, Paris; Confederation of Passenger Transport UK; Department for Transport (Tom Worsley); easyJet; European Bank for Reconstruction and Development (Philip Cornwell); European Commission Directorate General for Transport DG-TREN, Bruxelles/Brussels; Eurostar (UK); Eurotunnel; First Group (Moir Lockhead, Justin Davies); First Great Western (Alison Forster, Tom Stables, Chris Kinchin-Smith, Mike Carroll); HMSO (for reproduction permission); Ingrid Nyman; Lithuania Ministry of Transport; Michael Woods; Juliet Solomon; Ministerie van Verkeer en Waterstaat; NEI Netherlands Economic Institute, Rotterdam (Michael Gommers); NS Reizigers; Oxfordshire County Council (Roger Williams); Peter Morrel (Cranfield University); SNCF (Peter Mills); Stagecoach Holdings; Vilnius Gediminas Technical University (Prof. Ramunas Palsaitis, Dr Algirdas Valiulus); Virgin Atlantic Airways; Ymgyrch Diogelu Cymru Wledig/Campaign for the Protection of Rural Wales (Mervyn Williams).

My thanks also go to Professor Richard Neale, my head of department, for his support and encouragement in the preparation of this book, and to him and Professor Sir Adrian Webb for both establishing the Wales Transport Research Centre and supporting my direction of it. Also to my colleagues in WTRC, Sarah Kendall, Andrew Olden, EmmaJane Mantle and Christine Rivers, who have helped me in general to make the Centre a success and have encouraged this work; Dave Gould, whose ability to create presentations for me never ceases to amaze; and Delyth Willis, for so efficiently typing the new material and the amendments from the last edition. My thanks also to Helen Moss who edited the material so efficiently.

My final and greatest thanks go to my late mother, Gwennie Cole, and to my father, David Cole, who have always provided unlimited support and encouragement for my career, broadcasting, writing and this book.

Introduction

The earlier editions proved popular and the best of their characteristics have been retained but the third edition has been largely rewritten to reflect the many changes in the transport market and in the industry since the publication of the second edition. However, it retains its basic purpose. Its approach is to introduce the reader to economic theory through the *application* of those concepts. It is designed for managers, policy makers and those economists who wish to see the use of economic tools in providing practical solutions, and students of transport, economics, business, management, public policy and business strategy.

The previous editions have been welcomed for providing an approach that does not dwell extensively on theoretical aspects; rather it uses them to underpin decision making. All have found the example-led approach to transport economics using the minimum of economic theory and jargon gave them an understanding of the subject matter in a policy or management context.

This is intended to give managers and policy makers an insight into transport economics, into the use of a range of techniques in decision making and into the rationale behind such decisions, for example in fares policies or transport investment.

The approach in this book is to begin with the practical managerial issue, look at examples and then where necessary derive the principles and theoretical concepts in varying degrees of depth, thus making it easier to understand those concepts and their application. The case study approach which proved so popular in the first and second editions has been extended in this third edition.

In Part 1 on transport dynamics, the significant changes brought by low cost airlines are considered, with the consistent problem of meeting peak demand for a product that cannot be stored.

These chapters bring up to date case studies and data that explain economic concepts such as supply and demand, elasticity, cost levels and structures, pricing policy and market segmentation and forecasting within the business context.

Part 2 of the book applies economic concepts to the public sector – the evaluation of expenditure by public sector bodies on transport infrastructure or on revenue support. It considers (in Chapters 9 and 10) the techniques and methods of valuing the elements when carrying out economic

1

appraisal. The trend towards investment partnerships between the public and private sectors and the economic and financial issues that arise are dealt with in Chapter 11, based on the discussion of the techniques in Chapter 9.

Two contrasting aspects of transport policy – integrated transport and free competition and their impacts in different areas – are discussed in Chapters 12 and 13 together with the use of market forces in public policy (eg cross elasticity and price discrimination).

Part 3 looks at the role of transport in urban development and in economic activity.

The book also has a wide geographical range and uses the author's experience in applying economic techniques in the older European Union member states and in those states that have moved from the planned economy of the Soviet Union to the market led economies of the 'West'. It also uses experiences drawn from Africa, South America, Canada and the United States.

Each chapter is referenced to enable the reader to follow up the topic in more depth.

Part 1: Transport Market Dynamics

CHAPTER 1

Market Demand

TRANSPORT AS A DERIVED DEMAND

Transport is a service rarely in demand for its own characteristics. Demand for public transport, road freight facilities or airline services is usually derived from some other function. A company producing clothes or food sees transport as a means of moving its products from factory or warehouse to the retail store. As the demand for products increases so the demand for transport facilities will increase.

As retail companies, such as Sainsbury, Carrefour and Marks & Spencer increase their number of stores, they increase the number of vehicles operated on their behalf, by contractors such as BOC Transmark and Hay's or through in-house fleets. A large national public house chain such as JD Wetherspoon delivers beer to its pubs and off-licence outlets; the number of miles operated and the number of journeys per day made by each delivery vehicle will depend on the demand pattern. At Christmas time or at major sporting events or during prolonged hot weather there may be two or three loads per day in place of the usual one. The Post Office hire additional vehicles to cope with the Christmas mail peak. TPG, the UK/Netherlands mail express and logistics company (TPG, 2003), indicates the seasonal experience where business is affected by public holidays and summer/year end plant closures (lower demand for the logistics division) and the distribution of Christmas cards and parcels during December (high demand for the mail division). In all these cases, the demand level for transport (measured in numbers of vehicles or vehicle miles) is related directly to the demand level for the product or service.

One objective of a transport operator (or in-house transport fleet) is to establish a demand pattern for its service. It also has to relate its prices to the perception and consequent demand of its customers, and derive a pricing policy and a development or operating strategy for the transport operation which will optimise the use of the fleet. This applies equally to National Express coaches, the Stagecoach bus group, Avis, Hertz, British train operating companies, SNCF, English, Welsh and Scottish Railways, TDG, Wincanton, Ryanair, BMI, British Airways, KLM, P & O cruise ships, Evergreen or Hapag Lloyd.

There are some markets where transport itself is the product demanded. The Venice Simplon Orient Express (VSOE, 2003) is a luxury train operating between London and Venice. Passengers do not use it simply to make the journey from London to Venice – it is more convenient, quicker and cheaper to travel by air (VSOE £2540; BA £105, business class £600). The Express is sold as a travel experience. The British train (British Pullman or Northern Belle) may also be used for excursions involving, for £170 in 2003, lunch of five courses with wine and a return trip in a luxurious moving restaurant.

A sea cruise is a close parallel to this. Luxury ships which were built to serve regular runs to Australia or to New York have been replaced by aircraft with a very high standard of comfort in business class or first class cabins. The cruise is a floating hotel and leisure centre with meals, entertainment, sunbathing and sports, as well as a form of transport to ports *en route*. Passengers on P & O's (2004) *Oriana* pay from £1500 to £9000 to cruise the Mediterranean, the Atlantic or North and South America, but the cruise and the ship's facilities are their reason for travelling in this manner. Similarly, travelling from London to New York by the *QE2* and (previously) Concorde (£3000) compares favourably in price terms with the return Concorde price (£7400), but the journey takes five days rather than four hours by Concorde. BA's Concorde operations ceased in 2003.

Two-hour Concorde final days' 'supersonic experience' flights around the Bay of Biscay (£800), the Palace of India Maharajas steam-hauled train, the Blue Train (South Africa), the Great South Pacific Express (Australia), the Canadian/the Rocky Mountaineer, the privately owned steam railways in Britain such as the Severn Valley Limited and the Great Little Trains of Wales narrow-gauge railways are other examples where there is no reason for travel other than the enjoyment of the journey itself. Here, transport is the end product.

FACTORS DETERMINING DEMAND

1. Physical characteristics

In the case of commodities, the choice of mode will depend largely on the physical characteristics of the goods. High cost, low volume goods are usually moved by air. Electronic component parts for machinery whose down time, particularly in 'just-in-time' contexts, has a high loss-of-output cost. Clothing (especially fashion goods), and food with short shelf life (eg fruits) will often be air freighted. Gold or diamonds will be air freighted in chartered aircraft which can provide the security level required, while urgent medical supplies are also likely to be moved by private jet or military aircraft. All these goods require urgent and guaranteed delivery internationally or internally. Companies (eg TPG, TNT, UPS) provide services involving the collection, storage, sorting, transport and distribution within 'specific timeframes' enhanced by data/document management systems (TPG, 2003). Low value goods (eg coal, cotton, steel) will be moved by rail and heavy tonnage ships. US railroads (eg Burlington Northern) have a large part of their business in moving such goods.

2. Price

The lower the price, the more people are likely to demand the transport service offered. That is generally true of transport as it is of most other products, with the exception of some exclusive goods and services. In a large urban area like London, the size of the passenger transport market will be determined by price. More trips will be made when fares and petrol prices are low than when prices are high.

The level of transport costs will also be an element in determining factory location. If transport costs are low compared with other costs, a company will be able to take advantage of lower land costs away from its large urban markets; thus more tonne miles are operated. The decision by Courage plc to close two central London and two other breweries and locate a 'megabrewery' near Reading was in part due to the lower land and production costs and easy access via the M4/M25 to its south-east England market, contributing to lower transport costs.

The reduction in air fares following Laker Airways' Skytrain service in the late 1970s led ultimately to lower fares, price competition and continued high levels of traffic on many routes. People who had never considered air travel at 'conventional' fares have been attracted by low cost services provided by such airlines as Virgin, easyJet, Ryanair, bmibaby, Go, Buzz and excel.

3. Relative prices charged by different modes or different operators

This transfer of business between modes or companies in passenger transport is determined to a large extent by the relative levels of fares on rail, coach, bus and air services, and the perceived costs of car travel (ie petrol prices and parking charges).

In the North American air travel market low fare operators (eg South West Airlines, arguably the first 'low cost' airline), and new companies (eg Jet Blue, Spirit America West) have attracted entirely new passengers or those who previously flew at higher prices (Field, 2003). For those passengers the inhibitors (such as Saturday night away) have also been removed giving more flexibility of travel. In Europe, easyJet and Ryanair still dominate the market. This has led to significant rises in demand (2002) for low cost airline services (a rise of 10 per cent in 2002 and representing 23 per cent of domestic capacity) and falls in passenger traffic

(RPK) of the 'continental' United States airlines: American – 15.3 per cent; United – 13.8 per cent; US Airways – 15.8 per cent; Continental – 6.3 per cent. Buzz and Go have been taken over and bmibaby has emerged as a fast growing airline. The overall European market has responded to low cost operators through own price elasticity (new passengers) or cross-price elasticity (passengers attracted from competitor airlines) leading to increased sales. Transatlantic fares have also fallen but other factors (eg international conflicts) have driven the operators' desire to attract passengers. Virgin Atlantic, British Airways, United Airlines, American Airlines and Asian airlines (eg Air India) have all introduced special deals and lower fares, which have attracted new travellers, but more are from Europe to the USA than the reverse.

Table 1.1 *Traffic growth: low cost airlines 2001–02*

Operator	RPK/M Change (+) %
USA:	
Jet Blue	226
West Jet	54
Atlantic Coast	49
Sky West	41
Spirit	20
European:	
Ryanair	45
Go	33
easyJet	25

Source: Airline Business, September 2002
PRK/M: revenue per passenger kilometre/mile

In freight transport the effects of different prices are confidential to the haulier and client. However, it is clear that given the same quality of service between, say, three national hauliers, the company with the lowest price is likely to get the contract.

4. Passenger income

Overall income available for travel and other consumer/business expenditure is linked to growth in gross domestic product (GDP), representing an income elasticity effect (see Chapter 2).

As income increases so the amount of travelling for both business and leisure (either of trips or number of miles) will increase. This reflects a higher income household or individual having more disposable income and increasingly likely to travel further on a summer holiday, make more and longer evening and weekend leisure trips, and take an additional winter holiday. This traveller is also likely to travel as part of a job particularly with multinational, City financial and legal organisations.

5. Speed of service

This is often analysed in qualitative terms for passenger traffic. Business people travel to New York in seven hours by Boeing 747 rather than four days because the firm or the person considers his/her time to be valuable. The development of new high speed trains in Europe (eg the Paris–Lyon Train à Grande Vitesse (TGV) service since 1984 and the London–Paris Eurostar since 1996) has led in both cases to a significant loss of airline patronage to the rail service (a reduction of 40% in passenger loadings in 1998 between Paris and London from a forecast 450,000 passengers in 1998 to 250,000 per annum.

The journey time from Paris to Lyon by train is 2 hours compared with 3 hours by air (centre to centre), while the Eurostar (ES 2003) has achieved 3 hours from London to Paris (2¼ hours with the high speed Channel Tunnel Rail Link). The air journey (centre to centre) with 2-hour check-in times is 4 hours. The train service has fewer hassle factors for business travellers (see Chapter 4) which contributes to SNCF's objective of 'offering customers rail safety, speed, comfort and steadiness' (SNCF 2002).

In operational cost terms, if a freight or passenger road vehicle can travel from London to Birmingham in three hours one way by motorway instead of six hours on a single carriageway road, then the number of journeys per 24 hours that the vehicle can make is four instead of two. Its productivity is increased and its capital cost per tonne mile reduced, with consequent reductions in operating costs and the tariff charged to customers. The lower price will encourage greater use by customers and the increased productivity will improve vehicle availability to meet the increased demand without the need to purchase additional vehicles.

6. Quality of service

(a) Frequency

The departure times or arrival times must be those which the customer requires. To be successful, commuter coaches must arrive at the central business district by 09.00 and depart after 17.30. To encourage long term growth there must also be departures during the day for those leaving work early, and in the evening for those staying on late, working or for entertainment reasons. A high frequency, rapid transit system (eg the Piccadilly line on London's underground); frequent, regular clock face, departures such as the 15 minute service on Stagecoach Oxford's Tube, which has maintained its passenger loadings since 1997, or the Nederlandse

Spoorwegen (NS) frequent direct services to most Dutch stations (including Amsterdam Centraal every 10–15 minutes) from Schipol Airport are examples.

(b) Standard of service

The quality of service provided has been a key marketing strategy of, for example, railways in northern Europe. French Railways have a reputation for time keeping enhanced by reliability and speed of the Train à Grande Vitesse (TGV) services. The strategic objective of train operating companies is focused on the principal competition in the market place – the motor car and the airline.

The competition between car and train is clearly illustrated on the western transport corridor from London. First Great Western (operating an intercity franchise) has identified their principal competitor as the private car, and it is from that market sector that growth will come.

The Great Western Trains franchise plan to have more trains above the Passenger Service Requirement, to increase the commitment to certain locations, to refurbish HST's as new, to provide a secure environment (in particular car parks at parkway stations), to provide integrated transport links with buses, cars, motorail and bicycles and to look at new trains 'and above all customer service excellence' was set out in 1997 and most have been achieved or are well advanced (Carroll, 1997).

Train company mission statements indicate a desire to make themselves 'first choice' through 'accurate, easily obtainable, up to date information; ease of purchase of the correct ticket; fast frequent direct on-time trains; platform information; clean, comfortable, enjoyable stations and trains and safety and security' – desires not dissimilar to those of airlines. The extent to which these changes are sufficient to stimulate demand varies according to investment levels. This level of quality will attract the traveller (including the high yield business traveller) from car or air transport.

Some of the world's major airlines believe an important way to enhance market share is to provide integrated service timings and ticketing resulting in the establishment of alliances. KLM and Northwest Airlines established a worldwide alliance in 1986 to link their strengths: KLM in Europe and to/from Europe and transatlantic; Northwest in transatlantic, internal US and Pacific (including the Japanese market). In similar markets the Star alliance, One World and Sky Team have the objective of increasing market share, and American Airlines are putting their case (1998). The impact can be significant in terms of the extension of the network. To be a global operator an airline now needs to have either by itself or more likely in an alliance a significant presence (ie 15% of market share) in four out of seven major markets in the world – Europe, TransAtlantic; United States Internal, Europe to South East Asia, internal South East Asia and TransPacific (Maynard 1992).

Table 1.2 *Airline alliances*

Airline/alliance	Passengers	Areas of significant operation						
		E	NA	TA	A	P	SEA	SM
One World:								
Air Lingus	6.3	*		*				
American	80.7		*	*				
British	40.0	*		*	*			
Finland	7.5							
Iberia	24.9	*		*				*
Lan Chile	5.2							*
Qantas	<u>22.1</u>					*	*	
Total	<u>187.0</u>							
World share	11.5%							
Star Alliance:								
Air Canada	18.8		*	*		*		
Air New Zealand	20.2					*	*	
ANA	38.4					*		
Austrian	4.9	*						
bmi	6.7	*						
Lufthansa	39.7	*		*			*	
Mexicana	8.5							*
SAS	23.1	*		*			*	
Singapore	14.7					*	*	
Thai	18.3					*	*	
United	75.4		*	*		*		
Varig	<u>10.5</u>							
Total	<u>279.0</u>							
World share	17.2%							
Sky Team:								
Aero Mexico	9.2							*
Air France	43.3	*		*				
Alitalia	25.0	*		*				
CSA (Czech)	2.9	*						
Delta	104.5		*	*		*		
Korean	<u>22.1</u>					*	*	
Total	<u>207.0</u>							
World share	12.8%							
Wings:								
KLM	16.0	*		*	*			
Northwest	<u>54.1</u>		*	*			*	
Total	<u>70.0</u>							
World share	4.3%							

Key: E Europe; NA North America; TA Transatlantic; A between Europe/North America and South East Asia; P Transpacific; SEA Southeast Asia internal; SM between Europe and South America.

Source: Airline Business, July 2002 (AB, 2002): ICAO traffic results 2000/01.
The objective of most alliances has been to maximise their position in six primary market areas (Maynard, 1992). The alliances above have achieved that in four or five. Thus, if countries served is a standard of service criterion, One World is ahead of Star (the largest in passenger numbers) in its provision of a global network (AB, July 2002). Wings, although the smallest alliance, provides the widest range of well used routes through a simple two-airline partnership.

11

Comfort

In the new millennium the standards of living of the majority must be reflected by passenger carriers if they are to continue to attract a demand for their services.

Reliability

A frequent reason for loss of patronage by both passenger and freight carriers lies in the failure to deliver goods on time or to get passengers to their destination or to a connecting service at the scheduled time. One factor put forward by SNCF (French Railways) for the high patronage levels on their trains is their good timekeeping.

Safety

This is always a concern of passengers, government authorities and most operators. The adverse publicity attached to coach or rail accidents reduces demand for the particular mode, especially in the short term. United States owned companies in many parts of the world have reduced executive travel, because of their perception of the terrorist threat and Middle Eastern instability.

The customer's dilemma

The quality of service in terms of all these factors – frequency, regularity, convenience, standard of service, comfort, reliability and safety – will act as a stimulus to demand if the quality is good and seen by the customer to give value for money. Demand is dependent on the operation of each of these factors and the operator company has to consider continually (Webster and Bly, 1980) what effect a change in price, income or quality will have on the demand for its services.

Meanwhile, the customer will often make a choice between price and quality in transport as s/he does in purchasing any other consumer good. A business traveller may decide that first class rail travel is worth the very large cost increase over a second class discount priced ticket. Similarly, the business class air passenger has a choice of services with better in-flight catering, while a tourist class passenger has restrictions on travel times. The business traveller needs flexibility and a work-like atmosphere on board for which companies may be prepared to pay a substantially higher cost.

A downturn in premium class passengers on British Airways (2003) is a consequence of several factors – global economic weakness, political instability, terrorism and downtrading to economy class or transfer to lower priced seats on the 'no frills' carriers such as easyJet and Ryanair.

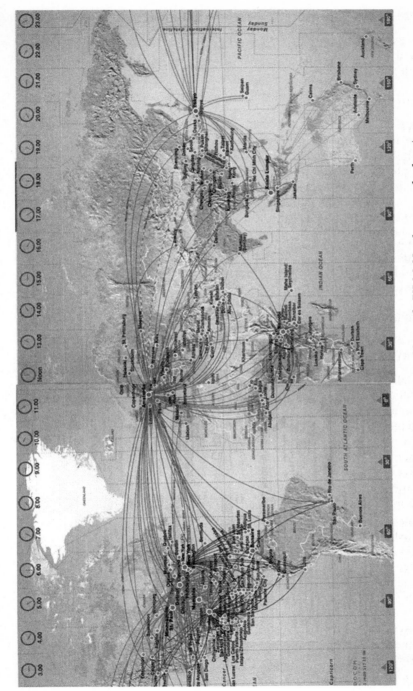

Figure 1.1 *Global Alliance Route Network (KLM, Northwest and others)*
Source: KLM

The very low advance fares and a perception of generally low prices led to ticket promotions during bank/school holiday periods by the 'conventional' airlines – KLM, Lufthansa, BA and others.

However demand is down in general (2003) and even 'low cost' airlines are being affected, with losses being made despite continual growth. Thus even low prices cannot stimulate demand to its pre-2000 level on some major routes.

A similar situation faces Eurostar trains (London–Paris/Brussels). Forecasts of 9.0 million passengers in 2003 are well above actual performance of 6.0 million (down from 6.6 million in 2002). Causes include competition from the low cost airlines between Paris and Luton/Stansted; and the link to economic slowdown (income elasticity) effects.

The market outside London has the characteristics of the customer's dilemma between price and quality. However, price and journey time from northwest England to Paris are both lower by air than by train. One journey time impact that ought to help Eurostar is check-in time for boarding, but this remains at 30 minutes compared with 5 minutes on international trains between those EU member states in the Shengen league.

Time/price comparisons: coach/air/train/car

The customer might also compare time and price in coming to a decision, as shown in Table 1.3, for a journey from London to Paris. Each customer will trade off time against cost and if there is a greater emphasis on cost, more

Table 1.3 *London (central) to Paris (central) 2003[1]*

Mode		Fares Return (£) Full[2]	Discount[3]	Frequency (daily M–F)	Journey times (hours)
Coach (National Express)		59	32	2	10.0
Rail (Eurostar)	1st	520	159	16	3.6
	2nd	318	59		
Air BA (LHR)	Business	530		6	4.0
	Tourist	372	95		
Air easyJet (LLU)		102	25–77	5	5.0

Source: Author's analysis of fare tables (BA, Eurostar, easyJet, National Express) and estimated timings.

Notes:

1. London Charing Cross to Paris Chatelot Les Halles, by specified mode and local travel to/from city centre.
2. Fully flexible for change of date, time, cancellation.
3. Lowest off-peak discount fares with restrictions booked up to one month before travel, but excluding cardholder discounts and special offers. Fares available May 2003. Note early booking fares of under £1 are offered by some low cost airlines.

people will travel by coach or car if available; while those travellers to whom time is important will choose the train or plane. The number of people likely to switch modes can be measured through demand elasticity (see Chapter 2).

The customer therefore compares one operator's fares with those of competing operators. In addition, there is competition from the private car where the difference between actual and perceived cost is important. The actual cost of running an average family saloon is estimated by the AA to be 33.4 pence per mile for a 1600 cc family saloon (2003). This includes depreciation, capital (and interest) repayments, servicing, tyres, oil, repairs, petrol (at £0.80 per litre) and parking. The perceived cost may be as low as 7 pence per mile and includes only petrol and possibly parking – those costs which the user relates directly to one specific journey. If two or more people travel together the perceived cost is even less.

Time valuation

The operator is able to reduce journey time with vehicles travelling at higher average speeds and reduced stops. Many long-distance motorway/autoroute-based coach services (eg National Express) provide on-board toilets and a snack service, thus eliminating the need for one or more 'natural breaks'. Direct services reduce the number of scheduled pick-up points *en route*. The passenger may, however, take convenience into account in deciding between plane, train, coach and car. The valuation of time is considered in detail as an element in road construction investment appraisal, but both leisure time and work time have a value either in opportunity cost terms or in marginal product terms. The consideration is the alternative use of the time involved and whether its value is great enough to justify the extra travel cost.

However, the entry of low cost airlines into the market has provided a competitor in terms of both price and journey time to all other modes. The central origin and destination points were selected as an 'average' travel point. For people living near appropriate airports the fare by air might be as low as £20 plus £20 tax with no other large travel cost. Coach fares are no longer necessarily the cheapest but have considerably longer journey time, although the advance booking requirements by low cost airlines to achieve the lowest fare can make coach prices competitive on a 'turn up and go' basis.

Even within the fare range of one operator (Eurostar) there are significant fares differences (see Table 4.2). This is also typical of airline pricing policies that make even more flexible fare ranges possible, through internet booking.

CASE STUDY 1: URBAN BUS OPERATIONS
Factors determining demand – urban municipal operator

1. Restructuring routes to provide higher frequency services along primary routes radiating from a city centre. This may result in some loss

of patronage from adjacent routes but traffic generation has outweighed this. A sense frequency of under 10 minutes results in passengers not requiring a timetable as the average waiting time is under 5 minutes.

2. Simplifying fees structures using zonal fares with no variation. Fare levels and therefore price elasticity appear to have little effect (LT 1993, 1997). This may reflect the low proportion of traveller's income represented by the fare in absolute terms.
3. Marketing – often reflecting a simple network and high frequency. This suggests a high service elasticity impact.
4. New vehicles with low floors guaranteed on these routes and advertised as such – service elasticity.
5. Reliability – quality of service/regular clock-face timetable/staff training as elements of service elasticity.
6. Concessionary fares (eg free travel for over 60s, students, disabled) may increase demand on a one-off basis following their introduction. This suggests an own price elasticity or cross-price elasticity effect from the motor car. However, this revenue increase has also provided a business case for higher frequency and newer vehicles. This is a combination of price and service elasticity.

Table 1.4 *Demand growth – urban operators: percentage change over previous years*

| Year | Passenger growth % | |
	Concessionary fares	Other (eg services factors)
2002/03	2.0	4.7
2003/04	0.0	5.0

Source: National Assembly for Wales

The national concessionary fares scheme had increased bus journeys across Wales by 5% from 104 million to 109 million per annum.

Table 1.5 *Peak vehicle requirement – Cardiff*

Vehicles	Morning	Evening
200	08.00–09.00	15.00–18.00
170	09.00–15.00	18.00+

Source: Cardiff Bus

The experience shown in the Bradford Study (Figure 1.5, Table 1.8) might illustrate: a different market between the two cities; and a shift in demand patterns with more off-peak travel for shopping, business and leisure, and the concessionary fares effect. Some companies currently make use of high capacity vehicles for a school journey followed by a peak-scheduled journey, affecting the peak vehicle requirement (PVR) by 25–30 buses. In this analysis, without efficient interworking of such vehicles the Cardiff figure could be a 230 PVR, putting it nearer to the Bradford position.

DEMAND PATTERNS NOT INFLUENCED BY OPERATORS

1. Peak demand

The peak in transport operating terms is the period of maximum demand and affects freight operators and passenger carriers alike. However, more data are freely available on passenger movement, so the examples here are largely taken from that sector of the industry.

(a) Time of day

The morning journey-to-work peak is related to the starting times of factories (07.30–08.30), schools (09.00), and offices or shops (08.30–09.30). The problem is slightly alleviated in towns with industrial and commercial activity, as one vehicle can make two peak journeys with high load factors. Large commercial centres (eg London, New York) will often have trains, underground trains or buses which only operate on peak load service.

(b) Day of the week

There is a summer weekend leisure peak on roads and on public passenger transport services. The pricing of most European main line discount tickets reflects their peak: for example, a Friday 'saver' ticket from London to Bath costs £40 compared with £33 on other days, but is not available on departures between 16.00 and 18.00, when the full second class fare of £80 applies (May 2003). There is also a peak period on the M4 out of London on Fridays between 15.00 and 19.00. Paris suffers the same problem with Friday outbound traffic, particularly to the south and west, setting off for *le weekend* from 14.30 onwards. The returning traffic creates problems on Sunday evening. Bank holidays present an added one day peak flow, particularly on roads, and are worsened by good weather. In towns serving rural areas (eg Marlborough, Groningen) traffic congestion often occurs on market days when they accommodate the market and its associated freight traffic.

(c) Seasonal peak

The seasonal peak results from a concentration of summer holiday traffic, with accentuates the weekend traffic flows on roads and from airports with a high percentage of package holiday traffic. Airlines serving the package tour market have average daily utilisation rates (CAA, 2002) for an Airbus 320 of 10.8 hours (Air 2000) but increasing to 12.6 hours for a Boeing 747–400 on transatlantic routes. This compares with a scheduled operations figure of 6.3 hours (BA) in the summer months to cover the demand on routes to Spain, Italy and Greece. Aircraft departures from Alicante to Luton and Manchester leaving from 04.00 hours are indicators of the summer demand pattern and aircraft utilisation rates. Their winter flight programme is considerably less frequent.

Coach operators have a similar weekend peak. For example, the coach departures from Victoria Coach Station, one of Britain's major hubs, have substantial increases in passenger throughput on Friday and Saturday and the major coach operator National Express's pricing policy reflects this. For example, fares from London to Manchester (May 2003) are £30 on Friday and Saturday but £25 on other days. This peak cannot be influenced by the coach operators and is serviced mainly through hired coaches.

This seasonal peak in northern Europe is at its highest point from late July through to the end of August, and corresponds with school holidays. Peaks in winter skiing holidays occur in January but are often moves to fill in the transport operators' period of previously low demand. Peak demand for passenger transport also builds up around the Christmas holidays. Operators may try to influence these demand patterns, through the use of off peak discounts (see below).

2. Changes in social habits

Leisure time has increased as a result of shorter working hours, increased unemployment and early retirement and in consequence, more leisure journeys are being made. The changed pattern of leisure journeys is outside the control of passenger transport operators.

The traditional British holiday destinations have been exchanged by many travellers for Mediterranean holidays, which has led to an increase in the demand for aircraft and airport accommodation. The increase in car ownership has changed social habits. It is now possible for people to make short visits and to travel to places not served by public transport. The development of out-of-town shopping centres and sports complexes has led to a demand for roads and car parks and a reduction in the demand for public transport for evening leisure travel. The 1950s pattern of social visits at weekends and evening trips to theatre, cinema and bingo has been largely replaced by a wider variety of car-based journeys. Demand for cinema seats has been superseded by television thus reducing demand for evening bus and train services, although in London there are still high load factors on central area route sections until late evening. The reluctance of car drivers to drink and drive has been exploited by operators such as Yellow Buses, Bournemouth (YB, 1984) and Gemeentevervoerbedrijf (GVB) Amsterdam and Transport for London (TfL) night bus network in campaigns such as 'sensible drinking can make you go yellow' – a map showing pubs and winebars together with bus routes passing their doors.

3. Changes in competitors' services or prices

The improvement in alternative services, particularly at a reduced price, may lead to changes in demand for a particular operator's services. Reduced prices by Laker Airways in the late 1970s led to some British Airways passengers transferring in the short term to Laker services. However, more recent changes in demand for European air travel have been influenced by the low cost airlines such as easyJet, Ryanair, Germanwings, bmibaby and excel. The 'conventional' airlines such as BA, KLM and British Midland established Go (sold via a management buyout to easyJet (Cassani and Kemp, 2003), Buzz (now part of easyJet) and bmibaby respectively in order to match the competitors' low fares. However, competition rules will encourage new entrants and the expansion of existing low cost operators at new hubs (eg Ryanair to Milan-Berganio; bmibaby to Cardiff). Changes in service quality such as punctuality, improved seating and at-seat films are now becoming part of the low cost airlines' branding strategy. Although price is the paramount selection criterion by passengers and has proved a successful strategy, greater competition is leading some brands towards a middle market image where airlines 'need to give more' (Bierwirth, 2003). In addition, the older established airlines are introducing low fares on their own routes with less limiting inhibitors such as an overnight Saturday stop (eg minimum of two nights away) (Pilling, 2003).

4. Changes in population distribution

Over the last 40 years, there has been a trend towards the construction of out-of-town housing and shopping developments, reflecting an expanding population and a need to replace older housing stock.

The construction of new housing estates on the edge of a town provides a bus or rail operator intending to serve such an area with two choices. It can operate services at a loss when a few houses are built in the hope that patronage will build up as the housing estate grows. Alternatively, the operator can wait for the estate to be complete, but by that time house owners will have purchased cars or arranged car sharing and the market is lost or difficult to retrieve. The desire for new housing in less crowded conditions is growing and increased car ownership in such estates cannot be influenced by the operator. Government intervention in the market place has then to be evaluated using forecasting techniques and socioeconomic cost benefit techniques described later (see Chapter 8, 9 and 10).

The changes in population may also be regional: from rural into urban areas and from the north and west of Britain into the more prosperous south. The decline in population means reduced demand for services in those areas and thus reduced supply unless government subsidy is forthcoming.

Operator attempts to influence demand

In most cases the causes of the changes in demand cannot in themselves be affected by the operator, but the transport company can try to influence the effect on its own operations or finances. There are two ways in which this can be done:

1. Price changes to encourage new travellers or to attract travellers away from other operators. The objectives of all operators are to maximise revenue and to compete more effectively in the whole travel market. In many transport areas the peak problem and its associated costs can also be influenced by pricing policy (see Chapter 3).
2. Improvements in the quality of service in terms of:
   - frequency – to gain more passengers by increasing convenience;
   - reliability – to help passengers and encourage regular traffic;
   - comfort – to match the quality of vehicle seating and cleanliness with the home environment;
   - feeder lines to extend the service area;
   - speed increases, for instance through electrification of railway lines or high speed train services;
   - regular interval clock face departure times to provide an easily remembered timetable. This has been exploited by, for example, the Stagecoach Oxford Tube coach service, and First Great Western: Bristol to London   ex Paddington – on the hour/half hour
   ex Bristol – on the hour/ half hour.

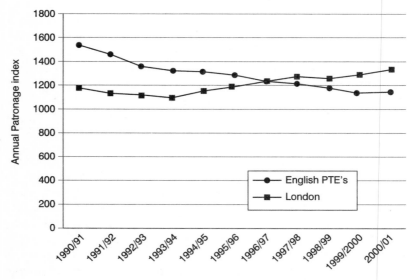

Figure 1.2 *Bus patronage 1990–2000*

Source: House of Commons HC 828, The Bus Industry 2001–2002, London

On some local London services the service interval varies and can lose passengers to more frequent and regular Underground competing services.

PEAK DEMAND

Why the peak problem is particularly bad in transport

There are various reasons why the problem in transport is particularly bad.

1. The transport product cannot be stored; it must be supplied when required and consumed immediately. Therefore, if a bus, train or plane has spare capacity when it leaves, this cannot be used later for the *same* journey. A similar problem occurs in freight transport.

2. Peak demand occurs on the London underground and mainline train commuter services into and out of major cities (from St Petersburg, Madrid and Johannesburg to Lima) from Monday to Friday. It is often the case that only ten loaded train journeys per week in total (five into the central business district and five out) are made by a commuter train set. To achieve a frequency which copes with demand, a far greater number of peak trains or buses is required compared with other times. In consequence there is over-supply in off peak. Operating companies servicing large cities have up to 60 per cent of their rolling stock in sidings or garages over a weekend and during the day or evening. The London underground or Paris Metro could have a similar problem, but the central area demand justifies a higher off peak frequency on most lines on cost/revenue criteria. Costs of depreciation, tunnel and track maintenance and some staff are not eliminated, and if variable costs are exceeded by revenue the service is justified. This same cost/revenue relationship does not often exist on mainline commuter railways except where terminals are in the very centre and where high frequency operations exist within the central area.

3. Transport has a derived demand, whose patterns are determined by the pattern of activities with which the demand is associated. For example, the journey-to-work peak results from working hours being mostly from 07.30–16.30 or 09.00–17.00, resulting in a peak at the start and end of the working day (Monday-Friday). In the case of holiday traffic, the peak demand for aircraft and terminal space for travellers to, for example, Greece and the peak demand for coach seats, additional trains and road space to southern France or Cornwall from major urban centres lasts from June to September with an excessive peak on August weekends.

   Freight transport operators face a peak demand for beer deliveries (summer and Christmas) and ice cream (summer) which results in fleets with reduced utilisation rates in the off peak. The Post Office avoids this by hiring vehicles to meet the Christmas peak from mid-December. There are daily peaks for retail outlets such as Marks & Spencer and Tesco, which require deliveries to stores by 07.00 hours; milk deliveries have an early morning peak, as do newspapers. The specialist parcel carries, eg TNT/TPG, also face an overnight demand peak at operating hubs with a 2200–0600 operating peak for equipment and trucks.

4. There is a cost implication – if, for example, a vehicle or train is used all day, costs are spread over 18 hours. With a peak-period-only operation, the costs must be covered in that period, for example four hours or two fare-earning journeys. The same principle applies to seasonal peaks. Peak services can therefore be loss making if the price charged is not enough to cover the additional costs. On a marginal basis, off peak operations may be more profitable, although demand in terms of passenger miles per vehicle per train/bus is less.

5. The sequential nature of vehicle running (an example of indivisibility of supply) leads in the morning to full 'into-town' vehicles which are nearly empty on return journeys towards the suburbs. The difference is often only one of scale from outbound buses (whether Chester or Dresden), trams (in Vienna or Amsterdam) to northbound trains from King's Cross Station, London, following high load factor inbound journeys. The reverse is true in the evening. Buses or trains may make only one peak trip in the morning with a high load factor, but some may make two, thus spreading the peak capacity and reducing the total capacity requirements. The indivisibility of supply resulting from track capacity, vehicle size and train size makes the problem more difficult.

Examples of the peak problem in practice

Commuter service operation in London

A typical electric commuter train operated by the West Anglia Great Northern (London) or SNCF/RATP (Paris) would make only one high yield peak journey during the morning and might spend the rest of the day operating low load factor services, or be out of service until the evening peak when it would make a high load factor outbound journey. On its return morning journey out of the central area terminus it might run empty to the depot.

Travel patterns on London Underground show peak (LT, 2002) demand to be three times that at midday when an average of 70 per cent of peak trains operate.

Underground travel increases sharply during weekday peak times, falling to much lower levels during the off-peak. Bus trips and troughs are less pronounced. Weekend travel patterns show a more even distribution of trips during the principal shopping hours.

Table 1.6 *People entering central London during the morning peak,*
07.00–10.00 (2001)

	Number (thousands)	%
All modes	1094	100
National Rail total	467	42.6
Transfers to LUL/DUL	204	18.6
LUL and DLR only[1]	379	34.6
Bus	81	7.4
Coach/minibus[2]	10	0.9
Private car	122	11.2
Taxi[3]	7	0.6
Motor cycle	16	1.5
Pedal cycle	12	1.2
Units:		
Average vehicle occupancy – bus	37.5	
Average vehicle occupancy – car	1.35	

Source: Transport for London, London Travel Report 2002

Notes:
1. In addition to journeys terminating in central London, all journeys passing through central London are included, except those entirely on London Underground.
2. Includes commuter and tourist coaches.
3. Unrecorded prior to 1996.

Table 1.7 *Main mode of travel to work[1] to main job by area: autumn 2001*

	Area of work place				Area of residence			
	Central London %	Rest of inner London %	Outer London %	All London %	Great Britain %	Inner London %	Outer London %	All London %
Car and van	12	38	66	41	70	25	52	42
Motorbike, moped, scooter	2	2	1	2	1	2	1	1
Bicycle	2	3	2	2	3	4	2	2
Bus and coach	9	13	11	11	8	17	10	12
National rail	40	16	4	19	4	12	13	13
Underground	32	17	4	17	3	27	13	18
Walk	4	11	10	8	11	12	8	10
Total[2]	100	100	100	100	100	100	100	100

Source: Labour Force Survey, Office of National Statistics

Notes:
1. Excludes people who work at home; those with no fixed workplace; those on government-related training schemes; and people whose workplace is not available.
2. Includes other models (less than 1% in each area).

81% of people working in central London travel to work using public transport. This compares with 46% for the rest of inner London; 19% for outer London; and 15% for Great Britain. 12% of work journeys to central London are by car, compared with 38% for inner London, 66% for outer London and 70% for Great Britain as a whole. 56% of employees living in inner London used public transport compared with 36% living in outer London.

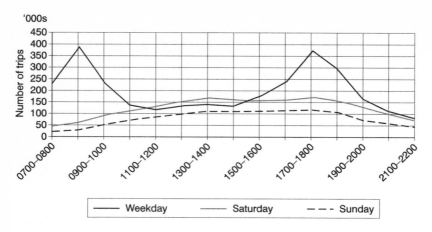

Figure 1.3 *Weekday and weekend Underground trips by hour 2002*
Source: Transport for London, London Travel Report 2003

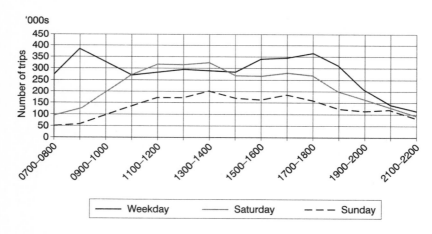

Figure 1.4 *Weekday and weekend bus trips by hour 2002/03*
Source: Transport for London, London Travel Report 2003

Bus operations in a large provincial town (Bradford 1976)

This analysis is based on the use of vehicles and the prospects for cost/ revenue ratios of operating under different criteria. Traditionally, bus companies have tried to satisfy peak demand and have run at a loss as a result. If these circumstances changed and a decision was made to operate only the number of vehicles required for the whole of the working day (ie to exclude peak only vehicles), then the financial position would be substantially changed. The Bradford Bus Study still remains one of the most comprehensive analyses of peak costs and the graph (Figure 1.5) is typical of many provincial town operations. However, some cities provide an even supply of newer vehicles through the day (eg Cardiff Bus) and use older vehicles for afternoon school journeys and evening peak operations (CB, 2005). Different companies will have a different graph in detail and low usage during the inter-peak daytime period can be used for preventive maintenance rather than more expensive night staff. In detail, there is often an earlier build-up in the afternoon with school contract work coming on stream at about 14.30; possibly a lower evening peak and a deeper 'dip' in the middle of the day. Many companies however operate high frequency minibus services with a higher level in the inter-peak period, eg in Edinburgh where the whole fleet is out from 07.00 to 19.00 and 50 per cent fleet operation thereafter. A similar demand pattern exists on the Den Haag tram network (Figure 1.8) where that supply reflects demand. On weekdays there are just over ten trains per hour passing the Ministry of Transport building in Madurodam with an expected peak at 18.00 and, unusually, on Saturday and Sundays there is a mid-afternoon peak caused by a demand for travel to Scheveningen – a popular seaside destination for urban dwellers. The consequences for costs may be derived using the same basis of analysis as shown in the Bradford Bus Study example.

Major British Airports

Major international airports provide a further example of peak operations in the handling of international traffic. The summer peak leads to higher aircraft landing and parking charges as does the morning business peak. However, such is the customer requirement for aircraft arrival times at the

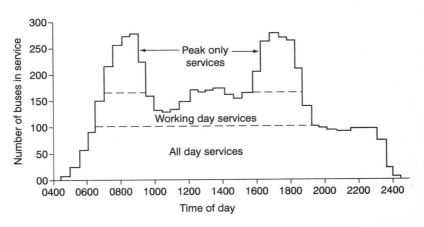

Figure 1.5 *Bus requirements for weekday bus operations in Bradford*
Source: Bradford Bus Study (1976)

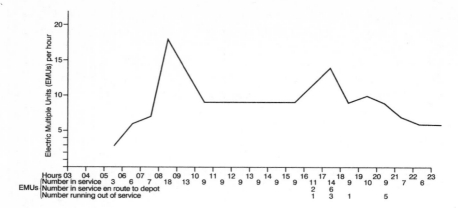

Figure 1.6 *Number of London suburban train units in operation up line to King's Cross/Moorgate (Monday–Friday)*
Source: Network Rail working timetable 2000

start of the business day that high landing charges are not a major factor affecting demand. More important particularly for the large international airlines in recent years (since 2000) have been low cost airlines and terrorist threats.

Smaller aircraft used on for example short haul regional services operating through major international airports may pay more per passenger than users of larger aircraft. However, the financial arrangements between low cost airlines and other airports have introduced a new competitive

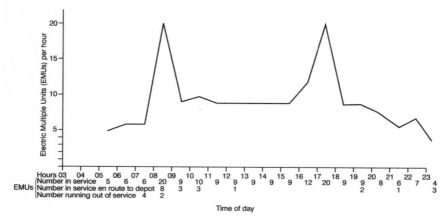

Figure 1.7 *Number of local train units (EMUs) in operation down line from King's Cross/Moorgate (Monday–Friday)*
Source: Network Rail working timetable 2000

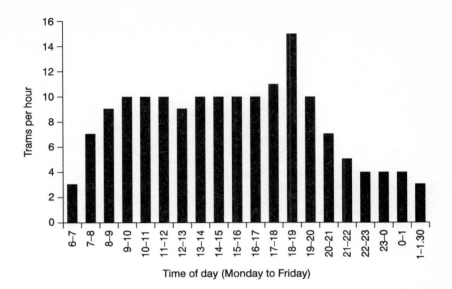

Figure 1.8 *Daily frequency of tram service Line 1/9 Centraal Station –*
Scheveningen, Den Haag, Netherlands
Source: HTM timetable, July 2002

position giving new opportunities to operators using lower capacity aircraft. There are also off-peak rates for aircraft at most major international airports. The lower costs of runway maintenance associated with smaller aircraft are not relevant in determining airport charges as such costs form a small proportion of airport total costs.

Airport operators (such as BAA) however were of the view that the economic basis of their pricing policy was the opportunity cost of using the runway which was dependent on the number of aircraft utilising it during a given period. The opportunity cost tended to be higher for a small aircraft

Table 1.8 *The main 'layers' of weekday bus operation in Bradford Resources*
required to operate weekday service for each layer

	All day	Working day	Peak	Total
No. of vehicles	99	65	111	
Cumulative	99	164	275	
% of total vehicles	36	24	40	100
Cumulative %	36	60	100	
Total payable hours	2087	892	672	3651
% of hours	57	25	18	100

Source: Bradford Bus Study 1976

Table 1.9 *Financial performance (Daily)*

	Satisfying peak demand (peak service approach)	All day and working day service layers only
Operating costs	26,000	12,970
Revenue	18,500	10,320
Reallocated revenue[1]	–	2,454
Total Revenue	18,500	12,774
Profit (Loss)	(7,500)	(196)
Cost/Revenue Ratio	0.71	0.98

Source: Data extracted from Tables 6.14 and 6.15 of Bradford Bus Study (1976) Reanalysis and revalued at 1997 Costs/Prices

Note:
1. Assumes reallocation of 30% of revenue to spare capacity during or either side of peak. Other 70% changes mode

because if it was following a large aircraft, it needed a larger separation distance on landing compared with two large aircraft in sequence.

Peak and off-peak pricing exists because of the demand characteristics at major airports (eg London Heathrow, Paris CDG, New York JFK) and an attempt by airport operators to even out demand through the day, the peaks continued to exist because of the derived nature of passenger demand to travel between 0700–1000 and 1700–1900.

London Heathrow and Gatwick Airports' monthly demand patterns (Figure 1.10) show the summer peak while the daily tables (Figure 1.11) for Heathrow (a major international airport) and Edinburgh (the

Table 1.10 *Index of airport charges for typical aircraft, 1996/97*

	Boeing 747–400		Boeing 737–400		% of total cost
	Peak	Off-peak	Peak	Off-peak	
Landing fee	334	316	400	284	26
Parking charge	871	290	82	27	14
Total landing and parking charge:	1316	606	482	311	40
Charge per departing passenger	10.95	4.20	10.95	4.20 ⎫	60
Total passenger changes paid	3219	1235	1217	467 ⎬	
Total per passenger	7.71	3.13	7.64	3.50	
Seat capacity	393		148		
Passengers carried (average)	294		111		
Parking time (hours)	3		1		
Flight	International		International		

Source: MMC: Based on report on BAA plc (June 1996)
Index based on Boeing 747–400 peak charge = 100.

government and financial capital of Scotland) has typical AM and PM business travel related peaks.

Peak pricing by package tour operators reflects two areas of leisure operations – airlines and hotels – which are hit by the peak demand for their services in the period July to August.

Those travelling to Greece with First Choice (London Gatwick Airport) or Reisen/LTU (Abflughafen, Düsseldorf) on 31 July are in a peak period, involve the operator in additional costs and consequently, should expect to pay a premium price for a holiday (Figure 1.12). Most leisure travel is very competitive with a high elasticity, but the summer family traveller on a holiday to the sun will find all operators offering the same price pattern (TB, 2003; JR, 2003). They have to travel when the schools are closed, and demand is likely to be more inelastic. Both these elements are taken into account by travel operators when pricing their holidays. This form of price discrimination is dealt with in more detail in Chapter 4.

Load factor variations are important in determining the profitability of airline operations. There are variations in mainline scheduled RPK's (see Chapter 7 for definitions) and in the passenger load factor – BA (1998) varied from over 80 per cent in June to 65 per cent in January. Although the airline can reduce costs by cutting services, the fixed costs representing

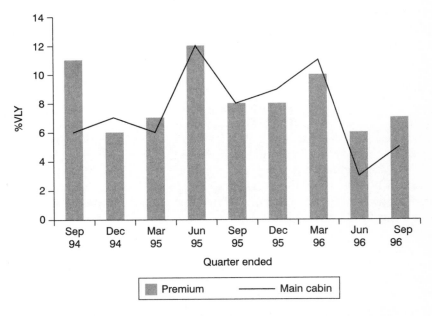

Figure 1.9 *Premium traffic trends – mainline scheduled RPK's: British Airways*
Source: British Airways, 1998

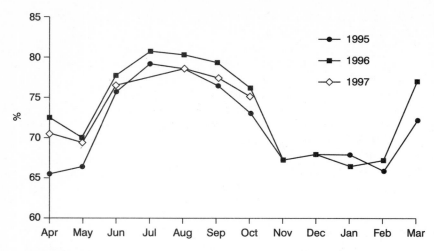

Figure 1.10 *Passenger load factor – mainline scheduled services:*
British Airways
Source: British Airways, 1998

nearly two thirds of total costs are still incurred (see Chapter 7). Thus these
short term variations in revenue passenger kilometres and in load factors
may be overcome using off peak pricing policies such as World Offers (see
Chapter 4).

Reducing the peak – possible action by the operator

The foregoing examples illustrate situations where peak demand incurs
costs by the operator and where, in some circumstances, that full cost is not
being paid by the customer. There are a number of options which an
operator can choose to reduce the impact of the peak on its operations.

First, the operator can decide not to provide the facility thus producing a
financially, though not necessarily socially, better result. Train operating
companies provide fewer extra summer services than twenty years ago
partly because demand has fallen, but also because of the cost of maintaining a back-up fleet of rolling stock to cover such demand. The interworking of services can also result in certain departures being
overcrowded because the train set capacity is only adequate for the
remainder of the working day (or even working year). Some Friday
afternoon peak journeys from London and services to tourist destinations
in the north of Wales or West of England provide examples of a decision
not to provide the capacity. In the latter case, if new, available rolling stock
with higher seating capacity can be interworked then the problem may be
solved.

Heathrow

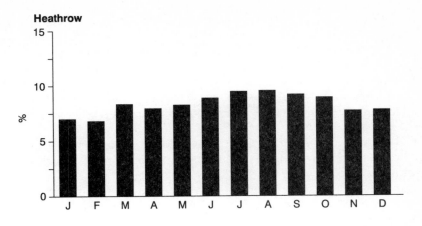

Gatwick

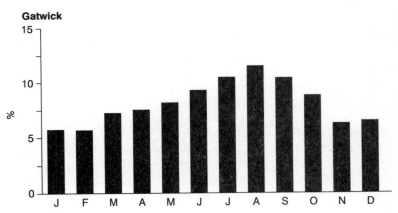

Figure 1.11 *Monthly distribution of passengers: London Heathrow/ Gatwick Airports*
Source: BAA Airports, Traffic statistics, 2001/02

In freight operations, the haulier has a contract to move goods at a given time and the contract price to the customer will reflect any peak operations of this type. Companies supplying haulage services to food and clothing retailers have delivery schedules clearly specified and these additional costs are likely to be catered for. The Post Office, faced with an increasing peak at Christmas time, brought forward its last guaranteed posting date and thus reduced the need for extra vehicles. By not hiring extra freight vehicles costs are cut, but the service level is reduced as a result of spreading the delivery over a longer period and flattening out the peak.

Other techniques have been adopted by operators to flatten out the peak or fill in the trough between peaks:

- Pricing through off peak discounts or a peak surcharge. Even if this policy does not flatten the peak, it may increase the overall demand level which may be a better alternative in revenue and profitability terms.
- Flexible hours are not popular with workers generally for family and social reasons. In some cases, however, they have been negotiated with education authorities to move the schools' transport peak, primarily in the afternoon.
- Out-of-service running on contra peak flow vehicles may enable an extra peak journey and thus reduce the number of peak vehicles and crew.
- Out-of-town industry and schools have been suggested as filling seats on out-of-town services and inbound evening services. This is not always a solution since the new demand pattern may not coincide with the radial route pattern.
- Private commuter operators can be used to supplement the existing operators. They are able to use low cost vehicles and staff or use vehicles for a commuter service to the city centre, then for private hire during the day (09.30 to 16.30), and finally on an evening commuter service out of town. In the present deregulated market some peak services will be put out to tender by county councils if demand is to be met.
- Bus lanes reduce bus journey times.
- The use of fully depreciated (usually older) buses, trucks and rolling stock at peak times, thus eliminating part of the financial burden of spare vehicles.

The policy which is most likely to produce increased revenue and (as most off peak costs are marginal or variable) increased profitability, is one aimed at filling in the off peak. This is particularly true if the basic system is retained (for example the London mass transit system).

The current fare structure in London does provide for off peak travel at a lower cost for single tickets and for short period travelcards. It also recognises 'core commuters' as the most important customers and provides a discount on their basic fare from home to work and 'free' additional travel within the zones on the Travelcard. This has achieved two prime objectives:

– increased overall patronage resulting from the convenience of a travelcard.
– the increased use of bus underground and train services during the off peak day, evening and weekend periods.

Package tour operators (Figure 1.12) in northern European states organising holidays to southern Europe have several factors determining their pricing policy:

Cost per person for two weeks – from Gatwick or from Dusseldorf

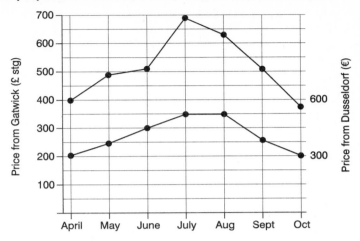

Location: Skopolos, (Cyclades Island), Greece
Price: Two weeks per person, two people sharing). £1 = €1.60 (2004)
Source: Average GB package holiday companies, Great Britain / Jahn Reisen – LTU Touristik Service, Munchen, Germany

Figure 1.12 *Holiday prices on a Greek island*

- Elasticity of demand is lower during the period 1 July to 31 August, compared with the rest of the year, because of the timing of school holidays and the coincidence of the warmest weather.
- Additional costs of providing extra hotel and airline capacity in that period.
- Competition (since about 1999) from low cost carriers and the availability of booking direct via the internet of both air travel and hotel accommodation. This availability of competitive, alternative and practical air travel has resulted in demand changes from cross-price elasticity. This has therefore affected the pricing levels of package tour companies and their airlines.

Figure 1.12 shows the application of peak pricing in Germany and Great Britain. A similar pattern is found in Italy and in Poland (Tousco, 2003) where package holidays have expanded rapidly following the end of the Soviet Union, the consequent freedom to travel and the rise of a new middle income group intent on taking full advantage of their much improved financial position (Table 1.11).

Table 1.11 *Package tour prices[4] in Crete from Italy, Poland and France (2003) (€)*

Country Destination	Italy[1] Creta	Poland[2] Kreta	France[3] Crete
Month:			
April	645	688	470
May	710	822	440
June	763	896	470
July	870	1002	650
August	925[5]	1002	720
September	–	984	440
October	–	801	370

Source: Operating companies

Notes:
1. Comitours, Grecia/Cipso, Estate 2003.
2. Orbis Travel, Lato Wycieczki Lotnicze, 2003.
3. Etapes nouvelles, 2003.
4. All are for two weeks (14 nights) per person in tourist class hotels.
5. 'Peak of peaks' price (3 August–16 August 1020).

REFERENCES

AB (2003) Alliances, *Airline Business*, April/July, Sutton, Surrey.

BA (1998) British Airways plc, Performance Report 1998, London.

BA (2003) British Airways plc, Performance Report 2003, London.

Bierwirth, A (Deputy MD, German Wings) (2003) Quoted in Price promise, *Airline Business*, April, Sutton, Surrey.

Bradford (1976) Bradford Bus Study, Final Report, West Yorkshire PTE, Leeds.

CAA (2002) UK Airlines Annual Operating, Traffic and Financial Statistics, 2001 CAP 734, Civil Aviation Authority, London.

CAA (2003) UK Airlines (CAP 672) Annual Operating, Traffic and Financial Statistics 2003.

Carroll, M (1997) Discussion with author on First Great Western.

Cassani, B and Kemp, K (2003) *Go, An Airline Adventure*, Time Warner Books, London.

CB (2005) Cardiff Bus Business Plan 2005–09, Bws Caerdydd/Cardiff Bus.

ES (2003) Eurostar, Performance Report 2003.

Field, D (2003) Network survival, *Airline Business*, March.

JR (2003) Jahn Reisen, Griechenland Preise (Greek Price brochure), München, Germany.

LT (1993) Fares and Ticketing Policy in London: From Travelcards to Smartcards Research Report 280, London Transport Planning Department, London.

LT (1997) Night time is the right time, London Direct (October), London Transport, London.

LT (2002) London Travel Report 2002, Transport for London.

Maynard R (1992), Director Corporate Strategy, British Airways. *Money Programme*, BBC Television; London.

P & O (2004): reference to brochures published by operators (eg P & O, Cunard, VSOE, BA Concorde, Great Little Trains of Wales etc.) Prices from operators.

Pilling, M (2003), Price promise, *Airline Business*, April.

SNCF (2002) Annual Report; Rapport d'Activité, Discussions with SNCF Département des Opérations Financières, Paris.

TB (2003) Tour company brochures – Comitours (Italy); Orbis, Travel Time (Poland); Etapes nouvelles, Objectif découvertes (France).

Tousco (2003) brochure.

TPG (2003) Annual Report 2002, TPG/TNT, Amsterdam, The Netherlands.

VSOE (2003) Venice Simplon Orient Express, Journeys of Distinction 2003, London.

Webster, FV and Bly, PH (1980) *The Demand for Public Transport: Study of the factors affecting public transport*, TRRL, Crowthorne.

YB (1984) Bournemouth Yellow Buses campaign 'Get around on the Yellows'.

CHAPTER 2

Elasticity of Demand

PRICE ELASTICITY OF DEMAND

Introduction

The term elasticity is one which may seem complex, but is clearly illustrated by the day to day marketing of the transport industry in the various advertising campaigns seen in the media.

Consider the range of train operator return fares per person from London to Cardiff and Newcastle.

Table 2.1 *Rail fare options from London (2004)*

Fare type (return)	First Great Western to Cardiff (145 miles)		GNER to Newcastle (270 miles)	
	1st (£)	Standard (£)	1st (£)	Standard (£)
Open[4]	169	107	264	176
Saver[4]	114	49		84
Super saver[4]		41		
Super advance[1]		36		62
Apex[3]	51	24		48
Off-peak one			59[3]	20[3]
Off-peak two			82[2]	34[2]
Off-peak three			102[1]	48[1]

Source: First Great Western (FGW, 2004a); GNER

Notes:
1. Booking at least a day before travel 1800 hrs.
2. Booking at least 3 days before travel.
3. Booking at least 7 days before travel.
4. 'Turn up and go fare'/'walk-on fare' with journey time rules.

The reasons for these differences are what price elasticity is about. In this case it will be the responsiveness of passengers or potential passengers to the prices on offer. The changes in those prices have to be measured to determine the extra passengers and extra revenue which will be achieved from this type of fares policy. Elasticity has a wider role than price, however. It is defined as the response of demand for a product to the change in one of its determinant factors. Rail passenger demand, for example, will be influenced by:

fares in relation to other prices;
fares in relation to other operators' fares and to car running costs;
consumers' income;
unemployment level;
car ownership level;
reliability and service level;
the image of intercity rail travel and the individual train operator

Demand is the amount of a service or product bought by a consumer. Only effective demand is of interest to the economist; that is demand which can be put into effect because the consumer is able to pay. The price of the services on offer and the income of the consumer will be important determinants of whether the consumer is able to buy. Once the purchasing power element is decided, the consumer then looks for service characteristics and value for money. Market demand is the aggregate of all individual consumers' demands, and it too will be determined by the same factors.

Own price elasticity – effects

This is the responsiveness of consumers to changes in the transport operator's own price. Generally it is applied to new consumers entering the market.

Cross price elasticity – effects

Cross price elasticity is a measure of the effect of a change in the fares or rates of one operator on the demand for the services of another. It can take place between transport modes, within modes or even within an operator if the transport company is offering a variety of fares for the same journey, but with different standards of service.

CASE STUDY 1: TRANSATLANTIC FARES

The reduction in air fares has led to a significant increase in demand. From the mid 1990s the 'low cost airlines' came to the fore. South West Airlines, easyJet and Ryanair led the field in the United States and the United Kingdom. But nearly 20 years earlier the same price elasticity effect had occurred when the reduction in transatlantic air fares led to a great increase in demand. A large part of the demand was from people who had never before flown on that route because they considered the fares were too high. When the transatlantic fares war began in 1979 with the start of Laker Airways' Skytrain service, the only fares available were standard fares and some limited discount fares. In 1939 Pan Am provided a dining room, sleeping berths and a honeymoon suite on its flying boat service from New

York to Southampton. But it took 24 hours and cost £140. Even in the 1960s, the airlines continued to cater for the higher income groups and transatlantic flying was for business people and the wealthy private traveller, not for the middle income family or the low income student.

1980 saw thousands of new British travellers preparing to fly to America on a trip which 30 years previously they could not have afforded. Table 2.2 shows how transatlantic fares have fallen. In 2004 prices the single fare by BOAC from London to New York in 1950 was £1500 (£125 in 1950 prices). The Laker airways price in 1980 was £50 (or £600 in 2004 prices). The low fares market had begun. Airlines bought larger aircraft (eg the Boeing 747 'jumbo') that they had to fill. Thus the fares were considerably lower in real terms in 2004 compared with 50 years previously. Just as important, the fares to earnings and income elasticity ratio enabled a wide market to develop, and the impact of price elasticity in the low cost airline market is clear (Tables 2.2 and 2.3).

The relationship to wages emphasises the fact that in 1950 few could afford these air fares and so demand was restricted, but in 1980 this new passenger market was opened up and has continued into the 2000's. The later developments in the battle for transatlantic passengers involved the bigger airlines in a price war with new low fare operators. Thus the trend begun by Laker Airways in 1980 continued to the present with airlines entering and leaving (eg People Express; Piedmont) the market and other major airlines introducing a low fare policy for economy class travellers.

The major 'conventional' airlines in the transatlantic market from Great Britain to the USA – British Airways, United, Delta, Virgin and American Airlines – have all tried to retain their share of the highly elastic tourist market. Despite recent agreements between some airlines (eg KLM-Northwest; British Airways – American Airlines) and the creation of 'alliances' (eg One World, Star Alliance, Sky Team) or code

Table 2.2 *Single transatlantic fares 1950–2004*

Year	Route/airline	Quoted fare then	Equivalent cost 2004 prices*
1950	London/New York BOAC	125	1549
1960	London/New York BOAC	91	774
1970	London/New York BOAC	87	497
1980	Gatwick/Miami Laker	50	82
1997	London/New York BA/ Virgin/AA (average)	165	196
2004	London/New York	110–250	180

*Adjusted for inflation

Sources: American Airlines, Virgin Atlantic Airways, British Airways. Laker Airways, author's archive, National Earnings Survey (2004).

Table 2.3 *Real cost of air travel*

	Air fare (£)	Weekly wage average (£)	Ratio to wages
1950	125	10	12.5:1
1980	50	100	0.5:1
2003	225	560	0.4:1

Source: Department for Employment, National Earnings Survey (NES, 1996, 2004)

share partnerships (eg KLM/Northwest; South African/Delta/Lufthansa) there still remains fierce competition to attract new travellers and to attract those who already travel with other operators.

CASE STUDY 2: COACH/RAIL COMPETITION

The London–Oxford passenger route is served by three main forms of transport:

- rail (Thames Trains);
- long distance express coach using the M40 motorway (Oxford City Link; Go Ahead Group; Oxford Tube; Stagecoach plc);
- private car using the M40 motorway

The introduction of lower fares on express coaches resulted in passengers transferring from rail travel to coach travel, particularly where comparative journey times were similar.

For all ticket types the fares were considerably undercut, so that a market which rail passenger service operators would normally consider their own – the commuter market – was likely to see passengers transfer to express coach. The coach services introduced by Oxford City Link in 1982 and subsequently by the Oxford Tube service still operate with high load factors and the fare differentials are still significant. In 1996, price competition between the coach operators reduced prices at one point to below the 1986 levels and increased total patronage (through own price elasticity). There was little cross-price elasticity effect as both companies' fare levels fell, indicating market saturation for leisure travel – the primary sector for long distance coach operators – and in that part of the commuter market prepared to accept longer journey times by coach (see Table 2.4).

Price competition between express coaches and rail is mainly in the leisure travel market. The railway advertising campaigns emphasise to the business traveller the significance of comfort, lack of stress, and the ability to work *en route*, but the importance of fares to the leisure traveller. If the travel brochures of Great North Eastern Railway (2004) are compared, the front cover slogans 'Business Travel – GNER First for Business' and 'Ticket Information and Fares Guide 2004' reflects the content. 'Quality,

Table 2.4 *London (Parliament Square) to Oxford (Carfax) return fares/costs, October 2004*

Fare type/car cost	Motor car £p	Coach (Oxford Tube)	Train (FGW Link) £p £p
Cost elements:			
Day return (peak)		12.00	31.00
Off-peak return		7.00	16.50
Season ticket[3]		4.20	15.00
Perceived cost[1]	27.30		
Actual cost[2]	55.76		
Quality elements			
Departure frequency (daily M–F)	Infinite	Every 12–15 mins	Every 15 mins
Journey time (mins)	77	100	60–90

Sources: Automobile Association, Oxford Tube (Stagecoach Oxford Ltd), First Great Western

Notes:
1. Petrol (£10.30); central Oxford parking costs (£12 per day); London congestion charge (£5 per day).
2. AA cost per mile plus central Oxford parking costs (deducted £11 if park and ride is used) plus central London congestion charge (£5 per day). Cost per mile elements: petrol 9.07p; other running costs 7.52p; standing charges (15000 miles pa) 16.85p. Distance 114 miles return.
3. Assuming 220 working days an annual rail season ticket costs £3300 or £15 per day; Oxford Tube 1-year ticket (including local Stagecoach services) £940 or £4.20 per day.

easy booking, business atmosphere, profit' are features of the GNER business travellers' world. Even ticket options relate to packages for add on meals, parking and Underground tickets. Options in GNER's leisure market relate to 'great value, extra savings, rail cards'. Excluding the glossy photographs, 66 per cent of the leisure brochure and only 5 per cent of the business brochure relates to price, thus indicating the relative magnitude of price elasticities in the two segments.

Rail operators' estimates of the effects of coach operations on their market share show an overall decline in the western corridor which is particularly marked on the Oxford route. The increase in the coach share of the market was due partly to price elasticity and partly to cross-price elasticity effects. The comparative fares of £12.00 (£7.00) by coach and £31.00 (£16.50) by train (see Table 2.4) for a commuter journey, despite a journey time increase of half an hour, would induce the transfer of some train passengers to the coach service. The cross-price elasticity is the proportion of rail passengers transferring in relation to the proportionate change in the coach fare. This illustrates the competitive reality of short to medium distance passenger travel. There is competition between coach and rail in some segments and between rail and air in others. However, the major competition for public transport is the motor car with its low perceived cost (especially per passenger when two or more share the vehicle) and its infinite convenience.

The relative costs of travel by car and public transport (see Figure 2.1) show motoring cost falling in real terms so that between 1992 and 2002 car travel prices have risen by about 2 per cent while public transport is up by 12 per cent. The cross-price elasticity impact has been seen; the income elasticity effect is also illustrated in the increased use of train services with annual increases of 8 per cent on some routes (see 'Income elasticity', page 64).

Passenger transfer effects may also result from a reduction in petrol costs, with passengers transferring from public transport to the private car. Cross price elasticity may also be seen where the relative prices of two modes change. If rail prices increased significantly and perceived car costs remained the same, there might also be a transfer of passengers.

An extensive compilation and assessment of elasticity studies in Europe in 1992 (Goodwin, 1992) reviewed 50 demand elasticities studies from 1980–1990 for car and bus travel. For urban bus travel the average value of price elasticity (impact of fares on patronage) was –0.41 but indicated a wide variation between the short-term and long-term impacts.

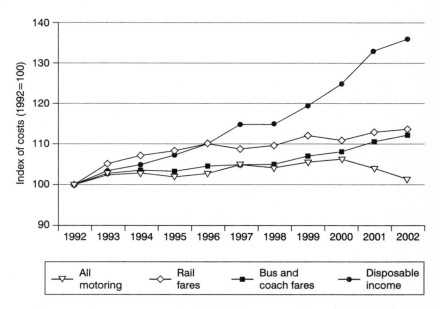

Figure 2.1 *Cost of motoring compared to public transport*
Source: Department for Transport Trends 2.3

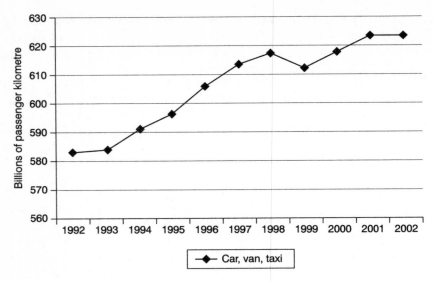

Figure 2.2 *Private vehicle passenger kilometres*
Source: Department for Transport, Trend 2.1a

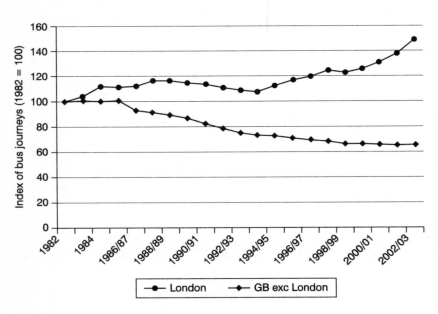

Figure 2.3 *Index of local bus journeys from 1982*
Source: Department for Transport, Trend 3.1a

Table 2.5 *Bus fare elasticities related to time period*

Time period	Average elasticity
around 6 months	−0.21
0–6 months	−0.28
0–12 months	−0.37
4+ years	−0.55
5–30 years	−0.65

Source: Goodwin (1992)

Rail elasticity studies are more commonly carried out for Inter City services rather than urban operations where as suggested in the Serpell Report and as indicated by London Transport underground price elasticities are relatively low (see also SNCB, 1997).

However, research carried out by Stagecoach Holdings PLC (HOC, 1995) into fare reductions indicates higher elasticities following substantial fare reductions but similar elasticities to the above (Table 2.5) for fares increases of 10 per cent.

Stagecoach doubted the urban bus fares elasticity of −0.3/−0.4, which public sector companies had used during the 1970s. An analysis of these figures showed different elasticities for small (−0.4) and large (−1.0) changes (Preston, 1998). A fares reduction of 50 per cent led to a ridership increase of 275 per cent even after fares were subsequently raised to 66 per cent of the original level. The Stagecoach data suggest:

- Fares elasticity can be greater than unity (although some of the increase might be the result of cross elasticity effects of transfers from other operators).
- Fares decreases and fares increases may not have the same elasticity for similar percentage changes.
- Fares simplification may lead to significant increases with an elasticity of −0.7, but with a more complex off-peak discount scheme there may only be a −0.2 elasticity.

Table 2.6 *Bus fare elasticity related to fare reductions*

Fares discount (%)	Passenger increase (%)	Elasticity
-50	+100	−2.00
-33	+50	−1.52
-20	+25	−1.25
-10	+4	−0.40

Source: Stagecoach Holdings plc

Table 2.7 *Long and short run elasticities*

Time of day	Long run	Short run
Early morning, peak am/pm	−0.24/−0.31	−0.16/−0.2
Saturday	−0.27	−0.2
Inter-peak	−0.55	−0.31
Evening/Sunday	−0.5	−0.19

This indicates a relatively inelastic peak journey demand in both the short and long runs. This may be due to the lack of alternative mode. Saturday traffic was also relatively inelastic, possibly for a similar reason. Inter-peak elasticities were considerably higher particularly in the long run due possibly to the journeys not being essential but unable to be curtailed immediately or because an alternative mode takes some time to establish.

Price inelasticity is not the only determent of demand. Journey purpose ticket type and service aspects (see below) also have an impact. Travelcard schemes' elasticity is affected by their characteristics (discount size, other ticket 'products' on offer), the short and long run effects, the extent to which the traveller sees a travelcard as better value depending on estimated use, the mode (bus is less elastic than rail), location and estimation methodology. The higher travelcard elasticity in London compared with smaller cities may reflect network size or possibly the high tourism content of the market. In a PTA study (ITS, 1998), disabled, elderly and adult fare elasticity is consistently −0.3 in respect of fares increases although adult demand elasticity for pre-paid tickets was −0.74.

The single fare price elasticity in the PTE studies (ITS, 1998; Preston, 1998) shows demand as considerably more elastic for shorter journeys with a long term elasticity of −0.83 where walking was a practical alternative mode, compared with −0.55 over much longer journeys.

European air fares

The real cost of air travel in relation to average weekly wages has fallen considerably from the 1970 level and since 1980 has been consistent, where one half of a week's wages represents a single discount price fare from London to New York. Similar patterns are found in Germany, the Netherlands and France.

On particular routes the arrival of new airlines (eg Flybe, easyJet and Ryanair) and lower cost operations of established airlines (eg Virgin Express, Go (BA, later bought by management, then easyJet) and Transavia (KLM)) have led to lower fares and an own price elasticity effect encouraging new passengers and/or more trips.

The lower cost airline effects

The decline in the airline market from the late 1990s was a result of economic downturn and to some extent consumer confidence in flying.

Some airlines have closed (eg Swissair); others have reduced jobs and capacity (United, British Airways, Air France) (AB, 2003b).

However, the increased demand achieved by low cost operators such as easyJet, Go, Ryanair and Flybe showed that:

- not all European aviation is problematic;
- low cost airlines continue to be successful;
- the airlines suffering most are those with business models ill equipped to cope with economic downturn and changing market conditions.

It is the third issue that concerns price elasticity. EasyJet claims 'people will fly if the price is right' (HOC, 2002a). Many airlines increased set prices when demand fell; easyJet sold 180,000 seats at very low prices in its primary markets in the UK, Netherlands and Switzerland. These low fares had several effects:

- Traffic volume increased but revenue per passenger fell (own price elasticity).
- Load factors remained high at 82–83 per cent (own price elasticity).
- October 2001 sales were 27 per cent above 2000 despite the consumer loss of confidence in air safety.
- Profits rose by 82 per cent.

The own price elasticity effect generated not merely replacement business but as Figures 2.4 and 2.5 show additional demand over the target for the period.

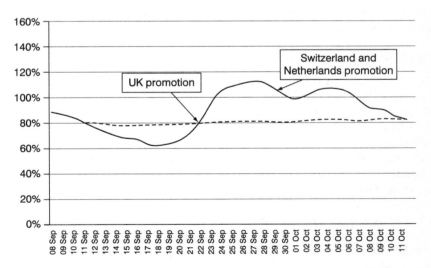

Figure 2.4 *Sales v capacity (rolling seven days), 2001 v 2000*
Source: House of Commons (HOC 2002a – easyJet)

45

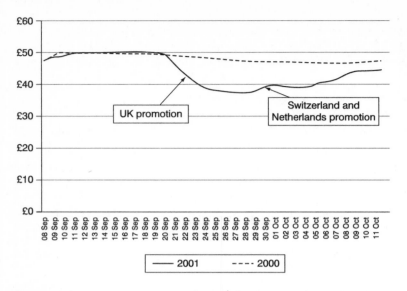

Figure 2.5 *easyJet – average fare (rolling seven days), 2001 v 2000*
Source: House of Commons (2002a)

The business models of several airlines were adopted to meet the low cost challenger (AB, 2004). This brought in both service elasticity and price elasticity elements. In domestic services Air Canada introduced its Tango low fares operation (2001); Air New Zealand discontinued its business class and meals, and replaced it with a single Express class with 20 per cent lower fares. In Europe (2003) British Airways changed its short-haul pricing strategy to offer simpler and cheaper fares, and SAS produced its Scandinavian Direct low fares (2003).

Business travel downtrading

A survey in 2003 (NBTA) indicated that, while US business travel revenues remain lower than in 2000, low-cost carriers have taken significant proportions of the traditional business market (cross-price elasticity). Corporate travellers are increasingly willing to buy restricted/non-refundable Apex fares to reduce air travel costs, thus reducing margins on once high profit travellers.

Business travel, according to the survey, will not rise until economic confidence is restored. Meanwhile 40 per cent of this survey said lower fares would boost business travel (price elasticity).

The cross-price elasticity effect (2003) is shown in the companies:

- using discount airlines: 73 per cent (2000: 43 per cent);
- requiring executives to fly economy class: 41 per cent;

- purchasing business class restricted non-refundable tickets: 54 per cent (2000: 25 per cent) (trend confirmed by American Express, 2004);
- using direct connection to the airline website: 19 per cent.

All but the last indicate a high value of cross-price elasticity. 'Low cost no longer means travelling second class' (BTC, 2003). This lack of feeling of 'trading down' means a long term cross-price elasticity impact. If those travellers do not return to the established airlines then the airlines (eg American and United) will reduce operating costs, introduce new fare structures such as refundable discounted fares in business class and incentive payments for frequent use corporations, and reduce fares, in some cases, to low cost airline levels. All these are an attempt to use cross-price elasticity to reverse the trend.

A further attempt by airlines to increase the cross elasticity effect has been a new trend to target the corporate market with web-based services and fares (eg Northwest Airlines, Corpnet Direct) previously directed exclusively at individual travellers.

There have also been cross-price elasticity effects such as the Dublin-London route where the introduction of low fares by Ryanair (from Stansted) was one factor in British Airways' decision to withdraw its Heathrow-Dublin jet service and move to a new lower-cost franchised operation from London Gatwick Airport (City Flyer Express, 1997). In the European market, as in other markets, major airlines such as BA have retaliated through low fares and franchised operations. Using sophisticated computer-based systems for booking, planning and forecasting of seat capacity the price advantage may move between the 'no frills' airlines (eg easyJet, bmibaby) to the medium-sized operators (eg BMI) to the major operators (eg BA). Thus on a particular date, shopping around may show, for example, BA is cheaper than easyJet. Cross price elasticity between these operators may therefore occur almost continuously in the price sensitive private leisure market. This may also result in passengers using different airlines' single tickets for outward and return journeys.

The initial impact (in the mid–1990s) was in the price sensitive off-peak leisure market, and routes from London to Dublin indicated considerable growth through own price elasticity creating new markets (Figure 2.7 and Table 2.8). However, the extension of networks by airlines such as easyJet has led to a loss of business travellers who take advantage of the lack of inhibitors (eg Saturday night away) imposed by the traditional carriers. These have reacted by removing such inhibitors or by reducing their fares for early booking by 50 per cent or more.

Overall however the world market for air travel continues to be problematic for the large airlines and successful for the new 'low cost' operators (Table 2.8).

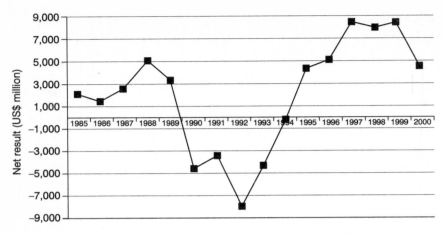

Figure 2.6 *Industry net profits, 1985–2000*
Source: IATA September 2001 briefing based on ICAO data

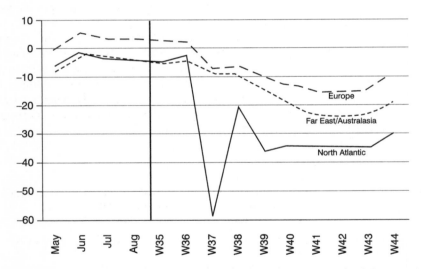

Figure 2.7 *Airline traffic in 2001 (RPK: revenue passenger kilometre)*
Source: AEA Weekly Traffic Monitor, November 2001; HUC 2002a

However, as Table 2.8 shows, the impact of transatlantic traffic and internal United States air travel has its effects on both traditional (eg United) and 'no frills' (eg South West) airlines but generally for non-price reasons.

It has been suggested that the reduction in passengers by UK-based charter airlines (eg Monarch, Air 2000) has come as a result of cross-price elasticity between them and for example easyJet, Flybe and bmibaby.

Table 2.8 *Passenger traffic, selected airlines worldwide (2000)*

Airline	Passengers '000 m	% change	Load factor
American	94	−5.1	70.7
United	68	−9.1	73.6
British	38	−5.0	71.9
Air France	39	−1.0	76.8
South West	63	−2.2	65.9
Monarch	5	−3.4	87.5
Air 2000	6	−7.4	90.3
Britannia	8	+1.4	90.9
easyJet	11	+59.5	85.5
Ryanair	16	+41.4	84.0

Source: Airline Business passenger traffic analysis (**19** (9), September 2003)

Using the internet, leisure travellers are able to book flights and hotels at lower prices in the more popular destinations. Thus the no frills airlines have benefited from both own price (new passengers) and cross-price elasticity (diverted from the other carriers) effects.

The international aviation industry demand pattern began its decline from about 1990. Many airlines operating across the North Atlantic faced capacity reductions, job losses and reduced revenues. British Airways makes 30 per cent of its profits on Atlantic routes. Many airlines, in easyJet's view, no longer have profitable European networks because they no longer meet consumer demand in an age of low cost airlines and high speed trains (HOC, 2002a).

Table 2.9 *Market comparison, October 2001*

Market	BAA total October 2000 '000	BAA total October 2001 '000	% change
Domestic	1,192	1,847	55.0
Eire	534	564	5.5
European scheduled	4,049	3,594	−11.2
European charter[1]	1,288	1,249	−3.1
North Atlantic	1,761	1,210	−31.3
Other long-haul	1,584	1,324	−16.4
Total	10,408	9,788	−6.0

Source: House of Commons Air Transport Industry Report HC 484 (2001–02)

Notes
1. Includes North African charter.
Origins and destinations are classified according to ultimate origin or destination of aircraft in the case of multi-sector flights.
Figures for the market sectors have been rounded. Totals as per Traffic Summary.

Table 2.10 *Passenger numbers (000s) between Dublin and:*

	1996	1995	% change
Heathrow	1,717	1,704	−1
Gatwick	422	339	+24
Luton	200	162	+23
Stansted	854	711	+20
Total:	3,193	2,916	+9

Sources: Civil Aviation Authority, CAP 671, UK Airports Annual Statement of Movements, Passenger and Cargo 1996. CAA April 1997

Table 2.11 *Passenger numbers 1991–1996*

Airport	Terminal passengers (m)		% change 1991–96
	1996	1991	
Heathrow	55.7	40.2	38.5
Gatwick	24.1	18.6	29.0
Manchester	14.4	10.1	42.5
Glasgow	5.4	4.1	31.7
Edinburgh	3.8	2.3	65.2
Cardiff	1.1	0.5	120.0

Sources: Civil Aviation Authority, CAP 671, UK Airports Annual Statement of Movements, Passenger and Cargo 1996. CAA April 1997

CASE STUDY 3: LONDON COMMUTERS

London – the Fares Fair policy 1980

The introduction of cheap fares on to London bus and underground services led to a change in shopping patterns in the capital. People who previously shopped in neighbourhood or suburban shopping centres began to make trips to the West End for casual shopping. This was because the fares were lower and were therefore available to new travellers who had not previously made the journey for this purpose. (See Chapter 12 for the use of market price policies to achieve public policy objectives.)

The demand for commuter transport is inelastic, particularly in the short term, and where the train or metro is the only practical form of travel into the central business district of a large urban area (LT, 1995).

Price elasticity – two variables in the rail industry

A study by AEA technology (Woods, 2003) suggests that London commuting demand may be more price elastic than has been previously supposed. Peak period rail travel has always been dependent on central

London employment and the economic cycle. If the capacity (supply) is set aside then the unconstrained demand will be subject only to price.

Figure 2.8 suggests that different real terms price increases would make a considerable difference in demand patterns thus suggesting that price rises of RPI+1 would have a considerably lower elasticity than RPI+3.

In cross elasticity terms one then needs to consider the relative cost increases of travel by car and by public transport (HOC, 2002b) while car travel has been at or near the retail price index (RPI), from 1981 to 2001 (Index 100:240) bus and rail fares have risen by 100:310. This partly accounts for the continued cross elasticity effect between the public transport and motor car modes.

The Serpell (1983) Report suggested fare increases of 40 per cent in London and south-east England, with little loss of passenger numbers and an increase in revenue because of the inelastic nature of the demand.

The 1980 Transport Act provided for express coach service deregulation and in particular, commuter coach services into London. The fares were those which the operator considered gave the best financial return and were considerably below those of the train operating companies, resulting in cross elasticity impacts on passenger demand with about 2.5 per cent of commuters transferring.

The introduction of cheap fares on London Transport resulted in a transfer from British Rail to LT (mainly underground) services, but when LT fares were increased in 1981–82 passengers transferred to alternative British Rail services (LT, 1984). This is more likely to have taken place on the lines

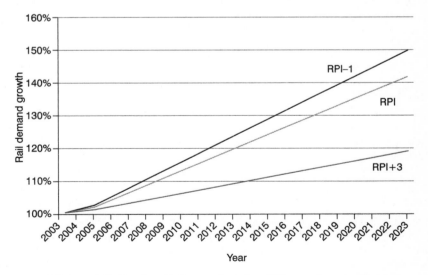

Figure 2.8 *Peak rail demand under different fares policies*
Source: Woods (2003)

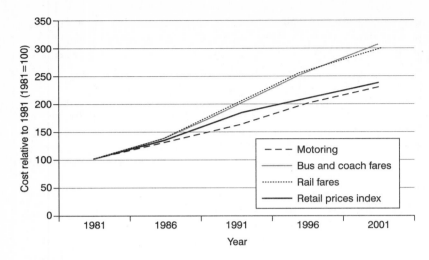

Figure 2.9 *Cost of bus, rail and motoring between 1981 and 2001*
Source: Passenger transport and price, Social Trends 32, Office of National Statistics

where British Rail and LT have common services into Central London such as Upminster, Richmond, Ealing and parts of Enfield and Barnet.

The presence of cross elasticity is also shown in the demand patterns between London Transport fare changes and the number of car commuters into central London, where the relative cost had fallen (Fairhurst, 1986). When LT prices fell so car use fell, and when LT fares were almost doubled in 1981 the number of commuters travelling into London by car increased by 14 per cent (see Chapter 12, Table 12.1).

In earlier studies it was clear that the passenger market in urban areas is one market with segments between which customers will move. Their actions are determined by price elasticities, fare structure changes (TfL, 2000), service elasticities and income elasticity (see pp. 64 and 70).

In the London area the own-price and cross-price elasticities indicate a degree of transfer between one public transport mode and another (the cross price elasticity effect) and that, for example, the cross price elasticity between Underground and rail is considerably less (+0.08) than in the early 1980's (+0.17) so that the modal shifts referred to above would have been less in the late 1990's than in the earlier period.

Recent research by Transport for London (TfL, 2002) and DETR (1999) has highlighted a more complex demand elasticity relationship. Although overall the elasticities have changed little (TfL, 2002) other than a reduced cross-price elasticity between Underground and bus (Table 2.12), the short and long term elasticity effects indicate that 85 per cent of the total impact occurs within one year and the remaining 15 per cent over a much larger period and are reflected in the DETR (1999) model for bus elasticities.

Table 2.12 *Comparison of bus and Underground price elasticity (all elasticities at 2000 fares levels; fares deflated by earnings)*

Elasticity	1979–1985	1971–1995	1971–2000
Bus:	(R266)	(M(97)71)	(TfL 2002)
Own price	−0.40	−0.60	−0.64
Cross price with U/G	+0.10	+0.12	+0.13
Cross price with National Rail	+0.05	+0.14	+0.15
Conditional[1]	−0.25	−0.34	−0.37
Underground:			
Own price	−0.54	−0.48	−0.41
Cross price with bus	+0.21	+0.20	+0.12
Cross price with National Rail	+0.17	+0.07	+0.08
Conditional[1]	−0.16	−0.21	−0.21

Source: London Transport Reports R266 and R273 (LT, 1986; LT, 1993), M(97)71; LT, 1997; TfL, 2002

Note:
1. Conditional on bus, Underground and National Rail fares changing by the same proportions

Table 2.13 *Local market bus fare elasticities*

Short run (1 year)	−0.4
Long run (7 years)	−0.9

The demand curve becomes more inelastic as time progresses.

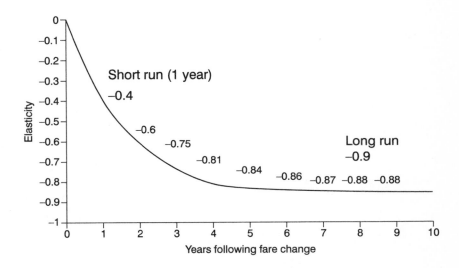

Figure 2.10 *Dynamic bus fare elasticity*
Source: DETR (1999) Bus fare elasticity project

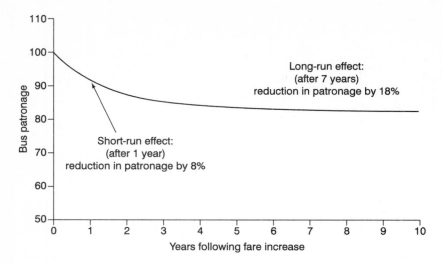

Figure 2.11 *Bus patronage over time resulting from a 20 per cent increase in bus fares*
Source: DETR (1999) Bus fare elasticity project

Note: The effect of bus fare increases is largely immediate, for example a 20 per cent increase in fares has a short term effect of an 8 per cent reduction in demand in year 1 but on average 1.4 per cent per annum reduction thereafter.

The factors affecting demand for any public transport mode are not restricted to price only. The primary factors involved are:

1. *Fare variables*
   - own mode fare (underground or bus respectively)
   - cross-fare (ie bus fare/underground fare)
   - train operating company fares
2. *Timescale*
   One important issue is the extent to which passenger responses to fare changes differ between the short term and the long term. In London the data suggests that the impact of a fare change is immediate and there is no further effect. However, long-term the 'lagged' effects are difficult to measure as they may be affected by other factors over a long period. Local variations in price elasticities have also been detected. Where the Underground (with lower fares) provides an alternative to main line rail services then the cross elasticity is greater than on those routes further out in the commuting area.
3. *Personal income* (see p. 64)
4. *Service Level factors* (see p. 70)

5. *Economic demand side factors*

(a) Employment in Central London is a key factor in determining demand, particularly in those central business district areas served by the Underground. On main line railway operations peak demand arrivals are more closely correlated with service sector employment than with total employment in Central London.

(b) *Tourism*

Market research (LT 1996b) suggests that about 9 per cent of Underground travel is by non-UK residents and a further 8 per cent are visitors from other parts of the UK. The proportion of non-residents using buses is much lower. Demand elasticity for tourists is relatively low at –0.05 reflecting relatively short journeys.

The European Commission (EC, 1996) examined a series of public transport demand elasticities in several EU member states and reported as follows:

Table 2.14 *Summary of public transport demand elasticities*

Relationship	Conclusion
Urban public transport elasticity	range –0.3 to –0.4 (SR)
Long/short-run ratio	50–200% higher
Peak/off-peak ratio	30–100% higher
By country	little variation
By size of city	no clear relationship
Source of increased/reduced public transport demand	possibly 20–40% derived from former car travellers (maybe less in peak periods)

Source: European Commission, 1996

A study by Halcrow Fox (1993) examined:

- price elasticities of car users when different levels of road price charging was introduced
- the cross price elasticities of demand on public transport modes

London Transport's analysis (LT, 1984) of changes in fare paying journeys from 1980 to 1983 subdivided the effects into several different categories (see Table 2.15). The performance of London Transport buses and underground during the 1980 to 1983 period resulted in a better than forecast cost-benefit return from the May 1983 fares packages and a financial outcome which substantially exceeded the forecast return (LT, 1984). The factors responsible for this were:

- the recovery of traffic lost to BR in March 1982 when LT's longer distance fares became higher than BR's;
- the success of travelcards in generating new traffic and revenue;
- the effects of the underground zonal fares structure.

Table 2.15 *Changes in fare paying journeys (end 1980-end 1983) (%)*

	Bus	Underground
Fares and price effects	+8.5	+8.9
Service level and quality	+1.2	−0.6
Economic factors:		
unemployment	−2.6	−1.5
consumer spending	+0.4	+1.0
Planning factors:		
car ownership	−4.0	−1.5
tourism	+0.6	+1.5
residual trend		
(population decline etc)	−4.5	−2.1
Other factors	−0.6	−0.2
TOTAL CHANGE	−1.0	+5.5

Source: London Regional Transport (LT, 1984)

Table 2.17 shows how different levels of urban road charging has a price elasticity effect on car travel, varying by purpose of trip, employer's business, and short work trips which are either optional or have an alternative mode (eg train, tram or bus). (See Factors affecting magnitude of price elasticity, p. 83.) At higher rates of charge the price elasticity is higher.

In examining these journeys, the evidence of transfer is also clear. Table 2.17 shows the impact of road pricing on public transport usage and the size of cross price elasticity involved. A low charge of 0p–5p per mile would give an elasticity of +0.05. Thus a 5p charge per mile would represent a 50 per cent increase in the cost of car travel, and lead to a 2.7 per cent increase in bus use, 6.7 per cent increase in rail patronage and a 2.7 per cent increase in Metro passengers.

There is an associated income elasticity effect to such a policy. For low income families the cross-price elasticity will be greater than for those

Table 2.16 *Breakdown of fares and price effects (passenger miles) (1982/83 to 1990/91*

Effects of	Bus % change		Underground	
	Revenue	Pass. mile	Revenue	Pass. mile
Changes in real fares level	−11	+10	−17	+13
(fares reduction)				
Changes in fares structure	+4	+20	+16	+33
TOTAL	−7	+30	−1	+48

Source: London Regional Transport (LT, 1993)

Table 2.17 *Road price point and arc elasticities (London 1993)*

Market Sector	Elasticities at Different Road User Charges			
	0.0p/mile	0.5p/mile	0.15p/mile	0.35p/mile
Work/radial	−0.09	−0.10	−0.37	−0.47
Work/orbital	−0.05	−0.06	−0.12	−0.40
Employer' business	−0.06	−0.10	−0.15	−0.33
Education	−0.15	−0.20	−0.42	−0.87
Shopping/personal business	−0.24	−0.35	−0.46	−0.81
Social	−0.20	−0.31	−0.38	−0.67

Source: London Transport

on higher incomes so the overall impact of road charging will be determined by the relative importance of different income levels (see page 64).

THE MEASUREMENT OF PRICE ELASTICITY

Price elasticity

The size of the change in demand has to be measured if elasticity is to be used in making pricing policy decisions within a firm. This measurement is obtained by dividing the proportionate change in the quantity demanded by the proportionate change in price.

$$Ep = \frac{\text{proportionate change in quantity demanded}}{\text{proportionate change in price}}$$

In the short run elasticity of demand is likely to be relatively low (−0.1 to −0.4) or inelastic, because locations of producers and consumers are fixed and they have no alternative but to make the journey. In many cases there may at first be no alternative mode. For example, if there were increases in bus fares in a provincial city such as Chester, bus travellers would have to save enough to purchase a car.

In the longer term other factors determining elasticity can vary. People can change jobs or housing, buy a car, or other operators can appear on the scene. Trade activities may change if transport costs change and a new motorway may lead to the relocation of industrial activity.

The Serpell Report suggested fare increases of 40 per cent for London commuters; it also indicated that demand was fairly inelastic, and that price elasticity was as low as −0.15 on some routes. If this were so the revenue effect of such a policy could be calculated:

$$Ep = \frac{\%\Delta q}{\%\Delta p} \quad \text{where } \Delta q \text{ is the change in quantity demanded}$$
$$\Delta p \text{ is the change in the price}$$

$$-0.15 = \frac{\Delta q}{40\%}$$

Therfore $\Delta q = 6\%$

Table 2.18 *Hypothetical data – Bristol to London services*

	Fare (£)		Daily (weekday) No of passengers making whole trip	
	National Express	FGW (Saver)	Coach	Rail
Before fare change	28	45	180	500
After fare change	21	45	280	400
Percentage change	−25%	0	+55.5%	−20%

Note: FGW: First Great Western (train operating company)

The fall in demand will therefore be 6 per cent on present passenger levels but revenue will increase by about 34 per cent.

Cross (price) elasticity

Cross elasticity (Ec) is expressed in its simplest form as:

$$Ec = \frac{\text{percentage change in quantity demanded of our service}}{\text{percentage change in price of a competitive service}}$$

The effect of these fare changes could be positive or negative. If rail prices increased, feeder services would lose revenue since they are complementary. Road services, however, would gain more business because they are competitive alternatives.

The cross elasticity of demand for a train service from Swansea to London is the rate of change in the number of train tickets sold on that route in relation to the percentage change in the price of an alternative mode, such as National Express services. If the latter's fares were reduced from £28 to £21, the extent of the transfer of First Great Western passengers on Saver tickets (£45) compared with the change in price would give the cross elasticity of demand. The cross elasticity would be limited by the availability of alternative services. If some simple calculations are made to express the changes shown in Table 2.18:

$$Ec = \frac{-20\%}{-25\%} = 0.8$$

Such a high cross elasticity would indicate at least part of the market to be very responsive to hypothetical price changes. Competition on long distance express services has an impact on passenger figures which require a continuous update of pricing policies.

Estimating elasticity – theoretical problems

It has been established that in the case of inelastic demand, the proportionate change in price is greater than in quantity demanded and if demand is elastic, then the proportionate change in quantity demanded is greater than that of price.

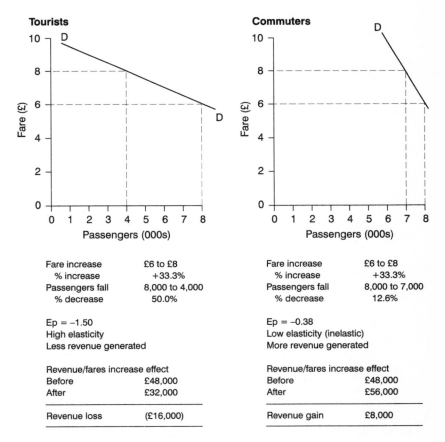

Fare increase	£6 to £8		Fare increase	£6 to £8
% increase	+33.3%		% increase	+33.3%
Passengers fall	8,000 to 4,000		Passengers fall	8,000 to 7,000
% decrease	50.0%		% decrease	12.6%

Ep = –1.50
High elasticity
Less revenue generated

Ep = –0.38
Low elasticity (inelastic)
More revenue generated

Revenue/fares increase effect			Revenue/fares increase effect	
Before	£48,000		Before	£48,000
After	£32,000		After	£56,000
Revenue loss	(£16,000)		Revenue gain	£8,000

Figure 2.12 *Varying elasticities in different markets*

Demand for commuter travel into the centre of a large city is inelastic. Demand for tourist journeys to holiday resorts is elastic. This is illustrated graphically in Figure 2.12. This form of analysis is a useful practical way for the operating manager or the transport economist to estimate price elasticity. However, at lower levels of demand, although the actual change in quantity demanded may be the same, the proportionate change is greater. The elasticity (that is the slope of the curve or the rate of change) will change along the curve and the elasticity at one fare level will not be applicable at a fare level above or below it.

A measurement of arc elasticity has to be used because fare or rate changes invariably occur along the curve and measuring a point along the curve is therefore inappropriate. In order to measure the elasticity along a curve it must be assumed that the elasticity is constant. A further difficulty arises when very large fare changes take place, for example, the changes in London fares between 1981 and 1983 and some European air fares in 1995–97 (see pp. 50 and 44). In addition, if fares are high and form a large item of expenditure, demand will be elastic, whereas with low fares, demand will be relatively inelastic. This relationship must be taken into account when there are changes from very low fares to high fares (as in South Yorkshire PTE services in 1986).

Measurement methods and problems

1. Market research surveys may be carried out on an operator's own vehicles before and after the introduction of price changes. This provides actual data for the calculation of price and cross elasticities.

Table 2.19 *Indicator of price elasticity magnitudes*

A. Fares Increase

	Elasticity	Increase in price %	Fall in demand %
−0.3	Medium	+10	−3
−0.1	Low	+10	−1
−0.8	High	+10	−8
−1.0	Problem	+10	−10
−1.2	Serious problem	+10	−12

B. Fares Reduction

The research from Stagecoach Holdings (HOC 1995 and Table 2.6) into price elasticities relating to fares reductions would change the above situation to one where elasticities greater than unity would be commercially, economically and environmentally (if cross price elasticity between car and bus exists) advantageous.

2. The modal split on a route between one service and another before and after the price change will enable cross elasticities to be calculated; for example, the effects of an operator's policy on rail, bus and car modes used by peak period commuters into the central business district (Grayling and Glaister, 2000). If data is available on all movements, the effects of competition between coaches and trains (see Table 2.4), and in particular the effects of lower InterCity saver prices on coach patronage, can be measured.

3. The reduction in patronage may not be solely the result of fare increases. Factors such as employment increases or higher car ownership levels can cause changes and present problems if they occur at the same time as the fare changes.

4. Inflation may influence the longer-term impact of fares increases. The analysis of price elasticity should relate to fare changes in real terms after allowing for inflation. For most products inflation is a gradual process, but in the case of fares there tends to be an annual increase. As a result, fares increase sharply when introduced but their real terms effect wears off as other prices catch up. Thus the traveller may react to this sudden real terms fare increase by stage shedding (ie walking part of the journey), or, if he/she lives near a zonal boundary, travelling to a less convenient station in an adjacent zone. However, in the long term he/she will probably return to their previous travel pattern.

5. Other factors are also associated with fare changes. A reduction in fares within, for example, an integrated transport policy instigated by government (see Chapter 12) requires a parallel investment in buses and trains. This increases frequencies and a service elasticity (see below) effect increases demand even further. The introduction of zonal fares, travelcards and other convenience factors at the same time as fare changes may exaggerate the effect of fare reductions or lessen the demand and reduce effect of a fare increase.

The sales of capitalcards increased significantly during 1985 and the effect was seen in British Rail's decision to retain the rail service into Marylebone Station to cope with the added demand from the western commuter sector into London. This increase is among those people to whom convenience rather than price is a decision making factor. Travelcard sales have similarly increased again despite fares increases.

6. Fares experiments can be used to provide data, but problems can arise if the fare changes are advertised as an experiment. The temporary nature of the reductions may not attract all possible potential customers. Regular travellers in car pooling arrangements would not want to jeopardise those arrangements for short term gains.

7. It is possible to carry out an analysis which measures the effects of several changes simultaneously. Such analysis might consider different types of journey (work, shopping, tourism, school), travellers' choice of mode and their valuation of time, as well as price changes.

Elasticity studies

A series of studies (BR, 1992; SRA, 2002) has been undertaken into rail travel elasticities in respect of fares and of quality. Quality factors are measured using stated preference techniques. They include:

- journey time;
- interchange (ease of, and delay times with preference for cross platform interchange, the removal of a need to change (ie through trains) rather than more convenient interchange with the maximum time before a fares reduction would be expected of 19 minutes for business travel and 35 minutes for optional travel;
- frequency;
- access to/from final destination at points of origin as passengers do not start or finish their trips at railway stations;
- rolling stock quality;
- station facilities (such as clean waiting rooms open in the evening and at weekends);
- reliability – this varied between different types of traveller where experienced travellers allowed a small contingency for late running and business travellers have a higher value of delayed time and leisure travellers' value of time depended on the leisure activity and its time sensitivity (eg: film starting time vs weekend away);
- overcrowding;
- seat reservation;
- cleanliness;
- passenger security;
- information;
- staff attributes/attitudes.

All these factors are taken into account in forecasting the revenue and passenger numbers using a variety of currently available models (OPRAF, 1997; SRA, 2000). The data quoted here are taken from earlier BR/TRL reports and more recent private train operating and company information. It is commercially valuable information, no particular routes are identified and the data are average elasticities and variations were found between different routes (TOCs, 2004).

In the case of fares elasticities there would be variations and movements between first and second class ticket purchases which are not shown in these figures. Such cross elasticities with down trading for full fares or even up trading to off-peak discounted first class fares have also to be taken into account when examining fares elasticities.

The impact of quality factors and of growth in GDP may also be measured in estimating service and external environment elasticities. In assessing the demand trends the consequences of these factors may be more important than fares elasticities.

The relatively high elasticity of the demand for leisure or non-commuting tickets appears reasonable because of its high optional nature while the low elasticity for full fare travel and for first class travel may be a result of the large element of business travel involved.

For towns close to a motorway running into London, the fare elasticity in each ticket type was larger than the average for other towns. This appears to reflect the increased competition between car and rail when there is a convenient motorway to speed up car travel. However, care should be taken against rationalising some conclusions because of the non-significant nature of some of the variables other than price. This should be borne in mind when considering the finding that London main line rail season tickets (other than to Waterloo) were significantly less elastic than flows from the other regions, while cheap day journeys into Waterloo were less elastic than cheap day travel in other regions.

Price elasticities amongst bus operators in the shire counties average –0.30 (ie if fares increase by 10 per cent patronage falls by 3 per cent) in the short run and over –0.6 in the long run. Demand elasticity varies considerably from one place to another. A DETR (1999) analysis of bus fare elasticity did not detect a particular type of area (eg rural, densely urban) as being a determinant.

The price and cross elasticity examples used here have been taken from the passenger sectors of the industry. These were chosen because data are more readily available on fares and because it is an area familiar to most transport industry employees and students. However, the principles can be applied in much the same way to the freight business in whatever mode of transport. The effects of rates increases on customer demand will be similar: if your company puts up its rates your customers may not ship goods at all, or find another haulier, or try to negotiate shared or return load discounts.

The simple equations in this section are merely used in explanation – the measurement techniques themselves are more complex and require rigorous testing of market research data before use in forecasting the effects of changing rates or fares.

Table 2.20 *Fares elasticities by market segment*

Category	InterCity	London area (eg NSE)	Major conurbations (PTE areas)	Regional Services
Overall				
Non-commuting	–0.8	–0.7	–0.7	–1.0
Commuting	–0.3	–0.2	–0.4	–0.5
Business	–0.4	–	–	–
Leisure	–1.1	–1.0	–0.9	–1.1

Source: BR, 1992; TOCs, 2004

Table 2.21 *Quality and external factors: elasticities by market segment*

Services	Quality elasticities[1]*	Elasticity to GDP[2]
InterCity (from London)	−3.5 to −1.5	+1.5
Other InterCity and 'Regional' Express	−3.5 to −1.5	+1.0
London area – commuting	−0.5 to +0.5	
PTE areas – other	−3.5 to −1.5	+1.5

Source: BR, 1992; TOCs, 2004

Notes:
1.* The demand levels are in a direct relationship to quality (ie quality rises demand is expected to rise; fall in quality: fall in demand.)
2. As GDP rises so demand rises (the derived demand concept outlined in Chapter 1).

INCOME ELASTICITY

This is the responsiveness of demand to a change in income. Income elasticity for personal movement is generally positive. As income increases so demand for travel, measured in number of trips made or number of miles travelled, increases. This is true for car, train and air travel which are used by higher income groups, while bus travel can suffer from negative elasticity as incomes rise and people use more comfortable or faster modes of transport. Long distance coach travel is likely to have a negative elasticity; as customers' income rises so they switch to a faster or more convenient form of transport. However, among lower income groups (the main bus users are women, children and retired people), as income rises so the number of trips made increases, giving a positive elasticity. The exception is unemployment (with its consequent reduction in income) when in one PTE area an elasticity of demand of −0.05 was found in the relationship between percentage rise in unemployment and percentage use of public transport (ITS, 1998; Preston, 1998).

Car use

The relationship between cars/car use and real disposable income from 1952 to 1992 is shown in Figure 2.14. The line representing an elasticity of 1.0 is also shown. Up to the early 1970's car ownership and use increased more rapidly (at about 8 per cent pa) than income, indicating an income elasticity of about 3.0 if the whole of that increase was linked to a 2.5 increase in income. This period was one of change to a consumer-led society and a parallel rise in car ownership. From the 1970's onwards, the growth in income, car ownership and car use all rose at about 2.5–3.0 per cent per annum thus indicating an income elasticity (on the same assumption) of 1.0.

Figure 2.13 *Price elasticity based discounted tickets*

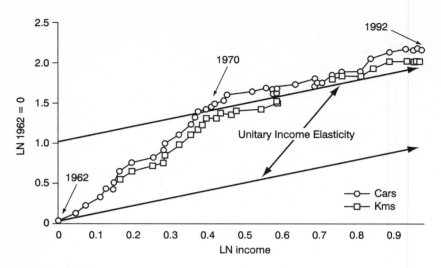

Figure 2.14 *Cars and passenger kms related to income*
Source: RAC Car dependence 1995

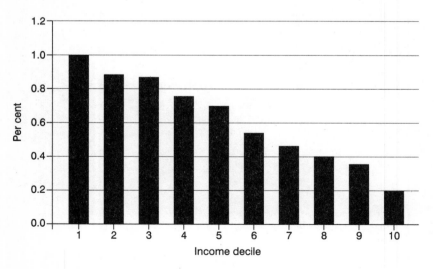

Figure 2.15 *Bus expenditure share by income group*
Source: RAC Car dependence 1995

Income elasticity effect in public policy

A flat rate congestion charge would in proportionate terms have greatest impact on lower income groups. An analysis of the proposed £2 daily charge scheme in Edinburgh (Cain and Jones, 2004) could indicate an increase in motoring costs by 11 per cent for the lowest income households. Thus only car users in the 30–40% decile or above could continue to work within the charges zone. Income elasticity here is based on affordability when trips fall as income falls.

Table 2.22 *'Affordability' for different income groups*

Decile	Proportion of income spent on motoring %	Additional money available for motoring (£)	Affordable number of charged weekly trips
0–10%	62.5	−17.18	−8.9
10–20%	31.5	1.11	0.6
20–30%	26.6	9.06	4.5
30–40%	26.4	12.04	6.0
90–100%	16.3	145.53	72.8

Source: Cain and Jones: Congestion charging and low-income car users, January 2004, Newcastle upon Tyne
Thus, car users working within the charges zone would only be able to continue in those jobs if they were in the 30–40% decile or upwards. The income elasticity test here is based on affordability and, for a fixed charge, possible trips fall as income falls.

London public transport

Evidence (LT, 1997; TfL, 2002) shows that an increase in personal income has the following effects on demand:

- direct: fares become more affordable with more trips or longer trips
- indirect: activities such as shopping or leisure are encouraged so generating more travel
- longer term: car ownership increases resulting in a shift in modal split from public transport to car (see Table 2.15).

This last effect is marked for buses because higher car ownership and use results in increased traffic congestion thus affecting bus operations. Underground speeds are not affected and so travel on it is relatively more attractive in the long term so offsetting the expected negative effects of increased car ownership on Underground demand.

Assumptions/Issues

1. Each 1 per cent increase in earnings results in 0.6 per cent increase in car ownership per head.

2. Increases in personal incomes encouraging shifts to faster modes were not estimated.
3. The normal close positive correlation between earnings, retail sales and car ownership per head has not affected short-term demand changes during recession periods and thus has a limited effect on demand.
4. Demand effects resulting from people's perception of the value of time resulting from earnings increases and consequent shift to faster modes have not been included in the LT model as they tend to be relatively longer-term effects. There is a body of research that suggests that car owners travel more (trips and kilometres) than non car owners. This is a reflection of convenience, wet weather not playing any part in the decision to travel and car owners in general having a higher disposable income to spend on travel compared with non car owners.

Figure 2.16 shows the relationship between car ownership and income levels in London and in other major cities (eg Manchester and Birmingham). The

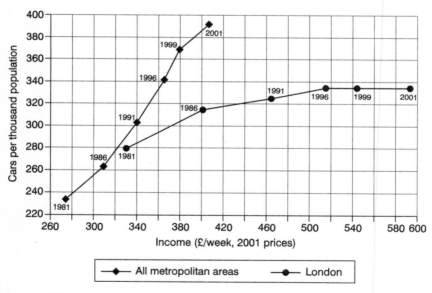

Figure 2.16 *Car ownership and income levels 1981–2001*
Source: Department for Transport; Transport for London, London Travel Report 2002

Table 2.23 *Estimated income elasticities for London Bus and Underground demand (2000 fares/earnings levels)*

	Bus	**Underground**
Income elasticity	−0.54	+0.40

overall position in the UK is shown in Figure 2.14. The London figures indicate the importance of high income and low car ownership in central London. Here the service elasticity in favour of public transport is strong; income elasticity therefore has a lower impact than in other major cities. This indicates the ways in which service and income elasticities can 'pull' against each other in an area where public transport is and is perceived as, frequent and safe, operates until late or has night bus services and where it is a socially acceptable means of transport for the wealthy.

Main line railway

The reports (BR, 1992, SRA, 2002) on the elasticity of intercity rail travel found income elasticities of 0.10 for season tickets, 0.15 for cheap day returns and 0.10 for full fares, thus indicating a close link between increased incomes and increased travel.

There are several reasons for this. For example:

1. People in lower income groups (say under £6000 pa) make basic trips to doctors, shops, etc, and as their income increases or they obtain employment or better paid employment they are able to consider more leisure trips.
2. People in higher income groups (£35,000 to £50,000) have increased their travel mileage as their income has risen, either because they have moved to better homes further away from their work, because they travel further to their holiday destinations or because they have more in-work travel.

Consequently, income elasticity is generally positive, unlike price elasticity which involves a negative relationship. There are limits on income elasticity because travel is limited by the amount of time available, and it has been suggested that although business, journey-to-work, and leisure travel increases with income, there comes a point when the demand curve flattens out or even begins to fall when limits are placed on the time available for travel.

GDP and income elasticity

The concept of income elasticity may be applied to personal/household income or to national income (GDP) as similar impacts on travel may occur.

The terrorist activity on 11 September 2001 in New York and Washington has had a significant impact upon US and North Atlantic traffic (see Table 2.8). However, the downward trend in passengers and freight carried by air had begun prior to that (see Figure 2.17).

The economic downturn in the United States and its impact on incomes and trade resulted in transatlantic freight tonnes falling by 2.3 per cent (2002) with trade between North America and Southeast Asia down by

10.9 per cent. Because few airlines own their aircraft (most are leased) there is no capital asset to sell off to improve cash flow. In consequence, even if demand is expected to recover in the medium term, aircraft will be 'mothballed' and application made to governments for financial aid.

The reduced economic growth rates will have an income elasticity effect on the overall demand for air travel reflected in the rates of growth of 'low cost' airlines compared with conventional airlines, which indicates a desire by the business sector of the air travel market to look for lower cost travel options.

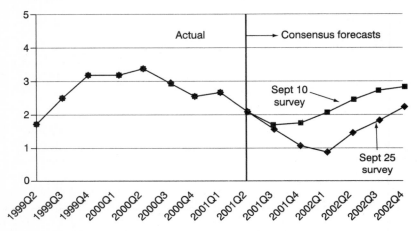

Figure 2.17 *UK GDP growth forecasts (percentage change year on year)*
Source: Concensus Forecasts September 2001, House of Commons Air Transport Industry report HC 484 (HOC 2002a)

SERVICE ELASTICITY

This is a measure of the effect of service standards on demand for an operator's transport facility.

If a road freight haulier is persistently late with deliveries it is likely to find its contract either terminated or not renewed on expiry. An unreliable bus company will lose customers to other companies, to rail or most likely to the car.

CASE STUDY 4: ANALYSIS OF EUROSTAR AND EUROTUNNEL MARKETS, 1992–97

London–Paris Eurostar market

There are two main reasons for the doubling of Eurostar's market revenue from £300m in 1992 to £700m in 1997:

Table 2.24 *Passenger movements 1995–1996 (000's) London Heathrow to major European destinations*

London Heathrow to:	1996	1995	% change
Vienna	573	549	4
Copenhagen	724	693	4
Paris (CDG)	1893	1.972	–4
Paris (CDG ex-LGW)	314	352	–11
Frankfurt Main	1355	1.308	4
Madrid	681	615	11
Rome	1024	986	4

Sources: Civil Aviation Authority, CAP 671, UK Airports Annual Statement of Movements, Passenger and Cargo 1996. CAA April 1997

1. Created traffic primarily in the leisure sector, from passengers' perception of a 'hassle-free' trip together with a special or novelty trip basis particularly in First Class (on discount fares).
2. Diversion of leisure travellers and some business traffic (harder to get because of air miles/business gold card especially if the traveller is making the decision). Hence the Eurostar frequent traveller scheme. Eurostar has proved itself stronger in attracting the leisure market especially for weekend visits to Paris in place of a weekend by car to a British destination.

In terms of yield management Eurostar has achieved respectable volumes but mainly at the discounted £100 return fare end of the market rather than the high yield (£180–£280) business market segment.

Following the introduction of Eurostar services (1995) between London and Paris/Brussels there was a reduction in demand for air services between London (LHR/LGW) and Paris (CDG) while demand for Eurostar services increased (see Figures 2.18 to 2.20). This is likely to have resulted from service elasticity effects (perceived convenience, single mode trip and journey time between city centres) and cross price elasticity. This reduction in demand was in the context of overall increases in air transport demand of at least 4 per cent between London and other major European Union capital cities from 1991 to 1996.

London–Brussels Eurostar market

In this market, air traffic appears to have suffered little from the introduction of Eurostar services while the latter has benefited from overall growth in traffic. However, the reduced journey time to 2h 25m may divert more business traffic as will connecting services via Thalys trains to Amsterdam and other SNCF services via Lille. The reliability factor will

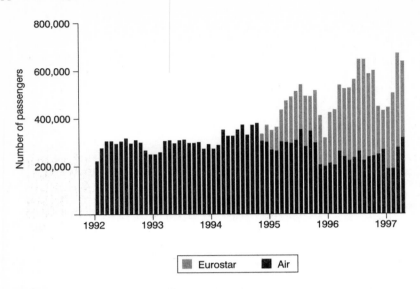

Figure 2.18 *London–Paris/Brussels: airline and Eurostar passenger numbers*

Source: Eurostar

also become significant if passengers perceive high speed trains as preferable to air travel. The changing image of rail travel (into a suitable business mode) and more sophisticated pricing policy by rail operators will have both service and cross-price elasticity effects.

Eurotunnel market

The car/coach/truck cross-Channel service through the Channel Tunnel competes directly with the cross-Channel ferries operating between Dover and Calais, attracting primarily mid-Britain to mid-Europe movements using improved infrastructure at either end. Eurotunnel is also operating in a growing market because:

- of an easier, more frequent option provided by Eurotunnel
- GDP is rising and trade is therefore higher
- the cost of transport is declining as an element of total production cost and thus production stages may be at several locations.

The decision by users to choose Eurotunnel rather than the ferries appears to be a mix of (Kendall, 1997):

- ease of loading
- frequency of departures
- time critical material, eg fresh bread, German yoghurt

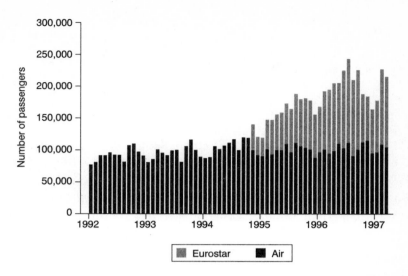

Figure 2.19 *London–Brussels route: Eurostar and airline passenger numbers*

Source: Eurostar

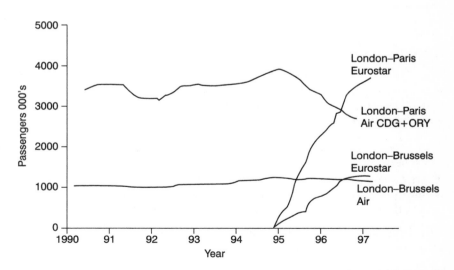

Figure 2.20 *London–Paris route: Eurostar and airline passenger numbers*

Source: Eurostar

- JIT operators, eg a major Belgian distributor who previously used air freight via London Heathrow used Eurotunnel's later closing down time (23.00 vs 20.00 hrs) for evening distribution to Britain
- frequency and journey time for one-day return trips where the ¾ hour break on Eurotunnel is sufficient, particularly for small companies in south east England
- decisions to use Eurotunnel or ferries are made mainly by the company with tight controls on vehicle movement
- the major price discounting by Eurotunnel in 1995 had the intention of attracting ferry customers and growing the market; by 1997, however, ticket yields had returned to the pre-1995 level.

The use of discounts (and thus cross price elasticity) had little impact on the traditional (long summer holiday) traffic and was mainly aimed at the price sensitive segments where a high premium (eg £20) over the ferry fare could not be sustained. The 1995 price reductions did achieve market share but did not promote the product in terms of quality characteristics. This restricted its market stimuli to those affecting own price and cross price elasticity effects and not achieving any service elasticity benefits. This would achieve a higher market share in the longer term through the high retention rate indicated by market research.

The generated traffic from the initial 'curiosity/novelty' market has been replaced by more regular travellers but who are in a price sensitive market which might be the cause of reported passenger reductions (RAIL, 2004) in Eurostar flows.

Market segments (for rationale see Chapter 4)

1. Short break:- medium yield (£90); several trips per year; long weekend is an expanding segment.
2. Day trip:- optional; low yield (£60); impulse visits from London and south-east England.
3. Long stay:- high yield (£130+); two to three weeks; very conservative market segment; have always used the ferry; book 6 months in advance; this traditional market has to be Eurotunnel's primary objective in the attempt to gain market share.
4. Club class:- fast track; business market is bigger than expected; Eurotunnel has 80 per cent of the cross-Channel business car market primarily related to speed and frequency. The ferry is not seen by the 'business suit' traveller as a 'business' mode.

Bus and Metro

In the case of passenger transport, research has shown that where alternative operators or modes are available, unreliability leads to a permanent loss of passengers. In Cheshire (1979), for every one per cent of lost mileage, 0.6 per cent of passenger trips were lost permanently; the figure in Manchester (FGM, 1997) is more cautiously estimated at 1 per cent loss of passengers per 1 per cent lost mileage.

Service rationalisation (particularly where route changes are not understood by the travellers, or where publicity is poor) can lead to a reduction in demand. This is more likely to occur with less frequent travellers than with regular users, such as commuters, who see the changes advertised on the company's vehicles or rolling stock. This effect will also be found when timetables change from winter to summer services or where timetables are not available.

The bus industry has not always done enough to promote bus services and provide co-ordinated information for different company bus services and for train services, both in advance of and during journeys (WTRC, 2003; DOT, 1996). Marketing spend is at a lower proportion of turnover than other industries or other transport modes, for example, the provision of network information, interchange plans, timetable leaflets (which are easily understood), bus stop and bus station information (for individual stops as, for example, in Dutch systems) real time (eg Nice; Countdown, London) and bus information (exterior and interior). Research carried out in Manchester and the West Midlands (TRL, 1994) and in Wales (WTRC, 2003) indicated information as a potential enhancer of passenger numbers – a form of service elasticity.

London Transport studies (LT, 1993, 1997, 2002) of service elasticity have also used miles operated (as a measure of reliability) to relate to service quality as a variable affecting demand. There is no evidence that the effects of changes in service levels has a lagged effect, but rather that 90 per cent of the effect of a service change occurs within three months.

Service elasticity of bus services in London had increased significantly since 1970. Then high levels of unreliability and reduced mileage (TfL, 2002) resulted in service elasticities of 0.14 (1970–77); 1.15 (1977–79); 0.33 (1980–86: the GLC Fares Fair pricing policy and increased bus mileage); and 0.65 (1995 onwards with bus mileage increases). The local market bus service elasticities vary between short run (+0.4) and long run (seven years) (+0.9). The report (DETR, 1999) suggests that price and service quality changes where the former rises by 10 per cent and the latter falls by 10 per cent would give no change in patronage.

Table 2.25 *Estimated elasticity of demand to levels of operated mileage (service elasticity)*

LT bus	0.18	(+0.12)
Underground	0.08	(+0.06)

Source: TfL (2002)

A major problem in identifying the service elasticity for bus and metro modes as a whole is that the relationship between total revenue/patronage and total operated mileage will vary depending on the geographical location of the operations and the time of day, both of which affect reliability particularly of bus services in congested urban areas.

There is also some evidence of a cross-service elasticity where the unreliability of one mode may cause a change in demand for a more reliable mode (eg bus versus metro/train) particularly where the fare (eg travelcard-based) is the same.

Several bus companies have introduced enhanced frequencies, which have an effect on patronage. A new minibus service operating a five minute headway between Swansea and several middle-income suburbs where fares are the same as other routes but improved frequency and reliability has led to higher load factors and passenger numbers than the conventional bus service which it replaced (1991).

First Group has found that in its bus services reliability was twice as important as service frequency and bus quality, while fare levels were a significantly smaller factor in determining travel. The company analysed (NRM, 1997) factors that 'drive' satisfaction and the relative importance of each factor. The resultant 'weighting' (see Table 2.26) indicates their importance in determining service elasticity factors.

Table 2.26 *Weighting of service factors*

Reliability	34
Frequency	17
Vehicles	14
Routes	11
Fares	7

Source: First Group plc

In west London the introduction of a 607 high quality vehicle express service between Shepherd's Bush and Uxbridge along a 'normal' running 207 route led to some transfer between services but the total market in the corridor has grown (CWB, 1997). A similar situation has resulted following the introduction of the Leeds guided bus service whose patronage has risen by 30–40 per cent with some transfer from adjacent routes but primarily representing new customers.

The N29 bus route is part of the London night bus network travelling from Trafalgar Square, to north London. The change in frequency and the promotion of the fare level compared to a black taxi/minicab, its main competitors, has produced results primarily reflective of service elasticity.

	Before	*After*
Frequency Fri/Sat (mins)	15	10
Frequency Other (mins)	30	20
Cost/resources (%)		+25
Revenue (%)		+33
Passengers		+54
Cross elasticity from other routes ⎫		no significant
Transfers from other routes ⎬		change
Waiting time		less than for a taxi

The service elements involved were frequency and information thus indicating a relationship between the two (WTRC, 2003; TAS, 1995; NRM, 1997; BR, 1992).

In Oxford this combination of cross-price elasticity relating perceived car costs to bus costs and service elasticity resulting from bus priority and city centre penetration schemes has resulted in a major shift in the modal split of person trips (see Table 2.28). In 1995, park and ride (bus) accounted for 5.7 per cent of the bus figure.

This provides an example of how the price mechanism (cross-price elasticities) of car parking charges, service elasticity (bus priority) and elasticity of supply (restricting new car parking spaces) can be used to achieve public policy objectives. Their usage therefore is not restricted to achieving commercial/revenue objectives.

Bus usage in Oxford city increased by 40–60 per cent (on different routes) between 1985 and 1995 as a result of three primary factors:

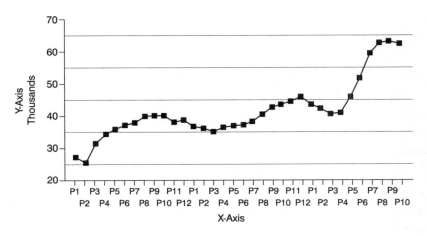

Figure 2.21 *N29 Passenger trends*

Source: Weightman (1997)

Table 2.27 *Elasticity indicators (service and cross price) – buses in Oxford (1985–1995)*

	% change
Bus patronage (Oxford)	+300
Bus patronage (GB) (outside London)	−29
Daily passenger trips (Thames Transit 1985)	+80
Park and Ride usage	+80
Traffic flows	0

Source: Oxford (1996)

Table 2.28 *Inner Oxford Cordon – person trips/excluding pedestrians*

	12-hour/two-way flow (%)		% change 1991–2001
	1991	2001	
Bus	27	44	+63
Cycle	11	11	0
Cars and taxis	54	39	−28
Motor cycle	2	1	−50
HGV	2	1	−50
LGU	4	4	0
	100	100	

Source: Oxfordshire County Council in HC 828 (HOC, 2002b)

Note: Pedestrian movements account for 20% of cross-Cordon travel.

- arguably the most effective park and ride scheme in Britain was well publicised and with adequate capacity (600 spaces in 1975; 3500 in 1993; 5000 in 2003)
- deregulation and competition with significant increases in frequency (6–10 minutes in place of 30 minutes on most urban routes) with extended or new Saturday and Sunday services; and two major well run operators
- a policy pursued by city and county councils to control traffic flows in the central area, reduce off-street parking, pursue planning policies that restrict parking place numbers for new buildings, and increase car parking charges to levels nearer to those in central London than in a similar sized city. This change in relative costs of park and ride compared with city centre driving/parking (see Table 2.27) will have resulted in a cross price elasticity impact.

The frequency factor coupled with reliability, service coverage and new high specification vehicles in Dublin (Coufield and O'Mahoney, 2004) has indicated a significant service elasticity figure as reflected in Table 2.27 (Oxford, 1996).

If bus companies are to improve the quality aspect of their operations then additional investment is required by operators (in vehicles and their waiting areas) and by local authorities (in bus stations, shelters, bus lanes, park and ride facilities etc). In cities such as Oxford, Exeter and Ipswich where this has occurred, bus usage has increased.

First Bus (2003), one of Britain's major bus groups, in a pilot study (NRM, 1997) of its services in Glasgow (Strathclyde Buses), Bristol (Cityline, Badgerline), Ipswich (Eastern National) and Leeds (City Link) identified frequency, reliability and time-keeping as the customers' primary determinants of service quality (and probably service elasticity levels) while attitude and fares appear not to be major issues.

Table 2.29 *Growth in public transport patronage*

City	Dates	Increase	Current share	Investment (£ eqn)
Amsterdam[1]	1970 to 1992	+41%	30%	N/A
Grenoble	1975 to 1990	+150%[2]	15%	250 m
Hannover	1970 to 1980	+30%[3]	22%	925 m
Munich	1972 to 1991	+55%	25%	3.5 bn
Stuttgart	1979 to 1991	+29%	23%	1.7 bn
Vienna	1981 to 1991	+35%	37%	
Zurich	1950 to 1985	+50%		
	1985 to 1990	+30%	37%	1.0 bn

Source: Jones (1993)

Notes:
1. excluding NS services
2. from a very low base
3. most of 1980's stagnant; last three years + 15%

A series of pro public transport policies may also change the travellers' perceptions of it as an alternative to the car. These policies have included:

- buses feeding a rail-based system
- through ticketing on all public transport modes
- franchised private services are integrated
- good interchanges
- dense public transport network (including frequency)
- increase in rail network compared with road network (no further major road schemes)
- orbital rail services to reduce radial demand in central or near central area
- traffic restraint with pedestrian areas, better cycling facilities and better penetration to central area

Those cities which have invested heavily in rail-based public transport have had significant and sustained increases in patronage (Jones, 1993). This would indicate a high service elasticity where the customer has responded to improvements in frequency, reliability and density of operations.

The data for identifying variables in establishing the value of service elasticity on such services may be obtained in two ways:

1. with on-bus surveys. This will restrict the analysis to existing users, will identify core customers (often seen as the immediate market to satisfy), tourists and out of town users. A random sample will have a higher percentage of frequent travellers.
2. a random household (telephone) survey. This will obtain data on people in the catchment area of the services, including potential customers, competitors' customers (such as those of West Riding, Kingfisher and United in Leeds) and will tend to have a higher percentage of less frequent users.

The first method therefore concentrates on keeping the existing market while the second is likely to identify potential customers.

The objective of such surveys is to take action to improve service quality and to obtain the degree of general satisfaction with the service – the most important determinant of the magnitude of service elasticity.

This analysis is partly reflected in research by TAS (1995). The primary difference is the importance of fares and journey time for those with the option of using a car: especially when fares were compared with perceived cost (petrol/parking). Thereafter the findings were similar and in order of importance were:

a) reliability/timekeeping
b) availability of information
c) adequate waiting facilities
d) quality characteristics of the journey (eg noise, congestion, smoking)
e) attitude of the driver
f) quality of the vehicle

Main line rail services

Quality analysis is being used by Virgin Trains and GNER to qualify the extent of any mismatch between what customers expect and what they actually experience (Wicks, 1997) using the ServQual methodology. The analysis is also aimed at differentiating between data for different market segments and thus weighting quality gaps by segment in order to prioritise improvements.

A study by SNCB (1997) (Belgian Railways) into fares and quality elasticities examined the impact of railway service level improvements on demand and on price elasticity. It concluded that the greater the improvement in level of service, the lower is the price elasticity of passengers. For example if the overall fare level is increased by 15 per cent (in terms of on train journey time) to maintain patronage levels as before in revenue terms, if service quality is improved, higher overall fare level will lead to increased revenue; but even if service level is deteriorating, retaining fares at their basic level may also lead to revenue increases.

The introduction of Eurostar services from London to Paris/Brussels and TGV services within France have led to a change in modal split. This in the leisure market has been partly due to price competition but research (ES, 1997) indicates that the convenience and total journey time of train travel compared with air travel has been a major factor. The ease of check in, the city centre locations for arrival/departures and the shorter journey time (three hours by train; almost four hours by air from London to Paris) have been the most quoted elements in customer decision making. As a result of further journey time reductions following the completion of Stage 1 of the Channel Tunnel Rail Link cutting the London–Brussels time to 2 hours 20 (previously 2 hours 40) and London–Paris to 2 hours 35 (previously3 hours), rail now has a market share of 4.8 per cent of the former and66 per cent of the latter. Cancellations of Eurostar trains are 1.0 per cent and punctuality is now at 87 per cent since Stage 1 of the Channel Tunnel Rail Link was opened (2004). These elements form part of the service elasticity effect.

Airline service quality

The challenge of 'low cost' airlines and economic downturn with over 35 per cent of business travellers using low cost operators (IATA, 2002) such as easyJet and Ryanair in Europe and Jet Blue, Frontier and South West Airlines in the United States is based on low fares (price elasticity) but also better than expected amenities (service elasticity). The provision of individual, live satellite television and greater seat pitch (32 inches) rivals conventional airlines, and additional 'space' through wider seats or an empty adjacent seat often achieved by 3–3–3 seating replacing a 2–5–2 configuration on wide bodied jets were found to be determinants of operator selection by travellers.

While providing 'more room in coach' (American Airlines advertising campaign, 2003) it reduced capacity by 6.4 per cent but at a time when capacity reductions were required to reflect reduced demand.

For many of the 'full service' carriers, such as American, Cathay Pacific and BA, a new generation of in-flight products was necessary but which achieved a higher service level without adding costs. Adding overhead bin space for larger 'roll aboard' luggage cases (which eliminate the arrivals hall wait for baggage and reduce handling costs) is seen by many passengers as a service benefit. Catering provision varies considerably between short haul and long haul but the objective is primarily to reduce costs with improved service often seen as a 'bonus'. BA however see 'service excellence as our unique attribute; sticking to what we do well – being a full service airline' as the basis of what their brand stands for (AB, 2003a). Price competition and cost reduction thus appear to have to be within these parameters. But for some markets price is the key strategy element (see Chapter 4) while simultaneously maintaining the brand image (service elasticity).

Such branding distinction will take time and each airline will strive to differentiate itself from its competitors and create distinct levels of service. However, most airlines remain conscious of the need to reduce costs, use service elasticity as a reaction to cross-price elasticity and retain those passengers currently downtrading from full business class fares to discount economy class tickets or, worse, to the 'low cost' airlines (see Chapter 4).

Two African airlines, Kenya and South African Airways, have repositioned their service element by offering 'full lie-flat' beds instead of reclining seats in business class. Gulf Air sets its policy as 'taking all the icons of first class and putting them into business class'. Changing the meal service style in economy class 'will bring back some grandeur to economy class'. These are based on an analysis of service elasticity elements that affect demand. Swiss and Cathay Pacific see flat beds in 'premium' class; increased seat pitch to 33 inches (from 31) in economy class and the wide bodied jets such as the Airbus A340, Boeing 777 and the new 550-seater Airbus 380 'making a "step change" in interior design but which are also space efficient solutions' (Cathay Pacific, 2003).

Direct flights from provincial British (eg Cardiff, Manchester and Edinburgh) airports to European centres like Paris, Amsterdam, Brussels and Frankfurt provide a shorter journey time, and the service elasticity effect has resulted in transfers from London-originated flights.

The development of operations from such airports has indicated the convenience factor in those markets. The creation of airline alliances though primarily intended to achieve higher yields and lower costs (see Chapter 4) could improve service facilities for the traveller by offering a worldwide network of services.

Journey times

Service elasticity may be considered in journey times as well as in reliability and comfort factors – those most frequently applied to public transport. Journey times have become many travellers' measure of distance. Time is the factor expended, which can be valued in monetary terms, and the traveller will consider the journey times by road and rail between, for example, key English cities when making the modal choice decision.

The impact of increased car journey time can be measured in terms of service elasticity in respect of car use. If service elasticity was high, ie time was an important criterion, journey time increases would be expected to result in a reduction in car usage. In respect of rail travel if rail journeys are now relatively faster than the equivalent road journey then a strong service elasticity in respect of journey time would be expected to result in an increase in rail usage.

FACTORS DETERMINING THE MAGNITUDE OF ELASTICITY

Essential journeys

An essential service will have a relatively inelastic demand. For example, commuters in London, Paris, Rome or New York must travel into the central business district to work (LT, 1996a). Therefore increases in fares on mainline commuter services or Metro/Subway/Underground will not significantly affect the number of peak passenger trips if there is no close alternative mode.

If trips are non-essential (mainly leisure trips) then demand will be relatively elastic. Family trips to the countryside will be unlikely to take place if fares are high, while at lower fares or with a pricing policy (eg railcards) which reduces the price per person more trips will take place.

Alternative practical available modes

The elasticity of demand for totally essential journeys to work will be relatively low (ie inelastic) but travel by a particular mode will be affected if there are alternatives available. The availability of substitutes will also be a more generally applicable factor in respect of the elasticity of demand for a particular mode. For most big-city commuters there is no practical alternative to rail or tube travel; if fares increased and they all changed to using cars the road and car parks have insufficient capacity to carry the additional flows. The present London modal split of the traffic flows in the peak and in total are shown in Table 1.6. The opportunities for travellers in general to choose a non public transport mode are clearly greater in suburban areas or smaller towns where car/walking are predominant modes.

The London fare policies of the early 1980's provided a good example of cross elasticity between public transport modes and from car to Underground but modal transfers from public transport to private cars are unlikely in large capital cities. In towns with populations of say up to 100,000 the evidence suggests a high cross-price elasticity of −0.3 from bus to car. This has been particularly possible since the rise in car ownership from 1970 onwards in Western Europe. The effects were seen in practice during rail and tube strikes in Britain during recent years (1980's to 2004) when traffic congestion created traffic blockages which in some areas took several hours to disperse.

In the case of long distance business travel for distances of less than 200 miles, car and train provide alternatives but for longer journeys, air travel is the only practical option if a return journey has to made in one day. Consequently, if substitute modes are available then demand will be relatively elastic (cross elasticity).

Alternative supplier available

If only one operator, or a cartel, is providing the transport service then demand will be inelastic for those whose journey is essential. The London

Table 2.30 *Summary of elasticity effects with examples*

Elasticity	Effect	Example
Demand		
Own price	Responsiveness of the operator's market to a change in its own price	Operators increasing market share by price differentiation or reduction (BA World Offers; First Great Western/ GNER Super Saver & Business First)
Cross price	Responsiveness of the market to the change of price of one operator on demand for another operator's services	Operators entering the market with significantly lower fares than incumbent operators capturing market share and increasing demand (Virgin Atlantic; South West Airlines; easyJet)
Service	Responsiveness of the market to improved or decreased quality of service (frequency; restaurant facilities)	Operators increasing or retaining market share by improved service and quality of product (Eurostar; Gulf Air; P & O cruises)
Income	Effect on demand by an increase or decrease in disposable income of customers	Increased demand for higher quality product by high salary users (P & O cruises; airline business class)
Supply	Responsiveness of supply to price and product demand	Supply increases to meet market demand (but note price decrease as a result of overcompetition) (Eurotunnel/ Ferries – Cross Channel market; BA/Virgin – North Atlantic market; Ryanair/Aer Lingus – UK/Dublin market)

to New York air route when shared between BOAC, Pan Am and Trans World Airways (TWA) prior to 1980 provided the traveller with the only means of air travel at one set of fares, and cross elasticity was relatively low. Total demand was also low compared with 2004. New airlines (eg Laker Airways then Virgin Atlantic and more recently Delta, United and American) have entered this market.

There is a continuing cross price elasticity effect between operators as travellers 'shop around' particularly for leisure fares but also for business class seats as companies copy. This effect has also been seen as routes within the European Union following the liberalisation policy and increased competition from so called 'discount' price airlines. In general, however, corporate demand in the business market has remained relatively inelastic because of their concern for perceived reliability, image, in-flight service and personal preference.

Proportion of income

If transport expenditure is a low proportion of total income then demand will be inelastic. In the business market, despite a concern by some companies about travel costs (see above), for others a first class fare of £6,642 from London to New York had little effect since business travel was a very small proportion of the costs of the multinational companies using the service. An increase in car prices by 40 per cent is likely to delay the purchase of the ordinary family saloon, whereas it will have little effect on a millionaire's decision to buy a new Rolls-Royce.

If a transport expenditure item is a high proportion of family income then its elasticity is likely to be high (eg long distance foreign holidays, new car).

Many of these factors are interdependent. The demand for a journey which is essential, where there is no alternative supplier or substitute mode, will be relatively inelastic. If it is essential and there is an alternative way, then it will be inelastic with respect to the journey but very elastic with respect to the original mode used.

REFERENCES

AB (2003a) Smarter service and the new economy, *Airline Business*, January, Sutton.

AB (2003b) Continued descent, *Airline Business*, September, Sutton.

AB (2004) Air India gives low cost, *Airline Business*, July, Sutton.

BR (1992) *Passenger Demand Forecasting Handbook*, British Railways Board, London.

BTC (2003) Business Travel Coalition, reported in *Airline Business*, September.

Cain, A and Jones, P (2004) Could congestion charge cause hardship to low-income car users, UTSG Conference Proceedings, Newcastle upon Tyne.

Cheshire (1979) Cole, S, Survey data and analysis, Cheshire County Council, Chester.

City Flyer Express (1997), Flight International, London, 1995; British Airways information 1997.

Copeley, G (2003) Multi modal studies and the 10 year plan, *Transport Economist*, TEG, London.

Coufield, B and O'Mahoney, M (2004) The use of service measurements as a means to evaluate the performance of public transport operators: a case study of Dublin, UTSG Conference Proceedings, Newcastle upon Tyne.

CWB (1997) CentreWest London Buses, London.

DETR (1999) Bus fares elasticity project, TAS Partnership Ltd and Transport Studies Unit, UCL, London for the Department of Environment, Transport and the Regions, London.

DOT (1996) Better information for bus passengers, Department of Transport, London.

EC (1996) Pricing and funding of urban transport, Transport Research APAS report, European Commission Transport Directorate (DG VII), Brussels.

ES (1997) Research (unpublished) by Eurostar (UK) Ltd, London.

Fairhurst, M (1986) Travelcards and Zonal Fares in London, PTRC Annual Summer Meeting Seminar K, PTRC, London.

FGM (1997) First Greater Manchester Buses data; Mitchell, M (1997) Director – North West, First Bus plc – interview with author. Oldham, Lancashire.

FGW (2004a), brochures produced by First Great Western.

FGW (2004b), discussions with directors of First Great Western.

First Bus (2003) Annual Report 2002–03, First Bus plc, Aberdeen, Scotland.

GNER (2004), brochures produced by Great North Eastern Railway.

Goodwin, P B (1992) A review of new demand elasticities with special reference to short and long run effects of price changes. *Journal of Transport Economics and Policy*, May 1992.

Grayling, T and Glaister, S (2000) A new fares contract for London, Institute of Public Policy Research, London.

Halcrow Fox (1993) London congestion charging review and specification of model elasticities. Halcrow Fox and Associates, Accent Market Research, University of Leeds, HCA, London.

HOC (1995) The consequences of bus deregulation, Evidence by Stagecoach Holdings PLC to House of Commons Transport Committee, HC54, HMSO, London.

HOC (2002a) Air Transport Industry, House of Commons, Transport, Local Government and Region Committee, HC484 (2001–02), HMSO, London.

HOC (2002b) The Bus Industry, House of Commons Transport Committee, HC 828 (2001–02), HMSO, London.

IATA (2002) Annual Report, International Air Transport Association, Geneva.

ITS (1998) University of Leeds with Tecn Econ, Studies of passenger demand within three PTE areas in GB.

Jones, P (1993) Study of policies in overseas cities for traffic and transport (SPOTT); Final report prepared for Traffic Policy Division, Department of Transport, London. (See *Transport Economist*, Vol 21, No 3, 1994.)

Kendall, S (1997) Eurotunnel plc, interview with author.

LT (1984) The London Transport Fares Experience (1980–1983) Research Report 259, London Regional Transport, London.

LT (1986) Fares Elasticities Research Report 266, London Transport Planning, London.

LT (1993) London Transport Traffic Trends, Research Report 273, London Transport Planning, London.

LT (1995) *Planning London's Transport*, London Transport, London.

LT (1996a) *Planning London's Transport – to win as a world city*, London Transport, London.

LT (1996b) Market Report, October, London Transport Marketing.

LT (1997) *London Transport Traffic Trends, 1970–1995*, Research Note M(97)71, LT Marketing, London.

LT (2002) *London Underground and Bus Demand Analysis 1970–2002*, London Transport, London.

NBTA (2003) National Business Travel Association (a group of large US corporate travel managers), Business Travel Survey, New York.

NES (2004) *National Earnings Survey* 2003; Office for National Statistics. Fares based on airline data.

NRM (1997) Study of effects on patronage for First Bus (unpublished), Network Research and Marketing, London.

OPRAF (1997) *A guide to transport demand forecasting models*. Office of Passenger Rail Franchising, London.

Oxford (1996) Roger Williams, Chief Planning Officer, Oxfordshire County Council, Oxford.

Preston, J (1998) Public transport elasticities – time for a rethink? UTSG Conference Proceedings, Dublin.

RAC (1995) Car dependence – a report (by GSU Oxford and others) for the RAC Foundation for Motoring and the Government.

Rail (2004) Eurotunnel truck traffic rises… Passenger levels fall (Rail 480), March.

Serpell (1983) *Report on railway finances* (Committee Chairman: Sir David Serpell), HMSO, London.

SNCB (1997) Belgian Railway domestic passenger services study of impacts of services and pricing policies (STRAEC sa, Belgium, H Duchâteau and P Lobé), Brussels.

SRA (2000) Based on TEN and other rail industry forecasting frameworks such as PDFH (see BR, 1992) and HM Treasury. These are dealt with in more detail in Chapter 8.

SRA (2002) *Passenger Demand Forecasting Handbook*, Strategic Rail Authority, London.

SRA (2003) Everyone's railway – the wider case for rail.

TAS (1995) Bus Industry Monitor, The TAS Partnership Ltd, Preston, England

TfL (2000) *Effects of the 2000 Fares Revision on Bus Passenger Travel*, Transport for London.

TfL (2002) *London Underground and Bus Demand Analysis 1970–2000*, August 2002, Transport for London.

TOCs (2004) Several train operating companies in Great Britain agreed to provide information on a non-identifiable basis. The conclusions are based on those data.

TRL (1994) Transport Research Laboratory, Crowthorne, Berks.

Weightman, K (1997) Marketing Challenge: Transport of the last resort, TRaC/Transport and Travel Society lecture (December), University of North London, London.

Wicks J and Dekker C (1997) There's more to a railway than making the trains run on time, Research plus (October) Market Research Society, London. Based on work for Virgin Trains by MVA Consultancy, London.

Woods, M (2003) Commuter overcrowding alternative solutions, *Focus*, September, Chartered Institute of Logistics and Transport (UK), London; reference to M Lee, paper to Landor London Rail Conference, AEA Technology Rail, May 2003.

WTRC (2003) Information needs of the independent traveller for the Welsh Assembly Government, Wales Transport Research Centre, University of Glamorgan, Pontypridd.

CHAPTER 3

The Supply of Transport

INTRODUCTION

Source of supply

Transport services can be supplied by:

governments – at national, regional or local levels;

private enterprise concerns specialising in the provision of transport services;

manufacturing/trading concerns where the main interest is not in transport – they will purchase their own equipment to carry freight or employees;

individuals, ie cars.

The relative ease with which a substitute private supply can be made available poses, for existing transport concerns, problems which are not usually faced by the producers of most goods and services.

The supply of transport services usually involves the provision of track, terminals, and the operation of vehicles, but these are not always provided/maintained/controlled by a single supplier.

Modal differences

The ease with which the supply of transport can be increased or cut back depends on the nature of the particular mode. At one extreme, an individual can start a supply of road haulage with the purchase of a second-hand lorry. At the other, the provision of transport facilities where vehicles, terminals and track are involved, requires considerable capital expenditure and a long period of time to prepare for operation.

With the more complex forms of transport, there are problems involving the withdrawal or reduction of supply. In some cases, transport supply is very specialised. It is designed for a particular job and is not easily switched to another task. Other facilities/vehicles are more flexible, permitting some variety of usage.

Excess supply of transport

For several reasons, transport is commonly supplied in too great a quantity. Any unused production – such as empty seats or space for freight – is wasted and cannot be stored. If seats/freight capacity cannot be filled with traffic, the potential production facility cannot be carried over into the next period in the transport field – the same problem applies to electricity. In transport, production and supply are carried out at the same time, whereas with the manufacture of goods, supply can exceed current production by drawing on stock. The demand for transport services is often very uneven over time. Many transport services, particularly on the passenger side, are operated according to a timetable and vehicles depart whether they are full or not.

Another cause of over-supply stems from the indivisibility of supply. Track has a certain capacity and vehicles are manufactured in a limited range of sizes. Even if demand were constant over time, it would often be difficult to get the exact blend of track and vehicle capacity to match it without waste. In sparsely populated areas even the minimum facilities may provide more capacity than can be used, but their provision may continue as a social service to a rural community.

Technological progress may result in the supply of new vehicles which prove very difficult to fill. If supply exceeds demand as new airlines or new/larger aircraft are introduced onto a route, then discount fares schemes will follow as airlines attempt to sell that capacity. This may be a short term or longer term effect (see Eurostar forecasting process, Chapter 8). Competition appears to encourage operators to purchase the latest vehicle type in spite of the accompanying problems.

When new services/facilities are provided, supply will usually exceed demand until traffic is attracted. Sometimes traffic never reaches the antic-ipated levels when airlines purchase aircraft in anticipation of obtaining route licences, and this excess capacity can have disastrous financial results. But economies of scale often make it cheaper in the long run to provide capacity for future growth of demand, as in the case of motorways or airports.

In some cases, transport facilities are provided to encourage the economic growth or revival of a region, and capacity will exceed the traffic potential until such growth occurs.

As new superior transport modes have been introduced, they have partly generated new traffic and partly abstracted traffic from earlier modes. There are considerable problems in adjusting the supply of the earlier facilities to their reduced and possibly different roles; this is illustrated by the adjustments in the UK rail network from 1960 to 1990 (a fall in demand) and the 1990s to 2005 (a significant rise in demand). The closure of lines, the reduction of four-track to two-track and some single line intro-duction in the period to the late 1980s reduced capacity supply.

The increase in demand between 1996 (28 billion passenger kilometres) and 2002 (40 billion passenger kilometres) and a further forecast increase to 57 billion passenger kilometres by 2011 now show the very inelastic supply of rail infrastructure and relatively inelastic supply (in under five years) of rolling stock capacity. Particular infrastructure capacity problems arise at key locations, eg Birmingham New Street, Reading, Bristol Parkway and the lines into Euston. The capacity (supply) position has been partly relieved by opening additional services, but achieving the government target of 1400 million passengers per annum requires additional rolling stock and track capacity (Cole, 2004).

Over-supply can arise in situations where there is too much competition. In competitive situations, operators will not reduce the number of their departures without considering the service of their competitors, because their service will become less attractive and they will suffer a reduction in their share of the market. This is illustrated by the over-supply in air 'shuttle' services, where airlines must have standby aircraft; international air flights, particularly on the off peak midweek transatlantic services; and competition between railways on major intercity routes in 19th century Britain.

ELASTICITY OF SUPPLY

Factors determining elasticity of supply

1. The ease of entry into the transport market is a major determinant of supply elasticity. One of the main constraints on entry is the amount of capital outlay involved. In the case of a railway, capital investment in rolling stock and track is extremely high, the lead time is long, and cash flow will be zero/low in relation to total operating **and** funding costs for some years. The Channel Tunnel scheme illustrates this, and supply of such a facility is inelastic except in the long term. Road haulage and road passenger transport are easier markets to enter and supply in these sectors is therefore relatively elastic. Capital investment is relatively low for small scale air transport if the services envisaged are on local internal routes (eg Eastern Airways, 2001; Air Wales, 2003), and high for a Boeing 777 or the Airbus A340–600 long distance aircraft. However, aircraft for both types of operation are available in sufficient quantity, and as Virgin Atlantic Airways has shown, supply can be elastic in the medium (three- to five-year) term, despite a capital investment of £25m to £30m for a second hand Boeing 777, or $211m (£115m) for a new Airbus A340–600 (VA, 2004). The short time span within which low cost airlines entered the market also indicates a current relatively elastic supply of new and second hand aircraft (eg Boeing 737) resulting from an estimated 2500 spare aircraft currently (2004) available. Similarly, new aircraft orders can be deferred to match reduced capacity requirements (AB, 2004). Prices will vary depending on factors such as market conditions, quantity of aircraft leased or purchased.

2. If transport facilities can be easily converted from one use to another, for example from passenger to freight use, then supply will be more elastic than in a situation where transfer of equipment is difficult, expensive or impossible. In the shipping sector, the conversion of tankers to other uses (eg dry cargo or container transporters) will not help short term inelastic supply, but in the medium term (one to two years) supply will be relatively elastic as it becomes financially viable to make the conversions. Therefore, if alternative vehicles, aircraft or ships are available, supply will be relatively elastic. This principle also applies where alternative modes might be used. The supply of transport for coal was initially thought to be inelastic if no trains were available, but the UK rail and coal strikes showed that in the short term transfers could be made to road haulage.

3. The supply of extra capacity is often linked not only to the supply of vehicles or aircraft but also to the supply of energy. Thus, if the supply of diesel oil, aviation fuel or electricity is elastic, the opportunities for elastic supply of transport are greater. If these resources are inelastic then the supply of the transport facility is also likely to be. This is because transport is not merely the vehicle, it is the vehicle on the move.

Definition of price elasticity of supply

The price elasticity of supply is calculated as percentage change in quantity supplied (QS) divided by the percentage change in freight rate or fare level (F):

$$E \text{ of } S = \frac{\% \text{ change in QS}}{\% \text{ change in F}}$$

Elasticity of supply in shipping and aircraft charters

Consider a short-term situation on a global basis. If all available supply is being used and then a change occurs in demand (new demand curve), supply is likely to be inelastic. In Figure 3.1 the effect is to increase price by a disproportionate amount. In the short term, supply is almost totally inelastic and the only way to increase supply is to build new ships or aircraft, and these:

are very expensive;
have no alternative uses if the market slumps (there is no other way commercial aircraft or specific-use ships can be used profitably); have a relatively long construction period.

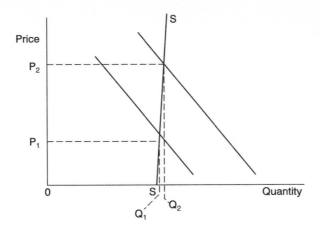

Figure 3.1 *Supply and demand in the shipping market (short term)*

The trade or commodity situation in shipping

The total number of ships in use at a particular time is OQ (see Figure 3.1). If the demand curve for the commodity they transport shifts to the right in the very short term (weeks) supply can be increased in the following ways:

increase speeds of existing ships;
increase turnround time in ports by using more dock staff or overtime.

In the longer term (months) supply can be increased by:

attracting vessels from other ports (nearby);
attracting vessels from further away;
possibly attracting other types of vessels into the trade, eg tankers might start carrying dry bulk or, in the case of aircraft, passenger carriers may start carrying freight.

Transport supply is now at a stage where all usable capacity has been exhausted. As a result of the shortage of supply, the freight rate may be increased, other ships/planes might be taken out of layoff, and ships and aircraft may be re-commissioned. It is still expensive to run craft that were too expensive to run before, but now they may be viable. At this point the industry moves from the short-term to the long-term position and starts building new vessels.

If new ships are built, then the short-run supply curve would change, and when the new capacity has been introduced it cannot subsequently be disposed of – except with considerable financial penalties.

CONCLUSION

A dynamic transport market is complex and volatile. It must accommodate frequent changes in incomes, tastes, fashion and prices. The transport manager must take many factors into account in decision making for two main reasons:

1. The transport product is complex. It is not merely a question of moving goods from a factory to a retail outlet, but it must be done safely and on time. The transport service itself is a mixed product with intermodal through freight and passenger arrangements involving road/sea, road/rail, road/air and any other combinations of the four modes. There are also short notice variations in the customer's requirements with changes in departure time, route or mode and this often will not fit into a simple price/product relationship.
2. The demand for transport is largely derived from other demand patterns; it rarely gives direct satisfaction, since people or goods are not moved to improve or satisfy them, but because of the demand for them elsewhere. People usually travel because they prefer to live some distance from their work, for holidays or recreation or on business; few people travel for fun. Transport operators therefore need to know about the basic demands underlying transport needs and if these can be forecast then demand for transport can itself be forecast more easily.

REFERENCES

AB (2004) Resisting the growth (in supply) temptation, *Airline Business*, March, Sutton.

Cole, S (2004) Right tracks, Agenda (Summer 2004), Institute of Welsh Affairs, Cardiff.

VA (2004), Virgin Atlantic Airways announcement of A340–600 purchase, 6 August.

CHAPTER 4

Pricing Policy

INTRODUCTION

The objective of the pricing policy of a transport operator is to maximise revenue. This can be done in two ways: first, by extending the market size and second, by attracting customers from other operators, thus increasing its market share.

The use of both own price elasticity and cross price elasticity described in Chapter 2 plays an important role in pricing decisions. The response from competitive operators will often lead to a price war. This can bring short term benefits to transport users in the form of fares reductions but the longer term consequences within the transport industry also need to be considered.

The pricing policies adopted by transport operators are important and this chapter will examine the policies pursued by, for example, Eurostar, First Great Western Trains, British Airways, National Express and local bus companies. The policies of passenger transport operators are easier for the reader to dissect because all the price information is known and the rationale behind the policies can then be analysed. In the case of freight operators, the charges to individual customers are not known and the analysis is often impossible to do from outside the transport company.

In both cases the charges are 'what the market will bear'. There will be different charges for different customers based on the degree of competition, the degree of necessity in the journey and the customers' ability (or desire) to pay a particular price; thus the transport market will operate forms of price discrimination and product differentiation.

PRICE DISCRIMINATION

Definition

Price discrimination is the term used to describe a pricing policy whereby a firm distinguishes between different groups of customers. Each group or market segment is charged a different price for identical units of supply. The policy need not reflect cost differences (although it might). It is based on a principle of 'what the market will bear' and thus it relates to differing levels of elasticity.

Market conditions required for price discrimination

1. The transport operator may have a *near-monopoly control* of the supply of the service. This is certainly required within one mode and may be required between modes. If a long distance express coach operator has sole control of a route then the discrimination it makes between customers will not be affected by other operators undercutting its premium prices.

   Perfect competition, on the other hand, provides for many suppliers and many consumers all of whom can freely enter or leave the market. The supplier is the price taker and therefore the firm cannot set premium or discount prices, eg a premium price would result in consumers turning to other suppliers.

   In Figure 4.1 the firm accepts the price Pe. At the premium price Pp sales are lost. At a discount price Pd profits are not maximised. The only point at which profits are maximised is at price Pe and quantity Qf for the particular firm. The price mechanism in a free market sets the equilibrium price Pe and the quantity Qf, as shown in Figure 4.2.

   Perfect competition, therefore, is unsuitable as a basis for price discrimination. Under monopoly supply, consumers wishing to buy the service have to do so at prices set by the firm. Despite deregulation and privatisation within the bus industry, in general this situation has continued (Cole, 2003). However in notable examples such as Oxford, two bus companies, equally well financed and managed, compete for the market although as in other urban areas the bus's main competitor is the private car. In Oxford city centre high parking prices with car use restrictions have provided the necessary pricing policy to reduce demand. In the road freight industry and in airline operations free market competition is well established.

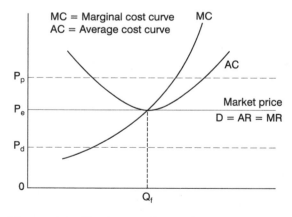

Figure 4.1 *The firm under perfect competition*

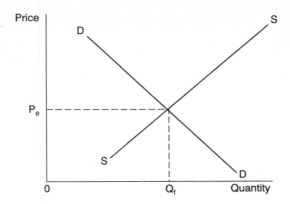

Figure 4.2 *The market under perfect competition*

There has however been a move towards a more competitive form of price discrimination but using the same basic principles described in this chapter.

2. It must be possible to *divide the market into segments* and thus separate different consumers within a particular market. This can be done by time of day, day of week, seasonally during the year or on a geographical basis. In doing this, however, operators must ensure (through the use of inhibitors) that high yield premium fare passengers do not 'down trade' to lower fares.

3. *Consumer surplus* is the amount of extra money over and above the market price which some consumers will pay for a product; it represents social preference and a willingness or ability to pay a premium fare. Price discrimination in this way transfers the surplus from the consumer to the producer.

As shown in Figure 4.3, the operator has identified a group of consumers who have a consumer surplus which they are prepared to pay for in cash, thus increasing the company's revenue. This can be illustrated by substituting actual prices and quantities in this example.

First Great Western, the London to South Wales/West of England train operator, sells saver tickets at a premium price on Fridays compared with other days. If fares are substituted as follows in Figure 4.3:

P1   = £30 (normal saver fare)
Pp   = £40 (Friday fare)
OQ1 = 5000 tickets
OQ = 9000 tickets
QQ1 = 4000 tickets

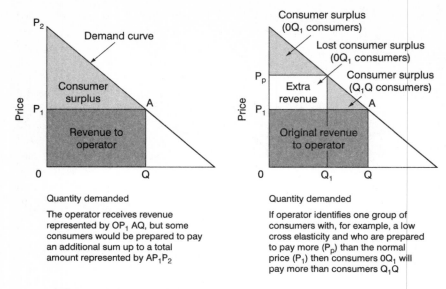

The operator receives revenue represented by $OP_1 AQ$, but some consumers would be prepared to pay an additional sum up to a total amount represented by AP_1P_2

If operator identifies one group of consumers with, for example, a low cross elasticity and who are prepared to pay more (P_p) than the normal price (P_1) then consumers $0Q_1$ will pay more than consumers Q_1Q

Figure 4.3 *Transferring consumer surplus to the supplier*

Then, revenue before price discrimination would be

$9000 \times £20 = 180,000$

but after market segmentation revenue has risen to

$5000 \times £25 = 125,000$
$4000 \times £20 = 80,000$

Total   205,000

an increase of £25,000.

This is possible because the Friday afternoon (weekend away) market is less elastic than on other afternoons. The market size is also greater and price discrimination may assist in reducing overcrowding or avoid increased costs from the supply of additional train departures.

Advantages of price discrimination

By charging the highest price that each market segment will bear, the operator's income will be maximised for three reasons. First, if only a standard fare is charged, there would be some travellers with consumer surplus who would be prepared to pay a higher fare; this revenue is being forgone. Second, if passenger demand is price elastic at the lower end of the price range, then a reduction at that level will generate new traffic from those who did not make a journey previously because they can only afford to travel at a lower fare. Third, if there is cross price elasticity between coach and train, then if some train fares are nearer to coach fares, some passengers will transfer to the train. Revenue will therefore increase with no charge in service quality. High yield and low yield passengers are distinguished so that the formers' consumer surplus is transferred to the operator and otherwise empty seats are filled by charging a lower fare.

Market penetration can also be increased using a similar process. At lower price levels, own price elasticity and cross price elasticity will encourage new passengers (eg on European airlines and on Eurostar) or attract passengers from competing modes and can be used to increase operators' revenue. Travellers with an inelastic demand can be charged high fares, particularly in peak business travel periods, contributing to peak costs where these are incurred. In situations of elastic demand, low fares can encourage more travel.

Fares on the Dublin–London route are the consequence of clearly defined market segments and calculated elasticities.

Demand for east-west travel in the four days before Christmas is high relative to supply and part of the market is highly inelastic in relation to the dates 21–24 December (see Table 4.1). The elastic section of the market requiring lower fares will not travel; will find alternative modes (eg car/ship where price differentials will also be found but a lower price per person); or will travel on cheaper fares before 21 December. It also illustrates the impact of low cost airlines entering the market.

Coach operators use some price discrimination but they have a more elastic market in general. SNCF (French Railways) standard fares are lower than those of British train companies but still have selective pricing within second class using a 'variable by day' fare structure. Railcards are an attempt to segment the leisure market for families, couples or senior citizens at off peak times.

Table 4.1 *London–Dublin Fares £*

Carrier	Normal fares Pre-Ryanair	Discount fares Christmas 2004[1] Christmas 21–24 December Now	Lon–Dub	Dub–Lon	Boxing Day St Stephen's Day Lon–Dub	Dub–Lon
Aer Lingus	110	69	195	69	69	101
B Airways[2]	110	–	–	–	–	–
B Midland	110	69	150	69	69	96
Ryanair	–	59	140	56	59	96

Notes:
1. A similar pattern of fares was seen in the previous 10 years.
2. British Airways withdrew from the LHR-Dublin route.

Source: Airlines

Social advantages can be obtained by providing cheap travel for lower income groups – families or elderly people. The increased use of spare capacity particularly at off peak times is achieved using off peak price discounts. In overall economic terms, resource cost savings are achieved if trains are running anyway and a change of mode from car to train will reduce congestion (and its costs), produce fuel savings, and give environmental benefits (see Chapter 9).

Disadvantages of price discrimination

Even in situations where the operator has a near monopoly of its mode, for example railway companies or airlines, a customer may move from being a high yield, first class passenger to being a lower yield, second class, saver fare passenger unless strong inhibitors are used to retain that passenger's high fare. The inhibitors may involve restrictions on the train the passengers can use with his/her lower priced ticket, thus excluding departures convenient for most business meeting starts. Such inhibitors are discussed later in this chapter.

An increase in demand in the discount price segment can create a peak in demand which results in overcrowding or the provision of an additional vehicle to meet the demand. However, the latter incurs increased costs, which may result in a loss making operation. The increase in fares on the services from London to Dublin at Christmas reflected excess demand over supply. In such circumstances where maximising revenue is the objective, then fares should be increased to a point where all the seats are full, and where standing (if allowed) is at an acceptable level. In air operations, an equilibrium price should be achieved where supply equals demand (when all the seats are full).

Passenger dissatisfaction may result from price discrimination where one passenger pays the standard fare and another travels at a discount, but both have exactly the same standard of service. Price discrimination with low fares may increase passengers but not revenue, whereas high fares may reduce passengers but increase revenue. Therefore if maximisation of revenue is the objective then price discrimination could act against this. Discriminatory pricing in existing market segments could lead to new operators entering the market at prices below the existing fare or with greater discounts or without segment inhibitors (eg Saturday night away). The existence of high cross elasticity combined with ease of entry into the market, or the abolition of a monopoly makes price discrimination policies a matter for careful consideration. Split tariffs can lead to increased administrative and advertising costs, but the benefit of price discrimination should be in excess of these.

So far, price discrimination has been considered from the operator's viewpoint. However, the passenger may be disadvantaged by its operation.

Passengers whose demand is inelastic may have to pay premium fares in order to arrive at work, or at business destinations on time. They or their corporate employers have little alternative but to pay the higher fare. This, however, merely returns to the discussion of consumer surplus and whether the operator should attempt to turn some consumer surplus into revenue.

The use of cross subsidy between routes, route sectors or between services at well-used and little-used times may be justified on purely commercial grounds. Express coach services may be used to subsidise otherwise loss making local bus services which pay a feeder role into profit making long distance routes. Similarly, an interurban route may have two profitable ends but an unprofitable rural section. Price discrimination may therefore be used to facilitate cross subsidy rather than have fares reflecting costs on a particular route. The result might be either overall increased revenue but not maximised profits, or both increased revenue and profits, depending on the market conditions and cost levels involved. In addition, cross subsidy may have a social rather than a commercial justification and price discrimination may be used to provide benefits in frequencies and fares for routes whose cost structure would not justify either.

Product differentiation

This can be justification for price discrimination, particularly in terms of the image of a carrier. It normally involves different standards of service such as first and second class on most European railways, or first, business and tourist class on airlines and is used as a means of segregating high and low yield passengers to avoid passenger dissatisfaction. To achieve increased profits from such an operation, there must be sufficient demand to justify the space taken on the vehicle with enhanced revenue per seat, and the additional service costs must be below the additional fare charged. The London–New York air return fares on British Airways (2005) varied from £200/£500 (non-refundable) for economy class, £1847 (non-refundable)/£4058 to £3694 (non-refundable)/£6642 in first class. Virgin Atlantic Airways Upper Class is around £4000 for 'first class service'. Concorde prices, were they still available, would be about £8200. The additional costs per first class passenger have to be substantially less than the fare differentials if such a complex product/pricing policy is to be financially justified.

CASE STUDY 1: RAILWAYS – MARKET SEGMENTATION/PRICE DISCRIMINATION

The objective of a market based fare structure where prices are based on 'what the market will bear' – eg a standard fare with discounts at the more competitive end of the market and a high fixed fare at the inelastic end – is to increase revenue, to encourage off peak travel, to compete more effectively in the whole travel market and/or to maintain or increase train operating companies' share of the market. The fares structure concentrates on the distinction between peak and off peak services with clear evidence of improved traffic. New types of fares (eg Advance, Super Advance, Virgin Value) based on the airline principle of a trade off between lower price and less flexibility have been introduced and railcards (for families, season ticket holders, senior citizens and others); special promotional offers with newspapers, other products or retailers; joint pricing on destination activity and price discounts on on-board catering to stimulate demand (eg FGW Forward vouchers, GNER restaurant vouchers). Some criticism has been made of the variety of fares on offer, and that the traveller might expect one flat (and cheaper) fare. In some cases, newspaper reports have made the fare structure sound confusing by using terms such as 'fares jungle' in headlines, while other reports have presented a clear analysis of the fare pricing policy.

There are three justifications for this price discriminatory policy. First there is a peak problem on most main rail (Intercity/grande lignes type) routes and fares can be used to dissuade some passengers from travelling at 17.30 on a Friday, or at 09.00 into a major city. Second, there are individual market segments which are prepared to pay different prices and without a policy of this type both revenue and passengers will be lost. Third, people no longer expect a standard price from any of the products they buy. There are no longer manufacturers recommended prices for consumer goods such as washing machines or foodstuffs, so that over the past 30 years people have become used to shopping around and looking for the cheapest possible price for a product or service. This applies to all but a few rail travellers. Travellers do not confine their choice to railways only but also examine the coach fare and the cost of travelling by car (if one is available), particularly if several people are travelling together.

Each major passenger service operator has also identified its competitors in its pricing structure. Family railcards, for example, provide a fare structure aimed at competing with the family car on the total cost of the journey. This competition is particularly effective for the day or short break journey where cross price elasticity is an important factor, while service factors such as convenience play a more important part in the annual family holiday market.

A comparison of Eurostar train fares provided 25 second class and 14 first class alternative return fares for most long distance journeys (with additional discounts for railcard holders). This pricing structure segments the market to achieve maximum revenue and off peak revenue. The same principle applies to all market-led railway operators.

The franchised railway operators in Britain inherited a segmented market from the market-led policies of InterCity. Price elasticity was seen as the most important issue influencing demand, yield management and thus maximising revenue and how to give most benefit to the 'bottom-line'. This leads to a pricing policy which is a mix of:

- a full price business market with favourable elasticity keeping prices hard
- high quality service and added value
- avoiding high demand levels in the peak. It is unrealistic to take more volume in peak periods as there is only finite capacity although some growth is possible on certain lengths of route at certain times and in outbound directions.

The leisure market (both first and second class) has the greatest opportunity for off peak growth and is also the time of day with greatest capacity availability (FGW, GNER, Chiltern Railways, 2004). The exploitation of these market conditions is best achieved by market segmentation within the price regulation of the franchised railway.

Rail industry-wide schemes use franchise agreements to provide through – ticketing for standard fares. This has advantages for the industry and the customer but constrains moves to innovate and provide different priced services. However pre-booking enables the type of yield management practised by the airlines to be introduced by identifying spare capacity on particular trains and selling that at discount prices as a means of stimulating demand through own price or cross price elasticity or service elasticity (upgrading aspects).

First class

In the 19th century first class was the domain of the aristocracy, the wealthy landowners and the emerging managerial class in the upper echelons of the new industrial companies. By the 1980's first class served the executive market with high yields and high peak journey load factors, which is still largely the case for full fare tickets (see Table 4.2 for Eurostar ticket range). However, two factors have influenced first class pricing policy: 1) companies being less prepared to pay high first class fares (London–Edinburgh £257 in 2003); 2) fares paid by the individual for private travel who prefers to upgrade to first class with inhibitors but at a more modest price (£59–£102).

GNER (2004), the east coast rail operator in England, had identified six market segments in first class travel:

- business travel: fully flexible;
- business travel: fully flexible with peak train restrictions;
- primarily private travel but some business travel: off peak limited availability;

Table 4.2 *Eurostar fare structure, 2004*

	Detailed fare list			
Fare type in GBP	**London/Ashford–Paris/Brussels (and any Belgian station (AB**			
	Standard Class		**First Class**	
	Single	**Return**	**Single**	**Return**
Business				
Premium (Paris only)	–	–	250	500
Business	149	298	210 (Paris)	415 (Paris)
Business Day Trip	–	219 (Brussels)	–	319 (Brussels)
Business Value	–	199	–	319 (Paris)
				299 (Brussels)
Leisure				
Leisure Flexi	–	169	–	–
	–	139	–	279
	–	119	–	239
Leisure	–	149	–	–
	–	119	–	–
	–	99	–	189
	–	79	–	159
	–	59	–	139
Leisure Day Trip	–	119	–	–
	–	99	–	169
	–	79	–	139
	–	59	–	109

Source: Eurostar

- leisure travel including a Saturday night away;
- discount fares (one-third) for over-60 travellers and the disabled (using railcards);
- leisure travel through upgraded standard class tickets to supply spare capacity at weekends and using yield management to increase revenue from that capacity.

The image portrayed by the business traveller is one of flexibility enabling him/her to travel at any time; one of dedicated waiting 'lounges' and meeting rooms with phone, email and fax; wide, more comfortable seats; a mobile office in which to work; package fares (for car parking, London Underground, meals); restaurant on key business trains and at-seat service. This is primarily a Monday to Friday market. The image is common to most of the main line companies (First Great Western, GNER, Virgin Trains, Midland Mainline).

A yield management model is then applied to off peak first class capacity. These may be 'shoulder' departures, ie just after the morning or just before the evening peak, used to retain first class travellers or attract back those whose companies downtraded in the face of high flexible fares. The business saver/saver first product available after 9.30 am was aimed at that segment.

The leisure segments (eg weekend first) contain those travellers wishing to buy a more comfortable seat with more space for a modest outlay. Initial supplements were low (at £1 to £5) and demand was high. As an income generator it was clearly able to produce a higher yield with single prices of £8 to £10 depending on length of journey and elasticity on the particular route.

The time of day inhibitor is built into the yield management model to discourage downtrading on business journeys where arrival times (eg in London) are determined by timings of morning business meetings and a desire to travel 'there and back in a day'. This element of service elasticity is paralleled by another – that of perceived superior travelling conditions at a more reasonable price (£176 compared with £264). Cross elasticity and the price/quality dichotomy (see Chapter 1) are also present.

The elasticities identified at different price levels are shown in Table 4.3.

The magnitude of price elasticity is low (relatively inelastic demand) not because of the necessity of journey or availability of alternatives as most of the trips will be optional but more that £5 or £8 represents a small proportion of the travellers' income for those requiring a more comfortable journey.

Thus a decision by some standard class passengers on a train to upgrade (service elasticity) would increase train revenue by 4.5 per cent through the capture of some consumer surplus (see above).

First Class is targeted at the business market which accounts for just over 80 per cent of that market segment.

The **First Class** brand has a long history and is strongly established amongst business travellers in Great Britain. It is available on all InterCity trains and offers segregated accommodation at a premium price. The

Table 4.3 *Elasticities for Weekend First tickets*

Price £	Price rise %	Illustrative Sales (tickets)	Sales (demand fall) %	Own Price/Cross Price Elasticity	Revenue £000	Revenue increase %
1		10,000			10	
3	200	8,000	−25	−0.12	24	140
5	66	7,000	−12.5	−0.19	35	46
8	60	6,500	−7.1	−0.12	52	49
10	25	6,000	−7.7	−0.31	60	15

specific physical attributes of and the emotional values associated with the First Class brand are summarised below:

FIRST CLASS

Physical Attributes

- segregated accommodation
- wider seats with more leg/arm room
- higher quality fittings/finish
- relaxing ambience
- enhanced catering service on selected trains
- InterCity magazine available
- guaranteed seat or refund to Standard fare

Emotional Values

- exclusivity/status
- solidity/tradition
- aspirational and to be defended when achieved
- feeling of a higher level of service

On selected trains and routes an enhanced level of service called First Class Pullman is offered. The attributes of First Class Pullman are summarised below:

FIRST CLASS PULLMAN

- a higher level of at-seat service
- the best staff, specially selected and trained
- guaranteed restaurant meal availability
- special luxury range of catering accessories (eg white linen)
- the best rolling stock (special attention to cleanliness etc)
- the best platforming arrangements
- often the fastest train

Extract from Business Products Plan 1992 (British Rail); Main line railway companies (2003).

Standard class

Most European Union train operators have their first (primarily business) class but with discounts on off peak/selected trains for private travellers. Standard (or second) class was primarily the preserve of leisure travellers but, as first class fares rose, many corporate customers transferred to peak period flexible standard class services at prices about 30 per cent below first class. This was the cross-price elasticity effect of 'downtrading' (see Table 4.4). This business market continues for these travellers whose desired arrival time (eg in London for a mid-morning meeting) requires an early start.

The peak demand pricing pattern is mainly directed at travel to and from large commercial centres such as London or Paris. Fares comparisons are shown in Table 4.1 and Table 4.4.

Table 4.4 *Morning peak (06.00–09.30) fares variations, standard class*

Route	Class	Company	Price £
Cardiff to London	1st open	FGW	169
Cardiff to London	Std open	FGW	107
Cardiff to Birmingham	Std	ATW	43
London to Birmingham	Std	VT	97
London to Birmingham	Std	CR	25
Birmingham to London	Std	VT	97
Birmingham to London	Std/disc	CR	62/25

Source: NRES

Key:
1st: first class
Std: standard class
FGW: First Great Western
CR: Chiltern Railways
ATW: Arriva Trains Wales
VT: Virgin Trains
Open: anytime travel
Disc: time restrictions

Most standard class travel continues to be for leisure purposes. Certain commuter routes (eg London, Birmingham, Manchester, Edinburgh, Cardiff) have a higher proportion of peak time commuters but overall on services such as Intercity they are a low percentage.

Interesting variations in pricing strategy appear in London. In the morning peak, inbound commuter trains have 120–150 per cent load factors but outbound services may be as low as 10 to 20 per cent. Companies like Chiltern Railways then see the advantage of low outbound fares, which through cross elasticity might draw Virgin Trains customers despite service elasticity (shorter Intercity journey time) drawing demand towards the latter operator.

Off peak fares on Fridays and on summer weekends are higher than on other days reflecting the large weekend and holiday market. Thus the distinction between the 'saver' discount and the 'super saver' discount reflects different elasticities in each market segment. Similarly, a range of low cost advance purchase tickets on some late evening Virgin Trains services from London to Birmingham reflects a segment whose demand position can be determined by the yield management model. Virgin, using systems similar to that for Virgin Atlantic Airlines, will sell Virgin Value tickets from £10 single through internet or phone booking for a particular seat/departure time. This may be a cross elasticity element in respect of long distance coach services whose primary market is price sensitive travellers with flexible travel options (eg students, senior citizens).

Intercity standard class is in competition with the motor car and coach/bus operators, in a price sensitive market. The own price elasticity and cross-price elasticity of individual market segments has therefore to be carefully measured. On longer routes, eg London to Scotland, or on mainland European routes, particularly those operating high speed (TGV, Thalys) trains, then price and journey time are factors determining demand.

The effects of price discrimination

The bulk of the competition in the long distance rail market comes from coach and car travel, with little air competition on shorter routes in England and Wales although on the longer Anglo-Scottish routes it has an important market share. The deregulation of the coach market has led to lower prices on main routes to and from London, but National Express has remained market leader.

The effects of saver tickets have been dramatic rises in volume and, more important from the railway's point of view, increases in revenue (see Table 4.5), but the extra costs incurred have also to be considered in assessing the impact on profitability. Where no additional resource costs are involved and spare capacity exists in the system, there will always be short run, marginal revenue benefits from gaining such traffic.

Table 4.5 *Volume and revenue benefits of London savers (Period: September 1981)*

	Liverpool–London	Manchester–London	Birmingham–London
Volume	+116	+92	+64
Revenue	+22	+10	+15

Source: British Rail

Some market segments with discount pricing relate to any off peak services (eg Saver) but certain aspects of segmentation are designed to use existing spare capacity (eg the First Class discount tickets, Saver First and Leisure First where specific trains must be pre-booked). Apex tickets on routes where trains already have high load factors in second class are restricted to a few trains per day which currently have very low load factors (eg early morning, midday, late evening). This form of pricing will also have an impact on market size where growing the market will be an important aspect of increased revenue.

Where extra sources are incurred, financial benefits will accrue if the net revenue generated exceeds the long-term, marginal costs of the extra capacity required.

The cost increase may result from the lengthening of several trains and/or the need for one or more extra trains per day in each direction. Reduced fares within a well researched market segment based pricing policy, where elasticity and consumer surplus factors are known can in fact reduce losses (and possibly subsidy) or increase profits.

The significance of market segmentation to InterCity operators is seen in Table 4.6.

Table 4.6 *InterCity travel income 1992*

Product	Percentage Business travel		Leisure travel		Total Revenue
	Journeys	Revenue	Journeys	Revenue	
First Class	21.7	44.5	2.3	7.2	21.5
Standard Single	10.1	8.4	8.5	11.9	10.6
Standard Returns	18.9	23.4	3.8	7.6	13.7
Savers (2nd class)	21.6	14.3	46.0	51.8	37.3
Cheap Day Return	16.9	3.1	21.0	6.3	5.1
Other products (eg Railcards/Seasons)	10.8	6.5	18.4	15.2	11.8
TOTAL	100.0	100.0	100.0	100.0	100.0

Sources: British Rail (1992): Business Products Plan; Leisure Products Plan (1992).

Notes:
No recent data is available at present as much of it is commercially valuable. This data precedes the introduction of First Class discount tickets.

The private companies with opportunities and a desire to improve performance have identified the current car and air user as potential customers. The long distance business market shares between rail and air were estimated as:

Table 4.7 *Long distance business market share 1992 (%)*

Between London and:	Rail INTERCITY	Air
Edinburgh	16	84
Glasgow	10	90
Aberdeen	8	92
Leeds/Bradford	85	15
Newcastle	57	43
Manchester	57	43

Source: British Rail (1992)

Clearly GNER and Virgin Rail have considerable scope based on journey time and convenience to increase their market share and GNER lead their incursion into this market on the basis of 'none of the hassle, frustration and delays you could encounter flying or driving … our service is fast becoming the preferred travel experience for business customers'. In some markets (eg Birmingham, Leeds/Bradford, even Manchester) that is true, but for the Scottish market it is a 'wish list' (*The Independent*, 1997) but one which must be achieved if business patronage and revenue is to increase on the east coast main line. Virgin Trains' plans (Rail, 2004) for its new tilt train service from 2002 together with an upgrading of the West Coast Main Line, is clearly designed to attract customers to/from Manchester and Glasgow by considerable reductions in rail journey time.

Summary

The rationale behind railway company pricing policy may be summed up as:

1. Maintaining first class on peak journeys as an exclusive 'business' class (with first class lounges at main stations) and charging a high yield fare in a relatively inelastic market. However on off peak journeys offering discount first class fares to encourage 'uptrading' with a risk that the inhibitors will be insufficient to prevent downtrading by a small percentage of high yield first class passengers.
2. Applying discounts to low demand periods to stimulate demand.
3. Simplifying off peak leisure travel fares to make them more easily understood by passengers.
4. Offering further leisure travel discounts for regular users through a variety of annual railcards aimed at the family, senior citizens, young persons, students, and regular commuter travel market segments, the last being marketed as a 'loyalty bonus'.

Product differentiation

In much the same way as the airlines have emphasised the differences between classes to justify price discrimination between market segments for what is essentially the same product, rail passenger operators are now trying to upgrade first class travel into a product which justifies a fare often three or four times the cheapest saver fare. At the same time it is trying to attract the leisure travellers and tourists away from car and coach travel with saver fares and railcard related price and use spare off peak first class capacity for new business and upgraded second class travellers.

The first class business traveller paying full fare provides 17 per cent of train operating companies' passenger income. Consequently, it is a market segment in which intercity train operators wish to hold their market share. Business travel has fallen and first class travel fell faster. The recession reduced the need for, and the frequency of, travel; many firms substituted second class travel (particularly off peak travel) in place of first class; and many self-employed professional people downtraded to reduce costs and overcame the departure time inhibitors by careful study of the timetable and arranging meetings to suit.

The product itself was becoming less differentiated from second class as new, high speed trains cut travel times, improved comfort and increased the frequency of service for all passengers, so that in first class the only advantage was more space, at-seat meals on some services and of course status. The first class product, in order to succeed, has to move towards the 'Pullman' concept – a high level of exclusiveness, standard of finish, comfort and quality of service to distinguish it from the normal train, rather than reduce the quality of standard class (which might be renamed 'leisure' or 'tourist'). Often the difference between users is people travelling first class when the firm is paying and standard class when they are paying themselves.

Marketing this new service successfully depends on how well it operates in practice, the efficient booking of tickets, and the building up of expertise in the business market with staff specialising in that market.

All these improvements will achieve product differentiation, but some problems have to be overcome. At-seat service in First Class has to be guaranteed on all weekday trains to avoid queuing, and preventing the passage of passengers through the first class seating area would make the train more comparable with the plane. The business traveller believes he or she should enjoy a better standard of service than those paying one-third of the first class fare. If it is not provided they may downtrade.

The final element in this product is the great British breakfast. Its price has been increased to cross subsidise under-utilisation of staff and equipment at other less popular meal times. Suggestions have been made to replace it with a continental breakfast, but it is part of the product and to some travellers an important part.

This may sound like a railway company advertisement but it is product differentiation. It is an aspect of market segmentation which can be effectively used to justify higher prices to those with consumer surplus available for transfer to producers, to increase revenue and profitability in a market which is relatively price inelastic and where the downtrading referred to above is likely to prove a small proportion of total journeys.

CASE STUDY 2: AIRLINE PRICING

Historical perspective

During the 1930s and the late 1940s, air travel was a luxury form of transport enjoyed by the rich, and until 1949 only a single fare was available. But in the 1950s, a new range of aircraft specifically designed for the civil air market became available and with it arrived two fares, first class which had existed previously and a new economy class. During the 1950s, British European Airways (BEA) and British Overseas Airways (BOAC) pioneered many changes in aviation pricing. A night excursion fare (the fly-by-night) enabled the aircraft's working day to be extended, thus spreading overhead costs over more services and represented the first segmenting of the market. During the 1950s, mid-week and weekend fare differentials identified two separate leisure markets and off peak, day excursion fares were introduced in response to a market segment with a higher price elasticity.

The airlines realised by the late 1950s that there is a business market and a leisure market with different price and cross elasticities. The business market represented the 'on-demand' passenger (of whom 30 per cent was non-business but required seat availability on the same basis as the other 70 per cent of that segment) and a set of rules was needed to separate it from the leisure market.

The late 1950s saw the development of the inclusive holiday package tour from Britain with, for example, British Eagle Airways offering a week in Palma for £39, including air fare and full board. The scheduled airlines had to compete with inclusive tour fares and cheaper excursion fares, but with self-imposed inhibitors such as sales only through a tour operator, a land arrangements' requirement and a minimum stay of six nights, to prevent downtrading and yield dilution. But charter operators were restricted by minimum tour prices. The real growth in European inclusive tours came from the mid 1960s, pioneered by Britannia Airways and its tour operator parent company Thomson Holidays. By 1964 packages which had been pioneered from the UK to Spain spread to other parts of Europe and were seen as a threat to scheduled airlines (eg BEA).

By 1970, price levels had begun to change as a result of increased capacity and the development of more efficient aircraft. In 1968/69 the first of the now familiar range of discount fares appeared. Called the 'Earlybird' (later Apex) fare (advanced purchase excursion) it was introduced by BOAC, first on its Caribbean routes and then on the other 'cabotage' routes between Britain and for example Hong Kong, which were regarded as 'domestic' routes between the territories of the same country.

In the early 1970s capacity increased when the Boeing 707 range was replaced by the Boeing 747 and other wide bodied, long haul aircraft. These more efficient aircraft had a lower cost per seat but the airlines were again having problems in finding more passengers to fill them as they had done when the 707 was introduced. In 1973–74, fuel prices rose sharply and fares rose with them; any new fares initiative had to increase passengers but not dilute existing revenue. Individual market segments have to be attracted, such as the student market or senior citizens. In those countries where deregulatory policies have been introduced such market pricing is being pursued by the airlines but conditions set down by Government regulatory authorities may encourage or may restrict such segmentation.

Many developments in airline pricing took place in the 1970s and 1980s with Laker Airways and new US airlines, among others, having an impact on the market. By the 1990s this transatlantic competition was being mirrored in European markets with low cost operators such as Ryanair, and easyJet (Rigby, 1997) and small aircraft, franchised or independent operators (eg City Hopper, Air UK – part of KLM) and Virgin Express entering the market with lower fares at all times of day and no inhibitors.

Current market and revenue management

By 1986, British Airways (BA) and other full service national carriers were closely monitoring booking patterns for particular fares, routes and departure times and predetermining the space available on an aircraft for particular market segments. This has led to a wider range of prices and varying numbers of seats available in each class or at each fare on a particular flight. The club class cabin on, for example, some European destination flights has a variable size, enabling the airline to provide extra space to take high yield traffic. For example, a Monday 08.00 departure to Paris or Frankfurt might have a 40 per cent business and 60 per cent economy seating configuration compared with 10 per cent business and 90 per cent economy on the 10.00 return departure to London. The full fare traveller demands flexibility for business travel and to be able to cancel or change reservations at short notice. This has important implications for planning load factors. In the economy cabin airlines can plan on a very high average load factor, which means low fares. For the on-demand passenger, the airline has to ensure late availability and take account of no shows giving a lower load factor and therefore high fares. The use of market segmentation and yield management to solve the problem is discussed below.

Competition in the market place

United States

Competition is generally regarded as bringing consumer benefits such as cheaper fares on high density trunk routes, but there is no evidence that its effects on secondary routes have been as widespread.

There is also evidence that 'low cost' carriers (LCCs) compete with rail companies and from them draw their business through cross-price elasticity.

With TGV services in France, the opposite has occurred in respect of air services through service and cross-price elasticities. SNCF services to Lyon and Marseille have led to the closure of some internal air services operated by Air France and Air Inter.

Comparisons should be interpreted in the light of qualifications such as exchange rates, fares conditions, the degree of availability of the fares, whether route by route comparisons are atypical of the market, and the likelihood of fares remaining at their existing levels. If an upturn in traffic took place in the USA, airlines would no longer need to discount fares to fill seats and with no regulatory fares 'ceiling', fares could increase dramatically. The same effect would result from the local monopolies enjoyed by the megacarriers.

Fares on US domestic routes have changed considerably since deregulation (Petzinger, 1995). On routes served by several airlines, and where new low cost airlines have entered the market they are not dissimilar to the UK – European equivalent fare per mile. On routes with weak or no competition, standard fares have risen faster than costs and fares are only 10 per cent below those in Europe. Some very densely trafficked routes, eg Pittsburg–Philadelphia, also have high normal fares.

Before deregulation in the USA, discount fares were few and the price difference from standard fares was small; since deregulation many new off peak and limited availability fares have been introduced. In the UK and Europe, very low fares are available as a result of charter operations and on competitive routes with new low cost operators. Comparison of all fares between routes is difficult because the range of fares varies between the two countries and on some comparisons UK-Europe fares may be cheaper. The range of promotional fares in Europe has always been greater than in the USA although they have become more widely available there since deregulation and are now used by the majority of passengers. The need to achieve maximum effects from yield management will also cause variations in fares per mile even within an airline (see above).

CASE STUDY 3: THE LOW COST AIRLINE MARKET (EUROPE)

The European and US markets also have another fundamental and vital difference. Most European routes are thin compared with those in the USA. The distribution of population in Britain, for example, lends itself as much or more to rail travel than to air travel. New low cost carriers may either operate during the lucrative parts of the day or will share the problems of low average load factors. Alternatively, a new airline will identify a segment of the market where, by offering a relatively lower price, cross elasticity will create either new business altogether or will attract some existing operators at the lower price range. On the

London–Dublin service, the two operators, British Airways and Aer Lingus, could not obtain Irish government approval for cheap fares. However, in 1986, a Ryanair service from Dublin to Luton with very low fares compared with the national carriers but which BA initially matched with low fares incorporating inhibitors was approved but subsequently left the route (see Chapter 11). The large increase in traffic resulting from the Ryanair low fares appears to have come partly from the other two airlines but largely from ferry traffic with passengers making a time/fare comparison and switching to air – a combination of service elasticity and cross price elasticities.

An example of downtrading as a result of cross price elasticity is illustrated by the easyJet advertisement 'Impress your finance director!' (see Figure 4.4). The move towards cutting corporate travel costs has led to a shift in demand (cross elasticity) from 'full service' airlines to low cost operators. This advertisement suggests a link between the two market elements.

The 'low cost' airlines on services into/from British airports included easyJet, Ryanair, bmibaby, Virgin Express, Go, Buzz, Flybe and others. There has been some **rationalisation**, with Go and Buzz being incorporated into easyJet and Ryanair. The older established charter airlines offering low fares as part of a package (eg Monarch, Airtours) faced new competition as customers found it possible to book (on the internet) both air travel and hotels themselves at lower prices without the need for a foreign language. Many seasoned travellers (previously using package tours) transferred – a cross elasticity effect. My Travel Lite was part of Airtours' response to this new competition (for cost aspects see Chapter 7).

The 'wealthy but cold' northern European countries tend to be the primary source of intra-European leisure travel, with the British, Dutch and Germans making up the largest part of this market and explaining why 'low cost airlines' have been most successful in these countries.

Figure 4.4 *easyJet business market advertising (2004)*

As low cost airlines enter a market, own price (new business) and cross price (transfers from other airlines) elasticity leads to increased demand. The consumer surplus is obtained by producers through additional travel rather than through higher fares with a new demand curve to the right of that in Figure 4.2.

Growth in airline passengers over the last 10 years has been, on average, 4 per cent per annum between major European destinations. The growth for several charter airlines has been negative (−7.4 per cent to −3.4 per cent) while easyJet and Ryanair's growth has been 4.5 per cent on average (see Table 2.8). This is due to low fares, more competitive frequencies, and an income in market size.

Low cost airlines base their marketing on the lowest price 'from'. Their rationale is to offer fares as low as 'four pence single' six months ahead of travel. This price will rise quickly to, say, £20 then to £50 and possibly up to over £100. Bookings made less than 14 days in advance of travel may have higher fares than those of 'full service' airlines. However, by this time the travellers' demand elasticity has fallen to a point where the trip is inevitable, eg a business meeting has been arranged, or the family has been told about the trip. This is particularly so in the summer peak period.

Yield management was traditionally based on the principle of what 'the market will bear' with market segments used to differentiate quality and price, and inhibitors to minimise downtrading. The full fares were sold through travel agents with corporate discounts but cheaper fares were available through the discount or 'bucket' shops.

The determinants of fare levels on a particular air route are the number, and the fares, of competitors. Existing operators, aware of the cross elasticity effects, adjust their fares to that particular market. In the international market, airlines will try to match one another in terms of fares.

The level of demand will determine the fare and, as all tickets are sold by phone or on the internet, this relationship is fairly easy to achieve. Most low cost airline prices are based on price banded seats sold on a 'first come first served' basis – those who book earliest get the lowest fare. The fare then responds to historical demand pattern for that service and adjustments to reflect actual demand for the particular departure can be made if demand

Table 4.8 *London to Glasgow – traffic growth 2003*

Low cost airlines' market share	44%
Growth per annum	5%
Low cost share	
– new/growth (own price elasticity)	66%
– transfers from other airlines (cross price elasticity)	34%
Fall in other airlines' share	26%

Source: Dunmare (2003) *Airline Business*, September

is higher or lower than expected. The airline will estimate the 'market' or 'willingness to pay' price for each inquiry and determine the 'strike price' where it expects to sell all or most of the seats. Some of the full service airlines have now responded (see Chapter 2) but only for economy class non-changeable tickets.

The high speed (TGV style) rail operation can still compete with airlines. Two services that have been offered on that basis with comparable travel times and competitive fares are London/Avignon by rail (five hours) at a return fare of £109 and Brussels to Cardiff (five hours) by Eurostar/FGW for a return fare of £87. The band range provided by railway companies (eg Eurostar) is less variable; its full range is published, unlike those of low cost airlines, although some internet additional discounts are available.

The fares and market strategy of low cost airlines vary but one might give some interpretation.

easyJet:

- new aircraft;
- flies to major airports (and consequent congestion at eg London Gatwick, Paris CDG);
- gives some compensation for delay;
- appears to be targeting business passengers (see Figure 4.4) for Monday to Friday business to balance its leisure weekend and holiday period demand;

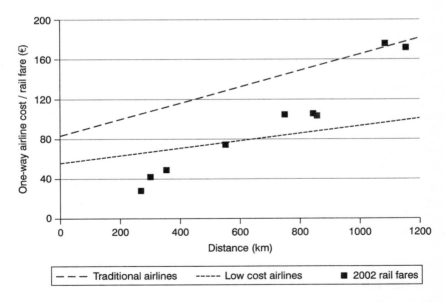

Figure 4.5 *Airline costs per passenger, and rail fares, from Barcelona*
Source: Dunmare, (2003)

- greater threat than others to established full services airlines;
- building up frequency.

Ryanair:

- lowest prices in general (though other airlines would contest this assertion);
- longer term aircraft age profile;
- expanding its network;
- generally serves secondary airports for its destination (Dublin, Edinburgh and Cardiff are notable exceptions) but with less possibility of congestion.

Other airlines such as Jet Blue in the US appear to have a market strategy aimed at both business and leisure passengers while Virgin Blue has a near 'full service' on its longest Australian routes.

Both easyJet and Ryanair plan to continue their present rate of growth. So did Buzz in 1998 (see Figure 4.6) (*FT*, 1998) when it forecast a market share of 25 per cent by 2016 with annual growth rates of over 20 per cent to 2006. These kinds of rates are currently being achieved by easyJet and Ryanair but in doing so the companies face several risks:

- Greater competition with other low cost and conventional airlines. The popularly named 'price war', which in economic terms refers to cross price elasticity of demand, might constrain growth.
- The costs associated with the change from low cost into major airline.
- The decision by BMI to establish bmibaby (Jowit, 2004), a low cost carrier, and also along with BA to introduce an economy class yield management model (and associated fares) similar to easyJet's but with continued inhibitors.
- Service elasticity effects related to unreliability (actual or perceived) with little or no compensation and no alternative flight for some time. The CAA reported time keeping (flights arriving within 15 minutes of schedule) on the London–Rome route as: BA 78 per cent; Go 71 per cent; Ryanair 38 per cent.

The low cost airlines are largely 'point to point', and travellers 'should allow 3–5 hours for connections' (Evans, 2004). The same elasticity impact for the business traveller then became apparent.

The changes taking place as far as the regulation of competition is concerned is the principle on which government agencies (like the CAA) will now accept a route and fare proposed by an airline.

The setting of air fares

The Government regulatory bodies (in Britain the CAA) tend to concentrate on regulating fares and conditions, and the lowest flexible on-demand

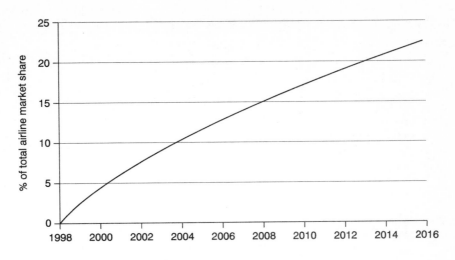

Forecast annual growth rates

1998 – 2002: 30%
2002 – 2006: 20%–27%
2006 – 2016: 9%–11%

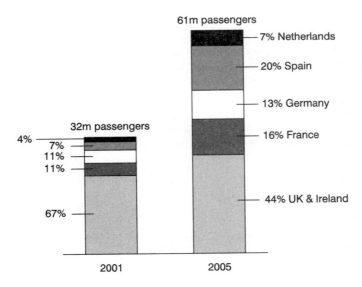

Figure 4.6 *Buzz – forecast annual growth (1998–2016)*
Source: Analysis of Buzz Forecasts, KLM, Amsterdam

Table 4.9 *Air travel growth[1] July 2003–July 2004 (passengers)*

Routes	% change
Total BAA[4]	8
North American destinations	12.3[2]
Other long haul routes	14.6
Other European[3]	10.8
UK destination[3]	6.4
Other European charter	−6.2
To/from London Stansted	10.2
To/from London Heathrow	7.9
To/from London Gatwick	6.1
To/from Southampton	8.5
To/from Scottish airports	9.5
Total flights	3.4
Total freight	15.3

Source: BAA (2004)

Notes:
1. The airports are those in BAA plc ownership.
2. This is from a relatively low base.
3. Includes low cost airlines (eg Ryanair at Stansted).
4. Passengers carried in July 2004: 14.2 million.

fare which the CAA tries to ensure is cost related and not excessively profitable. This can only be done by controlling fare increases; thus the fares can be reduced in real terms over time. The fare involved would be the full economy class fare or in its absence the business class fare. Other fares are generally commercial decisions in a deregulated market but may be subject to Government approval in controlled markets. (This is a simplified version of a far more complex procedure.)

Peak pricing

The most significant differences in fares are those between peak and off peak (eg leisure market demand is higher in summer/weekend periods compared with winter/midweek). Business travel peaks will be particularly high on short haul flights, and on 'breakfast-time' and 'end-of-business day' services on working days.

In the peak, airline charges are higher for two reasons:

1. *Cost.* The overall level of resources is increased to meet peak demand and therefore the people who travel in the peak should pay for it.
2. *Market.* Prices help smooth out demand encouraging off peak travel and so reducing the airline's resource costs. Differential fares between midweek and weekend departures are based on 'what the market will

bear' and use cross price elasticity of demand between time bands, within a day, between days of departure, or at different times of the year.

CASE STUDY 4: MA AIRWAYS LTD

Market application – segmentation and price discrimination

The division of an aircraft seating into segments with different charges for each segment (see Figure 4.7) is now a well established principle. This case study uses a simple pricing problem to identify the practical principles, although in reality pricing problems involve complex fare structure, route networks operated by a variety of airlines serving a wide range of markets. MA Airways (after Welburn, 1974) is a single route airline currently offering only one fare, but on which it proposes to offer a 10 per cent discount from 2008.

Marketing effects

A 10 per cent reduction in fare levels will have a number of immediate effects on the airline's operations:

1. increase sales probably above target;
2. increase traffic;
3. improve the cost/revenue ratio (ie increase profits which will depend on price elasticity);
4. it will be easier to sell to customers;
5. it will give MAA a competitive edge (until matched by a competitor);
6. travel agents will welcome it – discounts are always easier to sell (but it reduces commission);
7. it may compete with charter operators;
8. marketing opportunities will arise, eg. NEW LOW FARE!

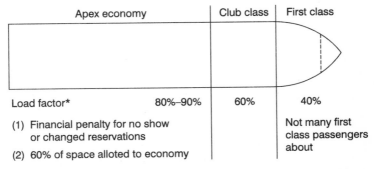

Figure 4.7 *Layout of an Airbus 340/Boeing 747 by market segment*

From a sales and marketing point of view then the policy has many advantages but a few problems.

Short term financial effects

Assume market research into price elasticities indicates that a 10 per cent fares reduction will result in a 20 per cent increase in traffic (see Figure 4.8). This traffic increase will generate an 8 per cent increase in revenue (see Figure 4.9). A further assessment of the effects on profits shows a remarkable increase in profits of 53 per cent by 2009 (see Figure 4.10).

Peak load factor

MA Airways peak load factors have always been held around 75 per cent in order to:

1. remain competitive in the market;
2. avoid turning away business;
3. discourage new airlines from entering the market to pick up surplus and perhaps non-surplus traffic;
4. provide seat availability for 'on-demand' passengers.

The peak load factor increases dramatically to nearly 90 per cent in 2009, as a result of the fare proposal. The airline finds this unacceptable and decides to introduce additional capacity in 2010 in order to restore the 75 per cent norm (see Figure 4.11).

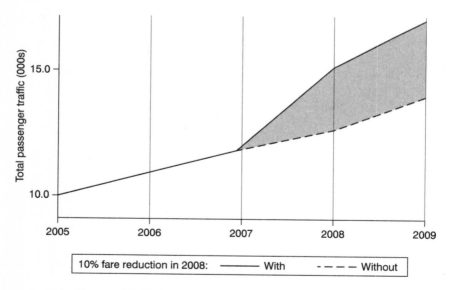

Figure 4.8 *MA Airways traffic forecast (short term)*

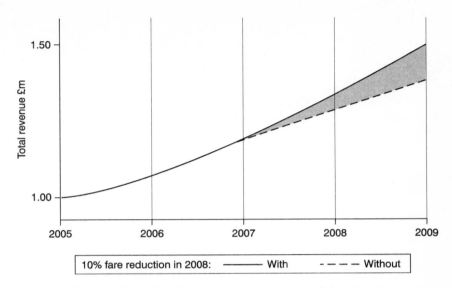

Figure 4.9 *MA Airways revenue forecast (short term)*

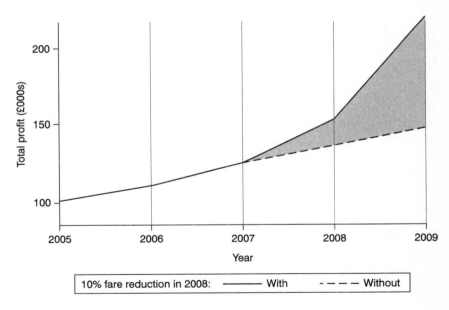

Figure 4.10 *MA Airways profit forecast (short term)*

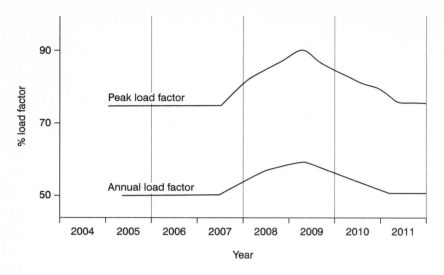

Figure 4.11 *Peak load factors – MA Airways*

Long term financial effects

The upsurge in traffic as a result of the fares reduction led to an immediate but small increase in costs of passenger meals, insurance and passenger handling but these are only 15 per cent of MA Airways' costs. However, when capacity was increased by hiring additional aircraft to cover the peak traffic period, costs began to increase considerably. The capacity lag meant that in 2009 the scheme was very attractive, but by the end of 2010 costs exceeded revenue and continued to rise in 2011 while revenue flattened out, as shown in Figure 4.12. As a result the 2009 and 2010 rises in profits were followed by a financial disaster in 2011 (see Figure 4.13). This long term change in cost patterns is often missed in fares policy evaluation.

Conclusion

The airlines looked at short-term results and concluded there was a positive reaction to its fares reduction policy. However, if no new competition entered the market and the airline decided to satisfy the new demand, the rise in sales would be at the expense of poor long-term profitability.

Satisfying peak demand

MA Airways in facing this new demand could decided just to operate at a 90 per cent average peak load factor thus incurring small variable cost increases, but in practice there will be some departures with potential load

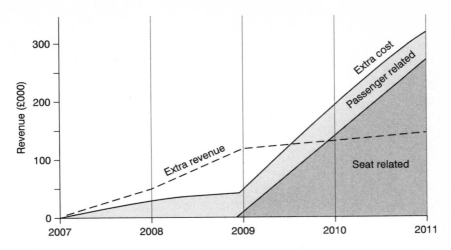

Figure 4.12 *Long-term comparison of extra revenue and extra cost*

factors of over 100 per cent and this means leaving passengers behind or not accepting their bookings. However, this is not the airline's policy (despite the fact that most airlines underserve the market) and for a number of reasons:

1. increased complaints from passengers unable to get a seat on demand;
2. increased complaints from marketing management about loss of business to competitors;
3. an increase in adverse press and consumer comment;
4. a risk that additional carriers will be granted licences to enable the peak to be covered but who will operate at times when load factors are well within MAA's capacity, so these will be reduced as a result of competition;
5. market share may fall as a result of this;
6. travel trade goodwill is lost, particularly if they previously booked first with MAA but now find them booked out too often;
7. seat availability falls and 'on-demand' passengers begin to look for alternative operators or modes.

Table 4.10 *MA Airways – summary of performance*

Year Analysis	0	1	2	3
Sales & Marketing	Good	N/A	N/A	N/A
Traffic	+15%	+20%	+20%	+20%
Revenue	+3%	+3%	+3%	+3%
Profit	+14%	+53%	–32%	–100%

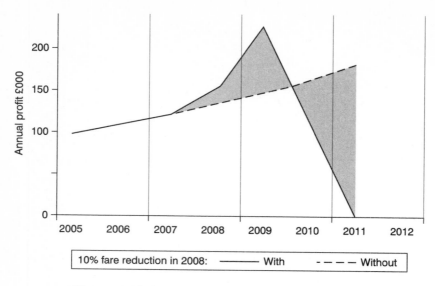

Figure 4.13 *MA Airways long-term profit forecast*

MA Airways' fare reduction brought financial benefits until the decision was taken to restore the 75 per cent peak load factor for the reasons shown here – which was of course not related to the initial decision. To achieve maximum profitability therefore the airline would put less emphasis on the marketing policy and consider overall profitability as the main objective. This often contradictory policy occurs when operators have to choose between market share and profitability.

SOLUTIONS FOR LOW PROFITABILITY AND LOSS OF MARKET SHARE

Fare increases

If costs are rising faster than revenue per passenger, the passenger should pay more. However as most leisure travel markets are price elastic, increased fares do not guarantee increased revenue. Fares increases may well restore profitability but as a result passengers with relatively elastic demand will no longer be carried, airline capacity will have to be cut, the frequency of departures reduced, and some economies of scale lost. There will be passenger resistance and dissatisfaction and a negative growth rate.

Table 4.11 shows how US airlines faced with declining patronage have made decisions on capacity to maintain a consistent load factor. Conversely expanding low cost airlines in Britain, Ireland and the United States have matched increased demand with increased capacity.

Table 4.11 *Comparison of passenger demand (RPK) and seat capacity (ASK) percentage change 2002–03*

Airline	Passenger traffic RPK %	Passenger number (m) %	Seat capacity ASK %	Load factor (2003)	% change
American	−1.4	−5.7	−4.2	72.8	+2.1
United	−4.6	−3.5	−8.2	76.5	+2.9
Delta	−3.3	−2.4	−5.2	73.4	+1.4
BA	+3.0	−5.0	+1.5	73.0	+1.0
Air France	+1.7	+1.9	+2.4	75.6	−0.5
Lufthansa	+2.4	+3.3	+3.5	73.1	−0.8
easyJet	+92.6	+85.7	+95.2	84.4	−1.1
Ryanair	+54.6	+47.0	+61.0	74.5	−3.1
Jet Blue	+68.5	+56.7	+65.4	84.5	+1.6

Source: Airline Business survey, August 2004

Capacity restrictions

There is excessive capacity particularly in the off peak and if seat numbers were reduced, costs would fall but revenue might remain the same. Airlines which often paid too little regard to costs in the mid-1990s are now matching capacity to demand far more closely as well as trying to recover their revenue position (2004) (see Table 4.11). However, capacity agreements set up by the airlines may be insufficient. Government imposed restrictions would lead to problems of national share and would restrict growth. From a market point of view, capacity control to push up load factors would lead to a reduction in the availability of seats, particularly to the high yield, on-demand passenger who generally books later than the discount fare passenger.

Market segmentation

This recognises that airline passengers are not an homogenous group but have a great variety of needs. Passengers requiring seats on demand at short notice can only be provided for if seats are kept in reserve. But this results in poor seat productivity and a load factor of 60 per cent or less in that accommodation (eg business class). However, there are other passengers who plan their journey in advance and will accept travel limitations which enables the airline to improve seat productivity. Exploiting these differences is essential to improve airline performance. On-demand seating is expensive and should be restricted to passengers prepared to pay the high cost of availability; low cost customers would pay a lower price. There are problems, such as the allocation of joint costs between different market segments, but these can be overcome. Market segmentation and price discrimination using yield management techniques is the only approach that can improve profits, consumer satisfaction and the rate of growth at the same time.

Yield management

So what techniques have major airlines (eg British Airways, Air France, Lufthansa, United, SAS) used to achieve the necessary improvements in performance or limit to financial losses incurred illustrated in Table 4.10?

The need to sell the right number of seats at the right price is essential for all airlines. This is done through a sophisticated seating control system which enables the booking agent in one of thousands of locations to identify today's price for a seat from say London to Athens. Such a system monitors controls and forecasts the sales of millions of seats thus maximising load factors, reducing costs per seat sold and increasing passenger numbers. Managing what airlines call 'yield' (the amount the airline receives for every passenger km flown) will result in higher profitability.

Airlines split their ticket sales into many yield bonds (between 10 and 20 is common) and using the computer system which monitors booking trends, adjusts fares and capacity on the whole network and forecasts global booking requirements for all flights. The highest yield passengers are business or first class users of whom 50 per cent book less than three weeks prior to travel while 75 per cent of low yield discount passengers book over a month in advance. If the system predicts too many bookings

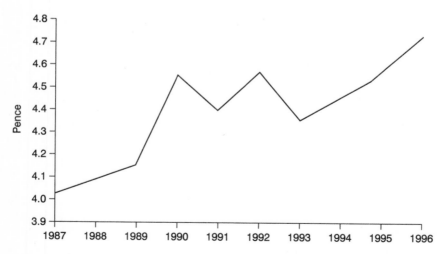

Figure 4.14 *Passenger revenue per ASK*
Source: British Airways Fact Book 1996

by high yield business travellers on the London-Athens flight, too few seats are sold to low yield passengers. They will be told that either no discount seats remain or that the price has risen to the next price band. They may transfer to (and perhaps experience favourably) another operator and when it emerges that seats remain empty it may be too late to sell them. If too few high yield late bookings are predicted an opportunity to earn extra profit is lost.

Many bookings are cancelled particularly where no financial penalty is involved so that on a typical BA Boeing 747 North Atlantic flight the airline may sell seats three or four times before the aircraft takes off. This continuous monitoring of cancellations avoids empty seats.

There are also a percentage of no shows (10 per cent on average) where a business traveller makes several bookings or extends his/her visit – they have complete flexibility and no financial penalty which in itself is one justification for high fares. To counter this airlines will overbook flights in certain markets where no show rates are included in the computer's availability profile for a flight. The consequence can be offloading and the payment of 'denied boarding compensation'. This is easiest done at destinations where there is a high tourist element amongst passengers and to whom a cash payment and an extra night at a luxury hotel is sufficient incentive to delay travel.

Exchange rates also have an impact where benefits may accrue from the country and currency of sale. The linking of an airline's own seat reservation and availability system to sales agents' (both airline and travel agents) offices has been revolutionised by direct access satellite-linked systems such as Galileo, Sabre, and Worldspan (Delta, Northwest, KLM). These provide for the major airlines and their franchisees direct point of sale data from which agents can immediately make bookings and produce tickets.

Differences in customers' needs

The business passengers are unable to plan far ahead. They have to react to fast changing business circumstances and need to be able to change travel arrangements at any time. From their company's viewpoint travel is a small part of its expenditure – even a relatively high business class or full economy fare is of less importance compared with the value of the executive's time and the travel convenience it provides.

The air passenger market has many people on modest incomes and this segment is a highly price elastic and income elastic market. The fare often represents hard earned savings and choice of flight is unimportant compared with price.

Airlines have also tried to attract business customers through techniques such as fast track check-in and arrivals. They have identified that travel to/

Table 4.12 *Differences in customer needs*

Type of traveller Customer need	Company executives on urgent business	Moderately high income holiday travellers	Ordinary holidaymakers (modest income), elderly people
Seat availability on demand	E	X	X
Freedom to change arrangements	E	M	X
Full range of departures (times, destinations, route, etc)	E	M	X
Low price	X	E	E

Importance of category of need
E = Essential
M = Moderately important/moderately unimportant
X = Irrelevant

from the airport, airport procedures, including two-hour check-in times, and 'hassle', produce the greatest frustration for them and why Eurostar has with far simpler procedures, and 30-minute check-in, attracted up to 30 per cent of air travellers from London to Paris. Aspects such as online late check-in and executive lounges (eg Virgin and BA) provide comfortable and time-useful locations to await departure. Many airlines and railway companies (eg FGW at Paddington) provide free phone and fax and coffee at their executive facilities.

Airlines are also improving the quality of inflight business class services with new seating, upgraded meals and entertainment systems. American has fitted new seats to its fleet of Boeing 767–300 North American service jets with new design and leather upholstery. United and BA have introduced the Boeing 777 to fight 'the battle for the business traveller across the North Atlantic' (Mark Schwab, United Airlines' GM in Britain).

Quality issues in relation to 'downtrading' by corporate travellers are discussed earlier in this chapter.

Cost based pricing

Cost levels vary in relation to different customer demands and prices charged in different market segments should reflect this. However, there may be circumstances where a direct reflection is not appropriate (for commercial or social reasons) and cross subsidy between one group and another could be justified, eg low price loss leaders and social inclusion and accessibility policies.

Costing each fare type might indicate that some lower fares are not profitable but, if fares were increased in price elastic markets, then passengers would be lost, assets under-used and the businesses would contract.

The costing basis

The current cost of flying a Boeing 747 from London to New York varies. Passengers can pay a wide range of fares from £200 to £3500 for this journey; the costs should be allocated to each of these fare types. The annual statement of costs is a useful summary of performance. The allocation of costs by expenditure category is necessary to ensure the control of those cost budgets. However they do not enable the fare to be directly related to the cost. The "externalities" (see Chapter 10) are excluded here.

The fare is the price per passenger and should be related to the cost per passenger (CPC). CPC is not simply an analysis of operating expenditure, it can also measure productivity. The scope for satisfying different customer needs by cost based price discrimination lies almost entirely in the two measures of airline productivity:

Utilisation   the proportion of available time that an asset is in use;
Load factor   the proportion of available asset capacity that is in use.

These measures apply to the aircraft, runways, check-in facilities, reservation systems, terminals and traffic staff. All have peaks and troughs and all operate on high and low load factors during different times of the day, week or year.

Market conditions

If fares are designed with consideration given to these two factors then a wide range of customer quality and fare options can be provided.

If passengers could only change bookings, cancel bookings or 'no-show' with a financial penalty, load factors would rise (particularly if predetermined space control was in use), productivity would improve and CPC would fall.

If passengers who were ultra responsive to price could be persuaded to travel on aircraft with low seat utility (caused by variations in demand during the day, week or year), then load factors could be increased. If there was also a market for a guaranteed flow of passengers on every flight, then such constant demand (often repeat business) could be profitable at low fares. The overall cost breakdown should also be examined to decide if there are some facilities which are only needed for certain market segments. Whereas computer systems are now used for all bookings including that of the package holidaymaker who decides and pays for travel months in advance, a more expensive, more sophisticated, worldwide, on-line, real time system is required for the on-demand passenger. These additional costs should therefore be applied to those passengers who require the service. Each of the market segments involves a different set of costs categories and will have different effects on airline efficiency and productivity. Thus, quite different costs per passenger will occur and this should be reflected in the fare charged.

The use of marginal cost pricing

If the airlines' objective is profitability pricing decisions should take into account what the market will bear and the cost of supply, thus enabling the profitability of the service to be measured. To achieve this, the cost of each activity must be covered or exceeded by the revenue from the customers for whom it is performed. If an airline decides to carry freight, the costs of providing the service have to be covered, and revenue must contribute to profitability. The same principle applies to a type of passenger traffic which requires two additional aircraft to meet peak demand. For that fare type to be viable: 1) the operating and overhead costs of the aircraft must be met; and 2) the fare (ie revenue per passenger) should be directly related to cost per passenger, which in turn is a function of the airline's costs and productivity.

In practice, because changes in transport capacity are discrete moves and one passenger less will rarely affect an activity, all passengers on one fare type should be taken together.

The use of marginal cost principles can now be introduced, by costing each fare type on the assumption that this was the only traffic. It would then be possible to identify:

(a) those fixed costs required to provide the service;
(b) the use made of these facilities and the variable costs involved;
(c) the load factor and the number of passengers over which each cost category can be spread;
(d) other costs incurred in providing the facilities;
(e) how total costs relate to revenue generated by the fare.

This will enable the airline to calculate the additional costs of providing a fare type and the additional revenue resulting from its supply.

Some would argue that cost based pricing is impossible because of cost allocation problems and pricing decisions should not be based on costs.

Determinants of fare type productivity

1. *Standard of service.* The commercial decision of most airlines is to provide adequate seat availability and freedom of choice for normal fare passengers. But many scheduled air passengers do not require these facilities, and if they had to meet their costs would certainly prefer to do without them. The demand for a high utility standard at a high cost is clearly required by some passengers on scheduled services. If normal fare passengers fail to obtain a seat on demand on more than five per cent of occasions, customer dissatisfaction increases sharply and reductions in choice are strongly criticised, resulting in loss of high yield patronage. But demand for low fare travel cannot be satisfied on a profitable basis by scheduled or charter operators unless service standards

are cut. Thus the cost of service standards for each type can be controlled (and a wide range of types used) by varying inhibitors and seat allocation. In order to guarantee seats to on-demand passengers, so that there is a 95 per cent probability of being able to book a seat 24 hours before departure some seats have to be left empty; this may result in a load factor as low as 60 per cent in the high fare cabin. These costs therefore have to be incorporated into the fare for the passenger who gets last minute seat access, incurs no-show and no-charge seat wastage, re-routes him/herself, gets a full refund on unused tickets, has full interline facilities and is allowed stopovers.
2. *Peak operations.* If there is a high peak demand for a particular fare type, whether regular, time of day, week or year, or unpredictable, then its productivity will be low in terms of load factor and utilisation.

Cost based pricing – summary

The application of cost based pricing requires costs to be allocated to each fare type so that the per passenger cost of the level of service provided by the airline is covered by the fare. With differential prices providing vastly different break-even load factors there is a need to distinguish one fare from another at all stages of ticketing. Seat requests have to be individually identified so that seat availability can be controlled and service levels specified.

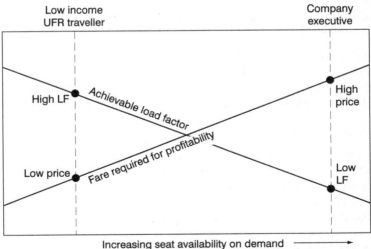

Figure 4.15 *Airline viability in different markets*
Source: British Airways

There are three ways of doing this:

1. Lower fare seats in a different class with physical differences on board or at least at the check-in. Business class and first class do this.
2. Sell these tickets through specified outlets much as charter flight tickets are sold.
3. Early booking or late 'standby' booking would identify low fare passengers particularly in the booking system. Their bookings could not be changed and high load factors should be achieved.

Sales revenue or profit

But while these prices might be maximising seat sales and revenue, are they maximising profits? In some markets prices have been set at a level which may be achieving the first two objectives but result in a financial loss. This failure to reflect costs in pricing policy led to heavy losses by most IATA airlines.

CASE STUDY 5: EUROSTAR

The principles outlined earlier in this chapter have been applied by Eurostar in setting its fares from London to Brussels/Paris. The fares are based on what the market will bear; are related to the primary source of competition, the airlines' fares; use the processes of market segmentation and yield management (see above) to maximise the yield per seat and try to enhance market share (see Table 4.2, page 104).

The basic fare may, as with airlines, be the standard second class fare between the two points of origin/destination. From this fare there are increases or discounts depending on local markets, service quality, perceived journey times competition, and segment elasticities. The discount fare stimulates demand while the fully flexible ticket and first class fares capture some of the consumer surplus in the market. As identified above, high yield passengers have to be discouraged from downtrading through inhibitors and limitations on availability on certain peak trains when favourable market conditions can achieve the required revenue and load factors at a higher price. As with the BA yield management system, all passengers have a reserved seat and thus historic data and holiday, weekend and sports event data, may be used to vary prices as sales for a particular train progress.

In addition the objective of off-peak first class fares is to maximise yield, to meet market expectations and to capture further consumer surplus amongst passengers who would not buy a full first class fare of £298 but are prepared to pay above a discounted second class fare (around £110). Special fares also apply to children and special offers through newspapers and other train operators, eg FGW offer standard class off peak Eurostar fares of £87, are intended to stimulate demand for products of both Eurostar and its promotion partner (see Table 4.2).

COACH PRICING

Long distance coach pricing

Long distance coach operators such as National Express, Oxford Tube or First Shuttle have a totally different market to local bus operators. The market place is very competitive with the car, train and several coach operators. There is invariably a peak commuter market into major cities but with evening leisure, business and some commuting markets outside the peak.

The commuter coaches introduced competition for train companies' commuter services in their traditional London market, through a fares policy (based on cross-price elasticity) clearly designed to attract rail passengers. The pricing policy is related to what the market will bear and discriminates between peak and off peak operations, or between segments with different price elasticities.

National Express long distance services have day return, period return and peak period return fares with reductions for children, students and senior citizens whose price elasticity is higher and whose cross elasticity with rail travel makes these fares a very effective railway competitive device.

A market analysis (Table 4.13) of several routes indicates that intercity coaches are used because they are cheap, direct, quick, frequent, reliable, relaxing and comfortable.

Some operators with a higher commuter patronage have a peak and off peak pricing policy. However, if peak travel is a relatively low percentage, the disadvantages of a more complex fares structure may outweigh any potential revenue benefits. Indeed, a regular traveller discount might be more appropriate, for example:

Table 4.13 *Intercity coach operation – market analysis*

Journey purposes %		Gender %		Social class %		Sources of awareness %	
Shoppers	36	Male 35	(43)	AB 21	(4)	Word of mouth	39
VFR	22	Female 65	(57)	CI 31	(24)	Advertising	18
Education	13			C2 18	(22)	Mailing	10
Leisure	12			D/E 24	(54)	On-bus ads	6
Commuting	9					Cannot remember	28
Social (evening)	1						100
Other	3						

Source: National Express Group

Figures in brackets indicate bus equivalent figures.

Fares:

Regular day return	£5.50
Weekly return	£25.00
Weekly coach and local bus	£30.00
Over 60's	£2.75 (this market segment is price elastic; it is however a recognised segment for several modes)

The new 'low cost' UK operator Megabus offers fares from £1 single in much the same way as easyJet does for the 'low cost' airline business. Megabus is similarly an internet-only pre-booking operation, able to use a more sophisticated pricing policy aimed at the price elastic markets, eg students, and Megabus termini are often at a university campus. Some of these customers will be new (own price elasticity) and some transferring from other operators (cross-price elasticity).

National Express is again a pre-booking operation through the internet, telesales and retail outlets. It has very sophisticated pricing systems, and segments its business market, its peak leisure market and its off-peak leisure market. It can for example charge a premium fare on Friday afternoons, Sunday evenings and morning peaks. There are a fixed number of passengers (seats) per coach, the maximum load factor is 100 per cent (as with airlines), and filling a Friday 16.00 departure from London Victoria coach station is considerably easier than a Wednesday 12.00 departure. As running extra peak vehicles incurs costs, the objective of a pricing policy is to sell a fixed supply at the highest price. In price theory terms, the demand curve moves to the right.

Most of the traffic on National Express services to London originates outside London. On the Birmingham route for example, 75 per cent of traffic is *from* West Midlands with only 25 per cent originating in London and the south-east. Rail operators on several routes between London and other cities have a London outward fare and a different London bound fare in leisure market segments. There are good arguments for this. In London, press advertising costs are higher, the market is harder to penetrate and the widespread nature of the home counties market often requires passengers to purchase two tickets for a journey via central London. The car might therefore be a competitor. Many existing passengers will adjust their travel times and pay a reduced fare. Higher income levels in south-east England result in travellers being prepared to pay higher fares, while in provincial markets it is easier to motivate coach travellers. As most are travelling to London's airports or central London, the market is geographically more limited and same-price centres can be identified. The price elasticity and cross elasticity of demand is higher (ie more responsive to cheaper fares) in relatively lower income areas than in south-east England and so demand is more income elastic.

Rail companies sell most tickets through travel centres, online or through travel agents, who are easily able to cope with selective pricing. National Express use a wider variety of retail outlets including many shops, which requires a relatively simple fare structure, and have a stronger market position in the south of Wales or the north of England than in south-east England.

While elasticity is high in the long distance coach market, the private hire market is highly price competitive. The large number of small operators can result in a company losing a large amount (possibly 40 per cent) of its work with a price rise of 10 per cent. The market too has reduced in size and a Henley Centre report indicated that the coach industry has little chance to manoeuvre. A major reason given by bigger operators is the growth of a cash payment market niche, eg amongst club and society outings, where quality of vehicle is not an important criterion (although safety remains so) where older vehicles are acceptable and where the price is low. Some discerning clientele (eg large companies, government departments) will require high specification new vehicles. Regional location of markets will also affect price; airport services in the south east of England may earn £550 per coach per day, compared with under £250 in the south of Wales or the north of England. The London market has a larger, higher income population able to afford higher prices. Where more small, low-overhead companies exist, costs (and prices) are likely to be lower, and the hourly charge may also vary between peak and off peak.

BUS PRICING

Bus fares may be determined in two ways:

- By the company operating commercial services and deciding what the market will bear having considered the competition from other bus companies (existing or potential), the motor car or, on long distance services, discounted rail fares. This is the position in most of Britain outside London, but through new contract arrangements there is an increased move towards transport authority integrated fares systems.
- By transport authorities determining fares, routes, frequencies and type of vehicle. All bus, tram and metro fares and in many cases local rail fares may be decided in this way. Bus routes are directly operated or franchised with multimodal, multiride tickets. This is the case in most large cities (eg London, Paris, Berlin, Madrid) in the 'old' European Union; most cities in the new member states (eg Vilnius, Prague, Dresden) and most South American (eg La Paz, Lima) and Southeast Asian (Hong Kong, Japan, India) cities. Despite the competition policy of the European Commission (in the UK pursued by the Office of Fair Trading), most EU member states have excluded bus and train operations.

Tendered services may be either full cost (fares decided by the transport authority) or net cost where fares are decided by the operating company keeping in mind its required level of income and its subsidy in order to cover its costs and profit. In some counties and PTEs fares on tendered services may be determined by the authority and subsidy is paid on a cost basis.

On urban services, fare scales will be tapered and lower than on rural sections of routes where prices will generally be high. On inter-town routes, particularly if there is competition from rail companies or other operators, fares per mile are generally low. As a general indicator, a monopolistic market and low usage will result in a high price while a competitive market and a high load factor will result in a low price. In many provincial towns, companies have introduced minibuses with simplified fare scales almost on a zonal basis.

There is evidence to suggest that passenger service elasticity can be high where services prove to be consistently unreliable or where service intervals are long. The replacement of conventional buses on an hourly or half-hourly headway with smaller vehicles with a 5–15 minute headway (depending on demand) has had an effect in attracting customers back to public transport.

There are no peak/off peak fare differentials in many places and in some industrial towns the highest peak has moved to 16.00–17.50 as a result of schools, industrial, commercial and shopper traffic (see Table 4.14). The morning peak has either disappeared or is now between 09.00 and 10.30 – the end of the industrial worker flows and the start of the shopping trips. This requires some enhancement of service, but not enough to justify the added complication of premium fares.

A flat fare in a small town on a high frequency (five-minute interval) route could result in lost revenue. The choice for some short distance passengers is between walking or a bus ride. If a flat fare is 25p they would use the bus, while a fare of £1.00 would be unacceptable. In larger towns (eg Nottingham, Cardiff, Newcastle) with, say, a seven- to ten-mile radius the average fare might be £2.50, but in competitive or potentially competitive routes fares may be kept at £1.50 for the same distance. Another option is to use zonal fares, but on short cross (zonal) boundary journeys

Table 4.14 *High flow route showing peak demand*

	Passengers per hour
08.00–09.00	250–300
09.00–10.30	470
16.00–17.00 (Friday)	500

Source: Cole (2003)

demand may be lost. Multiride tickets provide a similar facility to the London travelcard but are restricted to one operator and provide travel for a period in a designated area on both commercial and tendered services. They provide for work journeys with optional travel provided 'free'. An important element in this market segment are females aged between 16 and 24 with no car but who work in the central business district. They have work, evening social, and Saturday shopping trips as a typical week's travel pattern. This provides a ten-journey ticket for the price of eight single tickets, with additional free journeys. It also ensures the passenger will then ride on that company's buses rather than those of competitors.

Bus companies operate in quite different markets to rail and airline businesses. They have little or no executive high yield custom, most journeys are local low mileage trips and in competition, fares and costs have to be kept down.

However demand may be relatively inelastic even on competitive routes. Fare increases from 18p to 20p and 21p to 25p showed no change in patronage, despite the competitor company's fares remaining the same and thus lower. The issue may relate to the low value of 2p or 4p in relation to total fares or to wages. Fares might be increased on the day increases in fuel prices resulting from taxation were announced; thus passenger perception was also important in reducing resistance. Coincidentally, bus fares could be increased at the same time as rail fares and the latter perceived as relatively expensive by the existing bus users. Most fall in socio-economic groups C D with many younger people (with low spending power), low car ownership rates (48%) and low second car ownership (10%).

The young account for 35 per cent of passengers, elderly people for 20 per cent (most of whom have concessionary fares or free travel in many local authority areas) and a further 40 per cent are women between 20 and 60 years. Only 5 per cent of passengers on average are males between 20 and 65 excluding central London. For journeys to work, 95 per cent of passengers are women. Thus inelasticity in relation to price might also relate to the necessity of the journey and the lack of alternative modes.

Market segmentation is thus being used in provincial towns under the new conditions of competition. It is not as widespread as in the airline or British Rail sectors but it indicates a pricing policy which recognises that passengers are not a homogenous group but that different market segments exist and that price, cross and service elasticities have been identified for these segments.

CASE STUDY 6: UNDER-18 MARKET

The factors affecting demand showed price to be a minor factor to most travellers. However, there are certain market segments that are more price sensitive. The under–18 (non-school travel) market is one of these. Travel to school has an inelastic demand and is usually funded by parents or education authorities. This segment, although it may have the same individuals, has a totally different level of price elasticity.

The under-18 market during weekends and school holidays has the following characteristics:

- low income and limited travel spend;
- high desire to travel;
- flexible in times of day to travel;
- considerable spare time to go out to, for example, entertainment or visiting friends;
- high price elasticity of demand;
- maximising revenue from maximum volume.

One example is FirstBus all day unlimited travel offer of £1.50 in place of single tickets of 50p to £2.50 and the usual £1.90 under-18 ticket (see Figure 4.16). Advertising throughout Great Britain targets this specific market segment on *Hit 40 UK Chart Show* and *Smash Hits* with local advertising attractions, things to do, etc. Increasing patronage during the school holidays is largely own price elasticity.

There is a view amongst larger bus companies that the dormant young persons market would increase patronage by 5 per cent if the free bus travel scheme (currently available in Wales for the over 60's) was applied to that under-18 market segment.

Summary

The four essential prerequisites of price discrimination are:

1. Bookings for each fare must be easily distinguished from one another. The easiest way is to introduce advance booking, payment and return-fare-only sales, thus improving cash flow and reducing reservations cost.
2. To raise the load factor a limit is placed on the number of low fare seats, both in numbers of seats and the journeys on which they are available, thus predictable troughs of demand are filled first.
3. Raise load factors further by reducing seat wastage from no-shows, cancellations or changes in plan. Such facilities result in the forfeiture of part of the fare to offset the cost of this service.
4. Prevent competitive practices by other airlines in a particular market segment which will undermine the price discriminatory policies operated in that market segment (through monopolies or cartels).

This environment now puts the airline in a position of being able to operate price discrimination between market segments in a way which improves

Figure 4.16 *FirstDay under 18 – Leisuretime ticket advertising*

its profitability and market share. If it can do this, it is ready to market the concept to potential passengers.

Market segmentation

Market price discrimination

The increased use of market segmentation over the last forty years, the pricing policies which airlines pursue, the cost implications of market segmentation and the use of costs on a marginal basis to determine fares provides the rationale behind the customer's perception of airline advertising and in his/her choice of tickets.

Table 4.15 *Summary of analysis for each new fare*

Stage			
1	Inhibitors associated with fares	Fare (level)s	Control of competition
2	Service level (eg seat availability, choice)	Peak demand pattern (if any)	Elasticity and generation of demand
3	Route productivity (load factor and utilisation)		
4	Variable costs incurred for this fare's passengers/cargo	Interaction with other fares	
5	Fixed costs incurred for this fare's passenger		
6	Load related costs incurred generated by this fare		
7	Net yield of fare (excluding agents' commission)		
8	Costs generated by this fare	Revenue generated by this fare	
9	Overall financial effect of the fare (contribution to profit)		

This concept used in conjunction with yield management techniques (see above) will produce a variety of tickets based on market segmentation, with product differentiation elements based on service and choice constraints. The latter are the inhibitors to first or business class passengers downtrading to economy class. The service quality is designed to justify to companies the payment of higher fares by executive travellers.

The range of fares reflects the segments in the market (see Table 4.16). If two of the world's leading business routes, London–New York (BA) and London–Paris (Eurostar), are looked at in more detail, the price variation between segments but the similarity of rail and air segmentation can be clearly seen.

A series of questions remains unanswered.

The monopoly held by a railway franchise or bus company is apparent if it is the only company operating in an area. However, is this a true

Table 4.16 *Market segments pricing – comparative levels analysis*

Destination	First class	Return fares Business class	Minimum class economy
London to:			
Los Angeles	5498	4320	300
Johannesburg	4643	2489	675
Cairo	2655	1604	541
Amsterdam		382	85
Frankfurt		450	132
Paris		415	59
Brussels		398	59
Warsaw		638	150
Hong Kong	4521	3022	685
Tokyo	6174	3977	1053
Melbourne	5733	3999	829

Source: Airlines

monopoly? It may be a single mode monopoly but there is inter-modal competition particularly with a low cost mode – the motor car – whose costs have risen more slowly than those of public transport (see Figure 2.1).

The long distance market is growing with new operators such as Megabus and easyBus, with what consequence? Is there a dominant market in travel, which will be stimulated by price? Is the low cost airline business an example of this or is even that a medium term (three–five years) phenomenon?

Price discrimination is a technique which divides the market into segments and charges what each market will bear. In each segment the competition is different on each route, different competitors exist, thus requiring further discriminatory policies.

Figure 4.17 *BA discount fare advertising (November 2004)*

Table 4.17 *Market competition summary*

Routes	Class	Competition between			
		Train	Coach	Air	Car
London to:					
Edinburgh	Business	X		X	X
	Tourist	X	X	X	X
Bristol	Business	X			X
	Tourist	X	X		X
New York	Business		X		
	Tourist	X	X	X	X
Paris	Business	X		X	X
	Tourist	X	X	X	X
Oxford	Commuter	X	X		X
	Business	X			X
	Tourist	X	X		X

The concept also recognises that consumer surplus will vary from one segment to another and that price elasticity, cross elasticity, income elasticity and service elasticity are essential features of market segmentation and thus price discrimination.

REFERENCES

AB (2004) World airline rankings (financial and passenger), *Airline Business*, August, Sutton.

BAA (2004) BAA Annual Report 2004.

BR (1990) British Rail, Inter City Business Products Plan 1990/91. British Railways Board, London.

British Airways (2004) fares information and brochures.

British Rail (1992) Business Products Plan, Leisure Products Plan, market Analysis, British Railways Board, London.

Cole, S (2003) Survey of bus companies in Great Britain (unpublished). Management interviews.

Dunmare, D (2003) Strategies for low cost airlines, *Transport Economist*, **30** (2), Summer, UCL, London.

Eurostar (2004) Timetable and fares information and brochures, Eurostar, London.

Evans, M (2004), Martin Evans, managing director Air Cardiff Ltd (an air brokerage company), in discussion with the author.

First Great Western (2004) fares information and brochures.

FT (1998) KLM spreads its wingspan in the no frills market, *Financial Times*, London.

Global Network (2003), KLM/Northwest.

GNER (2004) Great North Eastern Railway, fares information and brochures.

Goodwin, P B (1986) One person operation of buses on London, *Transport Economist* (1), pp. 9–14.

Jowit, J (2004) Aviation's great survivor, *Observer*, 13 June, London.

Main line railway companies (MLRC) (2003) Discussing with FGW, GNER, Midland Mainline and Virgin Trains; for commercial reasons no references or data are ascribed to a particular operator.

Petzinger, T (1995) *Hard Landing – how the contest for power and profits plunged the airlines into chaos*, Times Books-Random House, New York; Arum Press, London.

Rail (2004).

Rigby, R (1997) Cheap and cheerful. *Management Today* (August), London.

Welburn, TAN (1974) The case study draws on Segmental Seat Scheduling, British Airways, Overseas Division, London.

FURTHER READING

Doganis, R (1991) *Flying off Course – the economics of international airlines* (2nd edition). HarperCollins, London.

Doganis, R (1993) *The Airport Business*, Routledge, London.

Hanlon, P (1995) *Global Airlines – competition in a transnational industry*, Butterworth-Heinemann, Oxford.

Jackson, T (1994) *Virgin King – inside Richard Branson's business empire*. HarperCollins, London.

CHAPTER 5

Cost Levels and Structure – Road Transport

PRICE VERSUS QUALITY

In a freely competitive transport market, the allocation of resources and hence the provision of services would be determined on the basis that operators produced at the lowest possible cost the service required by customers. This applies to both freight and passenger operations and in both sectors, the customer will select the service with the best combination of cost and quality characteristics, not necessarily the cheapest.

Chapter 4 showed how many passengers prefer to pay a higher price for what they consider to be a superior service, by travelling first class by air or train, or by selecting a more expensive car. In the freight sector the same price versus quality equation applies. Marks & Spencer spends a higher percentage of its costs delivering food to its shops than other retailers, and believes it has the most sophisticated and reliable food distribution service in the UK. Some critics believe it pays too much for the high service standards and questions if the benefits are worth it. Marks & Spencer says it guarantees freshness, and sees the distribution system as a customer service.

High quality services might be provided at a higher price and cost; those customers not concerned with comfort, reliability or particular departure times would be satisfied with either an inferior service or one provided at the supplier's convenience (at an off peak time), so long as it was cheap.

Private costs and public costs

Private costs are amounts of monetary expenditure incurred by individuals and operators in the provision of different services demanded by the market. The non-storable nature of transport services and different methods of providing and financing infrastructure and moving units (eg vehicles, aircraft, rolling stock) in each mode make transport industry costs more complex than in many other industries. The operation of a factory usually only affects land use on the site although it may in some cases, where waste products are exuded, affect land around it. Transport operations are based at a garage or depot but their operations can affect land uses many miles away along a motorway, railway or flightpath.

In consequence, there may be costs other than private costs and the free market may not be the most appropriate or efficient method for the allocation of resources. The non-private costs, called social costs or externalities, are imposed on other operators and on the economy at large following the actions of a particular operator. They are outside the cost structure of the operator and take the form of environmental pollution (noise, fumes, vibration, visual intrusion), social group severance or congestion costs imposed on one operator by another (see Chapters 9 and 10).

Private costs in different modes

When a decision is made about which mode to select, the combination of cost and quality on offer is largely determined by the difference in cost structure between various modes.

BUS OPERATING COSTS

Cost allocation

The costs of operating a bus or road haulage company can be segregated into fixed costs (those which are avoidable only in the long term), semi-variable costs which can be reduced if the company's operations are permanently to contract, and variable costs, which relate to the number of vehicles or miles operated. These can be avoided in the short term (in terms of hours or days), subject only to agreements on drivers' wages and working conditions.

Bus cost allocation model

The allocation of costs into these three categories provides the economist with the nearest existing approximation to marginal cost. The route costing system (see Table 5.1) enables bus companies to allocate costs directly attributable to a route or joint costs where shared facilities (including drivers or buses as well as engineering and head offices) and both route revenue determine route profitability.

Cost reductions in any of these categories will therefore have a varying impact on the overall cost level of the company. Cost Model A (Table 5.1) provides for the allocation of costs between routes and for an analysis of avoidable costs in a period when the size of the company is being reduced, and enables companies to compare route costs in different areas; it also enables major groups such as First Bus or Stagecoach to compare similar routes operated by different subsidiaries. It does not however, identify

Table 5.1 *Cost Model A: Bus cost allocation model by category to routes*

Allocation to route	Long term Fixed cost	Avoidable in the: medium term Semi-variable cost	Short term Variable cost
Bus hours	Administrative staff costs; education; medical and welfare benefits	Traffic operational staff costs; miscellaneous traffic expense; supervisory staff costs; vehicle maintenance (PSVs); miscellaneous garage and workshop expenses; Training Board levy grant	OPO drivers' wage and expenses; crew drivers' wage and expenses; conductors' wage and expenses; vehicle servicing
Bus miles			Fuel oil and duty; tyres; hire charge for vehicles (manned); TP insurance and compensation
Number of peak vehicles	Rent, rates, fire insurance, maintenance, power, light and heat – buildings, staff cars, vans, lorries; telephone, postage, stationery; professional fees and bank charges; miscellaneous general expenses	Tickets, ticket machines and equipment; publicity licence duties and fire insurance; vehicle depreciation (PSVs – replacement); leasing/ renting of vehicles (unmanned)	

Sources: CIPFA (1974), NBC (1993), First Group (2004), Cole (2004)

areas of overhead costs whose control is the responsibility of a specific manager; rather it puts all overheads as a separate fixed cost item.

In the Cost Model B, local management is responsible for all costs except those relating to Head Office. It includes local overhead costs as well as direct (variable) and semi-direct (semi-variable) costs and is a basis for more local managerial decisions. In the case of overhead costs, the effect of closing one of two depots and using the open yard of the remaining depot for overnight bus parking can be estimated and related to that manager's financial responsibility and targets. There are however certain decisions that continue to be made by Head Office and their conse-quences should be measurable. Bus allocation, for example, is made on a business case basis by calculating driver/usage hours, operating mileage and passenger/revenue projected growth giving an internal rate of return (IRR). For example, a concessionary fare scheme in a PTE or in Wales can guarantee a new revenue flow, thus justifying new vehicles. If such a flow is the result of increased passenger numbers, it can then be part of the justification for capital investment in new vehicles.

Cost Model B (Table 5.2) considers the expenditure categories by garage/depot or by route. It is a bottom-up model of particular use in preparing bids for operating franchises or tendered services such as those contracted by London Transport, Passenger Transport Executives and county councils. It identifies key cost areas and enables managers to reduce these costs where required to meet the expected price for a successful bid for a route or route-group contract.

Each of these models can be used to achieve different objectives. For large companies with many subsidiaries, efficiency indicators are required. Companies bidding for tendered/franchise routes have to be able to go through each line of cost and try to provide that at the lowest possible cost.

Cost Model B (Table 5.2) has also been used to compare the relative importance of different cost elements and differences between inner urban and suburban small town operators. Driver costs form the highest single element and are expectedly higher in big urban areas compared with operations in rural areas and smaller towns. Costs of tyres and materials are

Table 5.2 *Cost Model B: Large PLC group subsidiary bus company*

Profit/Cost Centre	Revenue	Overhead Costs
Group Head Office		(a)
Operating Subsidiary H.O.		(a)
Management Unit (one or more depots with identifiable responsible manager)	Advertising Sales Comm.	
Depot (may be a management unit in its own right)		(b)
Other revenue: advertising sales commission		
Route		
Hours – drivers (include training)		
Miles – fuel, oil, tyres, maintenance (parts/labour)		
PVR – motor insurance, road fund licence, depreciation, lobase finance costs		
Journey	Fares	
Overheads –		
a) rent, local taxes (rates), professional fees, bank charges, senior managers salaries, CVL		
b) rent, local taxes, traffic staff, utilities, building insurance, management salaries, publicity, tickets, office and engineering equipment, depreciation, radio charges, support vehicles		

Source: Cole (2004)

determined by contract negotiations and size of single deliveries (eg fuel). The model can also illustrate the impact on depreciation and on maintenance through the use of new vehicles. Capital costs have risen in percentage terms but new vehicle warranties have saved on parts, some labour and reduced engineering staff in total. Smaller buses with a shorter life expectancy and a shorter depreciation period *may* also push up that cost element depending on the type of vehicle and number of years (eg 26 seat Ford/Mercedes depreciated over 7 years or Dennis Dart over 14 years). Under National Bus there was pressure to push all costs down to network or route level to satisfy local authorities paying subsidies that the companies were doing their best to reach break-even.

Network subsidy procedures have now been replaced by contracts and internal cost control is paramount. Companies must also show to shareholders, banks and venture capitalists that budget and cost control procedures are in place and are effective. City analysts want to see costs under control, efficient management and maximum profits, and have little interest in the detailed running of buses, any more than in the detailed operations of how ICI makes chemicals or BP obtains and distributes oil. Costs and dividends are the key measures of company success from the investor's point of view.

Cost saving process

It has also become necessary for bus companies to identify profitable and loss making parts of the business either to make commercial decisions regarding local bus service operations or to determine the level of funding to be included in any bids for contracts from PTE's or county councils. In the case of a large bus company the allocation of costs, for example, to works contract service may determine the level of costs allocated to a tendered service, where the same vehicle, staff and depot facilities are in use.

The process of cost reduction is one of avoidable cost – what costs can be avoided and what timespan is required to achieve that objective? The reduction of labour costs may be initially achieved through one-person-operation (OPO) and later by reducing wage rates or removing inefficient labour practices. Labour costs (wages and pensions) are the largest single component of total costs, together with materials (tyres, maintenance) and insurance. Labour costs reduced considerably from 1985 to 1995 in both urban and rural areas. However, since then there has been a levelling off or even an increase in costs although not to 1985 levels in real terms. Costs have risen by an average of around 8 to 9 per cent from 2002 to 2003 although these have varied from 1.7 per cent (West Yorkshire) to 17.5 per cent (East London). This may partly be the result of wage rate inflation in southeast England but also an indicator that at low wages the supply of drivers has fallen below operators' requirements.

Table 5.3 *Cost Model C: Expenditure by route/garage/company (% of total costs)*

Expenditure category	Average	L CWLB	L ELBC	MC BTS	MC GMBS	BC CB	BC NCT	BC OBC	R W&D
Wages and labour/overheads	50	71	70	63	61	66	65	61	58
Traffic payroll	6					4			
Engineering	7								
	63					70			
Depreciation/leasing	8	9	6	8	7	7	10	6	10
Fuel	1								
Tyres	8								
Engineering	8								
Building cost	2								
Bus insurance	8								
Non-building overheads	10								
Materials/other	37	20	24	29	32	23	25	33	29
Total	100	100	100	100	100	100	100	100	100

Source: Transit (London publications) Business Monitor (2004); TAS Partnership Bus Monitor (2004); First Bus; Cardiff Bus

Key:
L: London
MC: Major conurbation, eg Manchester, West Yorkshire
BC: Big city (eg Cardiff, Nottingham)
R: Rural
CWLB: Centre West London Buses Ltd (First)
ELBC: East London Bus and Coach Co Ltd (Stagecoach)
BTS: Busways Travel Services Ltd (Stagecoach), Newcastle upon Tyne
GMBS: Greater Manchester Buses South Ltd (Stagecoach)
CB: Cardiff City Transport Services Ltd (Municipal)
NCT: Nottingham City Transport Ltd (Municipal/Transdev)
OBC: City of Oxford Motor Services Ltd (Go Ahead)
W&D: Wilts & Dorset (Holdings) Ltd (Management; Go Ahead 2003)

Category definitions:
Wages: wages and overheads (pension, National Insurance) for drivers, conductors, service controllers, administrative staff, engineering staff.
Depreciation – bus depreciation (replacement cost); leasing cost; building depreciation.
Materials: spare parts, consumables, warranties, external repairs, plant maintenance, utilities, building maintenance, rents and rates, training, catering and welfare, marketing, cash transfers.

Table 5.3 illustrates the relative importance of expenditure categories in different companies representing different operating conditions.
Table 5.4 analyses these same costs over a period of 10 years in price per vehicle kilometres (ppvkm) and shows how costs have changed over that period.

Depreciation however has risen considerably over the last 10 years as bus prices have risen, and from the demand for new buses resulting from increased revenue flows and low floor buses specified as a requirement in Transport for London and other transport authority contracts (a service elasticity impact). Fuel and tyre costs can be reduced in the short term with real fuel costs halved (net of fuel duty) as a result of frequency reductions or withdrawal from some routes, but some maintenance continues to be incurred on unsold vehicles. In the short term, therefore, some labour costs and some maintenance costs can be avoided. Restructuring costs of one off payments can be made to achieve future cost reductions through buying out inefficient conditions of employment, redundancy and early retirement (the last two as a means of reducing non-driving staff) (First Group, 1997).

The next stage in the company's plan to avoid costs is to reduce the fleet size. Surplus buses can be sold (where the market allows) or returned to the leasing company and this results in a reduction in supervisory and maintenance staff. There is no constant straight line link between bus sales and reduced labour costs; it is more a stepped link. At this stage, quite large garages can become (or be replaced by) outstations with minor servicing and cleaning facilities, while older garage buildings can be demolished to reduce maintenance costs and buses parked in the open rather than under cover as was traditional with most companies. Depots can also be closed and peak buses parked at the bus station standing area or private car parks and not returned to the depot. This will avoid some building maintenance and some labour costs.

The final stage in a plan that comes to terms with new market conditions is to sell land such as depots or office blocks. Offices can be moved to a small block within the garage complex where major mechanical work is carried out. Situations have occurred where a company which once had four large garages and a separate head office, after some interim measures, closed all except one garage and relocated the head office at that garage or at the main bus station (eg First Cymru, City of Oxford Motor Services). This is the avoidance of fixed costs. These stages, although applied here to bus operations, relate equally to road freight.

Company efficiency and performance criteria

Other variables are required to analyse the efficiency and performance of the company:

Efficiency
Costs per bus mile/km
Revenue per bus mile/km
Cost per passenger trip
Revenue per passenger trip

Bus miles per employee
Bus passengers per employee
Number of employees per bus
Bus passengers per bus

Output performance
Drivers' gross weekly pay
Fleet size by type of vehicle
Total passengers carried
Total scheduled bus mile/km
Total operated bus mile/km
Total staff by full time, part time and type of job
Total income by type of service (eg local bus, express, private hire)
Total expenditure
Number of peak vehicles required
Peak-interpeak ratio
Days of operation
Hours of operation
Type of operation and vehicle used
Number of routes
'Dead' mileage (to and from depot)

This range of unit costs has been further analysed and the efficiency measures most appropriate as a basis for management action are:

- total operating costs per bus km (cpbkm);
- total operating costs per local bus service passenger;
- total operating costs per employee;
- total operating costs per vehicle;
- total operating costs per peak vehicle.

Factors affecting cost differences

The efficiency criteria indicate how well or badly a bus company is operated and can provide both internal measures and inter-company comparisons. Whichever of these measures is selected, the reason for variations, either from budget or from a comparative base using another company's performance, must be carefully considered. The comparative statistic of operating costs most frequently used by bus companies is cost per bus kilometre (cpbkm). It, like all other measures, has its limitations as a comparison of efficiency but so long as these are realised then it is probably the one datum which is most generally available throughout the industry. Data on passenger trips is only available when more sophisticated ticket and data capture machines are in use and is made more difficult where multi-trip travelcards are used on different routes. Smaller operators

Table 5.4 *Local bus services:[1] operating costs (pence per vehicle-kilometre)[2] 1990/91–2000/01*

	London[3]	English metropolitan areas	English shires counties	England	Scotland	Wales	All Great Britain	All outside London
At current prices								
Excluding depreciation								
1990/91	167	89	70	90	75	59	86	76
2000/01	150	95	83	98	71	70	93	83
% Change	−10.2	+6.5	+18.6	+8.9	−5.3	+18.6	+8.1	+9.2
Including depreciation								
1990/91	177	97	74	96	80	64	93	81
2000/01	165	99	87	104	78	76	99	89
% Change	−7.3	+2.1	+17.6	+8.3	−2.5	+18.8	+6.5	+9.8
At 2000/01 prices[4]								
Excluding depreciation								
1990/91	222	118	93	120	100	79	114	101
2000/01	159	95	83	98	71	70	93	83
% Change	−48.0	−19.5	−10.8	−18.3	−29.0	−11.4	−18.4	−17.8
Including depreciation								
1990/91	236	129	98	128	106	85	124	108
2000/01	165	99	87	104	78	76	99	89
% Change	−30.1	−23.3	−11.2	−18.8	−26.4	−10.6	−20.2	−17.6

Source: Transport Statistics Great Britain 2003

Notes:
1. Includes traditional local bus services.
2. Net of fuel duty rebate. Although data are given to the nearest penny they are unlikely to be accurate to this degree.
3. Comprises services operated under contract to London Transport bus network.
4. Adjusted for general inflation, using the Retail Prices Index.

may not have this or much of the other efficiency data because their cost accounting systems are not sufficiently detailed nor do they use a cost-allocation model.

If costs per bus km (cpbkm) is used for comparison then it is necessary to consider the operating differences between firms. Those companies which concentrate on excursions, tours and private hire, have a high mileage per vehicle and higher operating speeds and thus a lower cpbkm than local bus service (stage carriage) routes, which are primarily served by the major groups (eg First Group, Stagecoach, Go Ahead), ex Municipal companies and LT, PTE or county council contractors. Rural based companies operating rural or outer urban routes will achieve higher speeds than the operators on urban routes whose costs are increased by congestion, more frequent stops and higher passenger loads, higher depot costs and, on occasion, higher labour costs. Higher speeds result in higher mileage per vehicle thus enabling more trips to be made. These differences may be identified on some routes which are entirely rural or entirely urban. Table 5.4 gives an indication of the differences (compare English metropolitan and English shires/Wales figures) but some routes are mixed between rural and urban so that averaging of costs per bus km/mile may be misleading.

Thus the profitability of urban services might be underestimated if average costs are used. In the regulated bus network operating in London, passenger figures have risen; costs however have fallen significantly (Table 5.4; UKRTSD, 1997). Comparisons using cost per bus kilometre take no account of hours of operation and the effect of evening or weekend working on costs. Linked to this is the level of vehicle utilisation and in particular the peak vehicle requirement which can significantly affect costs through the financial effect of underutilised peak vehicles. Cost per bus kilometre is a distance related measure whereas many fixed or semi-variable costs cannot be changed in the short to medium term.

The costs incurred often reflect the provision of a level of capacity by an operator. The peak demand pattern, if it is to be met, combines the period of highest cost per bus kilometre and the period of highest demand. Peak buses purchased to serve two short periods of high demand may be idle for the remainder of the day. Heavy peak loadings on buses may be in one direction only with low load factors on the return outward journey. The overall peak load factor on London Buses for example is 23.7 per cent (2001). Some coach tour companies with a suburban operating base in London have found that revenue can be generated from using morning spare capacity into the central business district to provide a commuter service, while commuter coach operators provide tourist related services between 10.00 and 16.00.

Under many old agreements bus crews required enhanced rates of pay for working a split shift system, particularly with large operators, but many operators have bought out such arrangements. Small independent companies employ part time drivers for time-of-day and seasonal peak traffic. Improved efficiency within the bus industry had to focus on wages and related overheads as 60–70 per cent of costs lie in that area. This applies to all companies. In the 1980s the National Bus Company operation had considerably more administrative staff and higher driver costs through more or longer layovers between journeys, spare drivers and breaks of 40 minutes per five-hour shift with a maximum number of working hours (see also under 'Economies of scale')

Depreciation policy will also affect cost levels depending on the period (8, 10 or 12 years) over which vehicles are depreciated (in effect paid for). Depreciation is now on a replacement cost basis rather than an historic cost basis. This increases asset (eg vehicle) replacement costs but is more realistic.

A distinction must also be drawn between running costs and standing costs. The running costs are those which are avoided if the vehicle stays in the depot all day. The costs incurred no matter to what use the bus is put are the standing costs. Seasonal fluctuations in demand often give coach operators a relatively high standing charge per vehicle while for urban bus operators the standing charge per vehicle is a low percentage of total costs, but because of low running speed and frequent stops, running costs are relatively high. However, overall, the private independent coach operator has a lower cost level.

The age profile of a bus fleet will have an impact on cost in two ways: 1) a newer fleet will incur higher capital costs (interest or leasing); 2) an older fleet will have higher maintenance costs. The average vehicle age profile has changed: it was 8.4 years in 1990, rose to 9.9 years in 1994 and fell to 8.4 years in 2002 (*Transport Statistics GB*, 2003). The main reason is the increase in new vehicle purchase since 1995; however, 20 per cent of buses are still over 15 years old.

Economies of scale – their effects on cost

In the last few years a number of bus companies have grown rapidly, largely by acquisition. In 1996, five groups – First, Stagecoach, Arriva, National Express Group and The Go-Ahead Group – accounted for some 65.7 per cent of UK bus market turnover.

There is contradictory evidence on whether or not larger fleets produce economies of scale because the conditions under which operators work vary considerably.

Labour costs will be the biggest determinant of overall costs per bus mile. Within the labour element, the rate per hour, maximum hours and pension costs will be the predominant determinants of the level of costs. A simplified example may be used to illustrate the position.

A bus company wishes to operate a service from 07.00 to 20.00 each day. To comply with drivers' hours regulations, two breaks are required. A small

Table 5.5 *Market shares of major bus companies by turnover in the UK, 1996*

	%
First	22.1
Stagecoach	15.1
Arriva	14.5
Go-Ahead	8.3
National Express	5.7
	65.7

Sources: Bus Industry Monitor 1996, The TAS Partnership Limited

Note: The shares in the table are based on the annualised turnover of all subsidiaries owned by each group at 31 August 1996. The annualised turnover figures are based on annual accounts for the year ending between July 1994 and June 1995.

private company may employ one person for the whole shift, thus measuring a single person's payments for pension, National Insurance, sick pay and holidays. A large plc with seven-hour shifts and two demand peaks to satisfy may employ two drivers 07.00 to 14.00 and 14.00 to 20.00. At best it involves one and a half shifts but, as the on-costs are charged on a per person basis, the large company doubles such expenditure from two employees.

A study in Newcastle indicated that cpbkm increases with the percentage of total operated km represented by stage services and with gross weekly drivers' pay. Income per stage km increases with the size of fleet, and with the number of employees.

These factors however are related to a number of characteristics of the industry. The larger operators tend to be in the large towns or conurbations where traffic speeds are low and passenger loadings are high, which produces higher income but increases costs.

Small coach operators or schools service providers have lower costs per bus kilometre and higher profit margins than do large local bus service operators. This is often due to the age profile of the fleet and lower administrative costs. Full management costs may not be attributed to the company and overhead costs can often be minimal. Bus purchase costs will vary between small and large companies.

A group (eg First, Stagecoach) may purchase a new Dennis Dart for £110,000 as part of a bulk order for 300 vehicles. Many purchase or lease arrangements of large groups are complex, making it difficult to assess exactly the cost per annum. However, a small company could pay a 20 per cent premium because its order is for three buses (£132,000). However, the age profile of a small company fleet tends towards older vehicles (often purchased from outside the company and whose maintenance records may be less than desirable) compared with a large group (where even older vehicles are cascaded within the group and high maintenance standards may provide corporate cost advantages and prolong vehicle life).

It has been shown that new vehicles can attract more customers. However, a vehicle costing £110,000 now will not attract seven times the number of passengers or revenue compared with a second hand bus in reasonable condition costing £15,000. New vehicle maintenance costs will be lower and some costs covered by manufacture warranties. Other factors such as image, staff attitude and information on services will also be factors in determining revenue. However, bus purchase (depreciation) accounts on average for 8 per cent of larger bus company costs.

Insurance costs have significantly increased over the last 20 years – due partly to high repair costs, increased road congestion and a consequent increase in number of accidents. Passenger litigation has also increased.

There is a tendency for large groups to centralise fuel and tyre purchase also. However, savings in fuel are as dependent on the size of each delivery as they are on total volume purchased. Several companies after privatisation and leaving the National Bus Company were able to reduce unit costs of fuel and tyres and also of vehicles particularly with a switch to minibuses using existing commercial (van) chassis where negotiations with different suppliers produced costs discounts for new buses.

Many smaller bus companies may cost each vehicle associated with a local authority contract so that a required margin (say 6 per cent) is achieved after all costs (operating, finance and dividend) have been paid. Pension schemes of large groups may be more expensive; in many, but not all, small companies there may be no pension provision. One of the large bus companies estimates its pension costs at 10 per cent of costs on top of its wages expenditure. The working times agreements may also vary.

An insight into the impact of mergers was provided by the inquiry (MMC, 1997) into the First Bus/SB Holdings merger. The company estimated operating cost savings of £6.3m based on existing operations. The manpower savings would be achieved by reducing numbers of drivers and maintenance staff, through improved working patterns (so reducing overtime costs) and voluntary redundancy. There would also be savings in costs of maintenance supplies as a result of improved control over offering supplies, bulk purchasing, changes in maintenance working patterns, new vehicles and a reduction in the number of spare vehicles (particularly if

Table 5.6 *Comparison costs: large and small bus companies 2003*

Cost element	Large co (PLC)	Small co (private)
Rate per hour	£6.50	£6.50
Holidays pa (weeks)	5	3
Sick pay (% of costs)	3%	0%
Pension (% of costs)	10%	0%
Uniform	Yes	No
Statutory holidays (pa)	8	8

Source: Author's survey of representative companies

such vehicles were moved between companies). First (the major bus company) also expected to make further savings because of economies of size, including saving nearly £1m on the purchase of 90 new buses (1997) and IT systems which First Bus already had thus avoiding duplication. There would also be a reduction of sixty vehicles but no service levels change and the percentage of spare vehicles for the new company would be reduced from 10 per cent to 15 per cent.

Similar arguments were put forward in First's takeover of Centre West London Buses (1997) and by Stagecoach Holdings (1994) in identifying the benefits of acquiring Busways Travel, the bus division of Tyne and Wear PTE. They included economies of scale in purchasing fuel, spare parts, insurance and other supplies and investment in new vehicles to help reduce maintenance costs.

Centralised companies once had a large head office staff, but the scale of these aspects and their costs are now low and limited to investment and financial control on the so called 'octopus' principle – small head, with subsidiary companies operating at arm's length with profit margin targets. But as companies enlarge further they need to ensure that head office over-heads do not grow and neutralise economies achieved through operating efficiencies. The group head offices of two major bus companies, First and Stagecoach, are not in Central London but in Aberdeen and Perth.

The final question is whether these operating efficiencies would have been achieved with the consequent improvement in operating margins without large scale operations. Could Centre West or Busways Travel (who had both pursued such policies) have achieved a 15 per cent oper-ating margin without being part of First Bus?

Size – the big group argument

The argument put forward by major groups is that discounts can be nego-tiated for fuel, parts and vehicles. However, small private companies may buy second hand vehicles, have no specification criteria (which require a minimum order of 100 vehicles to achieve a cost reduction), may have no workshop, no planning permission, cheap labour, pay cash in hand with no national insurance and park buses on the highway. Even excluding these types of operators, small management units can identify discount suppliers. Fuel suppliers base prices on a 29,000 litre load as being one delivery per tanker. The number of locations rather than the number of full deliveries is the more important determinant of price although there will be large-quantity discounts above the bulk load discount. Companies will then compare fuel storage and stock costs against discounts. However, fuel is only 1 per cent of total costs (see Table 5.3). In purchasing vehicles the percentage discount is maximised per vehicle at 100 vehicles with very little additional discount beyond that optimum number.

Raising capital is cheaper for larger companies as there is a better return to size of loan. Funding of a £20m or a £2m share flotation will cost a similar amount in management fees; interest rates will be lower for Stagecoach plc than for say a 50-vehicle company because the risks are lower; and the purchase of an existing company (eg London Transport, PTE or ex-National Bus Company) will be less costly in funding terms for a big group (bank loan 2 per cent over base rate) than for a management buyout (venture capital finance with interest rates up to 20 per cent pa).

The effect of vehicle size on cost

In some transport sectors, for example air transport, the size and type of vehicle is a major cost determinant but it was argued (Higginson and White 1986) that this was not so in road passenger transport except in extremes of size.

Many bus companies have pursued a policy of introducing minibus services on many of their urban services in small towns and suburban services in larger towns. Until then lightweight single-deckers were used on a small scale on some rural routes with a vehicle 'cascading' policy preferred by many operators. The predominant vehicle has become the larger single-decker with the double-deck fleet in decline (Table 5.7).

This has led to a much closer examination of the effects of bus types on overall costs and in particular the use of minibuses. The current view is that improved vehicles with a longer life, reduced maintenance costs resulting from standardised specification, mass produced vehicles and separate (lower) wage agreements have resulted in cost advantages.

A study of 'small' and 'big' bus costs indicated difficulties in making easy comparisons. The definition of a small bus which once referred to mini buses as commercial light van chassis may now be applied to a 36 seat Dennis Dart which makes the definition less clear.

In general, direct costs are less for smaller, single-deck buses; labour and tyres cost less, fuel consumption is lower, capital costs are less, depreciation is less even over 12 years compared with 17 and maintenance is simpler and therefore cheaper. However, as labour is the predominant cost

Table 5.7 *Size and configuration of buses (000s)*

| Year | Single deck | | | | Double deck | Total |
	Up to 16 seats	17–35 seats	36 plus seats	All S/deck		
1985–86	6.5	3.1	33.2	42.8	25.0	68.0
1995–96	8.8	16.5	30.8	56.1	19.6	75.7
2000–01	10.9	15.0	38.0	63.9	15.9	79.8

Sources: CIT (1996); BCSGB (2003); CPT (2003)

in a bus company it is that element which will finally determine the cost per bus kilometre and it is that element which has to be purchased as efficiently as possible (see Table 5.3).

Indirect costs show lower insurance premiums because claims cost less, there are more accidents per kilometre but they are less serious; garage costs are reduced with more vehicles in the same space and open yards at low priced land sites are used increasingly in place of depots or garages with no effect on the life duration of the vehicle.

CASE STUDY 1: COST REDUCTION (BUS INDUSTRY)

The effect of one person operation on cost

Cost saving techniques already discussed include the change in types of vehicle used. However, the effects of such reductions in costs are limited, because the cost of vehicles and depots are a relatively low proportion of the total and do not necessarily fall directly in the same proportion as reduced vehicle capacity.

Two main effects resulted from the introduction of OPO. The first was a reduction, though not as great as first thought, in labour costs. The second was an increase in journey time and, more important, a given stock of buses operating more slowly will perform lower total mileage and thus reduce frequency or result in a higher vehicle requirement. The elasticity of demand in respect of service quality will result in some passenger and revenue loss. London Transport estimated this at 3 per cent of total revenue.

The effects of OPO in London were measured by London Transport (1983) using an assessment framework based on established cost-benefit analysis techniques. The evaluation contained an estimate of the financial costs and benefits to LT and a social cost/benefit assessment for society. (See Chapter 9 for a fuller explanation.) London Transport's objective was to illustrate the financial effects of OPO in the face of increasing costs and the likelihood of reducing subsidy. The argument put forward by Goodwin (1986) was that time delay imposes a penalty which has to be taken into account when considering the economic implications of public sector policy and the study (Goodwin, 1985) estimated that this would delay an OPO bus by 10 per cent compared with the Routemaster bus.

REFERENCES

BCSGB (2003) *Bus and Coach Statistics of Great Britain*, Stationery Office, London.

CIPFA (1974) Passenger and Transport Operations: Recommendations on a Standard Financial Statement and Route Costing System, CIPFA, London.

CIT (1996) *Omnibus for All*, Chartered Institute of Transport, London.

Table 5.8 *Effects of increasing OPO from 53% to 65% in London*

	Benefits (£ million)		Costs (£ million)		Actual gains (£ million)
Financial effects	Conductors'		Drivers' pay*	5.7	
(LT only)	pay	14.2	More buses*	1.4	
			Revenue loss	0.7	
			Severance	0.4	
		14.2		8.2	6.0
Social effects					
Travellers	Fewer bus		Time losses†		
	accidents	0.5	(a) to passengers	1.0	
	Fares reduction	1.8	(b) to traffic	1.8	
		2.3		2.8	−0.5
					5.5

Source: London Transport

* Because of longer loading times and a requirement to maintain the existing level of service
†Standard social cost-benefit analysis was used for this assessment

Cole, S (2004) Survey of cost structure and levels of British bus and rail operating companies.

CPT (2003) *CPT Facts*, Confederation of Passenger Transport, London.

First Group (1997) Annual Report, First Group plc, Aberdeen.

First Group (2004) Annual Report, First Group plc, Aberdeen.

Goodwin P B (1985) *One Person Operation of Buses in London*, Greater London Council/Transport Studies Unit, Oxford.

Goodwin, P B (1986) One person operation of buses in London, *Transport Economist*, vol 1, 9–14.

Higginson, M P & White, P R (1986) The efficiency of British urban bus operations, Transport Studies Group Research Paper 8, University of Westminster, London.

LT (1983) One person operation of buses; London Transport Executive memorandum to Greater London Council, September 1983, London.

MMC (1997) Monopolies and Mergers Commission, London – First Bus plc and SB Holdings Ltd. A report on the merger situation, London.

NBC (1973) Operational Costing Manual, National Bus Company, London.

NBC (1993) Cost Allocation System, National Bus Company, London.

TSGB (2003) *Transport Statistics Great Britain*, Department of Transport, HMSO, London.

UKRTSD (1997) Making Connections, Report, January, UK Round Table on Sustainable Development, Department of the Environment, London.

Note
First Bus plc changed its name to First Group plc following an Extraordinary General Meeting on 23 December 1998. The author is a shareholder.

CHAPTER 6

Cost Levels and Structure – Railways

Definitions

There are several elements of railway costing which should be clearly defined prior to any discussion of how the costing system of an integrated railway should operate. This may be where ownership and operations lies with one company/state body or where, as is increasingly the case within the European Union, infrastructure and train operations are separated.

Cost allocation (or attribution)

In an organisation where different parts of the business use the same facilities, the total costs and revenues of the business have to be shared out between those parts. This is done through the operation of a set of predetermined rules and criteria.

Contributory revenue

In the case of a railway operation, feeder services may provide much of the traffic carried on intercity services. Similarly much of the traffic carried on local lines originates outside those lines. If it were not for the integration of local and national services much of this revenue would be lost. Consequently, services contribute revenue and traffic to one another. For example, rural rail services provide a local facility but also provide feeder services into main line routes (Table 6.1).

Avoidable costs

These are costs which would no longer be incurred if a particular service was withdrawn and can be viewed in terms of marginal cost, which in economics is defined as the additional cost incurred as a result of operating one extra unit (eg a train service). Avoidable cost is the reduction in cost achieved as a result of operating one unit less. The railway will try to achieve those cost savings with the least resultant reduction in revenue.

The concept of *opportunity cost* is regarded as *resource* costs in economics and is used to reflect the value of resources used in providing a

Table 6.1 *Sources of passengers – Wales' provincial railways*

	% of total trips Feeder trips	Local trips[1]
Aberystwyth-Shrewsbury	71.0	29.0
Cambrian Coast Line	20.6	79.4
	$(13.9)^2$	$(86.1)^2$
Central Wales Line	34.9	65.1

Sources: Mid Wales – a strategy for rail and air transport – Development Board for Rural Wales/ Steer Davies Gleave, DBRW (1981), DBRW (1997) Cole reanalysis (2004)

Notes:
1. which began and end within the line
2. if journeys to/from stations on the Aberystwyth-Shrewsbury line are included

particular service. The opportunity cost is not necessarily the same as the financial cost of producing a service; it is the value of output achieved if the transport facility was put to the alternative use giving the next best level of output. Transport economists often calculate opportunity cost on the basis of the cost savings achieved if a service was discontinued and the resultant cash available was spent on a more productive facility.

If a service makes a loss to the extent where it is not covering even variable costs then it may be 'financially' acceptable to close it. Withdrawing a late night service will save the running costs of a train unit (the extent will depend on the interworking of that unit and the next morning service it provides).

If passenger loadings are low (eg 50 passengers) compared with capacity an alternative lower cost train type (eg 2-car diesel set) may be used in place of an intercity 8–10-car set where the alternative is to withdraw the service. A departure west from London operated by Wessex Trains is met using a Class 158 set on Saturday to Thursday while First Great Western meets the higher peak demand patterns on Fridays using an Intercity 125 set.

This example of avoidable cost also illustrates the opportunity cost – cost savings which can be used elsewhere in the system to provide improved services. The avoidable costs here will be modest in comparison with those achieved if the peak and all other operations of that train unit are withdrawn, when both capital and running costs will be saved. If the peak high yield journey has alternatives (eg on commuter services) then most of the revenue may be transferred and the loss minimised. However, any joint costs remaining have to be shared between those railway services still using the line, increasing their unit cost and possibly affecting their profitability. In some circumstances, a reduction in traffic may lead to a reduction in the number of tracks, thus avoiding maintenance costs and generating revenue from the sale of high grade steel.

It can be seen that the avoidable (or opportunity) cost of a particular service level depends on the proportion of total costs made up by joint costs. If joint costs are a high proportion then the avoidable cost will be low. This is particularly so in the case of longer term fixed costs such as infrastructure where the normal replacement point may be many years away.

Joint cost and common cost

The joint costs of constructing, maintaining or operating railway services are those which are shared by two or more services (or operating companies), and which would not be significantly reduced if one of those services was discontinued.

Common costs are an element of joint costs and exist in circumstances where significant reductions would be achieved if one of those services was discontinued.

Joint costs are incurred where the operation of one service is linked to, or is dependent upon the operation of another service. This may be the whole service, a part of it or two separate services using the same track, rolling stock or stations. A negligible reduction in costs is achieved if only one part is discontinued. Costs jointly incurred by different services have to be allocated to individual services if their financial position is to be measured.

Joint costs exist under a variety of operational circumstances where:

- A vehicle or train makes several trips so that fuel, crew and depreciation are joint costs shared between each departure.
- Assets are used by different services, eg railway station, track, freight depot, bus/rail interchange (where another operator's costs are affected).
- Labour (eg driver) is used on different services during one shift. Wages are a joint cost and to avoid these the driver's duties would have to be removed or reallocated to other drivers as there is usually a minimum shift period.
- There are return journeys but often no return loads. This occurs in both freight and against-flow peak passenger services with low load factors. Thus joint costs may be allocated on a directional basis.

Joint costs – effects on commercial policy

The existence of joint costs will have an effect on the commercial policy of transport operators. Transport supply can only be reduced in stepped units, for example an HGV truck, a train set, a bus and in labour terms, one mechanic per several vehicles. Therefore, to achieve *large* cost savings there is little point in eliminating low use journeys without also removing peak trips which require extra capacity but also have a high revenue yield.

Joint costs are incurred in all parts of railway operation (as well as in road and air sectors). The low load factor return freight trip is a joint cost with the original delivery, for which the outbound customer ought to pay unless (or even if) a return load can be found. Passenger service operation is characterised with high load factor peak operation and low load factors or idle train units during the day, evening and weekends (Chapter 1). The joint cost problem is not merely one of revenue penalties but also a decision on sources of revenue. Revenue per trip will vary between peak and off peak and if costs are identical for all trips, then busy period passengers may cross subsidise off peak passengers (eg many InterCity operations into London have no peak vehicle provision and operate the same frequency from 07.00 to 19.00). Demand is more price elastic in the off peak leisure market; the user will not pay the full cost of the journey and price/quality adjustments are made to improve off peak load factors.

It has been argued that joint costs should be paid by the peak user or prime user since without them all other journeys could be withdrawn and the costs avoided. However, this form of marginal cost pricing would result in very high fares/charges to the peak or prime user and a much lower price for the secondary user. Even with high inelasticity of demand, customer loss could be great since the benefits (measured in consumer surplus or financial benefit) derived are lower than the full peak cost. Consequently, an assessment of 'what the market will bear' could be made and joint costs allocated accordingly, but because joint costs occur between journeys in different market segments and with different load factors a commercial (or pricing) solution is far more difficult in transport than in other industries.

New structure for Europe's railways

The European Union directive 91/440 (EU, 1991) required the harmonisation of structures, the development of the railway and access by all competent operators to the market. This requires separating the management of the railway infrastructure from the provision of railway transport services (EC, 1995). The Commission White Paper on revitalising the railways (EC, 1996) sees the need to bring market forces into play but also retaining network benefits and the provision of socially necessary services which pure market economics could not justify (Cole, 2002).

The traditional form of railway operation in non-EU countries and other parts of the world still remains as an integrated approach to railway management with the impact on cost structure and costing principles as dealt with in this chapter.

Structures used in individual systems

This section briefly explains two different options currently in use for the separated railway.

Germany

The process of implementing Directive 91/440 began with the establishment of Deutche Bahn AG (DB) and the separation of infrastructure and train operations through its division into four operators.

- track network
- long distance passenger transport
- short distance passenger transport
- freight

The basis of track charging is required to be fair and free from discriminations among track users with revenues covering all costs and charges being competitive. These seem to be mutually exclusive at present. Third track charges should ensure optimum use of track capacity. The DB track division is a monopoly supplier in terms of the train service companies, but their customers have a modal choice. The monopolist also operates in a market with decreasing average costs and charging on a marginal cost basis would lead to a deficit as marginal costs are lower than average costs (see Great Britain section below for public funding solutions).

If no public funding to cover losses is available then the track suppliers may use price discrimination in one of three forms.

These forms are:

1. Customers pay prices according to their willingness to pay using consumer surplus.
2. Charge customers on the basis of volume of goods purchased with different prices per product unit, eg two-part tariffs of electricity and telephone companies which have a major capital cost element included.
3. Customers pay prices according to price elasticities of demand.

The charging system introduced in 1994–1995 covers all infrastructure (track and stations) and is based on the quality of lines (ten types of line are identified covering curve gradients, maximum speed, technical equipment, signalling and telecoms) and the importance of the routes (track capacity, volume of passenger and freight transport on the routes, economic importance). The prices first vary according to different types of passenger and freight trains, and then according to requirements on reliability, use by very heavy trains (in relation to extra wear) and the operation of empty stock. There are also discounts for higher usage levels in terms of train kilometres.

The costs charged to the operating diversions relate to the track only (and exclude stations etc) covering capital costs (depreciation and interest) and maintenance and management costs. The approach adopted in Germany does not equate to the private company balance sheet but rather to a format which equates rail infrastructure to road and waterway assets. The infrastructure for all three modes was the responsibility of the state and a non-commercial, macro-economic approach was needed so that comparisons of costs between modes could be made so identifying distortions in the market between modes and to charge equalised rates. This concept is not dissimilar to that of the 'level playing field' between road and rail put forward in Britain (Reid, 1985).

Great Britain

This excludes Northern Ireland Railways where a totally separate policy of bus and rail integration exists with state ownership of all operations.

The 1993 Railways Act (UK) signified a radical period of change in the railway industry in Britain. The most significant change is the separation of infrastructure management and provision from the operation of train services, the process of vertical separation. A not-for-profit company, Network Rail, replaced the original private company, Railtrack plc. It owns and manages the track, signalling, other operational infrastructure and stations. It provides access rights, together with an appropriate charge, (see Table 6.27) to the train operating companies, subject to the approval of the Rail Regulator (Cole and Holvad, 1997).

Some train operating companies (TOC's) have networks based on the British Rail profit centres with no attempt to rationalise a system of costing and interworking based on an integrated railway. These are gradually being replaced by a series of logically structured independent companies (SRA, 2003), each based on a market analysis and financial evaluation carried out by the SRA (2004).

The decision to return the rail infrastructure in Great Britain from Railtrack plc, which was put into railway administration (a form of bankruptcy), by the UK government has changed the financial position of the track operator. Although it remains a private sector company it has a not-for-profit format and its policy decisions are clearly made with government agreement.

The company was profitable in 2000 (£364 million) but since then has incurred a loss of £2.3 billion. The loss for the year end March 2004 of £734 million would have exceeded £1.3 billion had it not been for grants (£452 million) and rental from land (£167 million).

Because of the changes in the company's legal persona comparisons over several years are difficult. Operating costs have risen by 51.4 per cent and revenue by 2.4 per cent (including government grants). To enable the

Table 6.2 *Infrastructure costs and access charge percentage*

Access charge component	Description	% of total access charge
Short-run variable costs		9
a) Track usage costs	Direct maintenance costs	3
b) Traction current costs	Electricity costs	4
c) Peak charges & hardwired charges	Charges which aim to reflect the value of services with special attributes, eg peak period services	2
Fixed common costs		91
a) Long run incremental costs	Long costs of maintaining and renewing rail infrastructure attributable to the operations of an individual TOC	37
b) Common costs	Route specific common costs, zonal costs and network costs	43
c) Station and depot charges	Charges covering costs in relation to maintenance and renewal of stations and depots. Not part of the track access charge	11

Source: Network Rail

railway to continue operating and to enable infrastructure investment, the government is guaranteeing borrowing, and access charges payable by train operating companies will rise.

Much of this investment (£13.7 billion over five years) has been required to counteract lower figures over previous years. However, the evaluation process introduced would be difficult to justify except on a long term cost-benefit basis. The final view of this investment would be best assessed in terms of opportunity cost (would bus investment give a better return on some rural lines?) and in quality of service (reliability), a form of service elasticity. All this has to be achieved within a pricing policy that does not

Table 6.3 *Social costs of operation and use*

	Costs incurred by Railtrack	Other costs incurred by society
Short-run variable costs	Maintenance costs, electricity costs	Pollution and accidents
Fixed and common costs	Sub-zonal, zonal and national, common cost, long run incremental costs	Administrative costs of regulation and safety, other environmental costs

Table 6.4 *Network Rail analysis of income and expenditure percentages*

Revenue	%	Expenditure	%
Access charges (passenger trains)	73	Wages	18.1
		Depreciation	18.0
Freight trains access	3	Interest	10.2
Government grants	17	Maintenance	39.4
		Leasing	2.2
Rental from property	6	Other	12.1
Other	1		
Total	100	Total	100

Source: Transit Business Analysis (2004); Network Rail Infrastructure Ltd (2004)

result in reduced demand – a sophisticated market segmentation policy. These key elements in economic analysis are now being practised in Britain's railways.

THE PRIVATISED/DISAGGREGATED RAILWAY

The question of ownership (see page 167) is in the hands of the member states. The position in Great Britain is that both parts have been privatised. Elsewhere in the 'old' European Union, the railway has been split but both parts are state owned. In other countries in the 'new' EU and in Northern Ireland the issue has still to be determined. This case study examines the consequences of this change. Two projects were funded by the European Commission in 1999 on the techniques for evaluating operations (EC, 1999a 1999b) together with the APAS report on rail infrastructure (EC, 1996).

To put these costs into a comparative context an analysis of revenue sources should be made.

The cost breakdowns between the different domestic services vary little. Labour costs are consistently around 28 per cent and rolling stock cost just under 20 per cent although track access varies between 20 and 30 per cent of total costs, on average. There are no interest charges as most of the train operating companies own few assets which require heavy borrowing. London

Table 6.5 *Cost structure: train operating company, 2001*

Cost element	%
Managed costs (internal)	45.8
ROSCO charges	16.3
Railtrack fixed costs	37.9
Total	100.0

Source: Cole (2001) Survey of representative companies (see also Table 6.7)

Table 6.6 *First Great Western (train company) 2003*

Income Sources	£m	%
Passenger income	270.4	74.3
SRA payment	34.0	9.3
Car parking		
Catering income		
Commissions		
Station access		
Station trading	59.6	16.4
Call centres		
Heavy maintenance		
Light maintenance		
Stabling & cleaning		
Other		
	364.0	100.0

Sources: First Great Western; Transit Business Monitor (2004)

Table 6.7 *Cost analysis (%) of selected railway operators*

	Train company						
Cost element	LC/RS SWT	LC CR	BC/RS CT	RS ATN	IC FGW	IC MML	CTRL L&C
Labour	36.1	27.9	22.3	23	22.5	27.5	10.8
Depreciation	0.6		0.5		1.3	1.3	7.9
Rolling stock leasing	17.5	20.6	14.7	12.4	34.8	17.5	
Track access	29.7	17.2	37.2	36.4	14.8	22.5	
Interest			0.7	4.5			44.7
Other (incl train maintenance)	12.0		18.7	23.7	13.6		0.5
Materials/electricity/fuel	4.1	34.3	3.9		13.0	31.2	36.1
Leasing (other)			2.7				
Total	100.0	100.0	100.0	100.0	100.0	100.0	100.0

Source: Transit Business Analysis (2004); Company accounts (2004)

Key:
LC London commuter
IC Intercity
RS Regional service
BC Birmingham commuters/regional service
CTRL Channel Tunnel Rail Link
CT Central Trains
SWT South West Trains
CR Chiltern Railway
ATN Arriva Trains Northern
FGW First Great Western
MML Midland Main Line
L&C London and Continental

and Continental Railways however has interest as its largest item of expenditure (44.7 per cent) and at £235 million this is about four times its labour costs (£56 million). The reason is its role as a private company responsible for operating the British-owned element of the Eurostar train fleet and for constructing the Channel Tunnel Rail Link (the source of interest charges) from the Tunnel to St Pancras station in London. The company pays a minimum usage charge to Eurotunnel (until 2006) and received the trains from British Rail for a nominal £1. The capital cost of the Eurostar trains remained in the British Railways Board annual accounts as a residuary amount of £1.3 billion (and was eventually written off by the UK Treasury).

CASE STUDY 1: COSTING THE INTEGRATED RAILWAY – A LESSON FOR 'NEW' (2004) EU MEMBER STATES

Historical development of the accounting system

The majority of the world's railway operators retain a single operator structure running both track and trains. Only within the European Union (and to some extent the United States) have track and train operations been separated. This principle will eventually extend to those member states previously in 'eastern' Europe that joined the European Union in 2004. By taking the accounting system used by British Rail, which evolved partly from identified market segments and partly from a need to satisfy government demands for information, this system reflects the economic/ accounting processes currently existing in the 'new' EU member states. Part of British Rail's operations were required to be profitable – InterCity, Freight & Parcels. Separating freight and passenger has clear managerial advantages, but it was also a reflection of government policy to make freight profitable. The division of the passenger business into three sectors stems from the Beeching studies when, as a general rule:

- long distance express services were generally profitable;
- commuter services were unlikely to be profitable;
- rural services were unprofitable.

The advent of the Passenger Transport Executives (PTEs) in 1968 led to a further need for cost allocation to those services. Consequently, a business sector based accounting system became lost in these geographic divisions.

The provision of financial information for decision-making in each business sector led to the identification of five requirements:

1. Sectors are responsible for all cost management.
2. The financial consequences of all expenditure on physical assets can be measured directly.

3. Regional operating management and business sector management use the same financial database and interpretation of data.
4. Management information provided at required intervals (daily, weekly, monthly, etc as appropriate).
5. The ability to trace decision makers.

There is an essential prerequisite for giving managerial responsibility for the bottom line to each market sector. The system for allocating costs within British Rail has changed over the years according to the perceived management requirements at the time, from full cost allocation to the last used method under BR of 'sole user cost allocation'. The system described here (in particular under 'prime user and avoidable cost' and 'sole user cost') imitates the current EC objective of separating infrastructure (region) and business/market sectors (train operation). It provides the state railways of 'new' (2004) EU members with the form of information required of them.

Full cost allocation

All costs, whether joint, fixed or variable, were spread over all activities on the basis of arithmetical averaging, weighted according to use. But the weights were uncertain and direct management action could not be taken to control cost allocation and joint infrastructure cost allocation was unclear.

Contributory accounting

This system replaced full cost accounting from which it differed in not allocating infrastructure costs unless they could be definitely attributed to one service. A block joint infrastructure cost figure covering these non-allocated costs was contributed to by each business. It was very difficult to calculate the level of contribution and no method of allocating responsibility was provided for.

Avoidable cost

This method attempted to relate costs to a particular activity by establishing what costs could be saved if that activity no longer took place. The major problem from an overall cost point of view was that the basic infrastructure cost, which was not related to any market sector, amounted to over 50 per cent of total infrastructure cost. This large amount could not be made the responsibility of any sector manager and was therefore unsuitable for business based profit centre management.

Prime user and avoidable cost

The concept of prime user considered the responsibility for infrastructure cost on the basis of which sector was most important in determining the characteristics and scale of the facility. Thus the cost of every piece of track, every station etc was the responsibility of a sector and affected its bottom line (Reid, 1985). Avoidable cost techniques were applied to secondary users. The method was somewhat unfair to InterCity, a significant prime user of the most expensive infrastructure (eg big town termini, expensive track) and did not identify any surplus capacity. The prime user method was considerably more robust than its predecessors, but it took no account of hidden surpluses and could not be used for future business decisions; it was replaced in 1985 by sole user cost allocation.

Sole user cost allocation

This has the same basis as prime user in that both have all routes assigned to a particular market sector. Thus, the question asked is, 'What facilities would this sector require if it were the only user of the line with a brand new infrastructure?' The prime user requirements are so determined from 'scratch' and any other requirements of secondary users are then added and the cost (eg for extra platforms at stations, slow parallel tracks) are allocated to the secondary user. All investment projects are now assessed on this basis and business requirements are established at an early stage. Any surplus costs derived from the needs of the secondary user are then added back and although the track, terminals, rolling stock, etc, remain in the 'ownership' of the operating region, all financial decisions concerning it are made by the sole user sector.

This last facility (called 'location costing' by BR) ensures where and for whom any expenditure is incurred. Prior to this, regional infrastructure expenditure was spread over all locations and specific costs were not related directly to specific locations. All costs incurred by operators and engineers (in regions) are now the result of discussion with, and payment by, a business sector.

Non-infrastructure costs

A new computer system (the Sector Performance Accounting and Monitoring System) replaced the old system of annual allocation exercises related to grant payments. The system gave sectors direct control over costs and provides a direct link between physical assets and the financial consequences of their management. The eventual outcome of this move was to (in 1990) transfer all assets to the business sector, giving the market servers total control over all costs. Every planned item of expenditure was controlled by sectors and every existing asset is the financial responsibility of one sector until another sector agrees to take it over (as in the InterCity redefining exercise in 1984). Poor utilisation of equipment was thus controlled and sectors were not adversely affected by the performance of others.

Cost structure and cost levels

For the integrated railway the last available data relate to British Rail operations in 1994. To provide the basis for comparison with the separate functions of the infrastructure and train operations aspects of a railway service Table 6.8 sets out the cost structure for the railway and a comparative analysis with bus costs (based on the survey of bus companies in England and in Wales).

Table 6.8 *Cost structure – bus and rail: general comparison 2003*

	% Total cost	
	Bus	**Rail**
Crew	55	12
Maintenance & garage/stabling	12	20
Fuel	8	4
Depreciation	10	7
Route infrastructure	0	38
(includes track, terminal & signals (Railtrack))		
TOTAL	85	81
OTHER	15	19

Sources: Train operating companies and bus companies annual accounts, average figures; Transit journal, Business Monitor

CASE STUDY 2: AVOIDABLE COST (RAILWAYS)

The Serpell Report 1984

The deficit on British Rail passenger services had reached £933 million by 1983, and the Serpell Report was an attempt to quantify the effects of different levels of cost savings on cost, revenue and subsidy required. A number of network options were produced and the results of each show the varying effects of line closures and service reductions.

From the figures in Table 6.10 it is clear that only large scale network closures can make the savings necessary to achieve a viable network or substantial cost savings. Service closures alone will only produce comparatively small savings in costs and subsidy requirements. Avoidable costs levels are therefore closely related to the area of savings. The difference between options C1 and C3 indicates the additional savings made from substantial cuts in route miles in addition to cuts in service frequency and removal of services but not track.

Table 6.9 *British Rail cost analysis 1994*

	£m	% Total costs
Train Operations		
Crew	468	12.4
Fuel	165	4.4
Train Provision	169	4.5
(Stabling, cleaning, fuelling etc)		
Operations Control	288	7.6
(Management, control, signalling operations)		
Train Maintenance		
Locos & HST's	173	4.6
Coaches	295	7.8
Other	113	3.0
Terminals	464	12.3
Commercial	99	2.6
Security	37	1.0
Route Infrastructure		
Tracks	449	11.9
Signals	152	4.0
Telecommunications	62	1.6
Catering	51	1.4
General		
Management	278	7.4
Depreciation	246	6.5
Other	266	7.0
TOTAL	3775	100.0

Source: BRB (1995).

Station closures, particularly country halts, will make little difference to current costs but when the asset requires renewal, its closure at that point will avoid considerable capital expenditure. Closure of route miles will avoid significant track maintenance costs and the cost of maintaining infrastructure especially embankments, tunnels and bridges to a standard high enough to operate a railway. Some costs will continue, such as those to maintain a structure to a standard comparable with public safety requirements prior to demolition or infilling. This is less of a financial burden in sparsely populated rural areas.

Savings in rolling stock or locomotives may also be made when they become due for renewal if this can be coupled with the discontinuation of a service, thus avoiding replacement costs. Scrapping existing rolling stock will save maintenance costs but not necessarily interest charges or depreciation costs. This principle applies to all fixed assets and such fixed costs will remain even in a variable network such as Serpell option A (see Figure 6.1).

Table 6.10 *Serpell Report – results of network options (1983)*

| Option | Deficit £m | | Route miles 1983 | Comments on closure proposals |
	passenger	overall		
Current position	933	–	10,541	Passenger miles: 18,300 m
A Passenger miles: 7900 m	32	(34)	1630	All services (inc PTE) with operating ratio above 0.85; 40% reduction in administrative costs. Major track closures, major service reductions, viable network; profitable with freight.
B Passenger miles: 9800 m	72	19	2220	Option A mileage plus the majority of London commuter services, ie those covering direct costs and allocated infrastructure cost: orbital routes and branch lines are the main closures. Resource costs (eg highway congestion) minimisation 'proxy network'.
C1 Passenger miles: 17,200 m	807	817	10,461	Network largely unchanged, worst performing services and track deleted. (Operating ratio above 2.0 except PTE services and those with growth potential or contributory revenue). Many lightly used stations closed and low load factor services deleted. Nearly all savings are in train services (direct costs).
C2 Passenger miles: 16,400 m	690	667	8781	Retain most of network. Some savings in infrastructure but most are direct cost savings.
C3 Passenger miles: 15,300 m	564	534	6120	Substantial cuts in the network including contributory revenue routes. Cost savings achieved are: direct 50%; infrastructure 40%; administration 20%.
D Passenger miles: 16,500 m	707	684	8400	All towns with population over 25,000 retain a rail service but frequencies and intermediate stations reduced.
H Passenger miles: 18,400 m	848	803	10,070	High level investment. Not fully evaluated for each option nor on cost/benefit basis. Investment in new track, reducing rolling stock life to half and increased capital expenditure on buildings thus reducing maintenance costs. Investment required £4000 million compared current plans of £2400 million (1982–1992)

Source: Department of Transport, Serpell Report (1984)

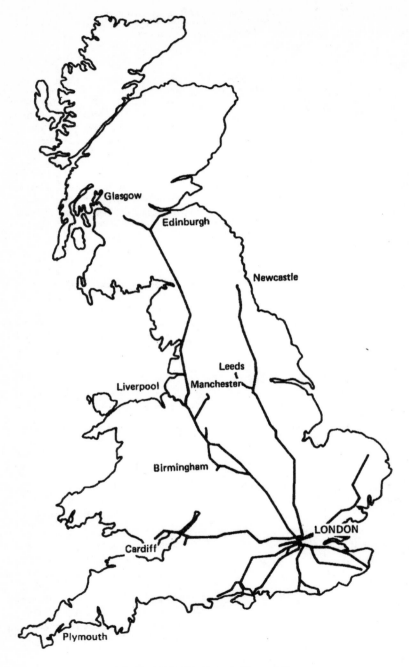

Figure 6.1 *Option A Network*

Figure 6.2 *Option B Network*

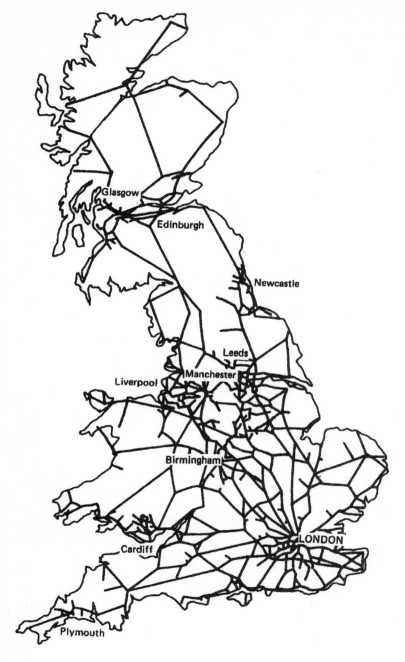

Figure 6.3 *Option C Network (1984)*

Figure 6.4 *Current train operating company services franchised by SRA*
Source: Strategic Rail Authority (SRA) (2003)

A programme of high investment in new track and new rolling stock can reduce the deficit as effectively as cost cutting. The main savings are in modern vehicles reducing the cost of maintenance and improving standards of reliability, image and revenue. (HOC, 1984)

However, as option B indicates (see Figure 6.2), the resource costs of closure have to be taken into account. A time constraint prevented the committee examining the full resource cost options which would have indicated the network to be retained if evaluated on a cost/benefit basis rather than a cost/revenue basis (see Chapter 9).

REFERENCES

Cole, S (2002) Survey of railway operations in Estonia, Latvia, Lithuania, East Germany (post-unification), Czech Republic and Poland (1992–2002). The Sonerail project (see Chapter 9) involved some of these states.

Cole, S & Halvad, T (1997) Track Cost Allocation for Railway Companies, Great Britain, World Congress on Railway Research, Rome, 1997

DBRW (1981) Mid-Wales – A Strategy for Rail and Air Transport.

DBRW (1997) *Developing an Integrated Transport Policy*, WDA, Cardiff.

EC (1995) The Citizen's Network: fulfilling the potential of public passenger transport in Europe, European Commission Green Paper, Brussels.

EC (1996a) A strategy for revitalising the Community's railways, Commission of the European Communities COM (96): 421, Brussels.

EC (1996b) Cost benefit analysis and multi-criteria for rail infrastructure, APAS Report, European Commission Transport Directorate (VII), Brussels.

EC (1999a) Evaluation of Socially Necessary Railway Services, APAS Report (Sonerail), European Commission Transport Directorate (VII), Brussels.

EC (1999b) Evaluation and Business Process Re-engineering of High Speed Railway Services, APAS Report (Prorata), European Commission, Transport Directorate (VII), Brussels.

EU (1991) European Commission Directive 91/440.

HOC (1984) Rail services to end in Wales, House of Commons Select Committee on Welsh Affairs, HMSO, London.

Reid, R B (1985) Organising the railways as a business, International Railway Conference Proceedings, Brussels.

Serpell (1984) Report on Railway Finances (Chairman: Sir David Serpell), Department of Transport, HMSO, London.

SRA (2003) Strategic plan, Strategic Rail Authority, London.

SRA (2004) Franchise Replacement Process, May, Strategic Rail Authority, London.

CHAPTER 7

Cost Levels and Structure – Airlines

In most railway operations terminal and track costs and train operations are the responsibility of one company. In others track and services are run by separate companies (TOC's; NS Reizigers (passengers) with NS Groep NV (track)). Bus vehicle and maintenance infrastructure is provided by the operator, while bus stations are often provided by another authority. The structure of airline costs is similar to both.

Within the European Union, an airline will own (or lease) and operate the aircraft, have its own maintenance facilities but pay for airport ground services and terminal facilities on the basis of use. In Britain the airport and terminal buildings are owned by private companies, for example BAA plc or by local authority companies (eg Manchester Airport plc), with National Traffic Control Services providing air traffic control facilities.

Away from its primary base an airline will usually use local maintenance facilities under contract, and other infrastructure is provided by local airport authorities. In the USA major airlines often operate their own terminal buildings, for example at JFK Airport, while smaller airlines use terminals provided by the airport authority or appropriate consortium. In all locations, transfer to and from the central business district is by helicopter, train, metro, bus or taxi, generally provided by other operators.

There are also instances at hub airports where one airline is the dominant user (eg Delta at Atlanta, Georgia). The cost of providing the additional capacity and facilities might be shared between owner and airline. There have been instances in Europe where the airport has funded the improvements in order to attract a particular airline, hoping that revenue from landing, handling and retaining will provide the financial return.

Cost structure

Costs of aircraft operation generally vary directly with the frequency of operation, the size of the aircraft, the type of route and the weight of the load. There may be differences between state owned and privately owned airlines since the former's cost structure may not be influenced by commercial considerations only.

Variable costs

These are commonly defined as costs incurred by individual flights which could be avoided if a single flight was withdrawn. Some of these costs are aircraft or crew related and vary with the departure frequency; other costs are load related and vary with the number of passengers and weight of cargo.

Aircraft related costs

1. Fuel.
2. Overflying and navigation costs.
3. Landing fees (these can be passenger related).
4. The variable element of engineering and servicing, eg greasing, pre-flight engineering checks.
5. Aircraft parking on airport land (as opposed to company owned sites). Handling costs are related to aircraft movement at airports where agents handle passengers.
6. Crew related costs; these include hotel allowances, meals, transport to and from the airport but *exclude* wages.

Load and revenue related costs

1. Passenger and security costs.
2. Catering costs on aircraft (food and drink element).
3. Insurance of passengers and cargo.
4. Commission for travel agents or freight forwarding agents (revenue related).

Fixed costs – allocated or apportioned?

These costs do not vary with the number of flights made. However, they can be segregated into allocated costs and apportioned costs. Allocated costs apply to a particular aircraft or route and would be avoidable if either was eliminated. Apportioned costs do not relate directly to the number of aircraft in operation. They may be reduced in a stepped form if several aircraft are eliminated and the airline company contracts in size or significantly reduces the extent of its route network.

Allocated costs

1. Aircraft standing charges:
    depreciation of aircraft;
    Civil Aviation Authority fees;
    insurance of aircraft hull;
    amortisation of technical spares;
    uninsured losses.

2. Semi-variable costs:
    pay and pensions;
    training.
3. Fixed costs:
    specific accommodation costs such as the crew reporting building.

Apportioned costs

1. Engineering costs:
    for example London Heathrow Airport and Gatwick Airport engineering bases;
    engineering staff costs at Heathrow, Gatwick and the airline's own staff overseas;
    other minor engineering costs.
2. Traffic handling at Heathrow, Gatwick and permanent offices overseas:
    costs of check-in staff for passengers and baggage;
    overseas managers;
    terminal equipment (including computer reservations systems).
3. Catering:
    staff costs;
    kitchen;
    catering equipment on aircraft where the trolleys are owned by the airline but serviced by an outside contract caterer;
    head office catering.
4. Cargo direct fixed costs (these are direct expenses which do not vary directly with the level of activity);
    cargo centre owned and operated by the airline.
5. Sales and marketing.
6. Central overheads (including depreciation on buildings and new aircraft assets).

There is a distinction to be drawn in the use of these costs. If British Airways is taken as an example, in the financial element of fares submissions to the Civil Aviation Authority, the sales and marketing costs and central overhead costs would be apportioned to route costs. However, these costs are not allocated in decision making on alternative route options. The functional costs of each head office service department (eg maintenance, catering) is apportioned to a route on the basis of the departmental cost plus the cost of activities provided for other departments or other airlines. Thus costs such as buildings, management information, telecommunications, catering and maintenance would be apportioned to a route to support decision making on route options.

The distribution of costs can be a significant factor in determining the profitability of a route. In many airlines, allocated costs are distributed in proportion to the schedule use of the aircraft over a year – this favours high aircraft utilisation. Apportioned costs are distributed on the basis for the gross weight of the aircraft, which favours high utilisation and a high payload to gross weight ratio (load factor).

If a particular service is withdrawn, on the basis of the Table 7.1 figures the fuel and user charges on that service (24.8 per cent of total costs) would be saved; fixed (allocated) costs would be reduced and possibly saved altogether if a group of routes was eliminated. In such a circumstance, however, 36.7 per cent of the costs would remain at least in the short to medium term.

Measuring output in the airline industry

A variety of operational factors affect cost levels in airline operation. As in the discussion of bus costing, a variety of output and productivity measures are available.

1. *Available tonne kilometres* (ATK) is the measure of transport output. The ATKs produced by a flight are the capacity for payload of the aircraft measured in tonnes (2,204 lbs) multiplied by the kilometres flown. They can also be used to measure labour and capital productivity. Some have suggested (HOC, 2002) that ATKs per employee as a key

Table 7.1 *Cost analysis by function – large international airline*

Cost type		2003 %
Variable costs		
Fuel	13.6	
User charges	7.2	
Cargo	4.0	
Fixed – allocated costs		24.8
Aircraft standing charges	15.3	
Crew costs	12.0	
Commission	11.2	
Fixed – apportioned costs		38.5
Engineering	9.0	
Passenger handling, catering	5.5	
Accommodation and ground equipment	6.5	
Sales and marketing	6.5	
General and administrative	5.0	
Other	4.2	
		36.7
		100.0

Sources: British Airways; BA Annual Report 1993–2003; CAA UK Airlines Annual Operating, Traffic and Financial Statistics 2003. Author's calculations based on this data.

indicator of productivity (it divides capacity by the number of employees) reveals little about the fundamental performance of the industry and gives little indication of how this figure translates into an improved operating result. It can also be affected by aircraft size, fleet mix and route length.

2. *Average flight duration* is the revenue hours flown divided by the number of revenue earning flights. There are 'dead mileage' flights associated with maintenance and aircraft relocation between airports.

3. *Average length of flight* is the revenue aircraft kilometres divided by the number of revenue earning flights.

4. *Break-even load factor* is the load factor required to equate traffic revenue with operating costs, excluding interest on capital. Break-even load factors assume that the whole operating surplus is attributed to the type of service involved.

5. *Load factor* is the revenue earning load carried divided by the capacity provided and expressed as a percentage; for passenger traffic the seat factor is the number of seats filled with revenue earning passengers divided by the number of passenger seats available on the aircraft. The revenue load factor relates RTK to ATK; the passenger load factor relates revenue passenger kilometres to available seat kilometres (see Table 7.3 and Figure 7.1).

6. *Revenue passenger kilometres* is the product of passengers carried and the distance over which they are carried (Table 7.3).

7. *Revenue tonne kilometres* (RTK) is the produce of revenue earning load in tonnes and the kilometres over which it is carried.

8. *Available seat kilometres* (ASK) is the product of seats offered for sale and the distance over which they are carried.

9. *Average daily utilisation* is the percentage of each 24-hour period the aircraft is in use (Table 7.2).

Average daily utilisation per aircraft in hours is an indicator of aircraft productivity although this may vary within an airline. (See Table 7.2).

The effects of investment, particularly on fuel consumption and maintenance, can be very significant (a comparison with the high level investment option in the review of British Rail finances illustrates this – Chapter 6, Case study 2). Airlines will therefore equate the higher purchase or leasing costs of new aircraft compared with the higher maintenance costs and possible lower rate of reliability of an older fleet profile.

Measuring productivity and efficiency in the airline industry

The world airline industry is not a homogenous industry with common objectives and measures of efficiency are therefore not straightforward. The Western world's major airlines are either privately owned or state

Table 7.2 *Average daily aircraft utilisation, scheduled/chartered operators –*
Europe (by aircraft type and airline)

Airline	Operator type	Aircraft type	Sector length (KM)	% available hours used
easyJet	L	B 737–300	791	49.8
Go	L	B737–300	1050	42.1
BMI British	S	B737–300	674	36.3
Midland			664	37.4
British Airways	S	B737–300	815	36.8
Airtours Int	C	B757	2311	53.6
Air 2000	C	B757	2289	50.8
British Airways	C	B757	799	29.2
Airtours Int	C	A320:100/200	2135	60.5
Air 2000	C	A320:100/200	2031	53.0
Virgin Atlantic	S	A320:100/200	2429	51.3
BMI British		A320:100/200	655	36.2
Midland	S			
British Airways	S	A320:100/200	769	25.6

Source: Civil Aviation Authority (2001)

Notes:
L: low cost airline
C: charter airline
S: scheduled airline

Table 7.3 *Revenue per passenger kilometre (2003)*

Airline	RPK (m)	% change in RPK (2002/03)	% change in yield per RPK (2002/03)
United	176.1	−6.2	−8.2
BA	100.1	−5.8	−1.3
Monarch	11.8	−8.5	+13.1
easyJet	9.2	+56.0	−0.9

Source: Airline Business Passenger Analysis, September 2003

owned, but profitability is not necessarily an indicator of efficiency if those airlines are in a cartel with revenue pooling agreements keeping up fares and load factors. The profitability of any privately owned transport business is however the requirement for its continuation. In 1995 the world airline industry moved out of the recession of the late 1980's and early 1990's but subsequently they reflected past cycles where airline profits are more in line with the five/six year economic cycle given that transport has a derived demand (Chapter 1 and Figure 2.17). The changes in airline prof-itability from 1997 to 2004 indicated a cyclical trend. Although the passenger market continued to be buoyant, the positive forecasts of charter airlines such as Monarch and Air 2000 in 1997 were challenged not only by trade cycles but by low cost airlines attracting leisure travellers through a cross-elasticity effect.

The measures described here are in some cases peculiar to the airline industry and in others more widely used in varying forms in the transport industry.

Total revenue passenger kilometre (RPK) does not in itself indicate success. The measure for a potential (though not guaranteed) profitability is yield per RPK (Table 7.3) and how that varies from year to year.

The *average stage length* although not a measure of productivity does affect profitability and has to be considered because short routes are operationally and financially more difficult. Profitability is generally low where the stage length is under 400 miles. The costs of ticketing, revenue accounting and reservations (sales and marketing) are a fixed cost per trip which gives a high cost per mile on short stages. Average aircraft speed is lower than on long haul routes and this reduces flying time utilization of aircraft and crews. Demand requirements interact adversely with supply. A doubling of aircraft size (for example, using wide bodied jets such as the Boeing 747–400) produces a 15 per cent reduction in seat mile operating costs. Short haul traffic demands a higher frequency of service but revenue hours are lower and there is a tendency to operate smaller aircraft. However comparing the costs of the Fokker 50/100 or BAe 146 with the Boeing 757/737–400 on short haul routes factors such as average hours per aircraft affecting capital cost per passenger and more frequently incurred airport charges affecting operating costs will impact on profits. As a general rule, the shorter the stage length the lower the profits on turnover. Fares may also be high but their level is limited because of cross demand elasticity with surface transport.

Departures per aircraft are higher on short haul routes but additional maintenance and support costs are incurred through greater engine and undercarriage use. A long haul trans-Atlantic flight might have three landings or take-offs per day while a short haul aircraft on a 'shuttle' route such as London to Edinburgh or Amsterdam to Frankfurt could expect five to seven movements per day.

Departures per employee also favour airlines with smaller aircraft operating on short high frequency route, since big aircraft require more staff per turnaround. However, in Europe problems of immigration, air traffic boundaries and other factors outside the control of the airlines contribute to departures per employee being lower than in the USA. If these were reduced under a deregulation policy or through increased membership of the Treaty countries, more departures, possibly of smaller aircraft, might be a consequence. Output per employee can be measured in total capacity (in tonne-miles) per employee or in seat-miles per employee. These measure total output, but the differences in short haul and long haul output have to be considered and the measure favours long haul operators, and despite requiring more staff more seat miles are achieved per employee.

Revenue per employee is the amount of income earned by each person and illustrates the relative profitability of long haulage and the lower staff to passenger (or cargo tonne) ratio. It will be affected, however, by the level of fares measured by the '*fare yield*'. This is the money received by the airline from a particular fare. It is not a particularly useful measure of efficiency but it does reflect the earning power of an airline. The yield can be affected by market segmentation, price discrimination, and price elasticity considerations, creating different fares on different trips between the same two airports.

Passengers per employee will be highest on short sectors, in densely populated areas with high average income levels and low fares. It is a measure of marketing effectiveness and can reflect the degree of competition and the level of fares. Low fares and convenient departures will result in a high passenger per employee figure. Staffing levels are also reflected in these figures and staff reductions in British Airways has improved its performance using this measure. American internal routes under deregulation have the highest passenger per employee figures because of the market conditions explained above, although it is also claimed to be the result of working practices.

Aircraft earn revenue and incur lowest operating costs when they are flying and aircraft *utilisation* (measured in revenue hours per aircraft) is a common measure of efficiency. Daily flying time of five hours (2000 hrs pa) for a short haul operation with more time on the ground might be considered efficient but unacceptably low on a long haul route. A long haul service between London and New York could expect to achieve up to 15 revenue hours per day compared with eight hours for the London to Amsterdam or similar internal European service.

Airline utilisation also will vary within an airline between types of aircraft as well as between airlines particularly those who operate different route structures.

The achievement of low cost carriers

The final measure to be considered is the cost level per unit of output. Low costs may be achieved by low cost start-up airlines with low overheads.

The air market analysis in earlier chapters of this book has referred to the impact on demand as a result of lower air fares. These have resulted from reduced costs of operation by 'low cost' carriers (such as easyJet, Ryanair, Jet Blue, South West Airlines) compared with the 'full service' airlines.

The analysis here looks at the role of operating costs in this competitive position with a low cost unit of output as the final measure to be considered. This may be achieved as follows:

- Low cost new start-up airlines 'with sound business plans and good management find the provision of finance is not a problem compared with the "legacy" (older) full service providers' (Texas Pacific, a private equity firm with shareholders in Continental, America West and Ryanair) (AB, 2004). The airline needs good management, clear, believable assumptions and a flexible strategy, and is often more able to deliver what the customer demands although 'majors' have huge network benefits (Morgan Stanley Bankers, and small airlines, eg Jet Blue, Hawaiian). To overcome these factors several major airlines launched their own low cost operator (KLM: Buzz; British Airways: Go; Air India: Charters).
- Labour costs and the cost levels in general have to be reduced. Labour can be 80 per cent of a major airline's costs and, as in the bus industry, it is the primary element upon which to focus.
- Reservation systems (global distribution systems) are profitable businesses in themselves. British Airways has (2004) negotiated reductions in charges expected to be around 15 per cent (1.1 per cent of total costs) and hopes to achieve a similar agreement with Amadeus and Worldspan. These sales represented 68 per cent of BA's booking and are through retail travel outlets. The low cost airlines have only direct-to-customer internet and telesales outlets.
- Hub-and-spoke systems will not bring down full service airline costs to those of low cost carriers but the market integration they bring provides a short term respite. However, longer term strategies are required.
- Standardised fleets (see below).
- Air terminal costs (including baggage and passenger handling, landing and parking charges and other costs) are minimised by using airports that have spare capacity or are prepared to construct a low cost terminal, eg at Geneva, Marseille, Singapore, Charleroi and Glasgow International. Landing charges are reduced from 11 euros to 6 euros per passenger (Geneva) with planned self-service baggage handling to the aircraft (Marseille) reducing the passenger charge from 6 euros to 1 euro per head. Other airlines are increasing the size/weight of cabin baggage through increasing the size of overhead lockers. These are seen by many airlines as serving the customers' needs. They want low fares and good service provided in a basic facility rather than a more glamorous one. Retailing malls can cut costs and, with often a one-hour cut-off time for low cost departures, travellers have time to spend time and money in shops, restaurants and bars. Incentives to attract such airlines have, in the European Union, to be within competition regulations but development funds created by the devolved governments in Wales, Scotland and Northern Ireland have led to new routes. The result has been significant passenger growth rates at London Stansted; Cologne/Bonn (44 per cent increase in 2003); Southampton (50 per cent growth as Flybe

expanded); Barcelona-Gerona (passenger throughput rose from 0.6 million to 3.0 million passengers following Ryanair's arrival in 2003); and Cardiff (1.6 million to 2.5 million since bmibaby began operations in 2002).

- An analysis of bmibaby's low cost characteristics (Davis, 2002) identified:
  - lower average yield;
  - no frequent flyer programme;
  - no premier lounge access;
  - no business class;
  - no connections with other airlines;
  - food is available on board to be purchased;
  - 'simple' point-to-point operations;
  - one aircraft type;
  - greater aircraft utilisation with fewer crew members;
  - short sectors;
  - lower distribution costs;
  - paperless electronic ticketing;
  - secondary airports.
- Short turnaround times of under 50 minutes, thus increasing utilisation. This can be limited by night flying bans at some airports and can adversely affect reliability if delays (eg traffic, airport congestion) occur as there is little or no recovery time in the operating schedule.

Operational factors affecting costs

The bases on which cost can be measured should be looked at in conjunction with the factors affecting cost levels. The ability of European Union airlines to control costs as a part of their marketing and competitive strategy has become crucial for their existence. Overall costs will depend on labour productivity (see above) and on factors such as fuel costs, route structure and aircraft size (*The Single Market Review*, 1997). The impact of the stage length on costs was discussed earlier. The size of an aircraft provides economies in terms of fuel and crew and may have possible utilisation effects because some aircraft types are more suitable, for example, for short haul routes while such aircraft cannot technically be used on long haul routes.

Load factors on chartered routes are much higher (90.6 per cent in 2003) than those on scheduled services (85 per cent on European routes, 75 on intercontinental routes) and given similar aircraft and similar total costs have an effect on cost and thus fares. The higher costs in the scheduled mode are due to sales methods, load factor, aircraft utilisation and aircraft configuration (Tables 7.2 and 7.4).

The load factor has an effect on cost per passenger and the fares airlines are therefore able to charge. This is of course in parallel to sales methods (direct selling, ie not through travel agents, thus eliminating commission), aircraft utilisation (high) and aircraft configuration. Table 7.4 shows how load factors vary between airlines and types of operation – low cost, charter and scheduled. The last of these has in general the lowest load factor but, despite reduced sales, charter airlines have reduced capacity to maintain a high load factor.

Table 7.4 also shows how quickly airlines can alter capacity either by returning aircraft to the leasing company or by acquiring additional aircraft. Both the new and second hand aircraft markets are well supplied. Charter airlines generally have higher capacity levels (achieved with a shorter seat pitch) as well as high load factors. It is now estimated that 2000 aircraft are 'mothballed' in desert airfields in the southwest United States. In the Mojave desert, aircraft (350 at present) have been stored for over 10 years as the market demand fell and travellers demanded newer aircraft. Some of the aircraft here are however brand new from the Boeing factory awaiting leases. Most are from US airlines but Virgin and BA aircraft are also to be found there.

Peak demand patterns occur in air transport as in other transport modes. Seasonal peaks occur largely in the summer holiday period and during the winter skiing season; time of day peak is related to morning and evening business travel on European and domestic flights and to weekend effects of both leisure and business travel on most sectors. The charter operations have greater demand variations but with a higher utilisation of aircraft in terms of flying hours and a higher load factor on those flights.

Table 7.4 *Load factors and capacity/passenger change (2003)*

Airline	Business sector	Load factor %	Passenger number % change	Seating capacity % change
United	S	73.6	−6.2	−9.8
Air France	S	76.8	+2.4	+2.2
Singapore	S	74.5	+6.0	+5.3
BA	S	71.9	−5.8	−7.9
Cathay Pacific	S	77.8	+9.5	+0.4
Japan	S	69.1	+5.5	+4.8
Virgin Atlantic	S	80.6	−4.9	−10.2
easyJet	L	85.5	+56.0	+53.8
Ryanair	L	84.0	+40.7	+36.1
South West	L	65.9	+2.0	+5.5
Air 2000	C	90.3	−13.7	−13.3
Britannia	C	90.9	−2.9	−3.3
Monarch	C	87.5	−8.5	−6.2

Sources: CAA (2003); *Airline Business* (September 2003)

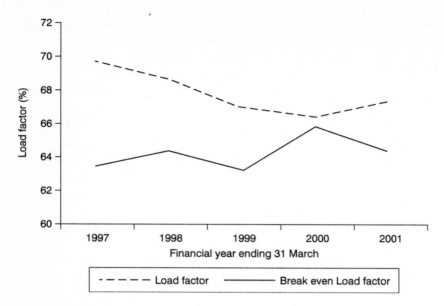

Figure 7.1 *British Airways' achieved and break-even load factor
1997–2001*
Source: Company Reports, HOC 2002a, Commerzbank Securities, 2002

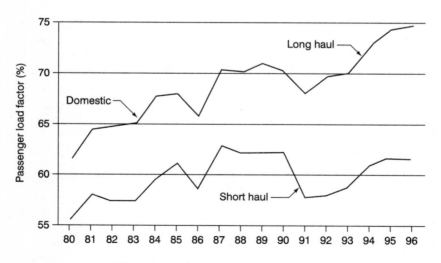

Figure 7.2 *Passenger load factors*
Source: Morrell *et al* (1997) *The Single Market Review Impact on Services – Air Transport*

The network shape is a determinant of cost per passenger mile. A compact network with high levels of route density and high load factor is one of the cheapest to provide and at the right level of fares, can be a very profitable undertaking. Some airlines transfer aircraft to achieve compensatory seasonality and thus increase annual utilisation – a charter aircraft operating in western Europe from April to September may be found work in North America from October to January and on western European skiing charter flights from February to March. This would be the ideal, but if some winter season work can balance the summer package holiday market, given the high load factors, the revenue per passenger kilometre can be high. The local costs of labour, fuel and user charges will also affect cost levels. Even within a region, user charges (parking and landing fees, airport passenger fees and navigation charges) will vary; for example, between London (Heathrow) Airport and Luton Airport.

Charges at London Heathrow also vary within the operating day and season. There is a peak passenger (departing) charge band during the summer and parking charges at Heathrow are also time band related. Landing fees are related to time of operation (peak pricing) and are also dependent on the weight of the aircraft. (See Chapter 1.)

Costs also vary between aircraft types and between short haul and long haul routes. Long haul operations are substantially cheaper per available seat kilometre compared with European and domestic flights. Concorde is an exception because of its high operating cost.

Fleet standardisation

There are a number of advantages in standardising an airline's fleet as far as possible within the needs constraints of its route network. The use of one aircraft type may allow standardised spares and maintenance procedures, leading to reduced costs. Even if different aircraft manufacturers are used an airline may standardise its engines with exclusive use of, for example, Rolls-Royce, Pratt and Whitney or General Electric. Flight crews are trained in one particular aircraft and variations within the fleet will have a flight deck which is incompatible with the airline crews' 'specific to type' licence. This will present operational problems in the logistics of crew scheduling. American Airlines currently (2004) has 14 aircraft types (with 30 sub-types). This is to be reduced to six types (with 14 sub-types) by 2006. The logistics in terms of crew training and interworking of crew and aircraft have proven a high cost factor. Even different aircraft of the same type, such as a Boeing 747 or Airbus, if built to a particular airline's specification may have a different flight deck to the others in the fleet.

Catering equipment is produced for particular aircraft. British Airways fly Boeing 747–400s and 767–300s and require two types of galley equipment including spare equipment at both ends of the route. The airline is continuing its investment programme in a common type of catering equipment which will reduce costs in this area.

There can be seat pitch and width differences in different aircraft which can present marketing problems when descriptions of the product are included in advertisements. These are important selling points in current advertising.

The seat configuration can differ between two aircraft, even of the same type, and this has to be recorded by the computer when seats are sold. It also presents problems at airports if the wrong configuration is input or the aircraft is changed from the type normally used on that departure, and overbooking can occur. When aircraft are leased, a Boeing 747 with a 400-seat configuration may be used in place of a 450-seat aircraft which is standard within an airline's fleet. Leased aircraft also present passenger perception difficulties with a different internal decor, particularly as many airlines have the refurbishment of interiors as a key marketing point.

Most of these elements affect costs, and airlines will try as far as possible to standardise their fleet with one aircraft or one type for similar routes or with internal specifications which are compatible. However the variations in route length and demand levels within a large airline's operations make this degree of standardisation difficult. A similar airline with operations of a homogeneous nature may find it easier to achieve.

Economies of scale

The comparison of costs per unit between small airlines and large airlines is difficult because of the inevitable variations in the kinds of service provided. A small airline operating 13 Boeing 757/767 and 9 Airbus A300/A320 jets on charter operations (eg Monarch Airlines, UK) will have a totally different cost structure to a larger airline operating turbo propeller Fokker 50/100 aircraft and BAe 146 small capacity (eg Buzz) jets or to a major national airline operating a combined Boeing/Airbus fleet of differing performance (eg aircraft range) on European and trans continental routes. Consequently, the type of route and aircraft operated are likely to be more important determinants of cost than scale. During the development of a new route not previously serviced, or where traffic potential is low, a lower standard and cost of service may be better than no service at all and economies may be achieved on a small scale.

The effect of differences of scale on the costs of operating any given kind of service does not appear to be significant. An analysis of airline performance (IATA, 2003) showed that of the world's top ten airlines in terms of turnover two were in the bottom five (of 150) in terms of margins, five had negative margins (ie made losses) and the remainder had margins of under 3 per cent. However, the limitations of profit as an indicator of efficiency are described above. The following explanations were given for the lower rate of profit:

- A large percentage of the services on the routes were subject to widespread competition, a demand for high operating costs and standard of service, low load factors and a major downturn in the North Atlantic and internal US markets as a result of economic and 'fear of flying' factors.
- A large proportion of services operated into major metropolitan airports with high charges and service costs, slow turnaround and frequent delays.
- The airlines cross subsidise a large number of unprofitable short haul routes either for public policy reasons or to maintain feeder services.
- There were major increases in aircraft insurance from £1.7 billion in 2001 to £6 billion in 2002 (IATA, 2002) and extra security costs particularly on United States bound services.

The effective marketing of a standard product by large airlines involves some limit on the number of classes available to passengers and a corporate identity. Marketing costs per passenger are reduced, with increased frequency and higher seat utilisation in a particular market. Standardising the product can involve similar aircraft and consequently operating and catering/cabin staff procedures. The advantages of staff specialisation on a particular type of service, eg package tour operations or business class scheduled services, enable them to become more efficient and reduce training costs.

The economies of large scale operations are largely concerned with discounted purchasing prices for aircraft or equipment and spare parts. Some of these economies can be achieved by smaller airlines by subcontracting maintenance and overhaul. This is a common occurrence and often takes place between major international airlines, thus avoiding the need for local permanent engineering staff. It does, however, involve a loss of control in a tightly scheduled, high capital intensive industry. This is particularly so in the case of package tour airlines who depend for their profits on high turnaround, high seat utilisation and high aircraft utilisation and it is becoming increasingly important in short haul 'shuttle' operations in Europe.

REFERENCES

AB (2004) Legacy load, *Airline Business*, June, Sutton, Surrey.
CAA (1996 to 2003) UK Airlines Annual Operating, Traffic and Financial Statistics, Civil Aviation Authority, London.

Davis, T (2002) What no frills carriers are looking for from a regional airport, Airports outside the south east [of England]: Towards 2030, Waterfront Conference Company, London.

HOC (2002) Air Transport Industry Report HC 284, House of Commons, London.

IATA (2002) International Air Transport Association, Insurance estimates for 2002, in *The Times*, London, 7 September 2002.

IATA (2003) Annual Report, International Air Transport Association, Geneva.

Morrell, P (1997) (with Alamdari F, Fewings, R, Hofton A, Pagliari R, Stockman I, Williams G) *The Single Market Review, Impact on Services – Air Transport*, Kogan Page (for the European Commission), London.

CHAPTER 8

Forecasting Transport Demand, Revenue and Expenditure

ECONOMIC FORECASTING

'Tu ne prévois les événements que lorsqu'ils sont déjà arrivés.'
(You can only predict things after they have happened.)
Eugene Ionesco, *Le Rhinoceros* (1959) Act 3

If economists, and in particular economic forecasters, had a full knowledge of all the elements affecting demand for each mode of transport and also had a full understanding of consumer behaviour predicting trends would be a relatively easy task.

This, however, is not the case. 'All forecasts are uncertain. This is the result of uncertainty in inputs, about assumptions and in the relationship used. Disaggregated data, while it improves the basis of the forecasts, brings increased recognition of the true uncertainty present through consideration of a greater number of inputs' (NRTF, 1997). Any company has a fairly good knowledge of the characteristics of its own service but not necessarily how they are perceived by customers, and a lesser knowledge of competitors' services but which might be increased by general market research and forms of research directed specifically at a competitor.

In the transport market much of the demand relates to leisure activities so the competition lies not only with the other modes of transport but also with other non-transport leisure activities. To achieve as accurate a forecast as possible for the demand for its own services a company must therefore be aware of demand characteristics for all its competitors, the particular aspects of its own business that affect demand and the general movements of economic activities within the country or countries in which that company operates.

Company forecasting is not the only predictive requirement. Governments too have to predict aspects of the transport market in order to provide for future demand or to develop policies which may change that demand pattern. Forecasts of car traffic growth have concerned governments in the European Union and North America for many years and policies to reduce the rate of growth are being considered or implemented. But without the forecasts governments would be unaware of the potential problem and have no basis on which to set traffic (and pollution/congestion) reduction targets.

Forecasting is based on a set of interactive elements brought together in an economic forecasting model. A transport model will have three general elements:

1. *Land use*

   This relates to the points of origin and destination of journeys and the reasons for those journeys. In freight the land use elements identify sources of raw materials processing plants and markets. These may be within one country but are often international. Similarly passenger traffic looks at home, work, leisure, educational, health etc activities and their location in relation to one another.

2. *Travel costs*

   The generalised cost of transport (including time and direct financial costs – see Chapter 10 for fuller explanation) will be a determinant of whether the journey is made at all and if so by which mode. This in the case of most companies will exclude externalities and in the case of private motoring may only include perceived costs as a modal determinant (see Chapter 1).

3. *Economic trends*

   These are the general movements in economic activity. As transport is a derived demand (see Chapter 1) its level of activity is in general related to the levels of output in an economy. Freight transport for example is directly related to production and sales, it being the distribution (logistics) link between the two.

These elements will change at different rates. Travel cost can vary very quickly as for example fuel or labour costs may change; land uses however change slowly. Thus the relative importance of the three elements depends on the timescale of the forecast; in the short term behaviour in determining travel or movement is influenced mainly by user cost; in the long term, fundamental changes in land use will alter the whole pattern of travel demand.

The model to be used depends on the funds available to develop and operate it. As a model becomes more complex so it becomes more expensive because of the more detailed level of data collection requirements. The model is the set of relationships between variables and each variable requires a value or values and a data set. The variables represent quantities and the relationship within the model represent the ways in which those variables will behave in the real transport world. For example demand for a service will be influenced by variables (or elements) such as rates of growth in the economy, prices offered (possibly themselves based on predicted costs) and the elasticities in the market. All are variables whose interaction with one another and with the final outcome in terms of expected demand level, revenue and/or market share is the essence of the forecasting model. The more detailed the model the more accurately it reproduces the real transport market or the real situation and thus the more reliable its output is likely to be.

This chapter now considers seven case studies of the application of forecasting models:

1. Forecasting bus costs and revenue in a shire county funding context.
2. The impact of Channel Tunnel international trains on domestic commuter services.
3. Road traffic forecasting – macro economic forecasts.
4. Forecasting rail passenger demand – elements in the model.
5. Forecasting for an integrated transport policy.
6. Forecasting air traffic demand.
7. Eurotunnel: forecasts of freight and passenger traffic.

CASE STUDY 1: FORECASTING BUS COSTS AND REVENUE IN A SHIRE COUNTY FUNDING CONTEXT

At present local county councils in England and in Wales (excluding London) are responsible for funding those bus services which cannot be justified on a commercial basis by private bus operators. Forecasts of revenue and expenditure are required for the tendered bus network in such counties. In areas such as London where there is a full cost tendering system (or network funding) revenue is received by the transport authority through the bus companies operating under contract. Here predictions of expenditure, revenue and revenue support (subsidy) are required.

Providing a forecast

The main problem in producing economic forecasts is that many factors, some external, influence future contracted payments. To show this, it is useful to consider separately forecasts of costs and revenue. Costs are a function of the level of service provided, general inflation, changes in real costs, productivity, wages policy and other specific cost elements. On the revenue side it is necessary to predict changes in demand resulting from other trends, population changes, unemployment, increasing car ownership, price changes and variations in level of service. Not all these relationships can be precisely quantified and assumptions need to be made. Each is the result of further factors (eg, income) and there are complex interrelationships amongst them. Ideally, therefore, forecasts need to be based on a fairly complex model.

Construction of such a model is not easy for three reasons. First, it would involve considerable research to fill the substantial gaps in knowledge of the factors discussed in the last paragraph. Time to do this may not be available despite its long term importance. Second, construction of such a model would be beyond the limited financial and manpower resources available to many county councils. This would also apply to smaller, private bus, rail and other transport companies. Third, this model would be cumbersome and costly to operate. Thus modifying it to allow for constantly changing circumstances and using it to test a wide range of policy options could be expensive. There is therefore a need for a simple forecasting model.

The model estimates separately expenditure and revenue for an operator based on external data, data produced by the operator, and the effects of policy decisions on matters such as fares and recession policy, which are within the province of the county council and the operator.

It is argued that whilst the model has several analytical shortcomings, it is practicable in that it is based on readily obtainable data, it can be updated and modified easily, is inexpensive to operate and can be improved as understanding of some of the basic relationships implicit in it increases. As a short-term forecasting tool it provides a much needed financial indicator on public transport operations for a shire county (Cole & Tyson, 1977).

Description of the model

Two problems common to cost and revenue estimates are that changes affecting them may occur part way through a year and that the operators' and county councils' financial years do not always coincide. To overcome them the effects of forecast change in revenue and costs are estimated on the basis of a full year and an appropriate fraction of them allocated to any financial year or part of a year, as appropriate. To operate the model, data is required, particularly on base years, from the operators.

Expenditure forecasts

The basis for expenditure forecasts for say 2006 was the expenditure levels being incurred by each operator in 2004 converted into annual sums. These base figures are adjusted for:

1. Cost increases,
2. Changes in service levels.

Cost forecasts may be based on an assessment of leading European forecasts including those of the London Business School, National Institute of Economic Research, National Transport Model, DG Transport and Energy (European Commission) and OECD together with Government statistics and forecasts on retail prices, wholesale prices and average earnings, and the pattern of cost inflation in a county is unlikely to differ from that for most 'old' EU member states or the UK as a whole. The balance between different cost components can be incorporated through weighting factors, since inflationary rates in labour costs may be different from those affecting other costs (for which the retail price index and forecasts of fuel price increases have been used as indicators). The timing of wage increases should be allowed for in the calculations as they occur at discrete time periods rather than evenly over the whole year.

The effects of agreed service changes and reduced mileage on costs should be estimated by the county council and the operators when the revisions are agreed between them based on a detailed analysis of the changes likely to be involved.

At this point it is appropriate to describe the prediction process used in the model. It is important to remember that the model is a simple one because the data available does not allow a high degree of sophistication, and is designed to be flexible and to enable options to be tested quickly. The process is as follows:

a) The increases in retail prices, fuel prices and earnings were predicted.
b) Based on these input data a forecast weighted average increase in these three parameters is calculated. The weights used are based on the proportion of total costs attributable to each parameter. An analysis of bus company costs (2004: see Chapter 5) suggests that salaries and wages (and other 'employee' costs, eg national insurance) account for 65 per cent of total costs, fuel and tyres approximately 8 per cent and other costs 27 per cent. The percentage increase in each cost parameter is weighted in the appropriate proportion to produce the weighted forecast.
c) The next stage is to predict the excess of the percentage change in bus operators' costs over the weighted change. The precise nature of this relationship over the years will vary but assume that major bus operators' cost increased by an average of 28 per cent per year more than the weighted average increase in the appropriate indices (see Table 8.1 below). Thus there has been an increase in operating costs in real terms ranging from 2.85 to 6.24 per cent. In the absence of evidence to the contrary it can be assumed that this will continue throughout the forecast period.

Tables 8.1 and 8.3 show the results of this forecast and for 2006 it can be seen that costs were expected to increase by 16.5 per cent and after allowing for the effects of service changes, the expenditure forecast was £10.047m. The excess percentage of 28 per cent was applied to the weighted average to produce the estimated increase in total costs at out-turn prices.
d) The estimated savings in expenditure resulting from service changes were deducted.

Table 8.1 *Expenditure parameters used in the model (percentage increase)*

| | Increase over previous year (columns 1–4) | | | | Percentage by which change in operators' expenditure exceeds change in weighted average (Col 4 over Col 3) |
| | Prices & fuel | Earnings | Weighted average | Expenditure by operators | |
	1	2	3	4	5
2003	10.3	12.7	12.0	15.2	27
2004 (A)	19.0	21.3	20.6	25.9	26
2005 (A)	24.9	25.0	25.0	32.8	31
2006 (F)	15.0	12.0	12.9	16.5 (F)	28
2007 (F)	10.0	8.5	9.0	11.5 (F)	28

(A) indicates Actual
(F) indicates Forecast
Note: All data values are illustrative and should not be taken to represent any particular bus company.

Revenue forecasts

The first stage in arriving at revenue forecast for 2006 was to calculate the full year effects of fares increases during 2005 which provided the basis for the revenue forecast for 2006. The forecast obtained in this way was adjusted for three major parameters:

1. trend changes in passengers resulting from car ownership and population changes
2. the effects of fare increases
3. the effects of unemployment.

An analysis of the relationship between car ownership per head and bus trips per head is carried out. Although this could not be based on the whole country because of lack of bus passenger data, the areas analysed revealed a price elasticity of bus trips per head with respect to car ownership per head of, say, –0.26. This meant that for every one per cent increase in car ownership per head, bus trips per head will fall by 0.26 per cent. This was then used to forecast percentage increases in population (supplied by the county planning department) as follows:

2006 – 1.04 per cent
2007 – 1.79 per cent
2008 – 1.66 per cent

These figures can be rounded to 2 per cent (to allow for the fact that the method of deriving them is only approximate) and were applied to the base revenue for 2004. Implicit in this was the assumption that an *n* per cent reduction in trips leads to an *n* per cent reduction in revenue.

Fare changes and service changes

The approximate timing of fare increases is agreed with the operators for the purposes of the forecasting procedure. In order to calculate the effects of the fare increases on revenue it is necessary to estimate price elasticity of demand. Studies may only have been carried out on a limited selection of routes, and revenue of the largest operators is monitored on a weekly basis to derive the implied elasticity underlying the revenue changes. From these analyses a price elasticity of say −0.4 is derived and used in the forecasting model, ie a 10 per cent increase in fares results in 4 per cent passenger reduction. If there is a fares policy set by the authority funding the services (eg PTE, county council, national government) then different fare percentage increases can be introduced into the model. These could be 2 per cent, 5 per cent and 10 per cent fare increase scenarios. This would result in different deficit (or profit) levels and enable a decision to be made according to the fare, total subsidy or congestion level policy in place. (Case Study 5 illustrates this.) The effects of service changes on revenue (and on costs) are estimated at the time the county council and the operators agree to the fares change. Usually such revisions only take place following a survey of travel patterns in the areas concerned at this local level. The likely effects on generalised cost of service changes are calculated using cost–benefit analysis methods.

Unemployment

High unemployment levels would themselves have an adverse effect on bus travel. In some counties unemployment exceeds 10 per cent. The overall effect of unemployment on bus travel is not clear cut. On the one hand, increased unemployment amongst non-car owners will reduce demand for bus journeys to work and, indirectly, the demand for non-work journeys also. On the other hand, if unemployment is sufficiently prolonged amongst car owners, they may be forced to sell or lay up their cars and thus their travel, albeit on a much reduced scale, would switch to public transport. It might be viewed on balance that unemployment would have an adverse effect on bus revenue. The key elements are thus apparent:

- the price elasticity effect of a fares increase;
- increased car ownership;
- unemployment (an estimate of 3 per cent fall in demand because of the reduced number of journey to work trips or the income effect of reduced earnings).

The effects of these three factors are summarised in Table 8.2.

Table 8.2 *Revenue parameters used in the model*

Year	Date of increase	Assumed fares increase %	Estimated reduction in demand %	Revenue increase for actual year over previous full year %	Revenue increase for full year over previous full year %
2006	Sept 06	10	5	2.3	4.5
2007	May 07	10	4	5.1	6.0

County public transport forecast

Using the public transport model outlined here the 2006 revenue forecast of £8.629 million and expenditure forecast of £10.047 million for the four bus operators assumed to be in the county were calculated. The model then applied the given parameters to the full year forecast and derived from that the forecast for 2007, except that no allowance was made for unemployment levels after 2006. The results of the forecast are shown in Table 8.3.

Table 8.3 *County council public transport forecast*

Year	Operator	Revenue £ million	Expenditure £ million	Deficit £ million
2005	Big Bus Co plc	4.932	5.971	1.039
	Citybuses plc	2.475	2.615	0.140
	Norbus Ltd	0.674	0.818	0.144
	MA Motors Ltd	0.004	0.006	0.002
	Total County	8.085	9.410	1.325
2006	Big Bus Co plc	5.022	6.241	1.325
	Citybuses plc	2.866	2.883	0.007
	Norbus Ltd	0.727	0.917	0.190
	MA Motors Ltd	0.004	0.006	0.002
	Total County	8.629	10.047	1.418
2007	Big Bus Co plc	5.301	6.855	1.554
	Citybuses plc	3.170	3.205	0.035
	Norbus Ltd	0.756	0.959	0.203
	MA Motors Ltd	0.005	0.007	0.002
	Total County	9.232	11.026	1.794

CASE STUDY 2: THE IMPACT OF CHANNEL TUNNEL INTERNATIONAL TRAINS ON DOMESTIC COMMUTER SERVICES

Rail links to the tunnel

As a result of changes in policy by the Government and a requirement to fund any rail links from private sector sources, the Channel Tunnel Rail Link, the high speed rail link for freight and passenger trains from London to Folkestone, has fallen far behind the similar links from Paris to Calais and from Brussels to Calais.

As a result of this delay British Rail and the Department of Transport decided to carry out substantial upgrading of existing routes at a cost of £1.6 bn. This included major engineering work on track, tunnels, bridges, signalling, loops and in Bromley the restructuring of Bickley Junction and major changes to the Orpington station layout.

The principal route used by the Channel Tunnel trains between London and the Tunnel will be the old boat train routes now known as CTR1 (Folkestone–Ashford–Tonbridge–Sevenoaks–Bromley–Herne Hill–Victoria). This has been improved and modified to connect with Waterloo International Terminal. At peak NSE periods, the trains can use an alternative route, CTR2 (via Maidstone and Swanley instead of Tonbridge and Sevenoaks). Both routes pass through the Bromley area and capacity constraints could lead to delays or reductions in domestic services used by people living there (NSE, 1994). This case study examines the position in the Bromley area as typifying the effects on the corridor overall.

Balancing conflicting demands

British Rail in 1986 (HOC, 1986) gave a general assurance that domestic services will not be reduced by the need to provide for international services through the Channel Tunnel so that 'existing services would not be curtailed in consequence of the need to find capacity for through international services.' However, under the railway usage contract with Eurotunnel, Eurostar (UK) Ltd (or its successors) will provide rail services through the Tunnel and these will achieve a certain passenger journey time between London and Paris. These two services could be in conflict when the capacity point of the network is reached and will be of great importance when the Channel Tunnel Rail Link is completed in 2005.

The traffic forecasts are crucial to this issue, since they determine the time when the capacity of the network is likely to be reached and the Rail Link needs to come into use. As the Rail Link would take at least eight years to plan and construct, it is necessary to decide its opening date that much in advance.

Passenger forecasts

Consideration of the passenger forecasts in any detail are outside the scope of this book but a summary of the assumptions and conclusions would be helpful.

Eurostar are likely to provide for a demand level equivalent to 80 per cent of that on the busiest hour of the busiest day of the year. Thus on about 55 days of the year passengers would not be able to take the first train of their choice (within the market segmentation inhibitors). The numbers of trains to be provided is thus dependent on the load factor assumptions (at present the InterCity European average is 67 per cent) within the forecasts.

A series of passenger forecasts have been prepared for British Rail, Eurotunnel and Eurostar (LCR, SNCF, SNCB) Union Railways with differences in the forecasts explained by differences in the following elements:

(1) assumptions about rates of growth in the economy.
(2) assumptions about cross-price elasticity between modes (particularly air to rail).
(3) assumptions about the reactions of the airlines and the ferry operators in respect of fares, frequency and service quality.
(4) methodology for passenger choice of mode, ie the criteria used by the passenger to make a modal choice and the weighting for each criterion.
(5) estimates of 'generated' trips.
(6) assumptions for growth in business and leisure travel between the UK and mainland Europe.
(7) weighting given to different elements of journey time (given the differences in interchange requirements between modes).
(8) the impact of high speed rail networks in Europe linked to the UK via the Channel Tunnel.

The forecasts indicate that patronage will grow fairly rapidly towards 2000 and slow thereafter unless a new Rail Link is built between London and the Tunnel. Thus market potential is likely to be lost but also passengers will have an increasingly reduced chance of travelling on the departure time of their choice since without a new line the growth between 2000 and 2040 can only be achieved by using spare capacity on, or increasing the number of, off-peak departures.

Capacity saturation

On the basis of the assumptions made, the numbers of train trips (see Table 8.5) for a typical summer weekday in 1995 and 2003 can be derived for the SETEC (1986), BR (1988 Low) and Eurotunnel (1991) forecasts, shown in Table 8.4.

Table 8.4 *Summary of selected international traffic forecast for the Channel Tunnel*

Forecast	Year	(Millions of one-way trips)		
		1993 Pass	2003 Pass	2013 Pass
SETEC[3]	1986	16.5	21.4	26.2
BR (Low)	1988	13.4	17.4	21.2
BR (High)	1988	15.9	20.8	–
Eurotunnel	1991	15.3	25.0	33.3

Table 8.5 *Equivalent passenger train trips for different forecasts*

	BR (BRB, 1988, 1991b)r	SETEC (BRB, 1998)r	Eurotunnel (ET, 1991)
1993	48	58	54
2003	61	75	79

Note: Train figures are the total in each direction each day, for a typical summer weekday. 1993 figures for passengers have been transferred to 1995.

Taking these adjustments into account, the years when capacity would be reached are shown in Table 8.6 below for each of the forecasts.

In the case of the SETEC forecast, the network would be overloaded from the outset and this is the reason for the range only being two years. No adjustment on account of domestic growth is required for the Eurotunnel or SETEC forecasts, as capacity is reached soon after 1993 in the former case and notionally before this in the latter case.

The British Government is of the view that capacity problems will not occur until 2005 on the local network. This is at variance however with the operators where British Rail and Eurostar see problems before the turn of the century and possibly even earlier if the rate of growth is faster than expected while Eurotunnel believe the problem will be very severe indeed by 1998 and overall constraints will apply from 2000 (ET, 1994).

Table 8.6 *Years when capacity would be reached for passenger trains*

BR (BRB, 1988)	SETEC (BRB, 1988)	Eurotunnel (ET, 1991)
1998–2001	1993–95	1994–97

Passenger demand

During the late 1980s passenger demand on Network South East (NSE) commuter services reached a high level of 470,000 in the morning peak having risen steadily and rapidly from 356,000 in 1984, but by 1993 had fallen back to 350,000 (Table 8.7).

Over the twenty years to 1994 a cyclical pattern evolved in NSE patronage reflecting changes in the London economy. National forecasts indicate an end to the present recession by the late 1990s and a subsequent rise in journeys to work.

This fall in demand over the last five years (1989–1993) is expected to be reversed and according to Network South East forecasts will rise to over 500,000 passengers by 2001 (NSE, 1993; Howarth, 1992), well above the 1989 levels, thus indicating that even that latter level of capacity will be inadequate.

The 1993 recession was seen as a 'blip' and an upward trend is anticipated from the late 1994 or early 1995. The level of demand on NSE services shows a clear link between employment predictions for the central business district and forecasts of rail commuting levels. The forecast for London is that of a generally buoyant economy, and NSE in 1992 (Howarth, 1992) indicated an expected rise in demand of '50,000 or probably even 100,000 extra commuters on lines in Kent'. Of these over 5000 are expected to travel through Bromley. This will be the requirement for extra capacity by 2001 on the basis of the assumptions in the forecasts (Serplan, 1989). Two sets of forecasts (NSE, 1991) predicted increases above the 1989 figure of between 18 per cent and 25 per cent by 2001 (see Figure 8.2 and Table 8.8) with even larger increases predicted for longer journey-distance services into Kent, despite the continued fall in demand since 1991. These forecasts are supported by the Central London Rail Study (CLRS, 1989) and the South London Rail Study (TPA, 1992) saw the area extending to Bromley as one with considerable rail development potential. The expected rise in capacity requirements in Bromley compared with 1992 is 1800 by 1998 and 5000 by 2001.

Table 8.7 *London area rail demand patterns (NSE, 1993)*

	Passengers (000s)	Change from previous year (000s)	(%)
1988	468		
1989	473	+5	+1.1
1990	461	−15	−3.2
1991	426	−35	−7.6
1992	397	−29	−6.8
1993	350	−47	−1.8

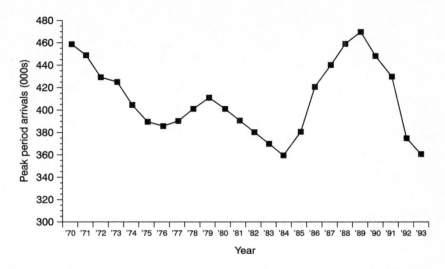

Figure 8.1 *London area rail commuting trends (Howarth, 1992)*

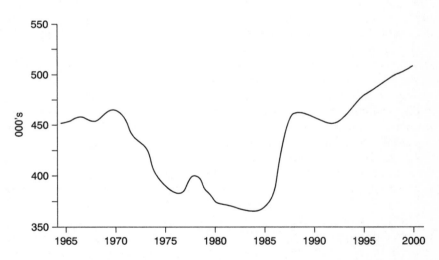

Figure 8.2 *London area rail morning peak arrivals in Central London –
actual and forecast (BRB, 1988, 1991a)*

Table 8.8 *Forecasts of Central London commuters (BRB, 1991a)*

| | | 000's journeys per morning peak (0700–1000) | |
| | | CLD/RT&P (NSE, 1991) | EPBRL/BSL (NSE, 1991) |
	1989	2001	2001
NSE			
Inner	227	259	245
Outer	222	302	285
TOTAL	449	561	529
South east sector NSE			
Inner	103	115	109
Outer	36	47	45
TOTAL	139	162	154

Train paths adjustments

The primary problem period for commuter services sharing the track with Eurostar is in the morning peak into London and the evening peak from London. At other times of day capacity is adequate until the period when it is anticipated that the system will be saturated in peak periods. It was therefore necessary for BR to adjust its planned NSE 1993 timetable which has become the established version to accommodate paths for Eurostar international trains.

British Rail/Railtrack plc have through investment in new track (eg at Bickley Junction) and other infrastructure investment tried to minimise the impact on local services. However some changes in service frequencies, timings and numbers of station stops have been required in order to create paths for the Eurostar trains and the reductions between the 1990 and 1992 timetables in train numbers operating from Bromley South to/from Victoria/Blackfriars in with-flow peak operations have been noticeable.

As an illustration of a wider range of changes the adjustments to commuter services for the CTR1 morning peak 'up' lines should be considered. The train graphs were produced by converting timetable data using the AUTOCAD technique.

The train paths for international trains are shown indicatively and super-imposed onto graphs for 1993. Those paths are based on 'flighting' two trains at thirty minute intervals (ie 4 trains per hour) and fit three criteria:

1) appropriate commercial departure times from London, Paris and Brussels.
2) a journey time of 70 minutes (or as close as possible to this timing) from the Channel Tunnel to Waterloo International Station via CTR1. The 70 minutes is derived from British Rail's publication of their intended journey time.
3) a path which best fits into the 1992 timetable.

At times in the am peak the planned Eurostar train flights on CTR1 cannot fit into the local service pattern, and an option to transfer to CTR2 was also shown. The study therefore derived the illustrative international paths to minimise the impact of the 'draft' (1992) local timetable. The 1990 timetable would have prevented many Eurostar trains operating without serious problems. In the pm peak international trains from London Waterloo have been diverted onto CTR2 because of conflicting flows south of Bickley on CTR1.

Operational options

The four trains per hour in peak periods in each direction by 1995 is possible with detailed adjustments. The analysis also indicated the possible need for a further train per hour in each direction to meet the higher passenger forecasts. These additional trains paths have not been plotted on the train graph as their operation causes conflict with local trains which could only be resolved:

a) by holding local trains at four track sections or at stations until the international train has passed (unacceptable to local commuters)
b) by slowing up (with added station stops) or by speeding up (with fewer stops) existing local trains
c) by cancellation of local trains (unacceptable to local commuters)
d) by extending the journey time from Waterloo to the Tunnel through lower speed of operation (unattractive to international passengers)
e) by holding international trains (unattractive to international passengers and unacceptable to operators)

In practice there is no capacity available for these additional trains. Neither is there adequate capacity for additional trains in future years following the growth of both international traffic and local commuter traffic.

It can be seen that the peak period operation is tight – there is very little leeway for delays resulting from non-routine operations. The international train movements for example inbound to London at around 0855 and 0925 at Bromley South are dependent on local trains being timed to run on the slow line or be stationary at Bromley station to allow Eurostar trains to pass. Railtrack and Connex South East will be under pressure from international customers, from SNCF, and from Eurotunnel to run the Eurostar trains on time and thus to give them priority over local trains in the event of any delays resulting from non-routine factors such as signal faults or points failure.

The effects of a resurgence of demand to 1989 levels

This level is expected to be achieved by 1998 as the recession ends and economic activity in London rises again. The main issues discussed in this section therefore are the comparison of train operations in 1990 (reflecting the 1989 demand level) and the 1992 position following the adjustments in commuter services to accommodate Eurostar train paths; the 1990 trains which can be reinstated or replaced by close substitute paths, and the trains for which no paths can be identified. Approximate indicative paths have been used to carry out this analysis; the expected demand trends over the next ten years; the expected increase in capacity resulting from reinstated or substitute paths/trains; the expected increase in capacity resulting from the introduction of Networker trains; the alternative investment policies available to Connex-South East/Railtrack; and the likely impacts of privatisation/franchising after 1 April 1994.

1990 and 1992 train graphs

The graphs show that in places Eurostar indicative train paths are times within 30–60 seconds from domestic services which indicated the limited number of available paths in the morning and evening peak periods.

It is not now possible for Railtrack/Train Operating Companies (TOC) to return to the 1990 timetable. As definitive paths have been allocated to the franchisees (including Eurostar trains) these are legally binding agreements between Railtrack and the Train Operating Companies.

There is likely to be a period of notice for changing paths available to both Railtrack and the TOC. There is also likely to be developed a priority system for path allocation which could be based on several factors including:

a) a need to inter-connect with other train services
b) a pricing policy of Railtrack in respect of premier paths especially in peak periods
c) external pressures placed upon Railtrack to achieve, for example, a given rate of return on a financial or on a cost-benefit analysis basis.

Reinstated trains

A total of eight trains were removed from the peak period timetable based on CTR1 and CTR2 am up line services between 1990 and 1992. Of these, it appears possible to reinstate or closely reposition five trains (see Table 8.9). However as the CTR2 am train graph indicated there was one path which could only be reinstated with difficulty. It may therefore only be possible to reinstate four paths.

Capacity following train reinstatement/repositioning

As indicated, the replication of the 1987 or 1990 timetable is no longer possible. However an approximate reinstatement/repositioning of some

Table 8.9 *Number of train paths: 'Optimistic' position am peak*

	Reinstated/repositioned	Lost paths	Total
CTR1	1	2	3
CTR2	4	1	5
TOTAL	5	3	8

trains is possible. The capacity increase however will not be sufficient to meet the increased demand forecast for 1998/2001. The existing ETB 'slam-door' rolling stock on Kent lines is to be replaced by Networker Class 465 rolling stock and the assumptions made below include an allowance for this investment.

The ETB total capacity has a planning standard of 10 per cent standees with 736 seats and total payload of 808 passengers; Networkers have a planning standard of 35 per cent standees with 696 seats and total passenger capacity of 938.

Alternative investment policies

A major assumption in the analysis of capacity increases is that four additional Networker trains would be available to the NSE services (or those of the franchisee) through Bromley. Such investment is by no means certain as the current investment plans are at best a replacement programme for old ETB 'slam-door' stock.

There are several options available to provide a solution to this shortage of capacity in relation to demand:

1) lengthen commuter trains from, for example, 8-car Networker, to 10-car Networker, or to 12-car Networker Class 465 sets, and in parallel lengthen platforms. This will require expensive investment with the TOC, OPRAF and Railtrack having to agree contractual arrangements. The 12-car Networker Class 465 set has a seating capacity of 1044 plus 35 per cent standees, giving a total of 1409 passengers. This would provide sufficient capacity in 2001 to replace the withdrawn

Table 8.10 *Capacity shortfall (NSE, 1993)*

am Peak Year	Bromley Train paths	Train type (8 car)	Total capacity available	Total capacity required	Capacity shortfall	No. of trains paths required
1989	8	ETB	6464	–	–	–
1998	5	NET	4690	6464	1772	2
2001	5	NET	4690	9700	5010	5/6

trains (7045 places) and enable a greater number of passengers to be carried compared with 1989, but with a planning standard of 35 per cent standees. The level of comfort is therefore a further consideration.

2) operate fewer longer commuter trains where there is a configuration for 12-car sets (eg Dartford line).

3) increase planning standards for passenger loading from the present 35 per cent to 50 per cent of passengers standing, thus enabling the TOC to say it is meeting the standards but does not provide a solution for the passenger.

A further option is to raise fares to dampen down demand increases. There is considerable evidence to show this is effective and the new private TOCs may well find this a financially more satisfactory solution. Profitability would be higher under a regime running current numbers of trains at higher prices than running an increased number or longer trains at present prices. It is however questionable whether a new franchisee would wish to make a financial contribution to additional rolling stock, new or extended stations or remodelling and signalling of junctions unless some payback was possible beyond the period of the franchise.

Given the reduced revenue (Figure 8.3), the almost nil property asset sales income and the External Finance Limit for NSE expenditure on additional trains is unlikely during the period of increased expansion. NSE's own forecast of investment requirements assuming a 20-year renewal period, against expected expenditure approval, shows a shortfall of £256m in 1994 and such evidence (NSE, 1993) suggests that the investment required to achieve the required capacity will not be approved.

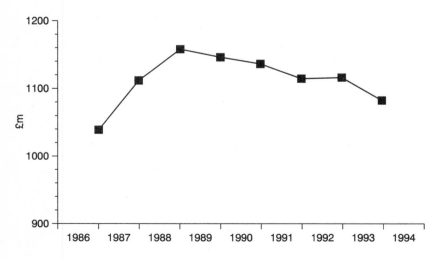

Figure 8.3 *NSE revenue 1993 prices (Howarth, 1992)*

Conclusions

It is forecast that demand on commuter services in south-east England will increase to the 1989 level by 1998–2000. It is unlikely that increased capacity either through additional Networker trains or longer trains with associated infrastructure changes will be available given current expenditure constraints imposed by Government. This capacity will need to be greater than that available in 1989 if the serious overcrowding of that time is to be avoided.

It is unlikely that the required capacity will be achieved, even with higher capacity Networker trains where planning standards of 35 per cent standees can be achieved. It is therefore unlikely that the 1989 level of capacity of ETB stock with a planning standard of 10 per cent standees will be achieved.

It is evident that without the investment programme there will be a shortfall of 1800 passenger places on routes in the Bromley area (or two trains) by 1998 assuming a return to 1989 passenger levels. Any further increases in demand will create even more serious problems for commuter movement by train until a new high speed link is constructed.

The train requirement for the increase in 5000 passengers forecast for routes through Bromley by 2001 will be five or six additional Networker trains (and paths) over and above the 1989 level of train paths in the morning peak. These are in addition to the reinstated/repositioned train/paths identified in the analysis.

Terminology

Network South East (NSE) was until early 1994 the British Rail train operating business in the London and home counties area. This was replaced by several Train Operating Units of which the relevant one in the study area is Connex South East. It is referred to as 'London Rail Area' for data covering years after 1995.

Railtrack plc was a private company which took over responsibility for track signals and most station property from British Rail.

CASE STUDY 3: ROAD TRAFFIC FORECASTING – MACRO ECONOMIC FORECASTS

This case study examines the elements contained in the traffic forecasting models adopted in industrial countries. The Department for Transport in Britain produced a long term forecast of road traffic for a 30-year-period; its primary purpose is to feed into the economic appraisal (cost–benefit analysis process for major road projects) to form the expected number of vehicles to which benefit values (at fixed prices currently 1997) (DoT, 1997a,b) are applied.

The National Road Traffic Forecast (NRTF, 1996) is published for total road transport (Figure 8.6) and freight transport (Figure 8.5) using two broad scenarios – the high growth assumptions (3 per cent pa) and the low growth assumptions (2 per cent pa) (see Figure 8.6). The details of these assumptions are dealt with in Chapter 10 where the application of these forecasts to an individual road investment scheme are dealt with.

There is however a close link between Gross Domestic Product (GDP) and traffic levels and this is evident in the forecasts of both total traffic and freight traffic. This becomes evident when the elements making up the GDP forecasts are identified. In a developed consumer economy (eg Western Europe, North America, Japan, parts of SE Asia) the levels of disposable income are related to levels of consumer expenditure of which personal car travel is an important part. Similarly, the wealthier a country (in GDP terms), the higher the outputs and consequently, as transport is a derived demand (Chapter 1), freight transport levels would be closely linked to the growth rate of GDP. However difficulties arise with the inaccuracy of any GDP forecasts (LTT, 1995).

The elements of traffic demand may be summarised as follows:

- Economic growth
- Household incomes
- Consumer expenditure
- Manufacturing output ⎤ relative weighting
- Commercial activity ⎬ in a particular
- Changes in land use ⎦ scheme
- Location of activities
  (CBD out of town shops/entertainment)
- Local population activity
- Unemployment level
- Interest rates
- Credit facilities

On a more localised basis these forecasts may then be applied using local data as a precursor to input of the forecasts into an individual scheme (see Chapter 10). The localised traffic forecast may then be based on:

- Economic growth in the area
- Car ownership   – 1st car
                   – 2nd car
                   – Company car
- Employment
- Income/disposable income/discretionary disposable income
- Industrial patterns

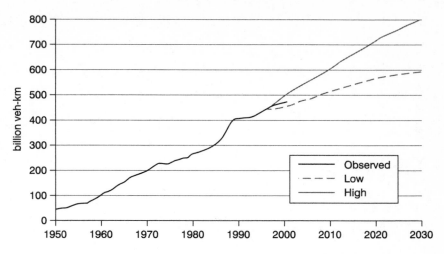

Figure 8.4 *Observed and forecast traffic growth*
Source: National Road Traffic Forecast UK, 1997

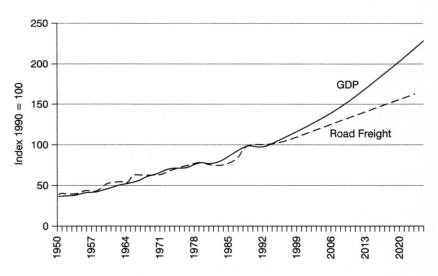

Figure 8.5 *Road freight and GDP forecasts: Great Britain*
Source: DETR, OPCI (1997a)

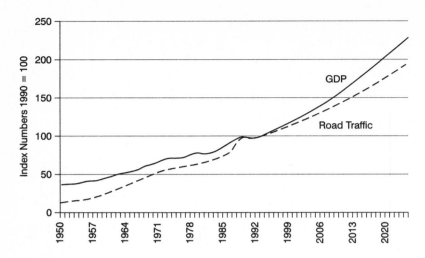

Figure 8.6 *Road traffic forecasts: actual, high/low scenarios*
Source: Derived from NRTF (1997) by the author; DfT (2002)

Table 8.11 *Forecasts of traffic growth and congestion (England), change 2002 to 2010*

Element	With 10-year plan[1] %		Without 10-year plan[1] %	
	Low	High	Low	High
Traffic (trips)	20	25	23	26
Congestion (trips)	11	20	27	32
Walk (trips)	1	2	–1	0
Cycle (trips)	30	37	–2	0
Bus (boarding)	11	12	–10	–6
Rail (pass. km)	34	49	18	30

Source: DfT

Note:
1. DETR 10-year plan. DETR (1998)

The application of assumptions is again clearly seen in the high and low forecasts that result. All forecasts should therefore be considered together with the assumptions.

CASE STUDY 4: FORECASTING RAIL PASSENGER DEMAND – ELEMENTS IN THE MODEL

A discussion of the elasticities involved in forecasting the rail passenger market is discussed in Chapter 2 using data from the Passenger Demand Forecasting Handbook (PDFH, 1986, 1996, 2002)

There are a large number of models which may be used by rail planners to derive future trends (SRA, 1997). This case study will be used to examine the role of the economic model in forecasting trends. The model tries to represent what happens in the real world using sets of inter-related data, changes in which will have different effects on the forecast outcome.

Within a framework of four basic elements, the model will tell the user the most likely scenario although all the elements might not be dealt with in one model.

1. number of train travellers in one area
2. origin and destination
3. mode(s) of transport to be used
4. service and/or route to be used

The model is made up of a series of data sets representing these elements, and based on different types of market research – this data collection and analysis forms a major part of the modelling process. Normally two types of data are required; for a train service these might include (SRA, 2003):

Data type 1 – operation

- frequency of train service
- station stopping pattern
- distances between stations
- train capacity
- speeds/journey times of the trains

Data type 2 – market demand characteristics

- existing demand levels
- existing demand patterns (on an origin-destination matrix)
- market segment data
- planning (eg housing, commercial, industrial developments)
- population forecasts
- intended fares policy by train operating companies or by the funding/integrating authority
- past travel patterns
- price elasticities
- generalised cost
- journey time (including on-time time, waiting time at stations; interchange time and number; journey time to/from stations. Comparisons may be made with other modes).

Models may also be one of two general types:

1. Aggregate models use past travel patterns and the generalised cost of different modes between each Origin–Destination in the model and

using econometric relationships (such as price or service elasticity) forecast demand (Case Study 2).
2. Disaggregate models calculate the individual travellers' options for travel between a pair of locations and the probability of the passenger using a particular route/mode and thus the number of passengers likely to use that mode.

Models may also produce forecasts of rail revenue, overcrowding, and transfers from other modes. These are input into the economic appraisal model to determine total user benefits (eg reduced journey time or overcrowding) and non-user benefits (such as a reduction in road congestion consequent on a new rail scheme). Such an analysis was used in the Central London Rail Study (CLRS, 1989) (see Chapter 9).

Models have to be tested (or validated) using past data to ensure their accuracy in reflecting actual movements. Applying past data and assumptions as trends in different elements, the forecast of passenger traffic is then produced.

But the recent changes in the rail industry in Great Britain mean that forecasting demand 10 years ahead is more than usually uncertain. The SRA expects that, once the priorities set out in its strategic plan have been implemented, passenger demand will increase substantially, rising by between 40 and 50 per cent by 2010 (see Figure 8.7).

In Great Britain, the SRA (2003) uses four primary models to forecast rail demand:

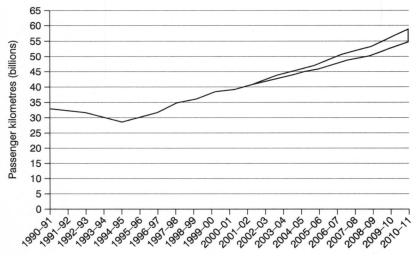

Figure 8.7 *Forecast growth in passenger rail travel*
Source: SRA (2002) The Strategic Plan

- The Passenger Demand Forecasting Handbook (PDFH) is the key model. It contains available research into rail market forecasting and recommends elasticities and other parameters which are incorporated into the main forecasting models.
- The SRA's PLANET provides strategic modelling for all surface rail, metro and tram systems and for bus services linked into the rail network. It incorporates journey times, crowding levels, the redistribution of new schemes and changing demographics. It can be used for changes to existing services, new services or major schemes.
- MOIRA is based on the elasticities and methodology in PDFH and considers the effects of timetable changes on revenue, journeys and travel miles. It can be input into a cost benefit analysis as the 'value of time saved/increased'.
- Rail industry forecasting framework (RIFF) is used to estimate the effects of external factors (eg car ownership) on demand, giving discretion to modify parameters, and can link into MOIRA to test timetable change effects.

CASE STUDY 5: FORECASTING FOR AN INTEGRATED TRANSPORT POLICY

The National Transport Model (NTM, 2002) for England has been developed to cover all modes of surface transport. It supports the integrated transport policy (see Chapter 12) by illustrating how different policies interact and their effect on modal split, congestion and pollution. The forecasts can indicate the effect of a long term plan (eg the UK 10-year transport plan, DETR, 1998).

The core of such a process is the demand model. This has information, for each mode, on total number of trips and the cost of travel, thus producing forecast trip numbers by distance, purpose and mode, and thus the option available to travellers with differing transport needs including how far they wish/have to travel, what area type represents their destination (eg central business district, rural, out of town) and which mode of travel they will use (car, bus, rail, cycle, walk).

A model of this type has to take account of a range of social and economic factors affecting businesses, individuals and households. As with all forecasts, uncertainty arises from factors affecting travel, eg how income growth and changes in the relative cost of each mode affect travel choices. This range of uncertainty reflects:

- how rising incomes affect prosperity to travel and reduce sensitivity to many costs of travel;
- assumptions about the rate of growth of the economy;
- the impact of 'soft' planning policy such as traffic awareness and planning;

- the impact of income growth on rail demand (versus cheaper, eg bus, or perceived cheaper, eg car, modes).

If assumptions on factors such as these are applied to the forecasts then high and low forecasts will be produced (see Table 8.12).

The key forecasting inputs to the NTM are:

- the impact of demographic factors (eg growth in number and location of households) on journeys made;
- census data and projections;
- employment growth (eg 7 per cent over 10 years means 2 million extra jobs) and impact on population distribution;
- percentage of adults with driving licences (8 per cent rate of growth from 2000 to 2010 gives licences to 75 per cent of over 17s);
- car fuel costs fall by 30 per cent (12 per cent fall in real terms fuel prices; 20 per cent improvement in fuel efficiency); uninterrupted world oil supply; no real terms increase in fuel duty; car manufacturers introduce agreed fuel efficiency;
- trunk road capacity increases from individual capital schemes (eg bypasses, road widening) and from network improvements, and bottleneck and junction improvements;
- capital and revenue expenditure on local transport policies and their impact on generalised cost by mode;
- regulated rail fares fall by 1 per cent per annum in real terms and unregulated fares increase by retail price index;
- bus fares outside London rise by 14 per cent from 2000 to 2010 in line with current trends;

Table 8.12 *High and low travel demand assumptions*

Factor	Low travel demand assumptions	High travel demand assumptions
Income increases lead to higher prosperity to travel and reduced response to changes in money cost of travel	No	Yes
GDP % points related to Treasury forecast for 2010	2% below	2% above
Soft planning policies' relative impact on travel behaviour	High impact	Low impact
Income effect on rail travel	Slow	Fast

Source: Department for Transport, London (NTM 2002)

- the rail forecasting model (see above) estimates the service elasticity effects of local heavy rail improvements; passenger and freight services are included as are rail links to freight generators, eg Channel Tunnel, Felixstowe, Southampton;
- London road user charging scheme in central and extended area; pedestrianisation in other cities;
- improvements in bus infrastructure and light rail/tram schemes for Transport Railways Directorate.

CASE STUDY 6: FORECASTING AIR TRAFFIC DEMAND

This case study is spit into two sections:

1. Methodology used by the Department of Transport, Great Britain
2. Examples of the outputs.

The forecasts prepared by the Department of Transport (DETR, 1997b) are used by government departments, the CAA and airlines alongside their own forecasts. The objective of the DETR forecast is to input into the future needs for runway and terminal capacity and the impact of capacity constraints on passengers and airlines; they also have a role in examining environmental and development impacts of growth in air traffic. The airlines will wish to extend the analysis along similar lines to Case Study 4 to include cost, revenue and profitability analysis.

Methodology

Air traffic forecasts are broken up into several markets for long and short haul traffic using data from for example the International Passenger Survey, given data on journey purpose, origins and destinations, CAA statistics for historical data and values, and cross Channel diversion rates from air to Eurostar (see Chapter 1 for detailed analysis). A series of international traffic forecasting models (16 in all) are used splitting for example between OECD and non-OECD countries, the highly industrialised countries, newly industrialised countries and less developed countries where the relationship between air traffic and its determining elements within real life and the forecast will vary between each set of origin–destination relationships.

Factors taken into account include:

a) Channel Tunnel diversion forecasts – these used recent historical trends applied to the London-Paris/Brussels market. This has currently produced a rail share of 63 per cent of the combined (air/rail) market to/from Paris and 53 per cent to/from Brussels. The advent of further high speed services (eg Thalys to Rotterdam and Amsterdam and domestic rail services to Birmingham and Manchester) may result in diversion rates being applied on these routes. The air-rail market shares use a relationship between rail and air fares, consumer preferences, frequency of service, marketing strategies etc to calculate cross-price and service elasticities thus determining demand patterns.

b) All the models included determinants of air traffic such as GDP, trade, incomes, air fares and exchange rates. Econometric analysis also involves judgements on the assumptions made, using economic theory, market maturity and statistical evidence. In the case of demand elasticities, many business markets have a constant elasticity while in the UK originating leisure trip markets, the use of declining elasticities reflects more accurately the current trends. These would include price, income and service elasticities. There are also one off or short-term effect factors, eg sports events, royal weddings or international incidents such as the Gulf War which require the use of dummy variables to explain the inconsistency of growth in GDP and fall in air traffic particularly in for example the transatlantic and leisure market.

c) The question of how mature is that market is very important. The degree of maturity in a particular market is often a significant determinant variable for air traffic forecasts in that a market develops in three stages:

Stage 1: low growth following initial introduction and limited consumer awareness and supply.
Stage 2: rapid growth as the service achieves greater awareness and its advantages are clearer.
Stage 3: slower growth (though still maintaining high sales as the service becomes established and the market approaches saturation).

These will vary by market segment and as identified in Chapter 2 (income elasticity) time constraints will limit travel, particularly in leisure markets. In UK-European travel some decline has occurred in well developed mass holiday markets but growth has continued in newer markets such as long-haul destinations, winter holidays and short breaks although in absolute terms these are still relatively small markets. The propensity to fly and number of trips per head were lower in the regions, Wales and Scotland compared with south east England; and in low income groups compared with high (DETR, 1997b, 2001).

The forecasts assume declining growth rates for the major leisure market segments, eg summer charter flights to the Mediterranean, and a modest reduction in business travel segments, while weekend city breaks are one of the fastest growing sectors.

Examples of outputs

The forecasts of total terminal passengers produced by the DETR indicate an annual growth of 5.0 per cent per annum between 2005 and 2020 under the mid-point scenario and 3.8 per cent and 6.2 per cent in the low and high scenarios (Figure 8.8). These reflect the uncertainties within the market but show that variations are possible.

However the wider the range between high and low predictions the less useful are the forecasts in determining capacity policies for governments and airports and business development policies for airlines.

The FAA (United States) view

The United States is by far the largest single passenger transport market in the world. It has a high income sector of its population with a high propensity to fly (albeit mainly inside North America). The growth forecasts produced by the Federal Aviation Authority (FAA) and the assumptions made by them are therefore worthy of examination (FAA, 2004; AB, 2004a, 2004b). The airlines' response to demand and revenue reductions is reduced capacity (see Chapter 7): forecasts, in the same way, have to change to reflect those conditions. A series of scenarios and assumptions lies behind the latest five-year FAA forecast:

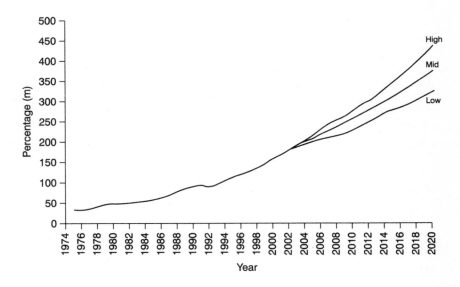

Figure 8.8 *Actual and forecast passenger numbers at UK airports, 1975 to 2020*

Source: HOC (2002); DfT (2003) The Future of Air Transport; DETR (1997b)

227

- Low cost airlines will carry about half of all air travellers by 2015. The growth of low cost carriers and the full service airlines' response have made the basis for the forecasts more complex.
- Low cost airlines' aircraft utilisation requires several flights per day with short turnaround periods and the ability to respond to new demand or lack of demand, thus changing airports and routes.
- This situation requires a new forecasting methodology incorporating socioeconomic and demographic trends – retirement patterns, new holiday times and destinations and general air transport trends. The location of home, places of work and holiday destinations, the increased popularity of leisure travel and increased opportunities for frequent travel coming from low fares had to be built into the forecasting model as a set of assumptions.
- Identifying airports that will reach their capacity over the next 10 years when US air traveller numbers are projected to rise by 50 per cent over 2004. Thus the FAA are concerned with airport capacity at the 35 busiest airports, which to meet the forecast must rise by 30 per cent by 2015. The figure for 2004 was 4 per cent.
- Demand from particular industrial sectors (eg high tech) has grown rapidly as a result of low fares and increased business activity expected to double by 2015.
- An associated pattern of regional airline operation is growth in the smaller aircraft, higher frequency market to meet the business demand. Regional services using smaller planes are expected to increase by 26 per cent in 2004, 16 per cent in 2005 and on average by 8 per cent per annum thereafter.
- The FAA may well try to model the impact of differential pricing for seats, air traffic services and congestion levels.

These developments put the model that the FAA has to create into context. However, the extent to which these are optimistic forecasts has been opened to question and illustrates how forecasts depend on assumptions – optimistic or pessimistic. The FAA short term forecast is for 6.8 per cent growth in 2004/05 and 6.1 per cent growth in 2005/06, falling to 4.3 per cent thereafter (see Tables 8.13 and 8.14). However, analysts in New York's financial area have suggested that 2.5 to 2.7 per cent is more realistic and that even 4.3 per cent growth projections may be optimistic.

The outcome is determined by the assumptions, and one needs with all forecasts to see these assumptions in order to assess the robustness of the forecast.

Table 8.13 *Domestic operations, US passenger airlines*

Year	Major airlines RPK (bn)	Change over previous year %	Total RPK (bn)	Change over previous year %
Actual				
2000	788	+5.8	825	+6.3
2001	778	−1.3	818	−0.9
2002	713	−8.4	761	−6.9
Forecast				
2003	729	+2.2	792	+4.0
2004	766	+5.1	845	+6.8
2005	809	+5.6	901	+6.6
2006	839	+3.8	941	+4.4
2007	868	+3.4	977	+3.9

Source: Federal Aviation Authority, Washington, DC (2004); *Airline Business*, May 2004

Table 8.14 *International operations, US major airlines*

Year	Market area					
	Atlantic		Pacific		All	
	RPK (bn)	Change over previous year %	RPK (bn)	Change over previous year %	RPK (bn)	Change over previous year %
Actual						
2000	140	+9.4	94	+4.1	293	+6.9
2001	139	−1.0	96	+1.7	294	+0.8
2002	120	−13.3	79	−17.5	255	−13.6
Forecast						
2003	118	−2.0	74	−5.7	251	−1.5
2004	132	+11.9	82	+10.8	280	+11.6
2005	140	+6.2	90	+9.4	300	+7.3
2006	147	+4.4	95	+6.4	318	+5.8
2007	155	+3.9	101	+5.4	335	+5.4

Source: Federal Aviation Authority, Washington, DC (2004); *Airline Business*, May 2004

CASE STUDY 7: EUROTUNNEL: FORECASTS OF FREIGHT AND PASSENGER TRAFFIC

This case study examines the competitive market of Dover–Calais to which the Eurotunnel forecasting model was applied. The Channel Tunnel operation from France to Britain is served by three supplying train companies:

1. Eurotunnel plc owned trains carrying cars, coaches and lorries between Coquelle and Folkestone.
2. Eurostar – the passenger train operating division of London and Continental Railways plc, SNCF and SNCB offering services primarily between London and Paris/Brussels with lesser services to Manchester, Birmingham, Glasgow, Cardiff and a ski train to Montiers/Bourg–St-Maurice.
3. Freight operators (eg SNCF, EWS, and others) operating freight trains through the tunnel for onward movement throughout the British Isles and continental Europe.

Eurotunnel's markets (ET, 1997)

Competitive environment

Eurotunnel's competitors

Eurotunnel's competitors on the DoCa route were P&O, Stena Line, SeaFrance and Hoverspeed. During 1996, ferry capacity on the DoCa route increased with 32 additional scheduled daily sailings being operated by the existing ferry operators during the peak summer period. As capacity increased there was a general reduction in ticket prices for cars, coaches and accompanied HGVs travelling on the DoCa route.

Eurostar

The market for Eurostar services is business and leisure passengers travelling in both directions between the UK and continental Europe. The market is varied, including business passengers travelling within the London/Brussels/Paris triangle, passengers travelling between the UK and France, Belgium, Holland and Germany, as well as a small number of long distance travellers to or from destinations such as Spain, Italy and Eastern Europe.

The London–Paris and London–Brussels prime air passenger market is Eurostar's target. Eurostar services connect London with the major centres of Paris and Brussels with a service that competes on duration, comfort and price with airline service. Other components of Eurostar's potential market are:

- those who use ferry services as foot passengers
- those who use coach services between the UK and continental Europe;

and

- those business and leisure passengers who travel by car between the UK and cities such as Lille, Paris and Brussels.

Table 8.15 *London–Paris and London–Brussels passenger traffic*

	1994		1995		1996	
	Passengers 000	Annual growth %	Passengers 000	Annual growth %	Passengers 000	Annual growth %
Air & Eurostar						
London–Paris	4021	10%	5550	38%	6584	19%
London–Brussels	1300	12%	1907	47%	2398	26%
Total	5321	11%	7457	40%	8982	20%

Source: Eurotunnel, TRC

Through freight services

Through freight services compete with most modes of sea and rail freight transport between the UK and continental Europe. Intermodal trains compete with load-on load-off ('LoLo') container services and with services for accompanied and unaccompanied freight offered by ferries and accompanied freight offered by Eurotunnel. In the automotive market, competition is from combinations of road, sea and rail modes in the UK and in continental Europe which are used to deliver cars from factories to retail outlets.

The growth of the target market for through freight services is set out below.

Table 8.16 *Cross-Channel freight traffic*

	1994		1995		1996	
	Million tonnes	Annual growth %	Million tonnes	Annual growth %	Million tonnes	Annual growth %
RoRo accompanied	21.8	10	24.2	11	25.2	4
RoRo unaccompanied	15.8	16	15.9	1	16.9	6
Other freight[1]	10.8	1	12.3	14	12.6	2
Total:	48.4	9	52.4	8	54.7	4

Sources: Eurotunnel, TRC.

[1] Includes sea container, new vehicles and through freight traffic.

Traffic and revenue

Macroeconomic assumptions

The Eurotunnel plc three year plan has been prepared in the context of the following assumptions relating to growth in gross domestic product ('GDP'), and using the following assumptions relating to inflation and interest rates in the UK and France.

Table 8.17 *Macroeconomic assumptions*

	Actual 1996	1997	1998	1999
Growth in GDP				
UK	2.3%	3.2%	2.8%	2.5%
France	1.2%	2.4%	2.1%	2.1%
Inflation				
UK	2.4%	2.9%	3.4%	3.6%
France	2.0%	1.5%	1.6%	2.1%

Source: Eurotunnel

Short-term projections 1996–1999

Table 8.18 *Projected Eurotunnel market share on the DoCa route*

	Actual 1996	1997	1998	1999
Traffic (million vehicles)				
Car	2.1	2.5	3.3	3.3
Coach	0.1	0.1	0.1	0.1
Accompanied HGV	0.5	0.3	0.7	0.8
Total:	2.7	2.9	4.1	4.2
Market share				
Car	41%	49%	59%	62%
Coach	29%	38%	45%	45%
Accompanied HGV	41%	17%	45%	43%
Total:	41%	42%	56%	57%

Source: Eurotunnel

Table 8.19 *Projected Eurostar and through freight market shares and volumes*

	Actual		Base case		Downside case		
	1996	**1997**	**1998**	**1999**	**1997**	**1998**	**1999**
Eurostar							
Million passengers	4.9	6.7	9.6	10.6	6.7	8.8	9.3
Market share	5.5%	7.1%	9.5%	10.2%	7.1%	8.7%	8.9%
Total London to							
Paris/Brussels	54%	63%	72%	73%	63%	66%	64%
Through freight services							
Million tonnes	2.4	2.8	3.2	3.5	2.0	2.1	2.3
Market share	4.4%	4.7%	5.0%	5.1%	3.4%	3.3%	3.4%

Source: Eurotunnel

Extended projections 2000–2006

Table 8.20 *Projected Eurotunnel market share on the DoCa route*

	Extended projections						
	2000	**2001**	**2002**	**2003**	**2004**	**2005**	**2006**
Upper Case and Lower case							
Tourist[1]							
(million vehicles)	3.4	3.7	3.9	4.0	4.2	4.4	4.6
Market share	63%	66%	67%	67%	68%	69%	70%
Upper Case							
HGV[2]							
(million vehicles)	0.8	0.9	1.1	1.2	1.3	1.4	1.5
Market share	42%	45%	52%	55%	57%	58%	60%
Lower Case							
HGV[2]							
(million vehicles)	0.8	0.9	1.0	1.1	1.2	1.3	1.4
Market share	44%	47%	50%	52%	55%	59%	61%

Source: Eurotunnel
Notes: 1. Includes cars and coaches
2. All HGVs are tractor unit and trailer accompanied

Projected market share

Eurotunnel's projections of Eurostar's market share and passenger volume and the market share and volume for through freight services are set out below.

Table 8.21 *Projected Eurostar and through freight market shares and volumes*

			Extended	Projections			
	2000	**2001**	**2002**	**2003**	**2004**	**2005**	**2006**
Eurostar							
Upper Case							
Million passengers	11.2	11.6	12.0	12.4	13.0	14.1	15.5
Market share	10.1%	10.2%	10.2%	10.2%	10.5%	11.1%	11.9%
Total London to							
Paris/Brussels	73%	72%	71%	71%	73%	76%	78%
Lower Case							
Million passengers	9.8	10.5	10.7	11.0	11.3	11.7	12.0
Market share	8.8%	9.2%	9.1%	9.1%	9.1%	9.2%	9.2%
Total London to							
Paris/Brussels	70%	70%	69%	69%	68%	69%	69%
Through freight services							
Upper Case							
Million tonnes	3.7	3.9	4.1	4.2	4.3	4.4	4.4
Market share	5.1%	5.1%	5.2%	5.1%	5.0%	4.9%	4.7%
Lower case							
Million tonnes	2.4	2.5	2.7	2.8	2.9	3.1	3.2
Market share	3.3%	3.3%	3.4%	3.4%	3.4%	3.4%	3.4%

Source: Eurotunnel

General market assumptions

For the purposes of its projections of traffic and revenue, and in addition to the macro-economic assumptions set out above, Eurotunnel has made certain general market assumptions, the most important of which are set out below:

(i)   current international agreements and conventions regarding trade and passenger movement will remain in effect;
(ii)   no significant downturn will occur in the UK or French economies;
(iii)   no significant incidents will occur which will abnormally affect cross-Channel traffic or otherwise lead to a material loss of revenue;
(iv)   no significant change will take place to the legal or regulatory environment in which Eurotunnel operates;
(v)   no additional fixed link across the Channel will become operational;
(vi)   ferry companies will continue to operate cross-Channel services, although significant rationalisation of capacity on the DoCa route will take place during the period and lead to enhanced yields;
(vii)   yields for Eurotunnel services will continue to be related to yields on the DoCa route for ferries;

(viii) no significant change in technology leading to a change in the competitive environment and, in particular, a reduction in competitors' journey times;

(ix)   new high-speed rail links will be constructed by the end of 1997 between Lille and Brussels and by the end of 2003 between London and the Tunnel; and

(x)   duty-free and tax-free sales to passengers will be abolished on 30 June 1999.

CONCLUSION – FORECASTING

The uncertainty of forecasts is unavoidable. However, the key to their successful use is monitoring predictions against performance. The forecast outputs in terms of passengers carried, freight moved, revenue earned and costs incurred have to be monitored. But with that, the assumptions have also to be watched carefully. Should any of these turn out to be incorrect (eg wages in the cost analysis; car ownership or income in the revenue/ travel analysis) then the forecast has to be recalculated.

Forecasts of air passenger travel prepared in the mid-1990's would hardly have considered the full effect of the low cost airlines. In 1997, several charter airlines were predicting a growth rate commensurate with disposable income available for travel. Those predictions were significantly reduced by low cost airlines.

Rail passenger usage in Britain and France was considered to be on a declining trend from the 1970's and 1980's. In France, the TGV network required a recalculation of those forecasts. The expected decline (at least by the governments of the day) in rail travel was to be reversed to the extent that rail travel now increases by 5 to 8 per cent per annum as a result of factors linked to income, GDP, road congestion, a desire for comfortable travel and environmental concern.

The economic and social bases from which both freight and passenger travel is derived are therefore the factors to be monitored. Because of its desired nature the more disaggregated the elements the more accurate is the basis of the forecast. Conversely there is an increased opportunity for one or more elements to have been incorrectly measured or forecast and thus adversely affect the outcome.

REFERENCES

AB (2004a) Banking on growth, *Airline Business*, May, Sutton.

AB (2004b) Passenger recovery, *Airline Business*, August, Sutton.

BRB (1988) British Railways Board; Channel Tunnel Train Services – BR Study Report on Long-term Route and Terminal Capacity (July).

BRB (1991a) Rail Link Project – Comparison of Routes, British Railways Board, London (June). The Rail Link Project became Union Railways Limited in 1993.

BRB (1991b) International Rail Services: Forecast numbers of trains (current and 1995 in London, Kent and Surrey), March, British Rail, London.

CLRS (1989) Central London Rail Study – joint study by the Department of Transport, BR Network South East, London Regional Transport and London Underground; Department of Transport; London.

Cole, W S & Tyson W J (1977) A forecast of public transport financial performance, *Transport*, Vol 37, No 9 (Chartered Institute of Transport Journal), London.

DETR (1997a) Developing an integrated transport policy; Department of the Environment, Transport and the Regions.

DETR (1997b) Air Traffic Forecasts for the United Kingdom 2000, Department of the Environment Transport and the Regions, London

DETR (1998) A new deal for transport; Department of Environment, Transport and Regions, London.

DETR (2000a) Transport 2010 – the 10 year plan, London.

DETR (2000b) UK Air Freight Study, DETR/MDS Transmodal, London.

DETR (2001), The Future of Aviation, Department of the Environment, Transport and the Regions, London.

DfT (2002), Delivering Better Transport Progress Reports, Department for Transport, London.

DfT (2003) The Future of Air Transport, Department for Transport, London (see Annex A: Air Travel Forecasts up to 2030).

DoT (1997a) Department of Transport COBA 10, Highway Evaluation Manual, London.

DoT (1997b) Department of Transport, Highway Economics Vol 2, 'Value of Time and Vehicle Operator Costs', London.

ET (1991) Interim Report, Eurotunnel plc, London.

ET (1994) Eurotunnel rights issue document, Eurotunnel plc, Folkestone.

ET (1997) Financial Restructuring Proposals (May), Eurotunnel plc Folkestone; Eurotunnel SA, Paris.

FAA (2004) Aerospace Forecasts 2004–2014, Federal Aviation Authority, Washington, DC.

HOC (1986) Channel Link, HC50, Transport Committee, Session 1985–86, House of Commons, London.

HOC (2002) National Air Traffic Finances, HC 789, session 2001–02, House of Commons, London.

Howarth G G (1992) Project Director, Rail Link Project, 'The Rail Link to the Channel Tunnel', talk, April, to the Chartered Institute of Transport, London.

LTT (1995) Whether forecasts? Ministers grapple with replacement for the 1989 traffic predictions. Barney Stringer in *Local Transport Today* (12 October).

NRTF (1997) National Road Traffic Forecasts. Department of Transport, London.

NSE (1991) British Rail Network South East passenger forecasts. Two separate sets prepared by (1) Coopers Lybrand Deloitte/Roger Tym and Partners and (2) Economic and Business Policy Research Ltd/Business Strategies Limited; 1991. The results are published in BRB (1991a).

NSE (1993) Network South East statistics department sources.

NSE (1994) Network South East management discussion and published train details, 1994.

NTM (2002) National Transport Model, Department for Transport, London.

PDFH (1986, 1996, 2002) Passenger Demand Forecasting Handbook, British Railways Board, 1986; TCI Operational Research 1996; SRA, 4th edn, August 2002.

Serplan (1989) The Channel Tunnel: Traffic Forecasts and the Transport Impact; London and South East Regional Planning Conference (Serplan), RPC 1480, London, June.

SRA (1997) A guide to transport demand forecasting models. Prepared by Transport Strategies Ltd for Office of Passenger Rail Franchising, London.

SRA (2002) *The Strategic Plan: Summary*, Strategic Rail Authority, London.

SRA (2003) *Appraisal Criteria: A guide to the appraisal of support for passenger and freight rail services*, Strategic Rail Authority, London.

TPA (1992) South London Rail Study Phase 1 (prepared for London Transport, London Borough of Bromley and others), Transport Planning Associates, London, July 1992.

Part 2: Public Policy

CHAPTER 9

Economic Appraisal – Techniques

THE ARGUMENT FOR GOVERNMENT INVESTMENT IN PUBLIC TRANSPORT

Public transport services are part of the basic mobility provision in rural areas and one means of reducing congestion and pollution as part of an integrated transport policy in urban areas. The only service likely to be profitable is one where there is intensive use, high load factors and a relatively price inelastic and service inelastic market. A few services (eg Heathrow Airport Express) fall into this category. It is unlikely to apply to rural railways or large commuter rail systems, and so places the evaluation of such services into the public policy context. Therefore, it is important to identify the impacts generated from services and to determine the social value these represent, as an objective basis for decisions on public funding (Cole *et al*, 1997).

Within the transport area a range of different forms of evaluation can be identified such as the financial analysis of service frequency increases on Eurostar or First Great Western or cost benefit analysis in the Central London Rail Study where rail evaluation was undertaken from a social viewpoint and not a limited private perspective. A social cost benefit basis is a comprehensive evaluation of modal options, where all relevant impacts are taken into account using social, rather than the private, benefits and costs. Two situations where public funding may be involved are:

- major infrastructure projects (EC, 1996; SRA, 2003; NR, 2003);
- loss-making services (EC, 1999; Cole and Holvad, 2001; SRA, 2003, 2004).

In both situations a private perspective could imply that the 'do-nothing' option is selected. However, if significant social benefits exist then these could justify public funding support; for example the evaluation of the social costs and benefits from services which are profit-making and where enhancement has external benefits, eg congestion or pollution.

Subsidies for public transport can be justified on the grounds of basic accessibility and social inclusion (particularly in rural areas) or reduced

Table 9.1 *Contractual payments by the French government/local authorities (regions) to SNCF*

Payment/income type	Percentage of total income	Percentage of state payment
1. *Compensation for tariff reductions* The revenue from passenger traffic includes amounts received from the state and local authorities as compensation for tariff reduction measures. The purpose of these payments is to offset the cost to SNCF of the mandatory free and reduced fare travel concessions granted to certain user categories such as large families, servicemen, and workers taking paid holidays. It also includes fare subsidies for Paris and other suburban services. In addition as part of its revenue from freight traffic, SNCF receives compensatory payments to cover the cost of providing services at rates set by the government under conditions inconsistent with the commercial interests of SNCF (eg the transport of newspapers)	6.2	18.3
2. *Infrastructure* A subsidy payment towards the cost of infrastructure and level crossings to ensure that SNCF rates are on a par with other systems of transport (eg road haulage) whose infrastructure is also provided by the government	10.6	31.6
3. *Public service obligation grant* This grant finances services required by the government or local authorities or at fares set by them, which would be inconsistent with SNCFs commercial interests. It also covers the development and maintenance costs of railway facilities surplus to those which SNCF considers necessary for operational requirements	3.7	11.1
4. Combined transport facilities	0.3	0.8
5. Additional operational funding	12.8	<u>38.2</u>
6. Total state payments	33.6	100.00
7. Sales of assets (eg land)	3.8	
8. Income from operations	<u>62.6</u>	
Total income	100.0	

Source: SNCF Annual Report, 2002 (Paris)

congestion as part of an integrated transport policy in a large conurbation (DOT, 1991; DETR, 1998; HMT, 2002; SRA, 2003). The technique used to compare the return on this form of expenditure with other state transport expenditure is called cost benefit analysis (OPRAF, 1996; SRA, 2003; Cole and Holvad, 2001). In the situation where total funds available are less than the total subsidy requirements, cost benefit analysis (or multi-criteria analysis which is merely an extension of CBA) can be used to determine a list of expenditure priorities.

The benefits derived from subsidies are those which enable existing services to continue or new services to start. They can be regarded in much the same way as the returns on investment in road or public transport infrastructure (see Chapter 11). In the case of new service developments the benefits are measured in relation to the cost of subsidy. When closure of, for example, a railway line is proposed, then the cost savings can be considered in terms of disbenefits to the community. If the net resource cost savings are lower than the loss of benefits this means that the continuation of the service will optimise the welfare of the community, ie there is an economic justification for the expenditure since it is likely that there are schemes where the benefits or disbenefits will be less than costs or cost savings. It has been assumed that any subsidy provided for a service will equate to the savings to be derived from the closure of the service. Through this the normal cost benefit analysis will relate to the savings disbenefit analysis (Cole, 1976).

Alternative transport options

In transport expenditure generally, there may be a number of options, but for a bus or train passenger service they are:

- to retain the service in its present form;
- to close the service;
- to rationalise the network (eg by amending or merging routes);
- to replace it with other modes;
- to use new technology (eg Geographical Positioning System – GPS) (BWCABUS, 2003).

In the case of SNCF (French railways), there is a series of contractual payments by the French government/local authorities (regions) to SNCF, as shown in Table 9.1.

COST BENEFIT ANALYSIS

Financial (cost revenue) analysis versus cost benefit analysis

A financial appraisal of public transport services assesses revenue generated (or costs saved) and cost incurred (capital and operating costs).

Provision of services will be considered if the revenue generated is larger than the capital and operating cost incurred. Obviously, financial appraisal excludes a range of different impacts which are of importance to society. Therefore, the appraisal form is more relevant in those situations where private capital is used (Cole and Holvad, 2001), eg appraisals undertaken by private operators. This may be in situations where the infrastructure is totally private (eg a decision by Stagecoach plc to purchase new buses or construct a new depot; on the road side a decision by CGDE to build the second Severn crossing) or where there is some private and some public funding as in the case of Manchester Metrolink where the private investors would have considered the financial return on their investment (Chapter 11; Ling, 1994). There was also an interesting dichotomy when Railtrack (1997), a private company, used financial objectives in investment appraisal but where funds for the track investment programme came from private and public sources. (Railtrack plc following administration was replaced by a state influenced, not for profit company, Network Rail.)

In the cost benefit study of the Victoria line, part of London's underground system, benefits to road users from reduced congestion were taken into account. The travel time and vehicle operating costs (through reduced traffic flow) of those who continued to use their cars were also taken into account since values can be attached to travel time and car operating costs. In this case, some of the people benefiting from the scheme contributed to it by way of fares, whereas those who continued to use their cars made no direct contribution to London Transport revenue. This was a distinctly different approach from those who constructed the Metropolitan Railway in the 1860s, when the only factors considered were cash flow and a profitable return on capital. No account of road users' travel time improvements were taken by the proposers of this scheme, although fast rail journey times were highlighted in train service advertising to attract new passengers. The profitable part of the business was the land development company, Metropolitan Country Estates Ltd (Chapter 14). Thus, items appear in the cost benefit analysis which would not appear in a financial analysis and conversely, some items in a financial analysis may disappear or may be substantially modified.

The projected increase in traffic congestion in Edinburgh and the estimates of time loss show a significant difference between the congestion delays index *with* road pricing (150 from a 100 base in 2001) and an index of 285 if *no* road pricing is introduced. It is generally accepted that alternative forms of transport are pre-requirements to such policies. A major investment programme (£1.3 billion) for bus lanes, cycleways, bus service improvements, heavy rail and two new tram lines is being evaluated using the Scottish Transport Appraisal Guidance (STAG) (SE, 2003; TIE, 2004).

There are therefore two alternative approaches to determining the network; one based on the network breaking even in market terms – that is, expenditure is equal to, or less than, revenue (from fares, parcels, advertising income, etc); the other takes into account the price mechanism but modifies the supply position to include the social costs involved and the subsidy provided by local authorities or central government. If forecasts of revenue and expenditure show an upward trend in the overall deficit, it is essential to have a formalised basis for allocating scarce revenue support resources to areas where they will provide the greatest benefit to the community in terms of the provision of public transport services. The comparative effect of basing fares and service level (ie frequency or size of network) on the price mechanism and on a social-cost-inclusive basis using a subsidy is shown in Figure 9.1.

The rationale for using different appraisal techniques for road and public transport investment relies on the principle (DOT, 1991) that road and rail serve different markets and have organisational and structural differences and this affects the choice of appraisal technique. This argument is weakened (SDG, 1992) since in many cases road and rail are close substitutes, and thus do not serve different markets. The separation of rail operations and infrastructure in the EU also makes the second part of the argument questionable. Road and rail infrastructure projects in consequence are competing on unequal terms for the limited funding resources with the potential of misallocating the available resources. Road investments evaluated using cost-benefit appraisal takes a wider range of impacts into account. The extent of discrepancy between financial and cost-benefit assessment is illustrated in the electrification of the Midland Main Line (SDG, 1991). A financial appraisal shows a net present value (NPV) of £1m while cost-benefit appraisal results in a NPV of £77m (including user as well as non-user benefits). Therefore when rail projects are assessed, through financial analysis user benefits not included in revenue changes, ie consumer surplus effects are ignored. In contrast, the appraisal of road projects includes consumer surplus effects through the inclusion of time and cost savings (Table 9.2 and Case Study 2, this chapter).

Cost revenue analysis

This considers the reduction in operating and overhead costs, the consequent effect on revenue, and the change in the financial deficit of the railway. The analysis is restricted to the costs and revenue and internal rate of return set down by the operating companies, and does not consider any community effects in economic, accessibility or environmental terms.

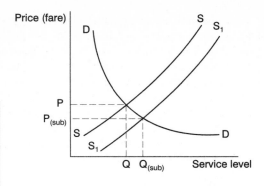

P = price (ie fare charged) determined by market forces
Q = quantity (frequency; size of network) provided on a financially viable basis
S_1S_1 = supply curve provided following subsidy
$\left.\begin{array}{l}P_{(sub)}\\Q_{(sub)}\end{array}\right\}$ = price and quantity supplied if a subsidy is paid

Figure 9.1 *Comparison of the effects of the price mechanism and subsidy*

Cost revenue elements in the analysis of public transport schemes (Cole, 1985)

The elements to be considered in a decision whether or not to close for example a railway or other bus/tram operation service would therefore be:

- Capital replacement cost savings (+)
     Infrastructure replacement (stations, track, bridges, signalling where these are avoidable (ie not joint) costs)
     Replacement of rolling stock (such as the new Class 150 'Sprinter' diesel multiple units proposed for use on the rural lines)
     Depreciation costs (depending on alternative rolling stock use)
- Operating cost savings (+)
     Labour costs (drivers, office staff)
     Fuel costs
     Maintenance costs
- Loss of train service revenue (-)
- Revenue transferred to alternative railway services (+)
- Cost of alternative bus services (-)
     Where additional buses are operated, as could occur in the case of a replacement express service
- Revenue generated by alternative bus services (+)

If the financial position is positive then in cost revenue terms the closure is justified. A further refinement sets a required rate of return on capital or on turnover. However, these techniques, developed for the private sector, are often unsuitable for wider public sector use because they are confined to the consideration of financial returns and cash outlays. This may also apply to a scheme which is not financially viable (eg Channel Tunnel Rail Link) and which will receive public investment funding determined on a cost benefit basis. Here non-financial benefits such as non-user benefits (eg reduced road congestion; reduced congestion on existing rail commuter routes) and user benefits from reduced commuting journey times (albeit at a higher fare, included in 'generalised cost' will accrue to the commuter transferring to the new service rather than to train operators whose fares will be regulated (EC, 1996; Walsh & Williams 1969).

Cost benefit analysis of public transport schemes

Traditionally the cost benefit analysis has been applied to those benefits to which an accepted basis of monetary valuation is available. In addition to this there are environmental factors (which may have a monetary value – see Chapter 10) and factors such as economic development (see Chapter 15), employment and energy use. This extension of cost benefit analysis has been referred to as multicriteria analysis and includes those factors not easily measured in monetary units (Nijkamp and Blaas, 1994; NATA, 2001; Cole and Holvad, 2001, DoT 1994; DfT 2004).

This technique contains elements similar to those used for new road infrastructure evaluation where community benefits (Glaister and Layard, 1994) rather than financial returns are taken as the decision criteria. The cost benefit study should compare the social benefits to be derived from the cost of continuing the rail service compared with the social disbenefits resulting from its withdrawal and the consequent saving to the community (Cole, 1985). Bus and rail services provide costs and benefits to both users and non-users in the community as a whole, so it is necessary to use cost benefit techniques to measure the effects outside the public transport operation, since these are also relevant (DOT, 1991; DfT, 2001).

A proposal for the closure of a passenger train service will have effects on the community and the effects to be considered are those incurred:

- by the existing users of buses and trains;
- by the existing users of other modes, eg private car drivers and occupants, and pedestrians;
- by transport operators and the authorities providing roads;
- elsewhere in the economy.

This means that there are factors not directly related to the service reduction under evaluation, eg increased congestion on nearby roads, which have to be taken into account (DfT, 2001). Both the direct effects on providers and users and the external effects are to be included provided they are spillovers, influencing the amount of output that others (eg non-road users) can get from a fixed amount of input. Costs and benefits affecting the 'real income' (or production in real terms) of a community should be included. Costs and benefits affecting the 'distribution of income' do not affect total output and conventionally were excluded, but an assessment of these effects should be made.

In many areas, financial appraisal in a private sector sense (cost revenue analysis) does not provide adequate consideration of the overall advantages and disadvantages of a project to the community as a whole.

Existing cost benefit/multicriteria approaches to evaluation

Using a wider technique extends the concept of cost benefit analysis to include other elements in the evaluation process and could encompass:

- time savings on trains
- accident savings on road
- overcrowding
- time savings on road
- employment impact

In a study of new rail infrastructure in one major city (CLRS, 1989) for example the following criteria have been considered:

- time savings
- crowding relief
- total public transport user benefits
- road use benefits
- additional rail revenue
- total benefit

The French Department of Transport and Société Nationale des Chemins de Fer Français (SNCF) in evaluating new TGV high speed train services (SNCF, 2003) used three main elements in the social benefit calculation:

- environment
- employment benefits
- commercial elements (such as the decentralisation of economic developments, transfer from other modes, leading to reduced overcrowding of, for example, other TGV, RER and SNCF services
- reduced journey time

It has to be remembered that the operators and users of these services may not receive the benefits which service improvements provide. Firstly the externalities (as they are known in economics) refer to benefits to the community (eg safety improvements; environmental improvements). Some types of investment benefit the user but not the operator where rail investment by SNCF will not, under its present tariff structure, allow SNCF to gain the consumer surplus accruing to the user. Thirdly calculating economic benefits to the community profits achieved by the railway may adversely affect the financial position of another transport undertaking (ECMT, 1992). For example the TGV Sud-Est service from Paris to Lyon provided substantial revenue for SNCF but resulted in almost total loss of passengers on the Air Inter (also government-owned) parallel service.

The financial position of the TGV network has, when incorporating contractual payments by the French State and regions, been satisfactory and is considerably improved when social benefits are taken into account (Table 9.2).

Basis of social cost benefit values

The evaluation process is carried out in terms of 'resource costs'. In determining these costs, the use of market prices is not altogether satisfactory since they can be distorted by a monopoly supplier in the market, by taxation or subsidies.

Some factors in the cost benefit analysis have no market value, such as journey time, life, or some of the components of accident costs. The resource cost is therefore the sum of the value of benefits produced by the resources (eg raw materials, labour, capital) with an allowance for their opportunity cost.

Labour cost savings

In the case of labour cost savings, if there is a general unemployment in the area where the reduction is to take place, then there is no opportunity cost, since in the absence of the railway or bus company the labour input would be unemployed. Unemployed labour is valued in cost benefit studies in terms of the value of its output in an alternative use. This gives a 'shadow' price of zero to labour and this is attached to the saving in labour costs.

Table 9.2 *Financial v cost benefit appraisal – TGV rail services in France*

TGV Service	Financial return %	Cost benefit return % (incorporating elements above)
Sud Est (Paris–Lyon–Marseilles)	17	33
Atlantique (Bordeaux)	12	20

Source: SNCF (French Railways) (2003)

That is, if the alternative is unemployment no opportunity cost should be subtracted from the cost savings.

The other factors affecting the value of this opportunity cost will be:

- the length of time the labour is likely to be unemployed;
- the extent of migration;
- the indirect effects of bus or railwaymen taking up jobs which other potential employees might have obtained;
- the multiplier effect of a fall in income;
- the increase in employment on the alternative passenger transport services (this is dealt with separately under alternative service resource costs).

If the area is one of plentiful employment opportunities, the labour made redundant will become a labour input in another sector and there will be an opportunity cost to use the labour in the area concerned. In most cases this will approximate to the payment made by the employer of the existing labour in the new employment and the total should be subtracted from the labour cost savings by the public transport operator to give the net resource cost savings. On the other hand, a financial analysis would count all savings in wage payments.

Some of the specific cost savings and disbenefits resulting from a service reduction should now be considered.

Capital cost savings

In the case of bus operators, these consist of savings in capital expenditure on buildings and new buses; in the case of railways, on stations, signalling equipment, track and replacement rolling stock and locomotives.

The capital cost savings on buses is achieved when the reduction of service A allows the bus used on service B. The use of buses on more than one service (joint costs) complicates matters and the calculation is further complicated by the allocation of vehicle depreciation and replacement costs on a peak vehicle basis. This will result in greater savings from peak service cuts. However, care must be taken in relating the cut in a peak service to the other uses of the vehicle on off peak services (if any) and the allocations of bus replacement costs to that service if no peak vehicle is available for use. Thus allowance is made for the remaining years of service of the bus, and savings in refurbishing costs and future replacement cost must also be allowed for. If the bus is sold, it is a transfer of use to another operator, and resource costs are saved, as the economy has to produce one less bus for the other operator.

Operating cost savings

In the short term, variable costs (such as wages and fuel) will be saved and in the longer term, semi-variable costs (eg vehicle maintenance costs) will be saved. Fixed costs will be reduced where larger scale rationalisation takes place and the savings will vary according to the alternative use made of the facility. These costs can be identified using bus and rail cost allocation systems (see Chapters 5 and 6).

Facilities which are used jointly by a number of services, eg bus stations, may only represent a cost saving if the operation is closed or replaced. There will be some staff savings at these locations but costs such as maintenance, heat and light and depreciation will not be avoided. In a cost benefit analysis the saving is made when the facility is closed. The savings attributed to a reduced service must be the resource cost savings. If joint costs are involved then the element of these which is not saved must be removed from the calculation.

Cost of replacing non-passenger services

It is necessary to deduct the cost of replacing any non-passenger services which are currently provided. Alternative services would be required and from the total cost saving resulting from a service reduction should be deducted the cost of providing this replacement service.

Feeder services

If some services are cut, then branch line feeder services may cease to be either financially viable or operationally practical. In such cases these too may be reduced and cost savings will accrue.

Loss of benefits resulting from the reduction of a service

The resource cost savings to the community resulting from a service reduction have to be balanced against the loss of benefit accompanying such an event. The approach to measuring this loss of benefit is to assess the effects on the existing users of the service when they take up the best alternative available to them after its withdrawal. They may choose to travel by other buses, rail, car, bicycle, walk or not to travel at all.

Whichever they choose, there will be effects on travel time, vehicle flow (and congestion), and so on, if the before and after situations are compared, and so benefits or disbenefits will accrue. The categories of benefit and disbenefit now require examination.

Time

One of the main effects of altering a service may be to change the time which is needed to make a trip. Every journey made incurs a certain amount of time and if a passenger is to continue to make the journey s/he must use the next best alternative mode. This loss in time is the loss in

251

consumer surplus to passengers who now have to make longer journeys. In areas of low car ownership this will involve longer walking time to the alternative bus service, possibly longer journey time and increased time spent waiting for connections.

The loss in consumer surplus may be evaluated using the Department of Transport (DOT, 1996a) values of time, per hour, for in-vehicle time in non-working hours (DOT, 1996b) (Chapter 11 has a full discussion). In the case of journeys undertaken during working hours, the value of travel time is based on the price paid for that person's labour. This is multiplied by the time involved, to calculate the aggregate loss in consumer surplus. The DOT data was based on behaviour studies which considered mainly journey-to-work trips and the choices made by people between, for example, lengthy trips at a lower cost rather than shorter trips at a higher cost.

The latest available prices are those for 1994 and the behavioural and resource values of in-work time show that bus passenger time is only 66 per cent of rail passenger time (see Table 9.3). This reflects the values people put on their time and reflects their income levels (as a proxy for resource values). Non-work time has lower values overall with no distinction between travel modes.

Consider a typical journey to work where the passenger at present has a choice of two peak services, one leaving at 08.00 hours and the other at 07.30 hours. The proposed service cuts involve taking off the 08.00 hours peak service leaving the passenger with no alternative but to travel on the 07.30 hours. The resulting changes in journey times and values are shown in Table 9.4. The loss in consumer surplus is £1.58 per trip. Assume 400 return journey-to-work trips per year, then the aggregate figure for this

Table 9.3 *Time values*

	£p/person hour 1994 prices Resources and behavioural time
Working time	
Car driver	12.89
Car passenger	10.70
Bus passenger	10.64
Rail passenger	16.19
Underground passenger	15.93
Bus driver	9.83
All workers	12.77
Non-working time	3.15

Source: Department of Transport COBA 10 Manual (DOT, 1996a)
These values may change as a result of DOT funded research in 1997.

Table 9.4 *Comparison of journey times and values*

		Present journey		Alternative journey
Depart home		07.50		07.20
Board bus		08.00		07.30
Alight bus		08.15		07.45
Arrive work		08.20		07.50
Desired time of arrival		08.30		08.30
Time	**Mins**	**Value (£p)**	**Mins**	**Value (£p)**
Walking/waiting } In-vehicle	40	2.10	70	3.68

passenger would be £632. This sort of situation is likely to be repeated for a large number of people on this and other services.

Existing road users

The transfer of passengers from bus to train into private cars has an effect on the existing users of roads along which the buses run. Their journey time will be extended by the increase in traffic flow on those and adjacent roads and the accompanying reduction in car speeds. The value of the increase of their journey time will also be a disbenefit following the withdrawal of a passenger service.

Journeys not made

Some people will find the alternative service too inconvenient or will not use it for other reasons (eg higher fares) and do not have access to a car and will no longer make the journey at all. Any journey incurs for the traveller the cost of the fare, the time spent travelling, and the disutility of having to travel. Together these form the 'user cost' of making a particular journey. Assume that the passenger was travelling by the optimum mode, then the user cost of an alternative bus service (or mode) is likely to be higher and one which the user is not prepared to pay. This means that the consumer surplus (Chapter 4 has an explanation) derived by the passenger as a result of his 'user cost' expenditure lies between the user cost of the two alternatives.

If a straight line demand curve is assumed (as shown in Figure 9.2), then the value of loss of consumer surplus will be one-half of the difference in travel time between the existing service and the next best alternative service (or mode) multiplied by the appropriate value factor for time. Where:

C_B User cost – existing bus service
C_N User cost – next best alternative mode
P_B Bus passenger journeys
P_N 'Next best alternative' passenger journeys
Loss of benefit = ½ (bus user cost – 'Next best alternative' user cost)

The value of journeys not made (J_N) is calculated as the total number of people forgoing the journey (P) multiplied by one-half of the difference in time taken (total walking, waiting and in-vehicle) to travel by the existing mode (E_T) and the next best alternative mode (A_T).

The aggregate loss in consumer surplus is:

$$J_N = P \times \tfrac{1}{2} (E_T - A_T)$$

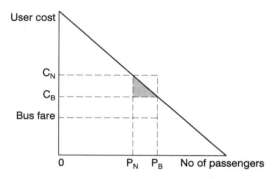

Figure 9.2 *Value of journeys not made*

Resource cost of loss of revenue by transport operators

If passengers transfer to travel by car or do not make the journey at all then there will be a loss of revenue to transport operators. This will result in increased expenditure in other sectors (assuming there is no saving). Some of this will be diverted to other travel sectors (eg car operating costs) and to avoid double counting, this cost will be excluded here as it is dealt with later. The loss of consumer surplus of the passenger who now walks is included in the time calculation. It is therefore correct to include here the fares paid by existing passengers who will not make the journey after withdrawal, and by those who walk when the bus is no longer available.

Insufficient details are known about consumption patterns and the relationship between expenditure on travel and expenditure on other items. However, if it is assumed that the marginal social cost of producing the alternative good is equal to its price, then the revenue not spent on transport appears as an increase in resource cost to the economy. In calculating the resource cost of the alternative expenditure, an allowance must be made for the indirect taxation element in the price of goods bought. This must be deducted from the resource cost. Revenue will be lost if the service to be withdrawn feeds passengers into other services. The same will apply to feeder services into the service to be withdrawn. In either case, the value of journeys not made will equate to an increase in resource costs and be counted as a disbenefit resulting from closure.

Additional public transport resource costs

If a bus service is withdrawn and other existing bus services have spare capacity to cope with the diverted demand with no additional vehicle requirements, there will be no additional bus resource costs. This is more likely at off peak times than peak times. If an additional, amended or extended bus service is required to replace the closed bus or train service then there will be the capital cost of providing the vehicles (where required), together with the appropriate variable and semi-variable costs. The resource cost will exclude revenue support from a county council, bus purchase grant and fares, as none of these will affect the resource cost of providing the bus service. The principles by which resource cost should be allocated to routes have already been discussed and these should also be used here.

Loss of output from unemployment

There may be an effect on resource costs resulting from people not travelling to work and therefore giving up work or changing jobs. If the passenger does not take up alternative employment and claims National Insurance and other benefits there is no resource cost resulting from his alternative means of support, as all such benefits are treated as transfer payments and do not incur any resource cost nor do they come as a result of any increase in output. This unemployment is separate from any redundancy of bus company labour which results in a short-term cost saving.

Additional car operating costs

The withdrawal or reduction of a bus service will result in some people transferring to car especially for their journey to work. This will mean an increased traffic flow (and therefore increased congestion) and a reduction in vehicle speeds, and since car operating costs are a function of speed they will be affected by the change in the volume of traffic. There will be two groups of car user involved. First, the existing user whose car speed will be reduced as a result of the traffic transferred from public transport. Here, the additional resource cost has to be calculated. Second, for the driver or passenger who previously did not use a car, the resource cost will be the whole operating cost. The formula for calculating car operating costs takes into account the cost of fuel, oil, tyres, maintenance and depreciation. (DOT, 1996b).

Road cost avoided by retention of bus/rail service

The withdrawal of a service will result in an increase in vehicle flow. This will result in some increase in maintenance costs, although road track costs vary more with HGV usage than with car usage. The largest increase in costs will result from the demand for new or improved roads especially those which are near capacity, particularly at peak journey-to-work times. There will also be additional capital costs of providing car parking spaces. These provide an increase in resource costs but against this must be balanced a saving of resource costs elsewhere in the economy represented by car parking charges. If the car parking charge for eight hours is £4.50 and the user previously used the bus service he must now divert £4.50 from other expenditure, giving the saving in resource costs. Again, the car occupancy rate will determine how much each passenger has to pay.

Accident costs

Accident costs are also a function of vehicle flow on a given class of road for particular types of vehicle. The rates and values are provided by the Department of Transport (DOT, 1996c).

Environmental implications

The increase in the flow of vehicles will have an effect on the urban and rural environment as it usually brings with it increases in vehicle noise, pollution, the numbers of properties affected, and conflicts resulting from the interaction of pedestrians and vehicles.

The elements used in cost benefit analysis of public transport schemes

Summary

If a railway service was considered for closure in conjunction with a bus replacement scheme, the elements to consider in public sector terms would be:

1. Capital cost savings (+)
    Infrastructure replacement (stations, track, bridges, signalling, where these are avoidable costs)
    Replacing rolling stock
    Depreciation costs (dependent on alternative rolling stock use).
2. Operating cost savings (+)

Labour costs
Fuel costs
Maintenance costs.

3. Replacement costs on non-passenger services (–)
   Freight and parcels taken by road transport.
4. Connecting services (+)
   Cost savings from closure of branch lines or reduction in main line frequencies.
5. Journey time increases (–)
   where bus journeys will usually be longer than train trips.
6. Journeys not made (–)
   (ie loss of mobility by individuals).
7. Increased car operating costs (–)
   from journeys transferred to car.
8. Increased congestion costs (–)
   from increased passenger and freight traffic flows.
9. Increased accident costs (–)
   from increased traffic flows.
10. Additional road maintenance costs (–)
    avoided by retention of rail service.
11. Resource cost of loss of revenue to British Rail (–)
12. Additional public transport resource costs (–)
    where existing bus services cannot cope or are not used to carry the diverted demand. This cost relates to additional vehicles.
13. Benefits in journey times (+)
    (i) rail passengers who have a bus stop nearer to their homes than the railway station and where the overall express coach journey time is less than the overall travel time using train as the main mode.
    (ii) existing bus users whose service is improved.
14. Loss of output from employment outside the bus industry.
15. Environmental implications
    The increased traffic flow will have an effect on the urban and rural environment with increased noise, pollution and pedestrian–vehicle conflict.

It has been suggested too (CPT, 1996a) that special consideration should be given to categories of costs or benefits that apply only to particular schemes. Some public transport services provide an alternative 'fall-back' route; the removal of others may have long-term effects on land use or the financial viability of town centres (CPT, 1996b) – the continuation of both types might be justified.

Period of evaluation

The evaluation should be carried out for the whole period over which a subsidy is to be paid (ie up to the date of renewal of the subsidy). This might be a five-year period, during which no replacement buses are acquired. A discounted evaluation over a 30-year period should also be carried out for comparison with other transport schemes. Certain costs will apply to particular years and these will be discounted at the factor applicable to that year, eg the purchase of new buses for a route every 14 years.

Standardised data

All data is provided in terms of annual aggregate sums and the same price base should be used. Currently in Britain this is November 1994. Because certain assumptions have to be made in forecasting changes in modal split or in forecasting journeys forgone, a maximum and minimum effect has often to be provided in cost benefit analysis, with a statement of the assumptions involved.

Conclusion

The use of a cost benefit appraisal technique might therefore justify the continuation of the service, although in terms of financial costs and revenue it is not profitable. If limited resources are available, cost benefit analysis can be used to allocate funds between services and assist in drawing up a priority list. There is a real danger when decisions are being made on the rationalisation of public transport passenger services that various criteria will be used, but the disbenefits accruing to the passengers may not be linked to the cost savings accruing from the withdrawal of services. In a situation where a public sector authority provides an operating cost contribution, the use of financial appraisal alone as a method determining rationalisation is limited. Its role lies in allocating the operating costs of the company to particular routes. The decision criteria for rationalisation should be a combination of cost benefit analysis and the overall policy and social considerations to be laid down by the appropriate public sector authority.

New investment in rail infrastructure/services

The analysis above considered rail closures. In evaluating new developments much the same criteria are used (SRA, 2003; Cole, 1976; NATA, 2001; Case Studies 3, 4 and 5). Appraisal of investments in the *commercial railway* is undertaken by financial criteria as this sector is operated according to commercial objectives. Thus no account is given to non-user benefits and user benefits are assumed to be captured in fare revenue changes. The appraisal of investments within the socially necessary railway uses different principles according to whether it is replacement investment (the most cost-effective way to maintain the service) or improvements (evaluated against the generated revenue from fares and other sources and where appropriate any non-user benefits are taken into account) with the assumption that user benefits can be measured by the fare revenue so consumer surplus effects are excluded.

CASE STUDY 1: COST BENEFIT ANALYSIS OF BUS SUBSIDY

A proposed change to a bus service can be evaluated on either of two bases explained above. Normally this will involve the assessment of a whole range of operating options, but to understand the analysis involved one option is considered using cost benefit analysis and cost revenue analysis.

The proposed merger to two bus routes is considered using both economic appraisal and on a commercial basis (Figure 9.3 and Tables 9.5 and 9.6). These are the forms of decision making processes which county councils and bus companies respectively should be using to make decisions following local bus service deregulation.

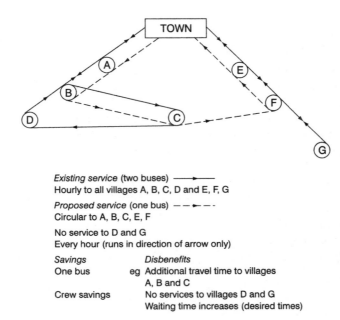

Figure 9.3 *Map of hypothetical routes*

On a cost benefit basis, the changes bring disbenefits and the county council can justify any contractual payments for tendered/franchised services. There will be a priority list for the allocation of contractual (or subsidy) payments. From a commercial point of view, the operation would continue to be unprofitable but with a reduction in deficit (Table 9.6). It could operate as a tendered subsidised service, or with some further changes become a profitable operation. The route costing statements (Chapter 5 Tables 5.1 to 5.3) provide most of this information for bus operations.

In a route costing statement the variable costs and some of the semi-variable costs will be directly related to the service land, but fixed costs can only be significantly reduced when a service level threshold is reached (eg when a depot, garage or infrastructure (eg railway line) is closed). However, the statement does not reflect opportunity cost and so an allowance has to be made for the value of the output in the next most remunerative use of the resources at present used in the production of vehicle-miles. There are a number of reasons for believing that the costing statement does not fully reflect opportunity cost, although it is fair to say that it comes near to an economic base and uses marginal costs to a great extent.

Table 9.5 *Example – cost benefit analysis (£ pa) Year 1 only. Impact on funding authority*

	£
Avoidable resource cost savings	
Capital	4,000
Operating (excluding labour costs)	10,500
Non-passenger services (replacement)	−1,000
Labour	10,500
Connecting services	1,000
Alternative public transport costs (including operating and labour)	−12,000
TOTAL RESOURCE COST SAVINGS	13,000
Loss of benefits	
Additional travelling time	8,000
Journeys not made (consumer surplus)	2,000
Loss of output from employment	3,000
Loss of revenue by operators	
(i) opportunity resource cost	3,000
(ii) feeder services (journeys forgone)	500
Additional car operating costs	3,000
Road cost avoided by retention	500
Additional accident costs	500
TOTAL LOSS OF BENEFIT	20,500
NET DISBENEFIT FROM ADOPTING THIS OPTION	−7,500

Table 9.6 *Financial (cost revenue) analysis (£ pa) Year 1 only. Impact on bus company*

	Existing service £	Proposed service £	Reduction £
Revenue	10,000	7,000	3,000
Expenditure			
Capital	4,000	2,000	2,000
Operating	10,500	5,000	5,500
Labour	10,500	5,000	5,500
Total	25,000	12,000	13,000
Profit (Loss)	(15,000)	(5,000)	10,000

CASE STUDY 2: GREAT BRITAIN – CENTRAL LONDON RAIL STUDY

The Central London Rail Study (CLRS, 1989) was prepared as part of the analysis of alternative transport modes in London and considered alongside the Traffic Assessment Studies (1989). It was a major step forward in the approach to public transport evaluation from the Victoria Line Study (Foster & Beesley, 1963) and provides a useful starting point in the evaluation of an integrated transport policy (Cole, 1976, 1985; Potter & Cole, 1992; Plowden, 1985).

The study considered seven scheme options whose primary objective was to relieve overcrowding on several key metro/national railways routes into London and to reduce road traffic flows. Cost estimates were affected by the tunnel diameter, the ground conditions and the number and complexity of stations. Rolling stock costs were dependent on the peak train requirement. Cross Rail for example would require few additional trains as through running would result in better use of existing trains. The Chelsea Hackney scheme would however require new trains, a new depot and sidings.

The benefits for each scheme include time savings to existing users, reduced congestion on trains and in stations, revenue from generated traffic relief of road congestion and a reduction in road accidents (Table 9.7). The Jubilee Line (in its original form, which is not the version as built) did not achieve any great reduction in journey time, particularly when compared with the Chelsea-Hackney Scheme and Thameslink Metro, whose main benefits derive from time saving and congestion reductions. The Cross Rail schemes all showed high reductions in over-crowding, road congestion and journey times into central London.

Thus while none of the schemes could be justified on a financial basis with revenue/cost ratios all under 0.3, the economic benefits/cost ratios in the cost

Table 9.7 *Estimated benefit–cost ratios of new rail schemes based on Tables 9.8 and 9.9*

Benefits as a proportion of total annual cost	To public transport users	To road users	Revenue	Total gain
Single Line Schemes				
Chelsea-Hackney	0.6	0.1	0.1	0.9
Jubilee Line Extension to Ilford	0.4	0.1	0.1	0.6
Thameslink Metro	1.5	0.3	0.3	2.1
East-West Crossrail	1.2	0.2	0.2	1.6
North-South Crossrail	0.6	0.1	0.1	0.9
East-South Crossrail	1.4	0.3	0.3	1.9
Two Line Packages				
Full Crossrail	0.9	0.2	0.2	1.3
East-West Crossrail plus Chelsea-Hackney	0.8	0.2	0.2	1.1
Rows may not sum up due to rounding				

Source: CLRS (1989); TfL (2003)

benefit analysis are considerably higher, at 0.6 to 2.1 (Tables 9.7, 9.8 and 9.9). The enhancement of employment opportunities or regeneration of inner city areas could also be included in the analysis through the most recent techniques (NATA, 2001). The land development and land value effects also need to be considered and the landowners who achieve development 'gain' should be part-investors in a new railway (CLRS, 1989) with investments as in the Docklands Light Railway and the Heathrow/Paddington Express. The experience of the final version of the Jubilee Line Extension (JLE) however showed that a figure of £400m investment capital put forward by property developers at Canary Wharf was very attractive if discounted over five years and applied to a total cost of £1 bn. However cost escalations and discounting of private capital over a longer period reduces the real value of such investment. The JLE was also seen as a factor in regenerating areas south of the river Thames at Bermondsey and Borough (HL, 2002).

The sensitivity analysis indicates that 'the results depend critically on the planning assumptions. Lower employment levels would deflate benefits roughly proportionately. If costs exceed the estimates, the case for the schemes would be similarly weakened. On the other hand, further employment growth would inflate benefits rather more than in proportion as crowding levels would become severe' (CLRS, 1989). The estimate of benefits may be more cautious than will ultimately prove to be the case. Despite the 1980s recession, travel into London has continued to grow and the forecasts (see Figure 8.2) indicate a higher rate of growth than was assumed in 1989.

Table 9.8 *Costs of new rail schemes (£m) 1998 prices*

	Capital cost of construction	Rolling stock costs	Equivalent annual capital costs	Annual operating costs	Total equivalent annual cost
Single Line Schemes					
Chelsea-Hackney (M)	1000	330	110	40	150
Jubilee Line Extension to Ilford (M)	560	80	55	15	70
Thameslink Metro (H)	260	70	25	25	50
East-West Crossrail (H)	870	15	75	10	85
North-South Crossrail (H)	650	50	60	10	70
Two Line Packages					
Full Crossrail Rail	1710	70	150	20	170
East-West Crossrail plus Chelsea-Hackney	1870	345	185	50	235

Sources: CLRS (1989); TfL (2003)

Notes:
1. Capital cost discounted at 7% per annum over 60 years (35 years for trains)
2. Construction cost spread over a five year period prior to line opening.
(M) Tunnel diameter Metro 3.85m.
(H) Tunnel diameter heavy rail 5.9m.

Table 9.9 *Estimated benefits of new rail schemes (£m p.a.) 1998 prices*

	Time savings	Crowding relief	Total public transport users' benefit	Road user's benefit	Additional rail revenue	Total benefit
Single line Schemes						
Chelsea-Hackney	60	30	90	20	20	130
Jubilee Line Extension to Ilford	5	25	30	5	5	40
Thameslink Metro	55	20	75	15	5	105
East-West Crossrail	30	70	100	20	20	140
North-South Crossrail	40	15	55	10	10	75
East-South Crossrail	55	40	95	20	20	135
Two Line Packages						
Full Crossrail Rail	70	85	155	30	30	215
East-West Crossrail plus Chelsea-Hackney	90	100	190	40	40	270

Sources: CLRS (1989); TfL (2003)

CASE STUDY 3: GREAT BRITAIN – STRATEGIC RAIL AUTHORITY

The elements used by the strategic rail authority (SRA) in Great Britain are those set out in New Approach to Transport Appraisal (Chapter 10, Case Study 1).

Table 9.10 *The NATA criteria applied to railways: five criteria and checklist of impacts*

	Passenger services	**Freight services**
Environment	Noise and vibration Local air quality Global atmospheric emissions Land and water pollution Landscape and townscape Biodiversity Heritage	Noise and vibration Local air quality Global atmospheric emissions Land and water pollution Landscape and townscape Biodiversity Heritage
Safety	Road and rail accidents Personal security	Road and rail accidents Security
Economy	Transport economic Efficiency Reliability and punctuality Economic regeneration Impacts Transitional costs of change Station facilities and rolling stock quality Crowding	Transport economic Efficiency Reliability and punctuality Economic regeneration Impacts Transitional costs of change Station facilities and rolling stock quality Crowding
Accessibility	Barriers to rail travel Quality of interchange Severance Option values Ticketing and information facilities	Access to the network Quality of interchange Severance Option values
Integration	Contribution 10 Year Plan objectives Policies and proposals for other modes Wider government policy Land use policy and proposals	Contribution 10 Year Plan objectives Policies and proposals for other modes Wider government policy Land use policy and proposals

Source: Strategic Rail Authority, Appraisal Criteria, April 2003

The objective is to find the optimum value solution based on a consistent set of assumptions across all projects which because of factors such as economic growth rate variations may not be possible. There is also a need for a comparative analysis tool (the base case) against which to compare the options. This may be, though not always, the 'do nothing' solution. The evaluation is also dynamic and may require several reviews (as in Case Study 4).

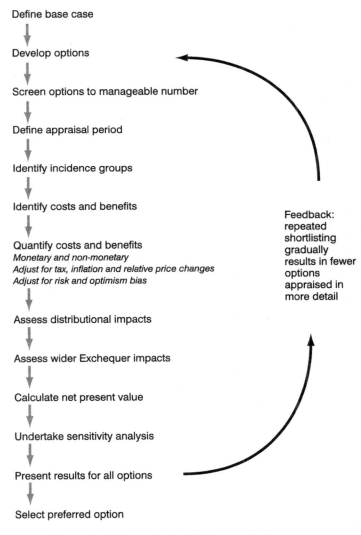

Figure 9.4 *Steps in the SRA appraisal process*
Source: Strategic Rail Authority, 2003

Table 9.11 *Checklist of incidence groups*

Consumers	Passengers	– Business
		– Commuters
		– Leisure
	Users of freight services	– End user
	Non-users	
		– Shipper
		– Travellers by other modes
		– Road hauliers
		– Non-travellers
		– Local residents
		– Non-UK residents
		– Different income groups
		– Minority groups
		– Businesses
Operators/providers	Network Rail	
	Train operating companies	
	Freight operating companies	
	Rolling stock suppliers	– Leasing companies (ROSOCOs)
		– Manufacturers
	Other public transport operators	
Funding agencies	SRA	
	Other central Government	
	Local government	
Private sector Partners Taxpayers		

Source: SRA

The appraisal process also identifies groups affected by a rail scheme.

Passenger service upgrade example

Consider a major commuter service with peak period overcrowding, where there are limited modal options and where journeys are dictated by working hours. This would be a case where fares might be used to move demand into the 'shoulder' or 'off-peak' periods but from a journey purpose viewpoint that would be unacceptable. It might also be prevented by fares policy.

The range of options could include:

- optimised use of existing capacity;
- larger trains;

- modifying the layout of carriages and crowding standards;
- changes to fare level and structure;
- increased capacity.

Capacity in this case study was initially increased through larger trains but the longer term best value solution was a higher service frequency.

Solutions may be appraised individually or together but the best value solution was a combination of:

- infrastructure upgrade, allowing an increase in service frequency;
- improving one large interchange station;
- refurbishing rolling stock to replace existing poor quality stock or to increase frequency.

The important aspects of the appraised process are:

- Cost estimates refined through a clearer knowledge of design and extent of the work to be done.
- Detailed risk analysis covering costs and revenue streams. The split of risk between private and public sectors is important as private funding requires a higher rate of return (see Chapter 10).
- Estimating the life of the assets, eg track infrastructure, 20 years; station buildings and platforms, 50 years.
- Calculating disruption costs.
- Rolling stock costs (usually leasing).
- Operating costs.
- Train operator margin and overhead recovery.
- Unpriced user benefits:
  - time related savings;
  - crowding relief;
  - reliability and punctuality improvements;
  - improvements in station and rolling stock quality.
- Non-user benefits:
  - external cost of road congestion;
  - environmental impacts.
- Accidents.

The analysis of these elements will result in a net present value (NPV) benefit/cost radio at 2003 prices (see Table 9.12).

The application of time values (Table 9.12) and other elements provides the overall numerical appraisal in the 'transport efficiency table' (Table 9.13). The passenger upgrade example is discussed here but the technique may be applied to freight and other passenger investments.

The final stage is to use the NATA (2001) appraisal summary table to relate the analysis of the passenger upgrade scheme to the Department of Transport, Scottish Executive and National Assembly for Wales integrated transport evaluation process (Chapter 12).

Table 9.12 *Time values in SRA appraisals*

Time	Market segment £p/minute/hour		
	Business	**Commute**	**Leisure**
In-vehicle (m)	0.24	0.12	0.09
(h)	14.2	7.2	5.4
Waiting (m)	0.41	0.20	0.15
(h)	24.6	12.0	9.0
Walking (m)	0.46	0.23	0.17
(h)	27.6	13.8	10.2

Source: SRA Appraisal Criteria (2003)

Table 9.13 *SRA transport efficiency analysis – passenger upgrade example*

Impact	NPV £000 2003 prices		
Financial impacts			
Capital costs	−42,849		
Operating costs	−8,153		
Rolling stock costs	−31,140		
Net additional revenue	11,248		
TOC profit	−4,930		
Net financial effect	**−75,824**		
Unpriced benefits			
General impacts			
Disruption costs	−1,144		
Residual value	62		
Passenger service impacts		Road	Rail
Time savings	37,743	5,422	32,321
Crowding relief benefits	72,113		
Reliability and punctuality	14,261		
Safety benefits	374		
Station quality	13,347		
Rolling stock quality	1,566		
Total unpriced benefits	**138,322**		
NPV net benefits	**62,498**		
SRA funding			
Capital grant	42,849		
Revenue support	28,045		
Total (K)	**70,894**		
Other funding			
Developer contributions	0		
Other government			
Grant/subsidy payments	0		
Tax revenues	0		
Total	0		
Benefit/cost ratio	1.7		
NPV/K	0.88		

Table 9.14 *Appraisal summary table – passenger upgrade example*

NPV £62 million NPV subsidy: £71 million

	Objectives	Qualitative impacts	Quantitative measure	Value PV £m
ENVIRONMENT	Noise and vibration	The proposal will have a marginal impact on noise levels for houses and businesses along the railway line because of the increased frequency of trains. GIS information suggested that 40,000 households are located within 500 metres of the track and therefore affected by higher frequencies early in the morning (6.30 am–9 am). Localised effects will be partially offset by the abstraction of passenger journeys from road to rail. Noise and vibration effects will occur during the construction of infrastructure works.	40,000 households located within 500 metres of the track affected. Low relative increase in frequency.	N/A
	Air pollution emissions	Provision of additional train services increase air pollution emissions at a national level via electricity production. Abstraction of passenger journeys from road to rail will contribute towards reducing air borne emissions and off-set localised dust emissions likely to occur during the construction of infrastructure proposals.	15,000 households affected by emissions during construction phase.	N/A
	Landtake (Landscape, townscape, biodiversity, heritage, water)	The proposal does not involve any additional landtake, and there are no significant biodiversity or landscape impacts to note. The station investment would have a minor impact on the façade of the main station building, which is a Grade 2 listed building. The capital cost of this work therefore incorporates the additional cost of complying with local planning restrictions.	N/A	N/A
	Greenhouse gases	Provision of additional train services will increase emissions at a national level. In principle, the abstraction passenger journeys from road onto rail will contribute to a reduction of carbon dioxide emissions. However, the scope for modal switch is limited and the impact on global emissions will be marginal.	N/A	N/A
SAFETY	Accidents	There may be safety benefits associated with modal shift, i.e. people transferring from road to rail and thereby benefiting from the inherently safety advantage of rail. However, these benefits are marginal given the limited scope for modal switching in this example. The proposal also includes some station investment on tactile paving and handrails, designed to help reduce the risk of passenger injury.	Accident reduction equivalent to one fatality every 50 years and one major injury every four years	PV £0.4m
	Personal security	The availability of additional staff at the station will help to improve passenger perceptions of personal security particularly late at night.	300,000 relevant station users affected every year.	N/A

Table 9.14 continued

NPV £62 million NPV subsidy: £71 million

Objectives	Qualitative impacts	Quantitative measure	Value PV £m
ECONOMY Journey time and frequency	This project is forecast to reduce journey times between certain origins and destinations. It will also increase service frequency, so that passengers are more likely to be able to travel at, or close to, their preferred departure time, and interchanging passengers will not have to spend as long waiting for their connection. The station investment will also benefit passengers by reducing the amount of time spent walking at their connecting station.	Average time savings per journey: 2 minutes in-vehicle 5 minutes walk time 3 minutes wait time	PV £38m
Crowding	Crowding relief is the main justification for this project. The train operator is breaching the PIXC limit of 4.5% in either peak or 3% overall. PIXC for TOC A is currently 6% during the morning peak and the project is expected to reduce it to 0.5% during the first year after opening.	PIXC reduced from 6% to 0.5%.	PV £72m
Performance	The additional capacity delivered by this scheme is forecast to reduce average lateness by an average of one minute on a number of flows, which would affect around 800,000 passengers.	Average lateness reduced by 1 minute per journey for 1.5 million passengers per annum.	PV £14m
Station facilities and rolling stock quality	The station investment will deliver better real time information, i.e. Information about actual arrival and departure times of trains relative to the timetable. More staff will be available on station platforms and concourse to assist passengers. This would benefit primarily passengers originating and interchanging at the station. Two of the refurbished units were not used to increase frequency, but rather to improve quality by replacing existing stock of a poorer standard. Therefore, a small proportion of passengers would experience better quality rolling stock compared with the do-minimum scenario and this benefit would not be reflected in revenue through fares increase.	1.4 million station users benefit per annum	PV £15m
Financial costs and revenues	It was estimated from demand forecasting work using Planet that revenue to TOC A would be PV £17 million over the appraisal period. Of this figure, PV£6 million represents revenue abstracted from neighbouring TOCs, giving net additional rail revenue of PV£11 million. These revenue figures compare with a risk-adjusted capital cost of PV£43 million, additional rolling stock lease costs of PV£31 million and incremental operating costs of PV£8 million.		Net financial effect: PV minus £76m

Table 9.14 *continued*

	Objectives	Qualitative impacts	NPV £62 million NPV subsidy: £71 million Quantitative measure	Value PV £m
ECONOMY	Wider economic impacts	This proposal does not affect any designated regeneration areas directly. However, it will have some impact on the labour supply to London by easing capacity constraints in the commuter market.	N/A	N/A
ACCESSIBILITY	Reduction of barriers	Station quality improvements will improve accessibility for some market segments.	200,000 relevant station users affected.	N/A
	Severance	Higher frequency services will increase waiting time at five level crossings along the route by approximately eight minutes per hour during the morning and evening peak periods.	Waiting time increased by 8 minutes per hour during morning peak at 5 level crossings.	N/A
	Option values	Not applicable	N/A	N/A
INTEGRATION		The station investment will create a better quality interchange and facilitate cross-modal interchange. The proposal is fully in line with the Government's objectives for the SRA and for transport in general. However, in terms of distributional impacts, it is likely to primarily benefit commuters, who comprise a relatively high-income group.	N/A	N/A

Source: SRA Appraisal Criteria (2003)

CASE STUDY 4: EUROPEAN COMMISSION – SOCIALLY NECESSARY RAILWAY SERVICES

Background and definitions

Background

The EC White Paper 'A Strategy for Revitalising the Community's Railways' concluded that a new kind of railways should allow for more customer oriented, less expensive, more efficient services being provided using less subsidy. Already a number of policy initiatives at national and European level are being implemented following the recommendations from the White Paper, including the framework for provision of public services. Several studies have identified that railways across Europe face problems due to declining market share, lack of response to market changes and customers' needs and related high subsidy requirements, and insufficient managerial independence which should be provided through contracts between state and operator, rather than obligations imposed by the state (ECMT, 1993). The key elements in these contracts are planned to be better value for money and more efficient services, with explicit and transparent compensation and limited time contracts. This development is supported through the EC Council Regulation 1893/91 although this regulation allows for continued public service obligations with respect to 'undertakings confined to the operation of urban, suburban and regional services'.

This case study will present the results from EC funded project SONERAIL (Fourth Framework) (Cole and Holvad, 2001) on the role of socially necessary rail services (not infrastructure), which under EC regulations 1191/69 and 1893/91 cannot be provided on a commercial basis and may therefore be financially supported by a member state. The project sought a definition of socially necessary rail services and the cost benefit evaluation criteria used in the specification of public service contracts for the future provision and support to loss-making rail services.

SONERAIL overview

The overall aim of SONERAIL was to examine the role of socially necessary rail services in order to improve the decision-making basis regarding the provision and funding of such services.

Its specific objectives were to:

- define concepts of socially necessary rail services;
- develop an evaluation methodology for socially necessary rail services;
- apply the evaluation methodology;
- identify and examine operations scenarios;
- consider passenger transport not freight;

- consider rail services not infrastructure;
- analyse the demand side rather than supply side;
- consider heavy rail with other forms seen as alternative public transport provision;
- address the issues in the countries represented in the SONERAIL Consortium (2000).

Definitions of socially necessary rail services

The SONERAIL definition of a socially necessary rail service is one with a positive net social value calculated with reference to the social benefits and costs identified for users as well as non-users of the service, although available literature on rail reveals that the concept of a socially necessary rail service is not clear cut. The basis of the definition is, therefore, where generalised costs are significantly affected by changes in level of service provision (reduction or increase) and where there are measurable externalities (such as environmental effects). Thus, the definitions are linked to the evaluation stage of rail services. A rail service will only be identified as socially necessary if evaluation shows a positive net social value. Calculation of the social value includes all relevant impacts which are measurable. Thus the definition phase provides an objective tool to assess socially necessary rail services without including either political factors or the common association between socially necessary rail services and their financial profitability in the analysis.

Usually, loss-making services are defined as socially necessary services. It is possible that profitable rail services are socially necessary, but are in a position to generate a financial profit without social benefits. On the other hand, it is also possible that a service is loss-making and not socially necessary. In this way, a service can be defined as socially necessary if:

- it is financially profit-making or loss-making; and
- the social benefits are larger than the social costs (see Figure 9.5).

The SONERAIL evaluation methodology

Overview of the SONERAIL evaluation methodology

Whether a rail service is financially profitable or not (ie whether a subsidy is required to secure the provision of the rail service) has to be determined, but the financial profitability of a rail service could be determined outside this type of methodology. The core element of the aim of the socially necessary railway evaluation methodology is a social appraisal of those rail services for which a subsidy is required and whether it can be justified and provided. This appraisal will consist of two stages:

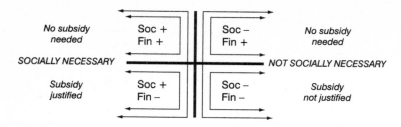

Figure 9.5 *Interaction of elements*
Source: Sonerail report, European Commission, 2001

- The social benefits and the social costs are assessed in monetary terms, for a given rail service. If the benefits outweigh the costs, the rail service is characterised as socially profitable in monetary terms, and a subsidy can be justified.
- The funding required to support all socially and monetarily profitable services is compared to the available budget. Only if a rail service is characterised as socially profitable in monetary terms and the budget is sufficient can a rail service be justified. An insufficient budget will result in subsidy being paid to rail services. This equates to the SRA's 'affordability' test.

The social appraisal can thus result in two outcomes:

- A rail service is socially profitable in monetary terms and there is a sufficient budget such that subsidy can be given.
- A rail service is not allocated a subsidy.

The second outcome can be caused by the following two reasons:

- A rail service is socially unprofitable in monetary terms.
- Insufficient budget combined with the existence of other rail services with higher social value.

If the budget is sufficient it may be possible to support not only the socially profitable services but also some of those for which the monetary benefits are less than the monetary costs. The extreme case is when the budget is sufficient to allow for support to all financially unprofitable services.

If the social appraisal of a rail service does not justify a subsidy a number of measures/policies can be suggested to improve its financial/socioeconomic position.

- business process re-engineering (BPR) of the rail service to reduce costs and/or improve revenue;
- to provide the service through other public transport modes with a better cost or revenue structure;

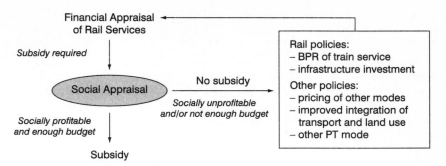

Figure 9.6 *Overview of the SONERAIL evaluation methodology*
Source: Sonerail report, European Commission, 2001

- through investment, eg by changing from diesel operated trains to electric operated trains;
- pricing of other modes;
- improved integration of transport and land use.

The applied pricing mechanisms of other modes can have an influence on the competitiveness of the rail mode, eg internalising the external costs of car travel, and land use policies could be utilised.

This methodology evaluates the service at present in socioeconomic terms. As Figure 9.6 shows, the next stage is to identify changes and re-evaluate the service to see if the cost improvements now justify a subsidy to cover the economic benefits. However, it does not include a BPR model. That is the next stage in the discussion process on whether or not to retain a rail service.

The appraisal is designed to provide recommendations for decisions regarding subsidies to financially unprofitable rail services, but the techniques should be applicable irrespective of the financial position.

CBA element

The CBA element of the SONERAIL evaluation methodology (SEM) assesses the monetary value of impacts following the closure of an existing individual rail service (or a complete network). Impacts are defined as the difference of having and not having the rail service and to which it is possible to assign monetary weights. Table 9.15 provides an overview of the impacts on different groups. Some impacts may have a net effect (shown as * in the table) but all should be evaluated.

MCA element

Multi-criteria analysis (MCA) is the next stage following the calculation of the net-benefit result for each rail service examined in the CBA.

Table 9.15 *SEM impacts*

	Costs of closure = benefits of retention	Benefits of closure = costs of retention
Former train travellers who change mode	Travel time change (commuter, leisure, business). Change in efficiency of business travel. Loss of consumers' surplus. Costs of other mode.*	Saving train costs (the fare).*
Existing car travellers	Change in congestion costs. Change in operating costs (fuel).*	
Train company	Change in revenues (excluding subsidy).* Change in subsidy.*	Change in costs.
Government	Change in costs of road maintenance.	Change in subsidy to train.*
Former train travellers who do not travel	Travel opportunities loss Loss of consumer surplus.	Saving of travel time. Saving of train costs (the fare)*.
Society	Change in emissions. Change in noise (inside/outside). Change in safety/accidents.	
Other		Change in revenues: oil companies/ garages.* Change in revenues: other transport modes*

Source: Sonerail report, European Commission 2001

Net-benefit value may be positive or negative. The rail services in the two groups will be ranked separately in order to ensure that the trade-offs between monetary and non-monetary impacts are reduced so that it is not possible for a rail service with negative net-benefits to be higher ranked than one with positive net-benefits.

The MCA elements are shown in Table 9.16.

In addition, the estimated net-benefit value is included as a composite measure for the monetary impacts.

Data for the non-monetary impacts can be based on quantitative or qualitative indicators depending on data availability and resources available. In most cases the non-monetary impacts related to the closure of a rail service will be measured through expert statements on the basis of an ordinal scale. The ranking procedure can be applied for both types of data source, but below the procedure will be outlined with reference to the situation with expert based statements about impacts. For each of the rail services the impacts of closure/retention should be recorded. The impacts should be indicated according to a seven-point scale:

+++	large positive impact
++	positive impact
+	small positive impact
0	neutral
−	small negative impact
− −	negative impact
− − −	large negative impact

A positive impact implies that the retention of a service involves benefits (eg higher level of employment compared to the situation without the rail service). Table 9.16 shows three services.

The ranking of the services will, in addition to the information about impacts, require indications regarding the relative importance of the various impacts (weights). The MCA ranking here is based on regime analysis (see Nijkamp and Blaas, 1994). This method is well suited in situations where some or all information is ordinally measured. The method is based on pairwise comparison of the rail services for the various impacts, and requires the relative order of the various impacts to be defined along

Table 9.16 *An MCA example*

	Service 1	Service 2	Service 3
Change in chemical pollutants	++	+	++
Change in flora/fauna	+	++	++
Change in visual intrusion	+	+	++
Change in vibration	−	+	++
Change in employment	0	++	+
Change in productivity	− −	++	+
Change in actual GDP as proportion of potential GDP	− − −	+	+
Change in stress levels for car travellers	+	0	−
Change in stress levels for inhabitants	+	0	−
CBA net-benefits (normalised)	0.7	0.3	1.0

Source: Sonerail report, European Commission 2001

with an assumption that the total weighting adds up to 1, a calculation outside the scope of this book, which assumes a weighting process for each impact based on the regime analysis.

The outcome is a ranking score for each rail service. This is the probability of a service performing better than the other services within the sample, so that the highest ranked service (the highest probability of best performance) is followed by the second one, the third one etc.

Recommendation for subsidy allocation could be based on the calculated ranking score as well as information about subsidy required for each service.

Application of the methodology

Objectives and approach

The SONERAIL evaluation methodology was applied to 25 rail services in the following countries:

- Great Britain (four rail services);
- Netherlands (nine);
- Czech Republic (three);
- Germany (three);
- Greece (three); and
- Italy (three).

Among these 25 services a total of 15 services appeared to be socially profitable in monetary terms, ie higher monetary benefits than costs. The annual net-benefits ranged from –4 million ECU to +5 million ECU, although only 4 services had net-benefits less than –0.5 million ECU. The results show that the main impacts associated with a rail closure were:

- avoidable rail costs;
- loss in consumers' surplus for the former rail travellers;
- travel opportunity loss for those travellers who decide not to travel;
- travel time effects;
- accident costs.

Avoidable rail costs and travel opportunity lost are the most important. Therefore, it is of crucial importance to estimate correctly the avoidable costs and the proportion of former rail travellers who choose not to travel if the rail service is closed.

On the basis of the results obtained it can be concluded that a socially profitable rail service (in monetary terms) is one with:

- high patronage;
- low cost of operation;
- relatively low journey times;
- lack of alternative modes.

Future scenarios

Possible scenarios

Future scenarios were identified on the basis of likely key influencing factors over a 10-year period covering the short, medium and long term. The scenarios reflect the range of policy initiatives currently being implemented or considered to revitalise rail services in Europe (TRaC/STM 1999). If policies are successful it can lead to reduced cost of providing rail services, increased demand and hence improved financial and social viability. However, the scenario assessment results indicate that the improvements might be insufficient for some rail services to show a positive social benefit value measured in monetary terms. Key elements in any improvement of the position of rail services appear to be:

- the extent to which cost efficiency gains can be achieved;
- the approach to infrastructure access charges, which can increase the cost of providing rail services and lead to the services becoming financially non-viable and/or requiring increased subsidies.

Action plans for case study services

Action plans for the case study services were specified on the basis of an analysis of key issues that would influence these services over the short, medium and long term period, reflecting the aftermath of rail privatisation, pending privatisation, state ownership and transition from a planned economy to a market economy for the eastern European countries. This results in a diversity of action plan proposals, which all evolve around the themes of increasing patronage, reducing costs and measures to instigate a reduction in car use through transfer from road to rail. The need to increase patronage (and revenue) and reduce costs is in general related to subsidy reductions and/or increases in access charges. On the other hand there is scope for increasing rail demand due to the possible introduction of road pricing combined with an overall increase in travel demand. Action plans could include:

- improvements in rolling stock;
- track and signalling to allow faster service speeds;
- station facilities;
- integration with other modes;
- consideration to provision by other modes, eg light rail or bus services.

CASE STUDY 5: SWEDEN – RAIL INFRASTRUCTURE COMPANY, BANVERKET (BV)

In January 1989 the state railway was reorganised into two separate organisations: Statens Järnvägar (SJ) responsible for operating train services, and the National Rail Administration, Banverket (BV) responsible for the provision and maintenance of rail infrastructure.

BV operates to social objectives since its income comes from the Government with approximately 16% originating from the track charges paid by the train operators and is used to finance operating costs and investments in infrastructure. The investment appraisal procedures take into account wider social costs and benefits within a cost-benefit analysis framework applied across all modes. Potential investments on main lines are proposed to the Government by BV. Investment principles, general goals and total investment volume are decided by parliament with BV taking decisions within the budget.

The evaluation manual assumes that values of costs and benefits are measured in fixed (eg 2004) prices and future costs and benefits are discounted using a discount factor of 4% over a project life of 60 years.

Each potential investment project is compared to a reference project (eg the do-nothing project or postponement of renewal investments) and cover new investments, renewal investments closure/reopening of lines. Several mutually exclusive projects are considered with the objective of selecting the best alternative.

The socio-economic appraisal includes the following elements:

- Construction costs
- Operating costs of rail infrastructure (including renewal investments)
- Operating costs of train services
- Revenue of train services
- Accessibility
- Travel time
- Frequency
- Road-rail crossings
- Accidents
- Road travellers' costs
- Non-corrected external effects
- Pollution
- Wear and tear (other modes)
- Accidents (other modes)
- Congestion including traffic monitoring (road)
- Noise
- Barrier effects
- Producer surplus for freight operators.

The definition of each of the elements is not dissimilar to that in the UK. Three elements in particular deserve additional attention:

a) The transfer of traffic from other modes to rail as a result of infrastructure investment can engender positive external effects on pollution, accidents and congestion, in particular for the transfer from road to rail. If the marginal costs of these elements are larger than the user charges per vehicle kilometre then the difference represents external costs. The transfer of traffic is a benefit to society and is valued according to the marginal external costs.

b) Rail investments can introduce so-called barrier effects in the form of visual disturbance, perceived risks, annoyance from increased waiting times and longer journeys in relation to road-rail crossings. To some extent these can be quantified following the procedures for the calculation of costs to road travellers as the result of road-rail crossings but many effects can only be assessed qualitatively.

c) The effects of rail investments on freight customers' producer surplus can be illustrated by the following example. A new railway is constructed between X and Y and this implies that enterprises which today send goods by road may transfer them to the railway with 100,000 ton goods expected to be transferred to rail. As a result the transport cost for this quantity decreases by SKR 20/tonne for the freight customers. The socio-economic value of the increased producer surplus will thus amount to SKR 2 million.

Spatial effects are not considered in the appraisal framework. Infrastructure investments can have significant impacts on employment during and after the implementation of a rail infrastructure project as well as other impacts on the regional economic structure.

The use of cost-benefit analysis implies less attention is given to impacts which cannot easily be translated into monetary terms. The extension of cost-benefit analysis to a form of multicriteria analysis (see Case Study 4) would establish a framework where such impacts are accounted for.

CASE STUDY 6: GERMANY – FEDERAL TRAFFIC INFRASTRUCTURE PLAN

Transport policy in Germany (1996) in the 1990s focuses on three main aspects:

- the link between transport and environment;
- German unification;
- European integration.

Specifically, the investment activities are focused on:

- the basic reconstruction and improvement of the infrastructure in the former DDR;
- the establishment of a high-speed network of the railways in Germany and Europe;
- the elimination of capacity bottlenecks in the railway network;
- investments in road construction in West Germany and the former DDR;
- an increase of the capacity of aviation.

Project appraisal procedures

The selection of projects is based on two central principles:

- overall traffic forecasts for all modes of transport;
- uniform criteria for the assessment of projects.

Four elements are involved in the project assessment:

- overall economic assessment (cost-benefit analysis);
- ecological assessment;
- down-planning assessment;
- additional criteria

The project assessment involves both a cost-benefit analysis as well as multicriteria-oriented elements (ecological assessment, town-planning assessment, additional criteria) these additional elements cover those project impacts which cannot be satisfactorily included in a cost-benefit analysis.

The *economic assessment* includes the following criteria:

- **Reduction of transportation costs**:
  - reduction of vehicle standing costs
  - reduction of vehicle operating costs
  - avoidance of modal shifts
- **Maintenance of traffic infrastructure**:
  - renewal of traffic infrastructure
  - maintenance of traffic infrastructure
- **Improvement of traffic safety**
- **Improvement of accessibility**
- **Spatial advantages:**
  - employment effects during construction of traffic routes
  - employment effects during operation of traffic routes
  - advantages of spatial structure
  - promotion of international exchanges on information and efficiency
- **Environmental benefits:**
  - reduction of noise
  - reduction of exhaust fumes

- reduction of separation effects
- reduction of impairment on living quality and communication
- **Benefits from other than traffic-related effects**
- **Investment costs**

The project impacts for these criteria are translated into monetary units according to standardised values. Total benefits and costs are calculated and the overall economic worth is summarised by the benefit-cost ratio (B/C). If the benefits are larger than the costs, the project is considered to be worthwhile from an economic point of view.

Although the cost-benefit analysis includes some allowance for environmental impacts it is required to undertake a formal environmental impact assessment and because additional impacts on urban areas are likely to exist, an urban development assessment is undertaken as well.

Criticism of project appraisal procedures

1. The evaluation emphasises only single projects without consideration given to the combined effects obtained as the result of implementing a range of interrelated projects.
2. Although other evaluation elements, in addition to cost-benefit analysis, are included in the project appraisal, the cost-benefit analysis has the most important role in determining the priority of projects. The priority of a project is determined by the benefit-cost ratio, while the other evaluation elements can only upgrade or downgrade a project according to definitions about the project impacts. An integrated approach could be achieved by simultaneous consideration to the different impacts of the project.

CASE STUDY 7: THE NETHERLANDS – RAIL SERVICE EVALUATION

The evaluation of contract payments (subsidy) to rail services in The Netherlands is looked at in two ways:

- cost revenue analysis by NS Verkeersleiding, the company operating passenger trains (along with its fellow companies covering cargo, stations and real estate in NS Groep NV) whose objective is to be financially viable
- cost benefit analysis by the Dutch Government

The Government determined to replace subsidy with contract payments and NSV have to identify which services would close if no payments were made. The Government then makes one of four decisions:

1) not pay at all and close the service
2) pay NSV
3) pay another railway company
4) switch to bus replacement

The evaluation criteria are related to peak demand where maximum use may justify confirmation of the service rather than replacement by a possibly more frequent bus service and to overall demand for the service. The financially profitable services continue to be operated by NS (1997) with some unprofitable feeder services; all unprofitable services are offered for contract operation on a franchise basis or on an innovation basis where demand is so low that a new approach is required, eg Lavers NV operation on the Haarlem-Iolanda branch line with improved marketing but no integration of tickets with the connecting service to Amsterdam Centraal.

In the evaluation of all lines only one (Almelo-Marienburg) with a cost coverage ratio of 16 per cent did not meet the required ratio based on a cost and revenue allocation model NS Riezigers (1997). The first evaluation is followed by a more sophisticated second level process (Case Study 3).

Second level social appraisal

1. Financial criteria: the cost coverage ratio must exceed 40 per cent of costs (excluding maintenance of infrastructure)
2. Transport related criteria:
   (a) peak hour use where the demand level has to be at a minimum to justify a train (300 passengers per peak hour). This implies that at lower levels of demand there would be more suitable modes (eg for 10 pax/hour a taxi frequency of 4/hour might be more appropriate)
   (b) overall use with high peak load factors and low off peak numbers.
3. Regional socially oriented criteria used by local government to maintain services through payment of the contract price. Local government would then decide between local bus or train services. This regional evaluation process might use different criteria or basis for contract payments (eg on the revenue earned or passengers carried).

Railned evaluation criteria

A report on infrastructure is produced every five years by Railned (1995) (the organisation responsible for capital investment in and operation of the rail infrastructure (track and signals)). Its particular set of criteria may vary between programmes but are essentially a comparison of costs and benefits using a priority list methodology (PLM) for infrastructure schemes comparing monetary values of benefits with the cost of the infrastructure investment scheme.

Table 9.17 *Criteria used by Railned in scheme evaluation*

		Measure	
A.	***Quality of Transport***		
	Criteria	PLM	
	Monetary values		
	Change in travel time (pax)	CBA	Minutes/year
	Change in freight journey times	CBA	Minutes/year
	Change in number of travellers	CBA	Total pax/year
	Change in tonnage of freight	CBA	Total tonnage/year
	Non-monetary terms		
	Reliability of network	MCA	Qualitative
	Comfort	MCA	Qualitative
	Reducing bottlenecks in railway system	–	
	Interchange with other public transport	MCA	Qualitative
	Water crossing for freight delays	MCA	Qualitative
B.	***Other Government objectives***		
	Criteria	PLM	
	Change in congestion	CBA	Part qualitative/ quantitative
	Change in car mileage	CBA	Number of miles
	New housing locations (near station)	MCA	Qualitative
	Better services for Schipol/Rotterdam airports	–	Qualitative
	Contracts for non-profitable services (rail)		Qualitative
	Environment	MCA	
	Rail safety	MCA	
	Future planning consistency		
C.	***Interest of transporters***		
	Exploitation costs	CBA	Monetary value (guilders)
	Return on investment (commercial)	–	Qualitative

Source: Railned Capaciteitsplanning/DEEL 1: Algeman-Bijlagen/Notitie Randvoor waarden/ April 1995.

The format used traditional cost benefit analysis criteria and multicriteria analysis for criteria now considered by the Dutch Government to be important in developing a sustainable transport policy.

CASE STUDY 8: EUROPEAN BANK FOR RECONSTRUCTION AND DEVELOPMENT (EBRD)

One objective of EBRD is to assist the transfer of ex-Soviet Union states in central and eastern Europe in the 'transition towards an open market-oriented economies and to promote private enterprise' (EBRD, 1991). It does this through structural and sector (eg transport sector) economic reforms, subject to an 'environmentally sound and sustainable development', using an Environmental Impact Assessment.

The environmental objectives are in line with European Union policy and all transport projects undergo environmental appraisal which like the economic, financial and technical issues is the responsibility of the project sponsor. The Bank's role is to:

- determine the type of appraisal needed;
- provide the guidance on how it should be conducted;
- review the results;
- ensure findings are properly reflected in operation financing and implementation.

The EBRD is however first and foremost a bank and its criteria are therefore different from those of the state agencies considered through other case studies in this chapter. Consequently it believes that financial and environmental sustainability are directly linked so that, for example, urban public transport must be financially and economically sound and so be able to compete with the motor car. To do this the operation must also be environmentally sustainable (EBRD, 1997).

Pricing is seen by the EBRD as a policy that promotes sustainability by:

- influencing overall transport demand
- encouraging the use of environmentally friendly modes of travel
- ensuring each mode is as 'clean' as possible within practical constraints.

For example, under the old Soviet regime Aeroflot passenger air fares were very low and generated high demand. As fares rose to meet cost levels, demand fell by up to 75 per cent over five years in Russia and much of that demand either disappeared or transferred to more economic and environmentally supportive modes (eg long distance rail). Airlines, eg LOT, were also able to modernise their fleets and introduce more fuel efficient, quieter aircraft. Pricing policies were introduced based on market forces and segmentation reflecting full cost recovery, subject to certain public authority policies.

Evaluation of subsidies

The move from 'subsidies' as a reflection of payments for urban public transport as a public service to 'contractual payments' to operators (whether in private or public ownership) provides a clear distinction between the elements in the provision of such transport facilities. As a bank, EBRD does not see its role as providing policy-based lending and sees it as the task of other public bodies to lead in policy development financial assistance. The need for a 'level playing field' in economic appraisal techniques (Reid *et al*, 1990) is paralleled by transport economists' use of 'externalities' of transport systems – those costs or benefits which derive from, or are received by, non-users. These may be supported by a bank which prefers economic to regulatory controls but does not see its role as funding such factors.

Eastern Europe and the former Soviet Union is facing rapid increases in car ownership partly resulting from increased disposable income by some sections of society and a decline in the performance of public transport made worse by increased congestion. The urban public transport system in eastern cities, eg Moscow, Prague, Vilnius, St Petersburg, are decaying due to lack of investment and to historically low fares covering only 25 per cent of operating costs with shortages, since the former days, of funds to pay wages and maintenance costs and none for reinvestment. EBRD is in such circumstances bound to be a part-investor; urban fares cannot be increased quickly as most of its customers remain on low incomes; cheap fares are recognised policy for the elderly or students in most EU states (WTRC, 2004). However it sees such policies whether for social or economic (eg congestion/pollution reduction) reasons as being funded through compensation payments by local authorities to urban transport operators.

The essence of EBRD and other similar bodies such as the World Bank is to provide loans which will be repaid on a commercial basis by operators whose viability may well depend on revenue streams from the farebox and from public contractual payments.

Critique of this approach

A potential problem with the EBRD (and other banks') approach is that financial criteria (cost revenue analysis) has to be reconciled to cost benefit analysis/multicriteria analysis relating to transition environmental and economic costs. Those projects whose benefits do not translate easily into monetary units tend to be excluded from cost benefit analysis and even more so from financial appraisal. Thus the difficulty arises from the relationship between monetary and non-monetary investment criteria in circumstances where the primary objective of the investment (eg urban public transport) is to achieve sustainability in the transition process. Put simply how to improve public transport fast enough to avoid the increases in car ownership and the 'reinforcement of the well known downward spiral' (EBRD, 1997) which the Bank recognises.

The projects in each area include:

- Aviation: runway improvements, navigation system, passenger and cargo terminal buildings; ground handling equipment
- Ports: basic infrastructure; primarily private sector investments; terminal for containers, grain, oil

- Railways: network: line upgrading (speed and capacity), if justified by traffic volume and economies; infrastructure maintenance/equipment renewal; signals and telecommunications
- Railways: operations: rolling stock (new and refurbishment); terminal improvement (especially freight and intermodal traffic); traffic/rolling stock management systems.
- Road transport: road infrastructure (private building, public operation); direct charging projects, eg toll motorways, tunnels, river crossings; vehicle fleets; priority for 'sound private sector' revenue-generating infrastructure problems.
- Urban transport: buses, trains, metro, heavy rail; eligible schemes are provided on a commercial basis with operator costs covered by revenue from:

  (a) farebox
  (b) compensation for travel concessions as a part of social policy
  (c) payments for predetermined services provided for public bodies (eg socially necessary services or public service obligation)
  (d) other earned revenue (eg rent, advertising)

Table 9.18 *Examples of EBRD investment projects*

Country	Project	Total cost (ECU m)	EBRD finance (ECU m)
Aviation			
Latvia (94)	Riga International Airport	9.0	8.4
Ukraine (94)	Bovispol Airport, Kiev	12.0	4.0
Estonia (94)	Tallinn Airport Rehab.	11.7	9.2
Georgia (95)	Tblisi Airport Refurb.	10.4	8.8
Azerbaijan (96)	Air Navigation	12.6	11.0
Railways			
Slovenia (93)	Railways	87.3	43.4
Lithuania (94)	Transport (inc. road)	37.4	15.2
Czech Rep. (95)	Railway corridor	695.5	43.1
Poland (96)	Modernisation	487.0	50.0
Roads			
Belarus (94)	Brest-Minsk-Russian border	69.2	43.0
Hungary (95)	M5 Toll m-way	369.1	112.0
Lithuania (96)	Via Baltica	94.3	18.6
Ports			
Ukraine (95)	Yuzhny Fertiliser Terminal	24.9	4.0
Kazakstan (96)	Aktau	59.6	43.1
Moldova	Giurgiulesti Oil Terminal	30.3	15.3

Source: EBRD (1997)

Social benefit to cost ratio

As a means of establishing the justification of a low fares policy a CBA framework can be established as follows:

Costs

Net costs to the taxpayers. These comprise for a fares decrease:

(a) the reduction in fares paid by existing public transport users; *plus*
(b) the extra operating cost of any additional service provided to cater for the additional traffic generated; *less*
(c) the additional fares revenue contributed by the extra traffic.

If taxation issues are left out, these three items cover the amount of resources consumed that taxpayers/ratepayers have to forgo to finance the fares decrease.

Benefits

These accrue both to public transport users and to all other road users. They comprise:

(a) the reduction in fares revenue required from existing public transport users which can now be spent elsewhere in the economy; *plus*
(b) the improved service (reduced waiting time) for all passengers as a result of increased frequencies to cater for extra demand; *plus*
(c) the reduction in congestion leading to reduced journey time (value), reduced vehicle operating costs and reduced accident costs as a result of increased use of public transport. These benefits apply to non-public transport users, passengers and operators.

At a given level subsidy using a hypothetical cheap fares policy and service land improvement, the results indicate that for each extra £1 of subsidy, the economic benefit to society might be £1.40, broken down as follows:

	£ p
Benefit to passengers through reduced fares	1.02
Benefit to passengers through improved service levels	0.23
Reduction in congestion and accident costs	0.15
	1.40

Thus the benefit cost ratio is 1:4 which compares favourably with ratios in road construction (see Chapter 10) and provides much of the explanation for the financial support given to urban public transport in the most major cities in the European Union.

CONCLUSION (UK)

Prior to NATA, the differential in criteria between road and rail investment in Britain (DOT, 1991) stemmed from the perception by successive governments that the railway is a business and the road a public service investment. Thus elements such as user benefits were subsumed into revenue elements rather than time/congestion benefits. This situation put public transport in Britain in a weak position when modal split changes are seen to be desirable (Harman et al, 1995) as a means of reducing car use. Changes in the criteria are intended to change the allocation of publicly funded investment resources (see Chapter 12).

CASE STUDY: SONERAIL CONSORTIUM (2000)

Transport Research and Consultancy (Project Co-ordinator)	United Kingdom
University of Pardubice	Czech Republic
Technische Universität Dresden	Germany
ZEUS European Economic Interest Group	Greece
Trasporti Mobilita Turismo Pragma Srl	Italy
Netherlands Economic Institute	Netherlands

The author acknowledges the contribution of the Sonerail Consortium to Case Study 4.

REFERENCES

BWCABUS (2003) *The Use of GPS Systems in Providing Demand Responsive Bus Services in Rural Areas*, Wales Transport Research Centre, University of Glamorgan, Pontypridd.

CLRS (1989) Central London Rail Study. Department of Transport, London Transport, British Rail, London.

Cole, S (1976) A cost benefit approach to the rationalisation of public transport services, *Transport* (November), journal of the Chartered Institute of Transport, London.

Cole, S (1985) Cost Benefit Analysis of Railway closure. Public Transport in Wales, House of Commons, Session 1984–85, HC 35, TSO, London.

Cole, S and Holvad, T (1997) Some aspects of Multicriteria Evaluation Methods, Proceedings, International Conference on Methods and Applications of Multicriteria Decision Making, May 1997, Mons, Belgium.

Cole, S and Holvad, T (2001) An evaluation methodology for socially necessary railways, Rail International/Schienender Walt, June/July, Vienna.

CPT (1996) Bus issues for unitary authorities, Confederation of Passenger Transport UK, South Wales Region, Caerdydd/Cardiff.

CPT (1996b) the role of the bus in the urban economy, Confederation of Passenger Transport UK, London.

DETR (1998) *A New Deal for Transport, Better for Everyone*, London.

DfT (2001) *Applying the Multi-Model New Approach (NATA) to Analysis of Highway Schemes*, Department for Transport, London.

DfT (2004) *Transport Users Benefit Appraisal (TUBA)*, Department for Transport, London.

DOT (1991) The role of investment appraisal in road and rail transport, Department of Transport, London.

DOT (1994) *Common Appraisal Framework for Urban Transport Projects*, MVA, OscarFaher TPA, ITS Leeds for Department of Transport, London, and Birmingham City Council.

DOT (1996a) COBA 10 Manual. *Design Manual for Roads and Bridges*, Department of Transport, HMSO, London.

DOT (1996b) Highways Economics Note 2, Value of Time and Vehicle Operating Costs, Department of Transport, HMSO, London.

DOT (1996c) COBA 10 Manual, *Design Manual for Roads and Bridges*, Valuation of Accidents, Department of Transport, HMSO, London.

EBRD (1991) Agreement Establishing the Bank, European Bank for Reconstruction and Development, London.

EBRD (1997) Transport Operations Policy; European Bank for Reconstruction and Development, London.

EC (1996) Cost benefit and multi-criteria analysis for rail infrastructure, APAS Report DGV11–15, European Commission, Brussels.

EC (1999) An evaluation methodology for public funding of socially necessary railway services (SONERAIL). European Commission; TRaC, University of North London, London.

ECMT (1992) Evaluating investment in transport infrastructure, European Conference of Ministers of Transport, OECD Publications Service, Paris.

ECMT (1993) *Privatisation of Railways*, Report of the 90 Round Table on Transport Economics, Paris.

Foster, C & Beesley, M (1963) The Victoria Line in *Transport* Ed Mumby D, Penguin Modern Economics, London.

German Ministry of Transport (1996) Macro-Economic Evaluation of Transport Infrastructure Investments: Evaluation Guidelines for Federal Transport Investment Plan 1992; Publication Series, vol 72, Federal Ministry of Transport, Bonn.

Glaister, S & Layard, R (1994) *Cost-Benefit Analysis*, Cambridge University Press, Cambridge.

Harman, R, Sanderson, G, Ferguson, G and Atkin, B (1995) Investing in Britain's Railways, Atkins Research and Development Ltd, Reading.

HMT (2002) *The Green Book: Appraisal and evaluation in central government*, HM Treasury, London.

HOC (2002) London Underground, House of Commons Select Committee, HC 387, Session 2001, 02, TSO, London.

Ling, D (1994) Manchester Metrolink – 18 Months On: *The Transport Economist*, vol 21, no 2, pp. 1–11.

NATA (2001) *New Approach to Transport Appraisal*, Mott Macdonald for Department of Transport, London.

Nijkamp, P & Blass, E (1994) Impact Assessment and Evaluation in *Transportation Planning*, Kluwer Academic Publishers, AA Dordrecht, The Netherlands.

NR (2003) Cost Submission, Update for the Business Plan (2003), Network Rail, London.

NS (1997) Annual Report, Nederlandse Spoorwegan, Utrecht.

NS Riezigers (1997) Author's interviews within economics department staff, Utrecht.

OPRAF (1996) Appraisal of Support for Passenger Rail Services: A Consultation Paper; Office of Passenger Rail Franchising, London.

Plowden, S (1985) Transport Reform – changing the rules, Policy Studies Institute, London.

Potter, S, Cole, S (1992) Funding an integrated transport policy, in *Travel Sickness – a sustainable transport policy for Britain*, Lawrence and Wishart, London.

Railned (1995) Tweede Tactische Pakket, Rail infrastructure, Railned, Utrecht.

Railtrack (1997) Annual Report and Accounts 1996–97, Railtrack plc, London.

Railtrack (1997) Network Management Statement: investing in Britain's railways, Railtrack plc, London.

Reid et al (1990) Reid, R, Reid, B, Horton, R (1990–1996) Chairmen of British Railways Board.

SDG (1991) *Electrification of the Midland Main Line*, SDG, London.

SDG (1992) *Public Transport Funding – How does Britain compare*, SDG, London.

SE (2003) Transport Grant (TG) Submissions 2002–2003: Guidance for completion of bids and appraisal criteria.

SNCF (2003) Rapport D'Activité; Etats Financiers, Societé Nationale des Chemins de Fer, Paris.

SRA (2003), Appraisal Criteria, Strategic Rail Authority, London.

SRA (2004) Franchise replacement process, Strategic Rail Authority, London.

TfL (2003) The cross rail business case, Transport for London, London.

TIE (2004) Edinburgh: Transport Initiative, A Burns and M Howell for Transport Initiatives Edinburgh.

TRaC/Symonds Travers Morgan (1999) Study of the Magnitude of Network Effects in the Trans European Rail Network, DG11, Economic and Financial Affairs, European Commission, Brussels.

Walsh, H G and Williams, A (1969) Current Issues in Cost Benefit Anaysis, HMSO, London

WTRC (2004) Comparative analysis of retail prices and incomes Poland and UK, Wales Transport Research Centre, Caerdydd, Cardiff.

FURTHER READING

APAS (1996) *Cost-benefit and Multi-criteria Analysis for Nodal Centres for Passengers*; Strategic Transport, Directorate General for Transport, Commission of the European Communities, Brussels.

APAS (1996) *Cost-benefit and Multi-criteria Analysis for Rail Infrastructure*; Strategic Transport, Directorate General for Transport, Commission of the European Communities, Brussels.

APAS (1996) *Evaluation*; Road Transport, Directorate General for Transport, Commission of the European Communities, Brussels.

APAS (1996) *Methodologies for Transport Impact Assessment*; Strategic Transport, Directorate General for Transport, Commission of the European Communities, Brussels.

DETR (2000) *Guidance on the Methodology for Multi Modal Studies*, DETR, London.

EC (1969) Council Regulation No. 1191/69, *Official Journal of the European Communities*, L156/1, 26 June 1969.

EC (1991) Council Regulation No. 1893/91, *Official Journal of the European Communities*, L169/1, 20 June 1991.

EC (1991) *Council Directive 440/91*.

ECMT (1998) *Rail Restructuring in Europe*, Paris.

Else, P (1996) Subsidy Requirements in a Restructured Rail Network, with Particular Reference to British Rail, *Transport Policy*, **3** (1/2), pp 13–15.

European Commission (1995) *The Citizens' Network – Fulfilling the Potential of Public Passenger Transport in Europe*, Green Paper (COM(95) 601 final), Brussels.

European Commission (1996) *A Strategy for Revitalising the Community's Railways*, White Paper (COM(96) 421 final), Brussels.

European Commission (1997) *EU Transport in Figures*, Statistical Pocketbook, 2nd issue 1997, Brussels.

European Commission (1998) *Developing the Citizens' Network*, COM (98) 431, Brussels.

European Commission (1998) *Fair Payment for Infrastructure Use: A phased approach to a common transport infrastructure charging framework in the EU*, White Paper (COM (98) 466), Brussels.

European Conference of Ministers of Transport (1995) Summary of Discussions, in ECMT (1995) *Why Do We Need Railways?*, ECMT publication, Proceedings of International Seminar 19–20 January 1995, OECD Publications Services, Paris.

Hillman, M & Whalley, A (1980) The social consequences of rail closures, Policy Studies Institute, London.

NAO (2003) Managing resources to deliver better public services, Report by Controller and Auditor General, HC 61, Session 2003–04, House of Commons, London.

OPRAF (1999) *Planning Criteria: A Guide to the Appraisal of Support for Passenger Rail Services*, Office of Passenger Rail Franchising, London.

Plowden, S P C (1983) Transport efficiency and the urban environment. Is there a conflict? *Transport Reviews*, Vol 3, No 4, London.

CHAPTER 10

Economic Appraisal – Valuation of Elements

PURPOSE OF INVESTMENT

The objective of publicly financed investment in additional capital infrastructure or vehicles (road and rail) (ie not replacement of existing capital assets) is to provide the basis for increased output and an increase in the real income of the economy often through a reduction in generalised cost. Generalised cost includes not only those directly valued costs such as fuel, capital utilisation and cost parking charges, public transport fares and costs, but also elements such as journey time changes and environmental factors. The analysis which follows identifies the use of resource cost as the basis for investment appraisal – usually seen as net of taxes and subsidy. However the user includes the fiscal (Owens et al, 1990) element in his/her costs although the principle of polluter pays has hardly been applied in the UK transport sector (Potter, 1993). Investment appraisal is the process of identifying the ways in which, and the extent to which, alternative projects will maximise the increase in real income and enables alternative projects to be compared. These valuation methods should be seen in the context of the techniques in Chapter 9.

AN APPROPRIATE EVALUATION TECHNIQUE

In Chapter 9 a distinction was drawn between the use of commercial and social criteria. Profit or financial returns can be used in transport in determining whether to operate a local bus route, a package tour airline or set up a road haulage operation. If there are alternative means (eg the use of different types of vehicles) to achieve the objective, each can be considered in terms of cost and revenue. Even in such cases a firm would estimate the time span for a sustainable market advantage, since if it successfully uses a particular type of vehicle, other companies will do likewise and the market advantage has to be shared.

However, there are three circumstances where this approach could not be used:

1. Where consumer surplus has to be taken into account in assessing social benefits.
2. Where no prices are charged (eg new roads and motorways) or prices are not related to cost because of subsidy (eg public transport) or are not related to market conditions and opportunity cost to users (eg bridge tolls); consequently the revenue is not equivalent to social benefits.
3. Where the project has external benefits, or cost disbenefits are created in other sectors of the economy, and these have to be taken into account. A road constructed to bypass a small town will provide environmental benefits to residents or town centre shoppers coupled with disbenefits to the area adjacent to the new road where issues of road planning and design emerge (NAO, 1994). Similarly, environmental disbenefits to residents can result from the construction of an urban motorway. Many of these cost/benefits are 'externalities' affecting non-users of the scheme but should be used in determining net social benefit (Kågeson, 1992). In neither case can the environmental values be established with the present state of knowledge. The London Underground Victoria line was built to reduce congestion elsewhere on the public transport system and on the highway system external to the scheme (Mogridge, 1990). The benefits to road users from this investment were not reflected in any payment and the revenue level on the Underground did not show total benefits (Foster/ Beesley, 1963). A recent (2004) example of this concept in small/medium sized towns is the concept of Yellow School Buses (First, 2004). These are evaluated in terms of reduced generalised cost of travel during peak school times resulting from the replacement of 'school run' cars.

Cost benefit analysis

Public sector investment resources have always been scarce, no matter what political party is in power; governments therefore wish to obtain value for money from investment expenditure and need a robust technique to make comparisons between alternative schemes. This enables the technique to be used in the preparation of scheme priority lists by, for example, county councils or the Department for Transport. The introduction of the package approach enables public transport traffic management and road investment measures to be used within the same scheme. From an appraisal viewpoint the package is therefore a group of policy measures designed to solve a particular problem or achieve an objective (LTP, 2004). The economic evaluation of different packages should determine each one's position in the priority list, testing for expenditure linked to objectives and targets (Gardner, 1997) which become an important element in the appraisal process. In the European wide context (SEC, 1995; Ministère, 1996), the concept of the trans-European transport networks (TENs) relies on the use of a similar integrated approach. In determining the trans-European road network (EC, 1995a) and the fourteen priority projects identified by the European Commission a cost benefit analysis evaluation process covering public and private investment is required (EC, 1995b).

Cost benefit analysis (CBA) compares the costs of road schemes with the benefits derived by road users and expresses those benefits in monetary terms EURET (1996). The use of CBA involves the same process as financial appraisal, whose main benefit is that it uses behavioural evaluation (ie it represents the real choice of consumers). The limitation of financial appraisal is that it does not cover all the costs and benefits of a scheme but is restricted to those financial effects on the producer. The major criticism of traditional CBA is that it is not comprehensive – yet financial appraisal is, if anything, even less so. CBA itself is only a partial technique; the type used in Britain is restricted to measuring value for money over a limited range of road user benefits and excludes non-user or environmental benefits (Cole, 1982) such as noise, pollution, vibration or community severance, and does not generally consider pedestrian delay effects. However, from the economists' viewpoint it does monetarise user benefits and thus provides a part of an appraisal technique.

Other factors which concern the economist also need to enter the analysis. Priority has been given to roads which aid economic development and generate employment (DfT, 1998, 2004; NAfW, 2001; SE, 1998) and a report highlighted the importance of good roads in the development of the UK tourist industry (DCMS, 2001). In addition, there may be political considerations involving the spread of funds on an equitable basis over a county or country and which change a priority list based on the evaluation process outlined here.

Cost benefit analysis in Britain was first applied to trunk road investment in the 1960s when the M1 motorway was one of the first applications (Coburn et al, 1960). This led to a computer-based technique called COBA, developed by the Department of Transport (DOT, 1996) to evaluate inter-urban road schemes. This particular use of the technique is still the most reliable and its principles have been applied to a wider range of road schemes in Britain and elsewhere but it has limitations. COBA is limited in its use to inter-urban schemes, because it is unable to deal with inconsistencies which may arise for peak and off-peak data, nor with the interaction between functions such as blocking back which are characteristics of urban traffic, but rarely occur in widely spaced rural junction situations. There are also lower minimum speeds and longer maximum time delays in urban areas which COBA does not make allowance for. To overcome this an urban cost benefit analysis technique (Urban Economic Appraisal – URECA) was developed to evaluate the economic effects of speed and traffic flow data derived directly from the assignment models. The issues of generated traffic and environmental factors are dealt with later (see page 303).

Selection of schemes for economic appraisal

Cost benefit analysis is used to find the best way of investing resources, particularly if those resources are less than the total required. In this way the right projects are selected, but the list of projects must be comprehensive. Some projects may not be included in the list, on the basis that the resources are not available to analyse every scheme. A balance has to be struck between using the resources for project analysis and ensuring that all the available resources are used in the best way. To avoid spending £0.5 million of a £5.0 million budget on analysing every single project, a 'first sift' simplified evaluation process is required, using appropriate but often crude criteria such as work flows or numbers of residents on particular roads. In evaluating a list for an LTP, an initial 200 capital investment schemes can be reduced to a priority list of 40, with a detailed cost benefit analysis for the top ten to determine the next two to three years' programme. A workable process for selecting projects can avoid some of the criticism made of urban transport investment programmes (APAS, 1996).

The cost benefit analysis (in whatever form) will have applications throughout the scheme preparation process, but it should assist with the following decisions:

- the assessment of the need for a particular road or corridor improvement scheme before it is considered for evaluation;
- placing each scheme in a priority list is based on the evaluation of economic returns and costs, and compared with other schemes in the county, region or country;
- the timescale for the scheme and its place in the current or planned construction programme;
- the identification of a 'top ten' list of schemes for consideration at public inquiries, by councillors or by ministers;
- the detailed design and engineering standards to be used.

The elements used in cost benefit analysis of transport schemes

Financial appraisal may be used where money is the only element required and where profit accrues to the investor. Cost benefit analysis covers a range of elements – some of which are non-monetary – and was developed for sectors which do not have a 'marketable output', and measures costs and benefits to society at large. In this country users are not charged for road travel, and therefore the roads sector is a classic case for cost benefit analysis. In Britain only the following road user benefits are measured in money terms and have been confined to those benefits or generalised cost changes which accrue to road users:

- journey time savings;
- savings in operating costs;

- accident cost savings.

In the case of a new motorway these user benefits will apply to users of the new facility and users of existing roads where congestion has been significantly reduced.

In the absence of any practical or extensive form of road charging based on use, the valuation of these benefits rests on a 'willingness to pay' principle using a 'consumer surplus' approach.

The user benefits of a scheme are then compared with its costs:

- Capital costs including land purchase, construction and temporary facilities (eg road diversions).
- Maintenance costs savings on existing road and future costs incurred in maintaining the road.

The COBA technique is used as a 'benchmark' test, even in circumstances in which additional economic factors not evaluated by COBA need to be taken into account. These additional considerations would arise where changes in traffic distribution, modal split or generation might occur. COBA is principally concerned with estimating benefits to road users. Construction and maintenance costs are paid by central or local government but the benefits of the improved system in operation are distributed more widely (Table 10.1).

The COBA technique calculates the first three categories of user costs. The analysis is confined to a specified road network over which the effects of the new road will be felt and where the traffic flows on each road are measured. A comparison is made of the situation before and after the construction of the road scheme under evaluation. Existing traffic flows are assigned to the different roads in the network before and after the scheme in question, using a modelling technique.

The travel costs of each traveller on each road and junction in the network are calculated according to the flows and junction movements along it. The aggregate component costs give the total travel costs over the road network.

Table 10.1 *Benefits arising from road improvements*

Type of benefit	Accrues to
Changes in travel time costs	Road users
Changes in vehicle operating costs	Road users
Changes in accident costs	Road users including pedestrians, central and local government, relatives and friends of those at risk
Environmental impact – noise, pollution, visual intrusion, severance, etc	The community at large, people living near affected roads.

Table 10.2 *Appraisal summary table*

Problems	Objectives	Public expenditure (NPV subsidy £m)	
		Quantitative measure	Valuation
ENVIRONMENT	Noise and vibration	eg households affected; change in dB(A)	Value of noise reduction: PV £million
	Air pollution	eg households affected; change in emissions	Value of air pollution reduction: PV £million
	Landscape, townscape, biodiversity, heritage, water	eg landtake in hectares	N/A
	Greenhouse gases	eg change in emissions	Value of change in greenhouse gas emissions: PV £million
SAFETY	Accidents	eg road and rail accidents saved	Value of safety benefits: PV £million
	Personal security	eg passengers affected	Value of security benefits: PV £million
ECONOMY	Journey time and frequency	eg in-vehicle minutes; saved walk/wait time; saved frequency improvements	Rail user time savings: PV £million Road user time savings: PV £million Value crowding benefits: PV £million
	Crowding	eg change in crowded hours	Value performance benefits: PV £million
	Performance	eg change in average lateness	Station refurbishment: PV £million
	Station facilities and rolling stockaffected quality	eg number of passengers	New trains: PV £million
			Net financial effect: NPV £billion N/A
	Financial costs and revenues	N/A	
	Wider economic impacts	eg additional jobs in designated regeneration area	
ACCESSIBILITY	Reduction of barriers	eg disabled or encumbered passengers affected	N/A
	Severance	eg size of community affected	Value of severance reduction: PV £million
	Option values	eg number of people affected	Value of option: PV £million
INTEGRATION			

Source: SRA

From 1991 the national transport authorities in Great Britain have introduced a 'New Approach to Transport Appraisal' (NATA). The principles are explained in Chapter 9. The COBA technique has been incorporated as part of a wider evaluation where monetary values are being introduced for a wider range of elements than those in COBA.

Use of resource costs

Before entering a detailed discussion of the principal elements of cost and benefit, it is necessary to ensure that all the assessment is being done in terms of resource costs. These are measured in principle by the benefits resources (for example, capital, labour, etc) could produce in their next best alternative use. For the most part market prices reflect this, but there are exceptions, the most important of which arises because of taxes and subsidies. If a bag of groceries costs £100 to manufacture (including production, distribution and profit) and sells for £117.50 including value added tax, the resource costs are still only £100 because only £100 worth of resources would be released for other uses if one fewer unit were produced. The tax is only a transfer from one part of the community to another. Similarly, if a bus costs £100,000 to produce but operators receive a 50 per cent purchase subsidy, this makes the financial cost to them £50,000 but does not alter the fact that it needs £100,000 worth of resources to produce it. Thus, taxes and subsidies must be eliminated when calculating resource costs.

Forecasting the elements

(Chapter 8 analyses forecasting techniques in more detail.)

Investment requires a consideration of the future (ECMT, 1992), because the expenditure on resources is either current or in the near future (up to three years), while the benefits or returns are spread over a longer term (30 years). A major problem in investment appraisal is to estimate the size of future benefits and to compare a 'do-nothing' (or 'do-minimum') position with a 'do-something' position. There are underlying causes of growth, both demographic and lifestyle, in transport demand, especially over the longer term. For example between 1951 and 1991 there was a large increase in the number of people over 16 and over the same period a 44 per cent increase in those aged 65–79. People have become wealthier in real terms since the 1950s, the consumer society has developed; people remain active longer and are more likely to welcome the comfort, convenience and security of travelling by car.

The primary sources of employment have also changed from manufacturing to service industries. There are also far more women in the workforce together with an emphasis on part-time work. But the fastest growing component in transport is in shopping, personal business and leisure, and use of the car is affected by location, with Marks and Spencer estimating that 90 per cent of customers arrive by car at out of town stores compared with 72 per cent at town centre stores. Changes too have occurred in the numbers of children being taken to school by car, with significant differences in traffic flows between term time and other times in suburban areas of major cities (First, 2004). Demand estimates for transport facilities are made on the basis of the particular mode used, the particular route and the time of day/week/year in which journeys are made. In considering the benefits of the M40 motorway, for example, a general forecast of vehicles per day is inadequate between, say, Warwick and Oxford (see Figure 10.2). There is a need to know:

- the traffic split between the A41, A429 and A34 roads;
- the modal split of cars, light goods vehicles, heavy goods vehicles, buses, and coaches;
- the peak demand periods, how long they last and the sections of the road that are involved.

The forecasts then have to take into account:

- the types of journey made (work, education, leisure) and the number of trips made under each type;
- the modal split of passenger and freight journeys, eg passenger journey forecasts by car, bus, train, etc;
- the trips expected to be made along each road or corridor;
- each corridor then has to be linked to form the road network which the new road is expected to affect;
- trips currently on the existing road network reassigned on to the new network (including the new road);
- generated traffic.

The data are collected from a range of surveys and computer modelling is used to represent the network and distribute the trips by route and mode.

Because of transport's essentially derived nature, forecasts of traffic flow also have to consider forecasts of economic growth, household incomes, consumer expenditure, output in manufacturing and commercial activities (and their relative weighting in respect of a particular scheme), changes in land use and the location of activities (eg the shift of leisure activities from the central business district to out-of-town shopping and entertainment centres), trends in local population activity and changes in the level of unemployment. These are determined outside the transport industry but have a significant effect on road traffic volume. The forecasting of transport demands and costs and a realistic appraisal of transport projects therefore requires a wide understanding of trends and developments in the whole economy.

The National Roads Traffic Forecast publishes forecasts for road transport split between car ownership and usage and freight transport giving high growth and low growth scenarios. In relation to the elements above, future economic growth (for example, high 3 per cent, low 2 per cent), future price increases in fuel costs and with no restraint on cars (eg road pricing; limits on usage etc.) were also included. The forecast for Great Britain is shown in Figure 8.4 and indicates that road traffic is likely to grow more slowly than GDP (a reverse of the pre-1990 trend) but will nevertheless be nearly double its 1990 level by 2025 (NRTF, 1997).

The M40 extension motorway from Oxford to Birmingham was justified largely on the basis of projected traffic flows which are not the same as 'generated' traffic. Many of the arguments at the public inquiry were based on the forecasts. It was suggested by those who opposed the scheme that the consultants' traffic flow forecast (in 1991) was an average of 28,000 vehicles per day compared with the minimum requirement for a six-lane motorway of 45,000. The DfT view was that 'taking high and low growth figures the scheme was justified on economic appraisal grounds' (ie the forecasts of the national economy and its impact on traffic flow) and the forecasts satisfied the minimum flows required to achieve an acceptable rate of return using the COBA technique.

Generated traffic

This last element comprises the trips which were not made at all before the expenditure but which are anticipated to be made as a result of it. Prediction of this traffic is necessary in order to estimate the effects on users. A procedure could be used, in the absence of reliable predictions, where traffic generation of 10 per cent and 20 per cent above existing levels is assumed, and the effects of this incorporated into the evaluation to test sensitivity of results. This also demonstrates the need for careful monitoring of different types of project in order to obtain an insight into actual generation rates.

The Department for Transport's model was previously based on fixed trip appraisal but the SACTRA report on generated traffic (IHT 1997; SACTRA, 1994) led to a new approach to the issue (NATA, 1999 – see above). The underlying question is whether improved trunk roads and motorways lead to increased traffic flows, whether those increases are significant in terms of planning design and evaluation, and if so which types of roads are involved and how does current forecasting and appraisal methods allow for generated traffic (SACTRA, 1994).

The impact of induced traffic has two possible forms:

1. adverse, where road improvement stimulates traffic but creates congestion elsewhere on the network thus overestimating the benefits of the scheme. There will also be adverse economic consequences

2. positive, where the increased flows on the new road will bring an increase in total user benefits and where no compensating congestion costs are incurred.

Thus it may have an effect of increasing or reducing total benefits but in the latter case the scheme may still be justified.

The traffic generative effect matters most (IHT 1997, SACTRA 1994) where:

- the network is operating or is expected to operate close to capacity
- the elasticity of demand in relation to travel time (service elasticity) or generalised transport costs (price elasticity) is high. This may happen where there is dormant demand which is suddenly released when network capacity is expanded
- where the implementation of the scheme causes large changes in travel costs.

The DfT is currently reviewing the National Road Traffic Forecasts and has accepted SACTRA's proposals which include taking account of the influence of road supply on road traffic demand.

In several recent studies of new road schemes, the existence of generated traffic has been shown subsequently. There is some traffic generation derived from the improved quality of the journey where the route is now easy and journey times reduced. The M25 London orbital motorway has generated, for example, leisure journeys from south-west of London to the north of London with traffic flows at weekends higher than predicted at the public inquiry, and traffic to and from London (Heathrow) Airport during the 07.00 to 10.00 peak traffic period has been generated. This has resulted in heavy congestion and a further appraisal of the width of the motorway west of London. These are journeys that were not made prior to the construction of the M25 because often the route was along poor roads with a complex route. The forecasts flows were 80,000 pcu's per day; the current figure is 190,000 pcu's per day, although the latter figure was similar to the higher forecasts of traffic flows prepared by the DfT during the planning stages.

Comparative scheme analysis

A proper definition of the project concerned is needed; whether it is a capital scheme or a system of revenue support, and to determine what schemes are compared. All economic evaluations effectively consider the net changes in costs and benefits as a result of the expenditure, ie to compare what the costs and benefits would be if the expenditure did or did not take place. This requires an assumption about what the situation would be if the expenditure did not take place, in order to set an alternative to the proposed scheme (the do-nothing/do-minimum versus the do-something scenarios).

In some cases it may be relatively easy. The alternatives may be to build a bypass for a town, or not to build it and by implication use existing roads. On the other hand, matters can be more complex. There could also be under consideration a scheme of traffic management proposed for the town. In this case, the cost and benefits of the bypass will depend on whether the traffic management scheme is to be implemented. If no firm decision has been made on the traffic management scheme, the correct set of comparisons is as follows:

(a) bypass compared with existing situation (ie no traffic management);
(b) traffic management compared with the existing situation (ie no bypass);
(c) bypass compared with situation after implementation of traffic management;
(d) traffic management compared with situation after bypass has been built.

If, however, the traffic management scheme is committed, then only comparison (c) is relevant. In this case it would be incorrect simply to compare the bypass with the existing situation (comparison (a)). In other cases it may also be necessary to assume completion of another project even though it has not been committed.

It is important to appreciate the existence of other schemes which will affect the costs and benefits of the one being evaluated, and to structure the evaluation accordingly. If this does not happen, double-counting of benefits or attribution of benefits to the wrong expenditure could occur, resulting in incorrect resource allocation or worse, making the analysis invalid.

The economic appraisal process

The final stage is to bring all the cost benefit elements into a form where they can be used for comparisons of different projects. The first step is to produce estimates on an annual basis and the second to obtain a time stream of benefits and costs and discount it, and finally produce a benefit: cost ratio.

Time streams

Most transport capital investments have long lives or will lead to consequences which could be difficult to reverse, so it is necessary to consider not only one year but a period of years. For this purpose, 30 years from completion is taken as the standard. In an evaluation, each of the elements of cost benefit analysis listed above needs to be estimated for each of the 30 years. In addition decision making also requires a careful analysis of past trends and their extrapolation, taking full account of all factors which affect the future situation (for example, population movements).

Economic assessment techniques

The wide variety of transport schemes proposed have to be evaluated on an equal basis. It is clear by now few of the benefits (though most of the costs) are quantified in monetary terms and some highway authorities have used a points system and a goals achievement matrix to assess schemes in terms of policy objectives.

However, if a test of monetary costs and benefits is to be used it has to be applicable to all schemes to ensure comparable assessment. There are a variety of techniques available.

1. *First year rate of return.* This assesses the benefits in the first year after the opening of the scheme and compares them with the total expenditure. In its simplest form it assumes all costs and benefits occurred in the same year:

$$\text{FYRR} = \frac{\text{total benefits in year 1}}{\text{total costs (assumed in year 1)}}$$

It has the disadvantage of only considering one year's benefits and even if the discount period from start of construction to the end of year 1 extends over, say, four years, the following 30 years' benefits (and maintenance costs) are not considered. However, it is a simple method of monitoring the performance of a road. It is also generally used for small schemes where the impact of the scheme is immediate and future discounted benefits are difficult to estimate and possibly small in value terms (for example, junction improvement schemes). Prior to the introduction of NPV, a 10 per cent FYRR was required for road construction schemes.

2. *Pay-back period.* The expected operating surpluses are calculated and projects ranked according to the period it takes for these surpluses to be sufficient to pay back the original sum invested.

3. *Surplus of revenue over cost.* This surplus is calculated as a rate of return on the sum invested and projects are ranked according to the average annual rate of return over the full expected life of the project.

4. *Benefits/cost ratio.* This is one of the most frequently used measurements. It comprises the net benefits of the project (ie the benefits achieved by the project less the disbenefits created) divided by the net capital cost:

$$B/CR = \frac{\text{Total net benefits}}{\text{Total costs}}$$

Schemes with a ratio of less than 1:0 have costs in excess of benefits. Road schemes would be expected to have a ratio of at least 1:1.
5. *Net present value (NPV)*. The present value of future benefits and costs resulting from the investment is compared with the present value of the sum invested.

The use in NPV calculations of a discounted cash flow technique (DCF) enables 'cash' inflows in the form of benefits measured in money terms to be compared with cash outflows to cover construction and maintenance costs. The use of discounting is necessary where cash flows (whether notional or actual) are spread over a number of years.

Discounting

Most people have a positive time preference (that is if offered £1 today or the same purchasing power in one year's time they would take the £1 today). To induce them to defer the use of the money until next year they will have to be offered more than the same purchasing power – in economic growth jargon, a real (as opposed to a money) increase. Thus, any sum of money (for example, £1 million) in future years is worth less in real terms than it is at present and in consequence the values of costs and benefits in future years have to be discounted to allow for this. A rate frequently used by government is 7 per cent per annum.

In addition, it is expected that certain elements will grow in value by more than the rate of inflation. Time is an example, as it is expected that as the country's economy grows we shall be able to produce more goods per unit of time worked (Table 10.3).

These time values are primarily related to levels of personal income and are assumed to grow in real terms in line with real rates of growth in the economy (GDP) per head. The rates of growth of time values, however, include an allowance for population growth and are therefore slightly below the GDP rate. It is, however, necessary to specify a year to which all costs and benefits should be discounted. For schemes planned and

Table 10.3 *Assumptions of economic growth rates (%) per annum*

	Low growth assumption	High growth assumption
2004–05	1.9	1.9
2005–10	1.6	2.9
2010 onwards	1.8	3.1

Source: Average of GB figures 1995–2020

programmed in say 2004 this would be 2002 and November 2002 price levels should be used.

Thus, if a motorway is expected to open in 2010 and yield a benefit of £30 million of time savings at 2002 prices per annum without any growth in traffic volume, the calculation would comprise:

1. Increasing the £30 million by 1.6 per cent in the low growth assumption (or 2.9 per cent in the high growth assumption) per annum from 2005 to 2010 and so allow for real increases in time values and at 1.8 per cent or 3.1 per cent thereafter.
2. Computing a figure for 2010 to 2030 allowing for this annual growth.
3. Discounting all these sums to 2002 at 7 or 8 per cent per annum. When selecting the rate for appraisal of non-trading public services such as roads, account has to be taken of the 'absence of market forces and the greater risk of appraisal optimism for projects where returns are primarily non-financial'. If a rate of 6 per cent reflects the opportunity cost of capital the appraisal rate will need to be higher. It has been suggested in the past (SACTRA, 1992) that instead of using one year (eg 2002) as the base, expressing the NPV in current prices and discount year may make the significance of the sums involved more readily understood. The values can be expressed at the price level shown in the latest retail price index (CSO, 2004). For example, if the scheme is submitted for consideration in February 2004 then the January 2004 index should be used to update, and the values stated 'in January 2004 prices'.
4. Aggregating them to give a discounted sum.

This would then be repeated (using correct growth assumptions for both volume and value) for the other elements in the cost benefit analysis. It is at this stage that the significance for the phasing of capital costs until as late as possible in the programme becomes apparent.

The appraisal methods using discounting techniques convert cash values occurring at different times to a common time base. The value of benefits gradually diminishes with each year, so that although the evaluation period is normally 30 years, 50 per cent of the benefits accrue during the first ten years, and 80 per cent during the first 20 years of the life of the scheme. However, the benefit:cost ratio can also be used to show economic returns on a yearly basis. The discount rate represents the opportunity cost of the capital to the investor which therefore takes account of any alternative investment option available to the government when allocating national resources.

All costs and benefits are reduced to their present value (or that of the base pricing year) and the project should be undertaken if the NPV of the return is greater than the NPV of the investment. Discounting does not take any account of inflation, which does not enter into the analysis in any way, and each £1 has the same real value in each year. The NPV gives a measure of the economic benefit gained from a proposal, but on its own does not give an indication of the return on the investment. This can only be indicated by a comparison of benefits and costs over a given time period using a ratio or rate of return.

Several evaluation options are available. The use of a benefit:cost ratio is recommended by several reports (CLRS, 1989; CR, 2003). The Department for Transport has used net benefit per pound (£) of subsidy to assess value for money in urban public transport revenue support; London Transport (CLRS, 1989) favoured either benefit:cost ratio or NPV:C ratio as a measure of value for money; while the COBA manual recommends a ratio of NPV:cost, where the equation is:

$$NPV/C = \frac{\text{Present value of total user benefits (PVB)} - \text{present value of total costs (PVC)}}{\text{PVC}}$$

The COBA manual concludes that 'the facility for estimating a stream of benefits arising over the life of a road scheme allows a sounder basis for evaluation than is afforded by single year measures. Such measures can be particularly deceptive since two scheme options may yield similar returns for a given year but perform differently as traffic flows change over time'.

ENVIRONMENTAL CONSIDERATIONS IN NEW INFRASTRUCTURE (ROAD, RAIL, AIRPORTS) INVESTMENT

The forecasts of growth in vehicle ownership indicate an increase (DETR 1997) in the future extent and severity of environmental impacts associated with roads and traffic. There is scope for reducing impacts by various policy measures – for example, by transferring some types of traffic to other modes and/or by the introduction of new low pollution vehicles – but these measures seem more likely to check the rate of growth of the problem than to reverse the long term trend. The Buchanan (1963) Report 'Traffic in Towns' focused attention on the problem, and noted that at the time there had been little opportunity to make special quantitative studies of it. In more recent years large investment in urban motorways, major urban road improvements and inter-urban motorways, has generated considerable debate on the assessment of benefits derived by the users of the network in relation to the capital expenditure and maintenance costs of the scheme.

Monetary evaluation techniques for user elements (such as travel time, costs, vehicle operating costs, and accident costs) are long established, and attention is now increasingly focused on the problems of measuring the environmental consequences of alternative schemes (Johannson et al

1996). This is because decision makers have required an improved judgement of the value of amenity to assist them in deciding on the need for a road and also its particular line. If environmental consequences could be quantified and incorporated into the evaluation, then the elements of cost benefit analysis using monetary values would become more comprehensive (Maddison & Pearce, 1997). It is important that a form of measurement is established which is not only valid, but is consistent with the user elements of cost benefit analysis and is seen to be realistic.

For the economist the ultimate objective in environmental evaluation is to establish the relationship between environmental perception and monetary index. This would enable the development of a procedure for quantifying environmental benefits and disbenefits in monetary terms with a view to incorporating them into the cost benefit analysis and so achieve a more realistic and complete assessment.

A study for the DfT (2004) considered applying monetary values to the environmental impact of transport, providing values for benefits derived from environmentally sensitive land and calculating the costs (including opportunity cost) of new transport infrastructure. This valuation would then be used in valuing the scheme's benefit: cost ratio and its NPV. Other work, for DEFRA in 2003 (see DfT, 2004), has included developing monetary values for carbon emission, local air quality and transport related noise.

Importance of the environment in transport decision making

The 'environment' includes noise, air pollution, the view from one's house, and the convenience of certain amenities and services (POST, 1995). Some or all of these elements are affected by capital investment projects. Environmentalists have, over the last few years, exerted increasing pressure and influence in the press and through the political and legal processes, (CPRE 1996; COL 1993; HOC 1995) so that environmental considerations now play a more important part in public sector decision making. This can be effectively achieved by reflecting environmental effects in the capital expenditure evaluation process particularly in transport construction projects (HOC 1995; SACTRA 1991). However the majority of investment with environmental consequences are new road or road improvement schemes; the principles apply to new airport investment (eg expansion at Schipol Airport Netherlands; London Heathrow Terminal 5; London Stansted Airport, England) or new railway investment (eg Channel Tunnel Rail Link, Cross Rail (2003) and Jubilee Line Extension, London). Such an evaluation process must be seen in the wider context of mobility or access for those with no car, the cross evaluation of road and rail schemes (see Chapter 9) and a series of policy elements including a supportive fiscal framework, changing personal behaviour, reducing the need to travel, changes in the decision making framework (DfT, 2002), setting environmental targets, promoting greener forms of transport, improving freight transport efficiency and increased research into sustainable development (Cole & Caldwell, 1994).

Experience has shown that the environment had become a secondary consideration in transport expenditure because it had no monetary value and because historically there was no way of taking it into account for grant purposes (Cole and Maltby, 1978). The government determines the initial priority lists for road schemes using rate of return and not environmental criteria. Therefore, if the environment is to be considered in a similar way to the traffic 'user' factors (for example, travel time is traded off against noise nuisance), a more precise and comparable measure than a general statement of noise or pollution is required.

Environmental statements (ES)

The requirement for all new transport schemes was set out in EC Directive 85/337 on environmental assessment (EC, 1985). The projects are divided into two groups, (a) where an environmental statement will always be required and (b) where the appropriate authority considers their characteristics should require an EIS.

The Environmental Assessment is the whole process required to reach a decision and involves consideration of environmental information from various services, and the Statement is required to indicate the main effects of the scheme and the measures envisaged to avoid, reduce and remedy the adverse effects. The effects to be considered cover those on human beings; buildings; flora; fauna and geology; land, water; air and climate.

The original Directive has been amended by EC Directive 97/11 in order to achieve a more even application across all member States (EC, 1997). This results in transport projects still being allocated to one of the two categories identified above:

(a) always required for construction of:
  • long distance railway infrastructure
  • airports (runway length over 2100m)
  • motorways and express roads
  • new road of four or more lanes or widening/realignment of existing road to 4 lanes if the road is over 10km long
  • inland waterways and ports for vessels over 1350t.

(b) required if so directed, for the construction of:
  • urban development projects including car parks and shopping centres
  • railways and intermodal trans shipment facilities (not in (a))
  • inland waters (not in (a))
  • tramways, elevated and underground railways, suspended lines; used exclusively or mainly for passenger transport.

The 1997 directive is intended to correct many of the failings of the EIA Regulations 1988 in relation to air pollution, ecological impact, route selection and mitigation (NAO, 1994) and to ensure the inclusion of environmental impacts in infrastructure planning (EC, 1995a, 1995b).

The more recent concept of risk assessment and risk management 'where decisions should be based on the best possible scientific information and analysis of risks' (DOE, 1994) is the use of such data to make decisions on the balance between costs and benefits and the probability of the occurrence of for example an environmental consequence (DOE, 1995).

The need for monetary values

The need for monetary evaluation is based on several arguments. First, the results of studies have suggested that road traffic noise (and other effects of high traffic flows such as atmospheric pollution, dirt and smoke) is a serious nuisance and that continued efforts should be made to reduce it (SACTRA 1992). Money has of course become a consideration through noise-insulation compensation, but this is not the concept of monetary evaluation under discussion. Instead, more precise measures of the value to be attached to environmental disturbance are required, for which money is the most appropriate measure.

Second, it has been suggested that an absence of monetary values prevents the environment being given the importance some sections of the community think it deserves. Road construction decisions are largely based on traffic criteria, independent of environmental factors. Thus, having made a case for the road, a route with a minimum environmental impact is chosen. This procedure makes the environment a secondary consideration, in that it may determine the final line of road but not whether the road should be built at all. By formalising the calculation of values attached to environmental effects a consistent approach may be achieved for all road schemes.

Despite the scepticism expressed by some people to the concept of placing cash values on the environment, in some form or another many environmental decisions are taken on a money value basis – in terms of capital cost versus saving lives or preventing pollution – even if the values are not explicitly stated. Indeed, all money values are merely an expression of value judgements.

The fundamental monetary value judgement in economics is market price derived under perfect competition. This price is the result of large numbers of consumers making judgements on how much a product is worth to them. In the same way, consumers can consider the 'worth' of the environment by comparing it with other possessions, eg the house or car, and can attach a value to it.

The third argument in favour of monetary evaluation of the environment concerns the effects of environmental disturbance on residents resulting from the construction of a new road or the failure to solve the environmental problems of an existing road. There is little evidence to suggest that the road user suffers any effects from the environmental characteristics of the area through which the road runs. The vehicle driver is more concerned with completing the journey than with the outlook, noise level and pollution on either side.

Earlier studies (UMPT, 1981; CTLA, 1971) have suggested that monetary evaluation of the environment can be based on the use of householder (consumer) surplus as a measure of value. The householder surplus then becomes the monetary estimate of the environmental impact of a transport investment. The environmental effects of the construction of a new highway scheme or the improvement of an existing highway can be measured in money terms by using the questionnaire techniques in which subjects are presented with hypothetical opportunities either for purchasing environmental benefits or for being compensated for environmental disbenefits. The use of such techniques as hedonic prices (POST, 1995) or revealed preference techniques may be appropriate in measuring environmental factors.

Establishing a monetary value

One of the objectives of some of the research was to establish the range in monetary terms within which householders provided values for their environment, bearing in mind that previously they had little or no experience of establishing such values. Certainly there is no market value involved, and other research has shown the impracticality of establishing values for individual environmental effects. Cost benefit analysis may be used at varying levels of decision making, whether it be at the policy level in determining whether transport expenditure should be incurred on roads or on highways, or whether it be at the operational level in determining where money ought to be invested. The methodology used in this research could be developed for use at the operational level as part of the economic evaluation process involved in drawing up a priority list for highway schemes; that is, which scheme provides the best return relative to the capital expenditure incurred in construction, in comparison with all the alternative transport uses of those financial and other resources.

The excess of the individual's subjective valuation of a house over and above the market price which was assumed in earlier studies (UMPT 1981; CTLA 1971), required an estimate of the householder surplus and it is this surplus which was measured in the research. Both of the studies found it necessary to establish either 'who pays to remove a nuisance' or 'who pays compensation for householders to put up with it'.

If consideration is given to the basis upon which those factors having no market value could be evaluated, two different approaches to obtaining an environmental monetary value emerge; should the approach be based on the householder's willingness to pay (which involves income constraints and the ability to pay), or should it be based on a form of compensation for the loss of amenity right (the amount he would have to be paid for being deprived of a pleasant environment or for putting up with an unpleasant one) (Cole 1982)? There may a large numerical difference between two such values. The most appropriate method is to consider whether people should be regarded as having a right to certain environmental conditions. To the extent that they are regarded as having such an amenity right they should be compensated for any loss or infringement of it. The selection of the principle to be applied – should it be 'willingness to pay' or 'compensation paid by government agency'? – must take into account the unequal distribution of income and wealth in society. The willingness to pay reflects a consumer's purchasing priorities in the market place and is widely accepted as a starting point for the valuation of non-market goods. It is important to note, however, that the payments made may be notional, and it was made clear in the research interviews that the compensation involved was a notional payment. Earlier research showed that the householder surplus values derived from questionnaire techniques given in response to 'willingness to pay' questions were restricted by actual income considerations and were in consequence lower than those values resulting from 'compensation' questions. The research was therefore based on the principle of compensation and concentrated on measuring housing behaviour and preferences. An important element in this was 'the measurement of the value attached by a householder to the undisturbed enjoyment of his house or the sum needed to compensate him for having to give it up wholly or partially' (UMPT, 1981), and maybe taken as the definition of 'consumer (or householder) surplus'.

DEFINITION OF THE ENVIRONMENT

There are three situations where the residents' amenities can be affected by highways. First, there is the adverse effect of the construction of a new motorway or road. Second, there is the effect of high traffic flows on an existing road and the unsuitability of the road for this, particularly in urban (including village) communities (Infras 1995; Nielson & Civitas 1992). Third is the use of traffic management schemes where the demand for capacity and the flow of traffic is controlled by a variety of fiscal and physical measures providing environmental benefits at relatively low cost and with no major infrastructural changes compared with new road schemes. These adverse effects may be caused by noise, visual intrusion, vibration, air pollution, community severance, land take, landscape and agriculture (IHT, 1997). The procedure for calculating the value of such adverse environmental effects entails estimating how much money the affected residents would need to receive in order for them to consider themselves no worse off than before.

If a person is moved from a house because of road development, the owner of the house loses the right to use that property and this right is transferred to the highway authority. In exchange the owner receives a sum of money (usually the market value), which is clearly to compensate him for his loss of property right.

If he is to be no worse off than before he should receive that amount of money which equals his valuation of the right he has lost, in compensation for its removal. From this property right (ie the right to use the house) can be derived the concept of 'amenity right' (ie the right to a peaceful and quiet environment).

There are two approaches to the evaluation of the amenity right and the quantitative difference between them may be substantial. First, how much would the residents accept to allow the nuisance to invade their privacy, or, in the case of a relief road not being built, to allow the existing nuisance to continue? In the latter case the question could be of the form: 'In your village there are a large number of heavy lorries travelling along a narrow road. To relieve this requires an expensive bypass. How much money would you be prepared to accept to allow this nuisance to continue?' There is also the notional right: how much as a maximum would the residents be prepared to pay to get rid of the nuisance or see it go elsewhere (ie the highway authority has a right to create a nuisance which residents have to purchase)? In this approach, income and wealth distribution become a major constraint in the evaluation, because residents have to pay from their own income. Thus the first approach is the more appropriate.

The concept of household surplus

The concept of household surplus in environmental evaluation is still in the development stage, although it was first put forward over forty years ago. In 1971 the Commission on the Third London Airport (CTLA, 1971) examined the newly proposed techniques which covered the consideration of social costs and benefits, such as the loss of agricultural output and the effects of noise, and an entirely new measure of social benefit, namely the 'consumer or householder surplus' attributable to residents in the vicinity of a new airport.

Where quantification is possible, the basis of the community's valuation of a factor is a price which the community would pay to receive the beneficial items, or the compensation it would accept for the disbenefit. Such valuations are chiefly derived from individual behaviour in a market situation or in conditions which simulate a market, ie people's revealed preferences.

The Urban Motorways Committee (UMC) research concentrated on measuring household behaviour and preferences using the amount of money in addition to the market value of that property which would have induced them to move voluntarily.

The UMC Report (UMPT, 1981), in its assessment of the alternative evaluation techniques, concludes that of the three it considered – environmental impact index, cost effectiveness analysis and cost benefit analysis – the last 'offers better potentialities' because 'it has the merit of using a common measuring rod to represent all the advantages and disadvantages of the scheme'. Thus, environmental benefits can be taken into account in exactly the same way as traffic benefits when transport investment options are being considered.

TRANSPORT INVESTMENT AREAS

Government investment in transport takes place in:

(a) highways and motorways (eg M40, M25, Hull Bridge);
(b) public transport infrastructure
   – railways and terminals
   – airports
   – bus stations;
(c) public transport subsidy.

There are also in these (especially in (b) and to the same extent in (a)) and other transport investments where the government is merely a sponsor or a part-investor and the bulk of the capital is provided by the private sector, for example the Docklands light railway, the Channel Tunnel, and the M25 Dartford-Thurrock (QEII) bridge.

Reasons for building a road

There are several reasons why a new road can be justified:

1. Improved access, which can be to industrial sites, housing estates or recreational facilities and can involve a new road or railway several miles long linking, for example, a new factory to an existing main network.
2. Reduced journey times.
3. Reduced vehicle operating costs.
4. Reduced accidents.
5. Improved traffic flow – this is linked to points 2, 3 and 4.
6. Improved environment both in rural areas and in towns and villages.

7. Economic regeneration; economic growth; employment.
8. Development of land; urban spatial expansion; development gain/land value increases.

CASE STUDY 1: THE VALUATION OF TIME SAVINGS

The M4 motorway north of Newbury, Berkshire

The effects of the motorway on existing users will be relatively easy to predict in terms of reduced journey times, accidents and vehicle operating costs, using the COBA technique. It also forms a part of the 'Economy' element of the New Approach to Transport Appraisal (NATA, 1999; DETR, 1998). There will be effects on the new road and on the existing surrounding roads with easier traffic flows. In this case study the reduced journey times are considered.

The A4 was a major industrial road linking London to Bristol and the West Country, which had a summer traffic peak with holiday cars and coaches. The flows on summer Saturdays prior to the construction of the M4 led to delays at several towns along the A4, including Newbury. The construction of the M4 north of Newbury led to the removal of these high traffic flows from the town itself, giving higher speeds on the M4 and the A4. The figures (Table 10.4) are hypothetical and based on assumed average speeds and journey times in 1968 (prior to construction) adjusted to take account of car ownership increases and assumed average speeds in 1996.

Calculating the value of time savings

The change in the time taken by traffic to pass along road sections is the major benefit item resulting from a road improvement scheme. It is necessary to put a money value on time savings in order to compare these with construction costs and accident and vehicle operating cost savings.

Travel time is distinguished between 'in-work' time and 'non-working' time, which includes leisure, education (except on courses in company

Table 10.4 *Through traffic journey times Thatcham Speen /equivalent points on M4**

	Average speed	**Distance**	**Journey time (mins)**
With M4	56 mph	4.5	4.2
Without M4	3 mph	4.5	90.0
	5 mph	4.5	56.2

* Based on estimated hypothetical traffic flows for 1996 on A4 and actual traffic flows on M4 on a typical August Saturday 09.30–12.30

time) shopping and journeys to and from work. Working time is valued on the basis of wages paid to the travelling employee, because the value of the output produced in working time must be at least equal to the labour hire cost to the employer. It assumes that savings in work travel time can be used for the production of output by the employee. This is the resource value of the time savings and is also taken to be the behavioural value perceived by the employee. The cost to the employer is given by the gross wage rate, plus on costs for that type of labour. Wage rate data is derived from the National Earnings Survey and the National Travel Survey. These values are estimated for different types of vehicle occupant, weighted to take account of the variation in mileage travelled by workers with different incomes.

Non-work time has no direct market value and so has been derived from studies of how people choose to travel when faced with a choice between a slow, cheap mode and a fast, expensive mode or between a short, expensive car route (such as over a tolled bridge) and a long, cheaper car route. These suggest that on average, in-vehicle non-working time is valued at 25 per cent of gross hourly wages.

Table 10.5 shows the value of time per vehicle adjusted for type of vehicle, occupancy rate and whether it is an in-work or non-work

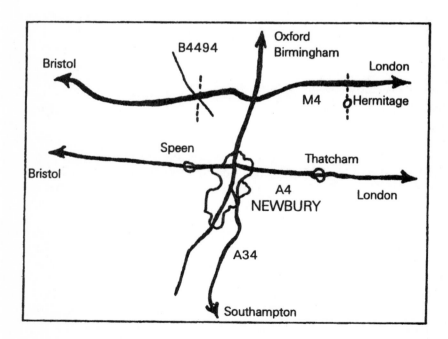

Figure 10.1 *Newbury in relation to the A4 and M4*

Table 10.5 *Values of time per person and per vehicle (£p) prices*

Type of vehicle	Occupancy		Type & value of time per occupant £p	Value of time per vehicle
working car	1.00 drivers	working	12.89	14.07
	0.21 passengers		working	10.70
non-working car	1.00 drivers	non-working ⎫	3.15	5.49
	0.87 passengers	non-working ⎭		
average car	1.00 drivers	16.7% working	12.89	
	0.76 passengers	83.3% non-working	3.15	6.73
light goods vehicle (LGV)	1.00 drivers	working ⎫	10.03	14.24
	0.30 passengers	working ⎭		
other goods vehicles (OGV)	1.00 drivers	working ⎫	9.45	
	0.20 passengers	working ⎭		
public service vehicle	1.00 drivers	working	9.83	49.00
	14.17 passengers	non-working ⎫	10.64	
	0.15 passengers	working ⎭		

Source: Department for Transport COBA 10 Manual (1997).

occupant. These figures will vary from year to year. They are related to the levels of personal income, and growth is at the same rate as GDP. To illustrate the use of these values in a calculation they have been applied to the hypothetical time savings case study at Newbury. The valuations and their application assume that even small savings per person are an acceptable basis for calculating total time savings. Thus, a saving of one minute per person should be included, as well as savings of 30 minutes per person because, over time, the development of a road network may produce a series of small time savings which can be aggregated to a large time saving. It would be inconsistent to ignore a series of time savings of, say, two or three minutes which, after several schemes were completed amounted to 20 minutes, and yet accept the savings of 20 minutes if they resulted from one scheme. There are also a number of studies which suggest that people place a value on small time savings.

The valuation of working time uses average pay, based on the assumption that savings in working time will result in increased output with the same level of employment rather than a reduction in employment (numbers of people or hours worked). It is also assumed that employees will 'pass on' savings to employers and not use travel time savings to extend a meal break. All travel in the course of work is assumed to be in the employer's time, so that time savings are valued on an 'in-work' basis. This applies, for example, to executives travelling back to base in the evening, for which they may not be paid overtime. A final assumption is that travellers do no productive work during travel (except transport workers on duty). This is a debatable assumption particularly in view of the 'mobile office' image portrayed by GNER, First Great Western and Virgin Trains (Chapter 4).

Non-work time covers a wide range of travel purposes but most of the studies on which the valuation is based relate to travel to and from work.

The calculation of user time cost savings in a 'do-minimum' or 'do-something' network is done in the following stages:

1. Disaggregate traffic flow data by vehicle category (car, bus, HGVs, etc) based on the flow of vehicles per hour.
2. Further disaggregate for each category by in-work and non-work trips: goods vehicles are all in-work: buses are work vehicles with a non-work passenger element; and car trips are mainly non-work (83.3 per cent).
3. The hourly flow of vehicles is shown for each link (ie section of road) by vehicle category and journey purpose.
4. The time cost per vehicle is based on occupancy rates.
5. The hourly flow of vehicles is converted to an hourly flow of people by multiplying the number of vehicles by the occupancy rate.
6. Time cost savings are calculated by multiplying the flow of each group of people by the value of their time.

Newbury M4: application of the technique

Using the figures shown in Table 10.5, the time savings shown in Table 10.4 can be evaluated (Table 10.6). The following assumptions have been made to assist in the analysis:

1. All vehicles achieve the same time saving by increasing average speed from 5 mph to 56 mph in the 'without M4' and the 'with M4' situations giving time saving per vehicle of 52.0 minutes.
2. The average daily traffic on a summer Saturday is estimated as 50,000 vehicles and for this analysis only Saturday time savings will be valued. The flow from 11.00 to 12.00 is given as 4,000 vehicles.

Thus, the time saving for that hour with that particular vehicle mix is £29,009. This is repeated over a sample of days using an 18-hour flow period (06.00–00.00) and for all links in the network. The example here illustrates how time values are calculated for input into benefits side of the cost benefit analysis.

Table 10.6 *Aggregate value of time savings*

Type of vehicle	Number per hour 11.00–12.00	Value of time per vehicle	Value (£)
working car	300	14.07	4,221
non-working car	3,490	5.49	19,160
light goods	100	14.24	1,424
other goods	30	9.45	284
public service vehicles	80	49.00	3,920
Total	4,000		29,009

CASE STUDY 2: WINNERS AND LOSERS

The M40 Oxford–Birmingham extension motorway

An examination of the M40 motorway between the original M40 east of Oxford and the M42 south of Birmingham (Waterstock to Gaydon) shows similar benefits over a longer stretch of infrastructure. The motorway is 48.2 miles in length and its construction cost was £375.3 million at out-turn 1990–91 prices – a cost per mile of £7.79 million.

The journey time for goods vehicles and working cars travelling between the Midlands, west London and Southampton docks along the A34 and the A41 has been significantly reduced, as have vehicle operating costs and heavy vehicles operating on unsuitable roads through small settlements, which resulted in an unacceptably high rate of accidents. A redistribution of traffic from the M1 London to Birmingham motorway was also included in the forecasts.

The Department for Transport calculates that traffic flows increase nationally between a low projection of 20 per cent and a high of 55 per cent over a period of twenty years. Even the low forecast would substantially exacerbate the already overcrowded routes in the corridor. The new motorway in conjunction with the improvements to the A34, Oxford to Southampton section, will fulfil the need and provide a higher standard route from the Midlands to Oxford, London and the south coast ports, particularly Southampton.

It is estimated that the new route will attract 15,000 vehicles a day by the year 2004, which would otherwise have used existing corridor roads.

The M1 is very heavily used, currently carrying up to 80,000 vehicles per day – more traffic than the design standard of a three-lane motorway. Frequent delays occur due to the lane closures necessitated by mainte-nance work. It is further estimated that the M40 will attract at least 10,000 vehicles a day away from the M1, a figure which will have increased since the assessment was made in 1979. The Department for Transport suggests that the M40 will be favoured by those travelling between West London and the West Midlands, as it will be the most direct route and because it will be a more pleasant and less heavily used road. It is also likely to be the favoured route for through traffic between the south coast ports and the West Midlands, as London can be avoided.

Table 10.7 *M40 Traffic Flow Forecasts 2004*

Section	Low growth	High growth
1. Waterstock to Wendlebury	30,000	39,000
2. A421 to A43 Baynards Green	46,000	60,000
3. A43 to A422/A362 Banbury	44,000	57,000
4. Banbury to B4451 Gaydon	41,000	54,000
5. B4451 to A41 Leamington Link	44,000	58,000
6. Leamington Link to A45 Longbridge	45,000	59,000

Source: Department for Transport

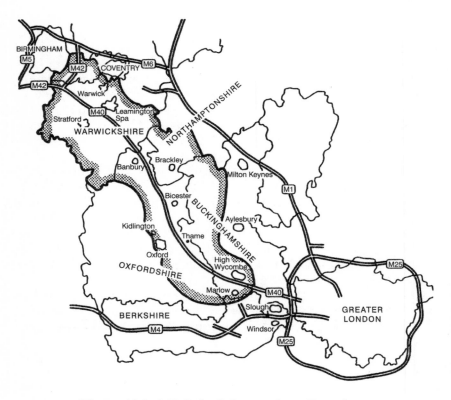

Figure 10.2 *M4 Oxford–Birmingham Corridor*
Reproduced by permission of the Aitchison-Rafferty Group. Extract from The M40
Corridor – A Location for Europe?

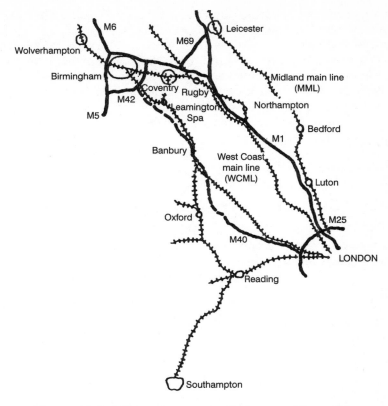

Figure 10.3 *M4 inquiry – map of relevant railway lines*
Source: Submission to the M40 public inquiry

For the first and last time British Rail opposed a motorway scheme, because it feared loss of revenue on its Paddington–Oxford–Birmingham corridor as a result of competition from express coaches making use of the M40 as an alternative to the M1. The main opponents, however, were the various environmental groups who are concerned with wildlife and historic sites, and local residents adversely affected by the line of route of the new motorway. Small settlements such Bishops Tackbrook and Shotteswell, which were peaceful English villages, now have a motorway through the parish which is easily seen and heard. They suggested a series of bypasses in place of a motorway. There is also concern in many towns and villages along the route that because journey times to Birmingham and High Wycombe will be considerably reduced by the new motorway, then new housing and distribution (retailing and warehousing) development will take place. These despite Oxfordshire County Council's policy of restricting growth and development to locations such as Bicester and

Banbury may increase traffic flows on local roads and change the culture of small rural settlements.

In favour of the scheme were towns such as Banbury, Warwick and Stratford which suffered most of the Midlands to Southampton goods traffic, on top of the local tourist traffic. The environmental balance was advantageous for several large towns but disastrous for a few smaller settlements. In population terms and in cost benefit (monetary elements) terms the scheme had disadvantages, but these were outweighed by the advantages (ICE, 1994). The question which remains is what kind of benefit cost ratio would a series of bypasses have achieved compared with the M40 scheme?

CASE STUDY 3: PRIVATE CAPITAL SCHEMES

(Chapter 11 considers these in more detail.)

Transport has been a leading area where proposals have been made to replace public finance with private finance (referred to in the UK as the Private Finance Initiative (PFI)) but where the principles apply in any country.

Schemes recently (1994–2004) completed in Britain have covered both road and rail schemes. For example the:

Channel Tunnel (c, p)
Dartford (QEII) Bridge taking the M25 over the Thames (c, p)
Second Severn Crossing (c, p)
Skye Bridge (c, p)
Birmingham North Relief Road (c, p)
Heathrow Express (c, p)
Croydon Tramlink (c, pg)
Docklands Light Railway (and Lewisham extension) (c, pg)
West Coast Main Line (p)
East Coast Main Line (p)
Channel Tunnel Rail Link (c, pg)
Midland Metro Light Rail (c, pg)
London Underground – Cross Rail (pg)
Manchester Metro (c, pg)

c – completed
pg – predominantly private sector finance with some Government investment
p – entirely private venture with transfer of assets at termination of concession

Under the PFI there are broadly three types of public private finance scheme:

1. Financially free standing projects where the private sector company undertakes all investment and recovers its costs through tolls charged to the road user (eg estuarial crossings; the Birmingham North Relief Motorway (M1) opened in 2004).
2. Joint ventures to which both public and private sectors contribute capital investment but which is operated by the private sector company. The public sector contribution will be made to secure non-financial benefits and evaluated on a cost benefit basis (eg reduced road congestion or air pollution (eg Manchester Metro; Channel Tunnel Rail Link; Croydon Tramlink; Network Rail Schemes).
3. Services sold to the public sector by the private sector and where the rental or shadow toll charges cover the costs of provision, (eg A55 Expressway, Ynys Mon).

Advantages:

- alternative source of funding when there are constraints on public expenditure
- private sector skills brought into planning and management of projects
- better value for money through economies of scale
- risk is transferred to the private sector (all risks including design construction, opening, traffic forecast and levels – though some of this may be faced by government) and maintenance risk
- close links between market demands and design and construction to maximise the return on the investment.

Criticisms:

- Is the scheme in addition or a substitute to an existing scheme?
- Does the scheme merely transfer capital investment to the private sector and the public sector guarantees an income over the life of the asset? A bridge built by a private company and charging tolls directly to users is a purely private investment project (eg Second Severn Crossing). However if the government is committed over the next 30 years to pay a 'shadow toll' then it has the effect of being a public sector scheme on a 'hire purchase' basis. There are many who are sceptical about the degree of risk taken in such circumstances by the private sector (*Economist*, 1995).
- Increased value for money is only likely if lower construction and maintenance costs will outweigh the cost of borrowing the finance compared with what the cost would have been through the National Loans Fund, which with government guarantees is the cheapest way of raising funds.
- An essential condition of the PFI is that risk is transferred to the private sector. However the greater that risk, the higher will be the risk premium (in the form of higher shadow tolls or guaranteed payments by the public sector) required by the private investor.

Finally it is necessary to consider the use of actual or of shadow charges. If the user is to pay for the benefits derived from the new road, bridge or trains (rather than it be a charge on tax revenues) then a pricing regime with forecast income streams and actual charges can be identified to cover funding costs and provide the required profit level. Therefore if the private sector provider can build the new bridge on time and within budget, the profitability is ensured (Broakes, 1988) through almost guaranteed traffic flows with very little risk.

A cost benefit analysis of passenger journeys from London to Paris gives high yields in journey time savings. Previously the surface journey time was five-and-a-half hours (up to seven hours) with changes on to the ferry and bus link at Dover compared with three hours on Eurostar. Vehicle operating costs for freight operators are likely to fall, with lower costs from better journey times giving improved utilisation of trucks and drivers.

The environmental impact has been considerable in the rural hinterland of Folkestone, Kent, as a result of the rail terminal, the rail link to the tunnel and the spur link from the M20 motorway. The rate of growth of traffic flows on the A20 and A2 are forecast as above average for the UK, even without the Channel Tunnel. Overall, however, there could be a fall in traffic flow on certain roads if there is a transfer of through passengers to rail. Thus, on a cost benefit basis the scheme would produce a higher rate of return than in a financial appraisal. The analysis of traffic and revenue for Eurotunnel plc/SA (1997), set out in the company's financial restructuring proposals, examined revenue in place of social benefits in five stages:

  demand analysis;
  total market forecasts;
  diversion estimates;
  competition and pricing;
  non-toll revenues.

The financial (cost revenue) approach, like cost benefit analysis, involves predicting usage and diversion, but there its similarity ends, since it considers the benefit flows to the company rather than to the community. Whether or not the scheme is financially viable, financial reports produced on the Channel Tunnel project will provide the transport economist with useful comparisons with cost benefit studies.

A further transport scheme already referred to was awarded to a private company, that of the high level bridge to carry the M25 over the River Thames at Dartford to relieve traffic congestion in the existing Dartford Tunnel. The plan was announced in September 1986 and was prepared by Trafalgar House Plc, who took over the two existing tunnels from Kent and Essex county councils and completed the bridge by 1990. The project is financed by toll fees and will be handed back to the government when all costs have been covered, by about 2005. This was the first significant piece of privately financed transport infrastructure since the railways were built in the last century. The public policy objective of this bridge is to relieve congestion and improve traffic flow and reduce journey times.

The one single difference, however, between public and private financed road schemes is quite simple. The Department of Transport objectives are to ease traffic flow and achieve benefits for the community as a whole, either on a minimum rate of return or at minimum cost and maximum value for money using cost benefit analysis techniques. The private investment company has to produce a profit on its capital equipment to pay interest or repay loans to the bank and to pay dividends to shareholders (HMT, 1995). A more open-ended arrangement such as the Dartford Bridge Scheme, which allows the whole debt to be paid before handing over the infrastructure, is less risky than the Channel Tunnel which is a purely private scheme. At least this is true in theory, but would the French and British Departments of Transport abandon a half-completed tunnel if the finance ran out?

CASE STUDY 4: ROAD PRICING: MARKET FORCES IN PUBLIC POLICY

Pricing formats

1. Road pricing including peak charges or occupancy charges (as in the United States)
2. Car parking charges at high levels in urban centres
3. Charging for entry into popular/attractive areas
4. Car parks for 'park and ride' schemes at low charges and low public transport fares
5. Low public transport fares on radical routes compared with generalised cost of car use (including journey time affected by bus lanes, fuel and parking charges).

Theoretical basis

1. The user pays the full costs
2. Generalised cost is used (ie not only personal cost but also congestion/environmental costs)
3. The charge equals the full generalised cost
4. Environmental benefits can be determined
5. Shadow prices can be used funded from the highways budget
6. All users are charged. Exceptions, though likely to be introduced to meet public policy objectives, distort the price mechanism and market pricing
7. The current method of allocating road space is through queuing; this would be replaced by the market mechanism.

Practice

An increased role for market pricing would reflect the inadequacy of supply to meet demand leading to road congestion and high generalised costs. Market pricing would reflect those cost levels and result in a more efficient transport system.

The variance in road capacity supply in relation to demand reflects the position in public transport and other real time service industries. The use of market sequestration and discriminating pricing can be introduced, and comparisons made by users between road prices and public transport prices. This might then lead to changes in the modal split and changes in expenditure patterns on transport infrastructure. (See Chapter 12).

REFERENCES

APAS (1996) Evaluation; Road Transport, Directorate General for Transport, Commission of the European Communities, Brussels.

Broakes, N (1988) Dartford Bridge finances: interview on *The Money Programme*, BBC, London.

Buchanan (1963) *Traffic in Towns*; a report for the Ministry of Transport by Colin Buchanan and Parties, HMSO, London.

CLRS (1989) Central London Rail Study, Department of Transport, London Transport, British Rail, London.

Coburn T M, Beesley M E & Reynolds D J (1960) The London Birmingham Motorway, Report RR46 TRRL, Crowthorne.

COL (1993) The Way Ahead: Traffic and the Environment, Corporation of London.

Cole (1982) *A Cost Benefit Approach to Environmental Evaluation of Transport Expenditure*, MSc Thesis (Supervisor Dr D Maltby), University of Salford.

Cole S & Caldwell N (1994) Wales needs transport not traffic/Angen Cymru – Trafnidiaeth nid traffig, Campaign for the Protection of Rural Wales, Y Trallwng, Powys.

Cole S and Maltby D (1978) Monetary Evaluation of the Environment in Transport Investment Appraisal UTSG, Annual Conference Proceedings, London.

CPRE (1996) Trunk Roads and Land Use Planning, Council for the Protection of Rural England, London.

Cross Rail (CR) (2003) Cross Rail business case and environmental impact assessment, Transport for London.

CSO (2004) Monthly Digest of Statistics, Retail Price Index, Central Statistical Office, London.

CTLA (1971) Commission on the Third London Airport (Chairman Lord Roskill), HMSO, London.

DCMS (2001) *Tomorrow's Tourism*, Department of Culture, Media and Sport, London.

DETR (1997) Developing an Integrated Transport Policy, Department of the Environment, Transport and the Regions, London.

DETR (1998) *A New Deal for Transport, Better for Everyone*, London.

DfT (1998) *A New Deal for Transport – Better for Everyone*, Department for Transport, London.

DfT (2002) *Delivering Better Transport*, Department for Transport, London.

DfT (2004) *The Future of Transport; The Future of Rail*, Department for Transport, London.

DOE (1994) Sustainable Development The UK Strategy, Department of the Environment et al, HMSO, London.

DOE (1995) A guide to risk assessment and risk management for environmental protection, Department of the Environment, London.

DOT (1991) The role of investment appraisal in road and rail transport, Department of Transport, London.

DOT (1996) COBA 10 Manual, *Design Manual for Roads and Bridges*, Department of Transport, HMSO, London.

EC (1985) European Communities Directive 85/337, *Official Journal* 1985, Brussels.

EC (1995a) The trans-European road; European Commission DG – Transport, Brussels.

EC (1995b) The trans-European transport network: transforming a patchwork into a network, European Commission, Office for Official Publications, Luxembourg

EC (1997) European Communities Directive 97/11/EEC, *Official Journal of the European Communities*, 14.3.97. No L 73/5, Brussels; DETR Consultation Paper on 97/11 (28 July 1997, London).

ECMT (1992) Guided Transport in 2040, European Conference of Ministers of Transport, OECD, Paris.

Economist, The (1995) Cooking the books, 28 October 1995.

EURET (1996) *Cost–Benefit and Multicriteria Analysis for New Road Construction*; Concerted Action 1.1, Directorate General for Transport, Commission of the European Communities, Brussels.

Eurotunnel plc/SA (1997) Financial Restructuring Proposals, Sections V and VII, Eurotunnel, Folkestone and Paris.

First (2004) *Yellow School Bus: Changing attitudes towards home-to-school transport*, First Student Ltd, London.

Foster C D & Beesley M E (1963) Estimating the social benefit of constructing an underground railway in London, *Journal of the Royal Statistical Society* Vol 126, p 46–58.

Gardner, K (1997) in *Transport in the Urban Environment*. Institution of Highways and Transportation, London.

HMT (1995) Private Opportunity, Public Benefit: progressing the Private Finance Initiative, HM (ie UK) Treasury/PFI Panel, London.

HOC (1995) Select Committee on Sustainable Development, Report, House of Commons (HL 72, 1994–95), London.

ICE (1994) *Managing the Highways Network*, Institution of Civil Engineers, London.

IHT (1997) Transport in the urban environment, Institution of Highways & Transportation, London.

Infras AG (1995) Reducing the external costs of transport, Infras AG, Zürich.

Johansson O, Maddison D & Pearce D (1996) Blueprint 5: *The True Costs of Road Transport*, Earthscan Publications Ltd, London.

Kågerson, P (1992) Internalised Social Costs of Transport, European Federation for Transport and Environment, Croydon, Swedish Society for Nature Conservation, Stockholm.

LTP (2004) Local transport plans in England are funding documents. In Wales they are the planning element only and a separate transport grant appraisal technique is in use. They are prepared at the county (unitary authority) or PTE level of government.

Maddison D & Pearce D (1997) Costing the health effects of poor air quality; Conference Proceedings: Determining the monetary values of environmental impacts in transport. University of Westminster, October 1997.

Ministère de L'Equipement du Legement des Transportes et de l'Espace, (1996) *Roads in France* (English version), Paris.

Mogridge, M J H (1990) *Travel in Towns*, Macmillan, London.

NafW (2001) *The Transport Framework for Wales*, National Assembly for Wales, Caerdydd/Cardiff.

NAO (1994) Department of Transport: Environmental Factors in Road Planning and Design; National Audit Office, London.

NATA (1999) *New Approach to Transport Appraisal*, Department for Transport, London.

Nielsen G & Civitas A S (1992) Nordic Transport and The Environment, Nordic Council, Copenhagen and Stockholm.

NRTF (1997) National roads traffic forecast, Department of Transport, London.

Owens S, Anderson V & Brunskill I (1991) *Green Taxes*, Institute for Public Policy Research, London.

POST (1995) Transport: some issues in sustainability. Parliamentary Office of Science and Technology, House of Commons, November 1995, London.

Potter, S (1993) Transport, Environment and Fiscal Policies: on the road to change? *Policy Studies* Vol 14 (2).

SACTRA (1991) Assessing the Environmental Impact of Road Schemes, Standing Advisory Committee on Trunk Road Assessment, DoT, London.

SACTRA (1992) Assessing the Environmental Impact of Road Schemes, Standing Advisory Committee on Trunk Road Assessment, Department of Transport, London.

SACTRA (1994) Generated traffic, Standing Advisory Committee on Trunk Road Assessment, DoT, London.

SE (1998) *Travel Choices for Scotland*, Scottish Office, Edinburgh.

SEC (1995) Instruction cadre relative aux méthodes d'évaluation économique des grand projets d'infrastructure de transport, La Circulaire du Secrétaire d'Etat aux Transports, Paris.

UMPT (1981) Urban Motorways Project Team Technical Paper 1 The Cost Benefit Approach (by R Travers Morgan Consultants), Department of the Environment, London.

Public Private Partnership (PPP) Investment

PPP FUNDING – ADDITIONAL INVESTMENT OR A SUBSTITUTE FOR PUBLIC SECTOR INVESTMENT?

It is difficult to demonstrate that something is additional to that which would have happened anyway.

For example, in 1996 the UK government's planned public sector expenditure was reduced when PPPs were seen to provide an alternative way of procuring that investment (evidence to UK House of Commons Treasury Committee, 1996). So, some PPP funding is clearly substitutional as some public capital spending is replaced.

However, investment may be additional when subsequent effects are taken into account. For example, public funds that are released from the capital programme by the injection of private investment can be used elsewhere and create additional activity. This could be additional spending compared with what would have been the case in the absence of a PPP scheme, even if the PPP projects were elsewhere. A second way in which PPP could provide additional spending is though efficiency savings, which release public funds for other purposes. Therefore as a subsequent effect, PPP spending may well be additional.

PPPs can offer governments options designed to disguise their spending commitments, and the timing of spending. If a project, such as a road, is publicly financed, the construction costs are counted as public spending as they occur; if it is privately financed, they are added to public spending years later, when the road is complete and the government starts to pay the contractor for it, perhaps through a 'shadow' toll pegged to how many cars use the road. And if a project, say a toll bridge, is financed by the operator levying a charge on users, its cost will never appear in the public-spending total. Even if successful in transferring risks to private investors and achieving efficiency gains, many PPP projects will simply be a form of 'buy now, pay later'. This will seem to reduce public spending in the early years. To 'prove' that a government is not using a PPP as an accounting mechanism, it will stress that PPP projects involve transfers of risk to private investors and detailed analyses of the efficiency gains achieved by recent projects. But this raises further questions. For instance, private contractors appear to be willing to bear risks over which they have no control. For example, in the case of a new road scheme the supplier will bear much of the risk of demand volumes. These might be lower than expected because of, say, the impact of taxation designed to reduce car mileage for environmental reasons.

The basis of the risk transfer is difficult to see and its impact difficult to assess because most PPP agreements are not in the public domain.

VALUE FOR MONEY

The rationale behind the private sector being involved in projects traditionally funded by the public sector, with associated complex legal structures and legal and financing fees, is that the private sector efficiency regime brings lower operating costs.

This has led to a general governmental view that PPPs will provide significant value for money gains. In order to identify that a PPP is the best option, a competition involving a comparison with a conventionally procured alternative (the public sector comparator) may be necessary.

Borrowing through a central government loan scheme, which comes with government guarantees and is backed by tax revenues and borrowing, is inevitably the cheapest way of raising funds. Proponents of PPPs have to justify how a PPP option should provide better value for money when public sector bodies have access to finance via a national loans fund. Moreover, because there is supposed to be genuine transfer of risk to the private sector, the private sector provider will insist on an adequate risk premium when setting its prices. The risk premium is an amount built into the contract to cover possible costs incurred. It may be seen as an 'insurance' premium and may indeed be financed by an external finance house. In any event it is likely to put an added cost into the project. The cost of capital (including the risk premium) brought to the project by the private provider will inevitably be more costly over the life of the project than that which could be provided from public sector sources.

Under PPPs, the public sector body may gain access to leasing and financing funds but the cost is unlikely to be as low as those from a government sourced loan. Therefore, while a PPP does not provide a cheaper source of finance to public sector bodies it does play a very important role in providing another source of possible funding, although probably at a higher capital cost. Under existing rules, public (profit-making) corporations cannot borrow and invest like private sector enterprises because their borrowing is treated by state treasuries as public expenditure.

Evidence for the value for money case would best be demonstrated by examining individual PPP projects, but there is very little detailed material on the performance of individual PPP projects.

TRANSFER OF RISK AND COMMERCIAL RISK PREMIUMS

An essential condition of a PPP is that risk is transferred to the private sector. Where the private sector is well placed to manage the risks, the public sector partner should transfer the following risks it would otherwise run if it were to construct and manage new facilities itself:

- construction costs overrunning;
- losses through completion delay;
- quality standards of facilities failing to meet performance targets;
- poor design that hinders effective delivery of services;
- problems through facilities failing to keep up with new technology;
- losses through capacity proving too large or too small for needs;
- costs of adaptation for alternative use;
- escalating maintenance and repair costs;
- failure to meet facilities management cost targets;
- income generation schemes failing to meet net income targets.

The higher the perceived risk that is being transferred, the greater the required risk premium that will be required by the private sector. The private sector will try and 'price' risk transfer. Therefore an efficiently designed PPP project will involve the optimum transfer of risk, on the principle that 'risk should be allocated to whoever is best able to manage it' and not risk transfer for its own sake. However, given that some risks are difficult to quantify it is difficult to assess to what extent real risks have been transferred, for example determining what liabilities are transferred back to the public sector should passenger and freight demand levels on the Channel Tunnel Rail Link fall below expectation, and whether an appropriate risk premium is being charged by the private operator for accepting a particular risk.

PRIVATE SECTOR ENTHUSIASM FOR PPPs

There has been considerable variation in the success rate in attracting private capital into PPPs. Much of the criticism relates to the process and the changes that would encourage them either to become partners or to increase their involvement.

The private sector's enthusiasm increased according to surveys (NAO, 1998; TRaC, 1999) of a small number of investors, based on the degree to which 'statutory' risk was reduced thus eliminating uncertainties which private sector investors could do little about. Projects for which planning approval, substantial technical design and construction planning were complete, and for which public inquiries had been held, were viewed more positively than those where such risks remained. The private sector was therefore most encouraging in its response where it was responsible for those financial, commercial and managerial related risks which its expertise was best placed to manage.

The reaction of bidders to private public partnerships established to construct major highway schemes (NAO, 1998) showed the procurement process had positive and negative elements (those that need to be improved are shown in italics):

- There was a high degree of interest in this form of financing and most bidders recognised the potential efficiencies in building up a PPP portfolio *but were concerned about the high cost of bidding.*
- Adequate information was given on the contractual arrangements. *However, the information on costs and traffic forecast information needed to be much improved and available to assist in putting bids together.* The public body (client) had tried to provide robust operation and maintenance cost data (but had not achieved this), and felt that its forecasts would make bidders too reliant on these estimates and inhibit bidders from putting forward innovative solutions.
- *Design aspects of the bid required from service providers was excessive*, but the client believed this was necessary to overcome political risk (eg public inquiry requirements). Such design needs should therefore be examined for all projects.
- *The availability of the criteria and their weightings on which bids were evaluated and an indication of how risk transfer was to be quantified would produce better bids.* The client believed that such information might stifle competition and that bidders would produce bids aimed at the most heavily weighted criteria rather than identify alternatives and put forward the best bid for the whole project. Such failure to communicate clearly makes bidding less attractive and might be a cause of so few bidders.
- *The use of a standard contract was found useful by some* as it focused on risk allocation, *but the time consuming, complex and expensive negotiation* was its down side. However, from the client viewpoint the use of compliant bids is a more efficient way of comparing alternative proposals.
- *Bidding companies considered they were restricted by public inquiry decisions* when adopting innovative designs and thus, apart from finance, kept to 'standard' approaches to minimise political risks.
- *There was a high cost of remaining in the competition as a reserve bidder* (who might be asked if the preferred bidder withdrew) but no reserve bidder withdrew.
- The allocation of risk contained in the standard contract was as expected except for legislative/political and traffic risks. The service providers therefore had a completely different standpoint to the client who believed the standard contract was in the public interest.

- A thorough discussion on a regular basis between past bidders and the public sector client is essential if investment in PPPs is to be achieved on a much higher scale than has been the case. Where there are few bidders the client must positively seek out potential bidders.

Overall, however, bidders were positive about these PPP schemes. The projects discussed were restricted to one EU member state, and other issues relating to international projects running between several member states. This was particularly the case with companies that had limited international experience and whose domestic experience with statutory related risks made them consider dealing with three or four legal systems a daunting task. There is a clear need to inform companies in all member states of the statutory risks and the assistance available to overcome them. However, this analysis of the process issues illustrates a need to meet the private sector's more dynamic perception of how bids and financial deals are made, particularly in relation to statutory (eg public inquiry delays) risk. The perception of these risks that the private sector could not control was that they were exacerbated when several legal systems were involved.

SOLUTIONS TO PRIMARY PRIVATE SECTOR CONCERNS

Delays in providing documents:

- The information pack for pre-qualification should be prepared on time and exactly identify the route.
- Tender documents should be designed and finalised well in advance of the process start date because of complexity of information.
- Preparing a standard contract takes considerably longer than expected; adequate time should be allowed.
- In awarding contracts public bodies must be aware of the unforeseen amount of negotiation and/or bringing financing arrangements to a close.

High cost of bidding compared with conventional contracts:

- The procurement process has to be less time consuming and the bidding costs reduced to a level comparable with traditional procurement (in which many companies were already involved).
- The costs for financial and legal advisers' fees following competition can be considerably reduced because the complexities and high construction costs became known.
- The experts' costs in traditional procurement are largely for technical advice on design and site supervision. The PPP concept is new and the cost of other advice (financial and legal) was, and is, often significantly

underestimated. A means to reduce these costs has to be found, eg by reducing the complexity of the process.

- The bidding costs for PPP contracts are high when compared with conventional road project procurement. New projects for road and rail using PPP require, for example, in addition to the new construction works, the capital and current maintenance of the road for the 30-year contract period and the raising of finance. Because additional skills are required, there is little opportunity to reduce these costs other than through the competitive market place (between supplying firms) or through economies of scale where bidders have several PPP projects and are thus able to negotiate better rates or employ an in-house team.

- The negotiated procedures of procurement regulations (set down by the EU and member state governments) required both private and public sectors to develop bidding methodologies. This can be a one-off cost and again is reduced through economies of scale related to several bids.

ANALYSIS OF BIDDERS' VIEWS

An ECMT (1999) study considered 13 schemes in different member states and accession states. The general conclusions were:

- Private sector investors and local or regional governments have to be involved at an early stage to ensure smooth running of the project and its completion on time and on budget.

- Forecasting over a 30-year period is unreliable as competitor reaction and traffic diversion (user reaction) cannot be forecast.

- User reaction (where the public or transport operators are not familiar with the tolls concept) can affect demand, but this can be helped by explaining the rationale behind private–public investment. The level of charges here needs to be balanced between public acceptance and company profitability through the PPP contractual arrangements.

- Additional costs may accrue to the public sector partner (eg link roads or feeder roads into the PPP scheme, upgrading of parallel roads, or in the case of an estuarial crossing the motorway on either side).

- Because of the links to the public road/rail network and because so many proposals are not financially viable, state investment is unavoidable.

- Good managers rather than experts are needed to monitor performance and civil service engineering and financial skills need to be improved to meet that need.

- If the specification is too high, it may be impossible to achieve the technical targets as well as financial targets (and therefore financial viability for the private partner), but flexibility is also difficult if the government wishes to retain high safety levels and quality. The consequences may be to increase the public sector's level of financial involvement.

- This leads to a series of financial issues inherent in PPPs. In addition to a clear separation of risk factors between the private sector and the public sector, there have often been demands by the private sector partner where a high proportion (or all) of the risk is underwritten by the state, without which such schemes have been difficult to finance.
- The action of local or member state governments as the primary legislative bodies involved and as the major suppliers of public funding are crucial to the success of PPPs. The international TEN-T (the Trans European transport network) adds a further dimension to this, as a co-ordination mechanism for budgets and rules will be needed through capital or revenue grants. In some cases 'corporatisation' (ie establishing a separate company part-owned by the government) rather than privatisation may be sufficient to achieve the private sector expertise and benefits.

Two further issues remain:

- A substantial public contribution is often required to bridge the gap between financial and socioeconomic viability so that appropriate rules and an attractive environment are needed to encourage private sector participation.
- The legal and financial arrangements both in individual member states and where a European Union TEN project involves several systems have been a discouragement in attracting private capital.

The conclusions of the ECMT study and the TRaC survey of investors provide a clear insight into the reasons for a reluctance by private sector partners to become involved in PPPs.

FINANCIAL APPRAISAL VERSUS COST BENEFIT ANALYSIS

The assessment of an infrastructure scheme using financial appraisal and cost benefit appraisal can result in four different outcomes as illustrated by Case Study 3 in Chapter 9 and Figure 9.4. A scheme not worthwhile in a financial appraisal nor in a cost benefit analysis would not be considered for funding. A scheme that is viable in financial appraisal and cost benefit appraisal would in principle not require a PPP as the private company could develop the scheme without public sector involvement. The third category where a scheme is worthwhile in the financial appraisal but not in the cost benefit appraisal would require regulation and implementation of mitigation of the negative effects but would not involve PPP arrangements. In effect, the only outcome that would be of relevance to PPPs is the one where the financial appraisal indicates the scheme is not worthwhile while the cost benefit appraisal suggests that it is worthwhile (APAS, 1996b). The reason for private sector involvement for schemes with these characteristics is the limited public funds available along with the possibility of enhanced efficiency in the provision of infrastructure and services. These differing assessment results would appear if the user benefits not captured in revenue are substantial and/or there exist significant external benefits (eg in the form of reduced pollution, accidents, noise and congestion). (See Chapter 9 for a full analysis of these issues.)

Public sector investment normally requires a return of 8 per cent, whereas private finance, because of the greater commercial risk involved, requires higher returns and/or a shorter payback period. The availability of private funding will be conditional upon the future income stream generated by the new investment, adjusted for an adequate margin for risk. Some projects will not attract private finance for the simple reason that there may be a mismatch between the private sector's preference for short payback periods or perhaps only a few years and that which the public sector can reasonably afford. Private operators may also require long term contractual commitments of several decades to reflect the long term life of the capital assets. Some public sector bodies may be unwilling or unable to make such long term commitments.

The underlying investment process of a PPP is in fact two investment decisions not one. However, this is not to say that the objectives of the private sector and public sector are opposed. The financial payback issues can be resolved for both sectors. The target is to identify public and private sector partners for whom a payback period of equal length may be identified.

CASE STUDY 1: FUNDING A PPP SCHEME (MAJOR URBAN RAILWAY)

The private sector will require an adequate financial rate of return. The public sector funding body will consider the social benefits to be derived from the investment. Thus two quite different output measures have to be included although the revenue flows may accrue to the public sector as they are a part of the monetary benefits with, for example, savings in travel time and vehicle operating costs (APAS, 1996c).

There are four key elements (see Figure 9.5) in any PPP transaction which will affect the achievement of the funding mechanism set out in Figure 11.1. The application of these elements will affect the differences in the outcome for any project in viability terms. There may for example be a situation where:

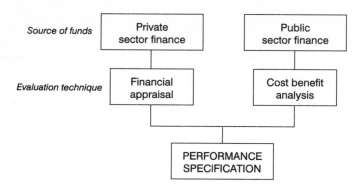

Figure 11.1 *A PPP funding package*

- financial appraisal alone rejects a scheme;
- cost benefit analysis alone justifies a scheme;
- cost benefit analysis and financial appraisal justify a scheme but may either enhance its quality, coverage etc or provide an opportunity cost saving enabling public sector funds to be available for another scheme.

The point at which a financially based investment proposal and one evaluated using cost benefit analysis are brought together into a PPP package is called the performance specification. This sets out the service provision and sets specific output measures or performance criteria that question the financial robustness of the scheme, value for money, affordability by the public sector investor and allocation of the risk.

CASE STUDY 2: EAST WEST CROSSRAIL (LONDON)

Given this framework a scheme can then be assessed from the investment viewpoint of both public and private sectors. Although not a TEN, the principle involved here can be examined using the UK government's Central London Rail Study, which involved schemes with total costs of several billion euros, thus putting them on the same scale as or bigger than many TEN schemes. The funding of these schemes is on the PPP principle.

The financial appraisal would be based on the revenue flow alone, would not provide an acceptable rate of return and would fail on a financial basis. However, were it to have been financially viable, it would not have been considered for part public funding.

The scheme has achieved viability on a CBA basis where the benefit flows to users were sufficient to obtain an acceptable return for both forms of funding.

Table 11.1 *Costs and benefits, East West Crossrail (1989 prices)*

Costs	Euro (millions)	Benefits	Euro (millions)
Construction	1,480[1]	Time savings	50
Rolling stock	25[2]	Crowding relief Public transport user benefits	120
Equivalent annual	130		
Annual operating	20	Road user benefits	35
		Added rail revenue	35
Total equivalent annual cost	150	Total benefit	240

[1] NPV at 7% over 60 years
[2] NPV at 7% over 35 years
Exchange rate £1 = Euro 1.7

Benefit/cost ratios (see Chapter 9)	
To public transport users	1.2
To road users	0.2
Revenue	0.2
Total benefit/cost ratio	1.6

Source: Central London Rail Study, London Transport, Department of Transport, Network South East, 1989

CASE STUDY 3: MANCHESTER METROLINK

The justification of the Manchester Metrolink in 1992 depended to a large extent on the appraisal technique used. The forecast of passenger usage forms a basic part of that analysis (Knowles, 1996). Table 11.2 (SDG,

Table 11.2 *Comparison of investment appraisal methods: section 56 and cost-benefit analysis for Manchester Metrolink*

Cost-benefit analysis	£m	Section 56 criteria (current DfT approach)	£m
Capital cost Metrolink	87.00	Capital cost Metrolink	87.00
BR capital cost avoided	41.44	BR capital cost avoided	41.44
Bus capital cost avoided	1.80	Tendered bus service saving	1.31
(Net capital cost	43.76)	Section 20 savings (payments to BR)	36.98
Operating cost savings	8.06		
User benefits			
(Time savings)	12.19		
Congestion savings	6.00	Congestion savings	6.00
Sub total 'benefits'	97.71	Sub total 'benefits'	87.73
Benefit to cost ratio:	2.23	'Benefit' to cost ratio	1.01

Source: SDG (2002) public transport funding

1992) shows the differences between a cost-benefit appraisal and the appraisal used for Section 56 grants by DfT, the technique currently used.

The cost-benefit analysis results in a much higher benefit-cost ratio compared to the method used by DfT for S56 grants caused mainly by the exclusion of time savings for users of the Metrolink in the DfT appraisal.

CBA/FA IN TEN PPPs – SOME CURRENT VIEWS

A survey of several private sector TEN/long distance rail infrastructure investors has identified three primary stakeholder interests. In the context of financial appraisal, they are:

1. Shareholders: share values and dividends through profits.
2. Customers (the passengers and freight operators): feedback through income streams and how the regulatory authority perceives operators' treatment of customers.
3. Social benefits derived from the business:
   - forms part of a licence agreement;
   - its view on the extent to which Network Rail works with local government;
   - opportunities;
   - the political dimension with consequent government direction to the regulator and then attitude to the operators.

These are of equal importance but private partners may set out with only (1) in mind but will eventually have to consider (2) and (3).

Appraising particular proposals

A private investor in a public private partnership will need to consider any proposal within a wider social context:

- *Stage 1.* The evaluation of the project from a whole industry viewpoint financially and from an economic (social benefit streams within the whole economy) position.
- *Stage 2.* The impact of the proposal for the investor in an overall current funding framework. The private company will develop and evaluate plans/options and determine the outputs from different route strategies seen in a long term operating context of say 10 years, 20 years and a whole life of the asset (30 years).

CASE STUDY 4: SPEED RAISING PROPOSALS FOR REGIONAL TRAINS AND INTER CITY LINKS BETWEEN REGIONS WITHIN THE EUROPEAN UNION

1. Evaluate potential enhancements to the route in the following terms:
   - in its broadest sense to achieve socioeconomic benefits;
   - in reducing the peripherality of the region to the European Union's highest GDP areas (the golden banana);
   - in increasing the possible use of the railway, eg stimulating passenger and freight traffic.
2. Factors in the evaluation:
   - sufficient capacity for growth;
   - the additional passenger numbers and revenue attracted by reduced journey times;
   - appraised in economic terms as well as a rail industry context, and so not restricted to a private sector perspective.
3. If a private operator decided to invest in a PPP it would consider:
   - Investment generated improvements to the region which resulted in sufficient passenger and revenue increase to justify them commercially. Therefore the *industry* also has a positive commercial return. However, in the context of vertical disintegration where track and train operators are separated (EC Directive 9/440) it is not always possible to attain financial information from train operating companies as the industry structure is not helpful.
   - On certain route sections journey time improvements led to a marginal payback in some sections, but none in others, especially with the higher costs of high speed train operations. Public sector funding is therefore required to close this gap after an allowance for revenue risk to achieve an acceptable return. Therefore, not all sections of the route will be financially viable. A PPP may be appropriate within a route as well as between different routes in a network.
   - Revenue risk: if there is a forecast increase in passengers, is there sufficient capacity and can current residual seat capacity be taken up? This may not be possible since, while there may be considerable capacity in a peripheral area, it is very limited at major cities which are significant en-route destinations or junctions. This makes the cost implications more complex than just the costs of direct services.
   - Non-user benefits: an impact on journey time, vehicle operating costs (road congestion), road safety costs and environmental benefits may also result. These would be evaluated using a cost benefit model of the SONERAIL type (see Chapter 9, Case Study 4) to enable the funding authority to decide where to allocate public investment funding.

In the evaluation of network enhancements some outputs are difficult to assess in terms of how they attract income. For example, investment in track and signalling may lead to reduced journey time but the impact of this on industry revenue is determined by train operators' service electricity effects (see Chapter 2) (eg through the stopping patterns, train operating speeds, marketing reduced journey times and how it is related to fares).

Access charges on some European systems may only be increased as a result of track quality enhancements. This requires operators' agreement as this may relate to a whole route. Consequently station improvements may not achieve a step change in output, as only the 'whole route' enhancement could produce an increase in access charges.

Demand risk

This is determined by the ability to extract value (often in revenue) from the investment. The infrastructure provider (Network Rail in Great Britain) has to forecast the level of demand for a new asset and what access charge can be achieved. If a large amount of new capacity remains unsold the risk of selling it in future is the demand risk. High capacity increase and high level demand give a low or zero demand risk.

Financial appraisal and joint funding

Within the European Union, joint funding issues arise which can affect the ease with which TEN PPPs may be created:

- A clear understanding of TEN/Objective I funding.
- More transparent evaluation criteria and weighting for schemes.
- Increase in concern about public sector achieving value for money.

Table 11.3 *Risk elements notes*

Demand risk	Train and track operators share the costs of enhancement. If a particular operator is not showing the enhancement costs then minimum on capital for remaining players is required.
Contractor risk	
Minimum return on capital	
Disruption to services during works	Element of cost charging for disruption to services.
Congestion/performance losses for new services	Regime in access contracts for delays to trains – a reasonable forecast of this.
Variable maintenance/operating costs	

- Some criteria are not clearly laid down so causing delays to new investment. Thus private partners may not be aware of the policy priorities being applied to particular schemes, nor of the shifting of priorities compared with a strict priority scheme based solely on economic rates of return.

Risk perspectives

If an acceptable payment model is to be derived, the objectives of the public sector service provider and the private sector partner/financier need to be considered.

'The financial "heart" of any PPP project is the payment mechanism and the cost components driving it through which the public sector sponsor remunerates the service provider and the basis on which financiers (banks and shareholders) lend money. The financiers' objective of achieving limited exposure remains fundamental when setting the structure and level of payments' (PROFIT, 2000).

For the development of the payment system to be successful, a number of areas are required to be thought through at an early stage. Such areas include:

- aims and objectives;
- payment mechanism structure and components;
- allocation of risk;
- interaction/triggers of components;
- practicality and measurement.

The complexity of the payment mechanism is developed over a period of time. Planning and understanding in the early stages create a more effective process in the long term.

Note

This chapter draws extensively on the output of a European Commission Research Framework 4 project 'PROFIT' – Private Operations and Financing of TEN's. The partners were: Netherlands Economic Institute (NEI); National Technical University of Athens (NTUA); Institute for Transport Studies (ITS), Leeds University; Transport Research and Consultancy (TRaC), University of North London; STRATEC Consultants Brussels. The author was a member of the project team.

REFERENCES

APAS (1996a) Cost-benefit and multi-criteria analysis for rail infrastructure; Strategic Transport, Directorate General for Transport, Commission of the European Communities, Brussels.

APAS (1996b) Pricing and financing of urban transport; Urban Transport, Directorate General for Transport, Commission of the European Communities, Brussels.

ECMT (1999) Public private partnership in the transport sector, report. Reference CEMT/CM (99) 21, European Committee of Ministers of Transport, Luxembourg.

HOC (1996) PPP's – Treasury Committee Report, House of Commons, London.

Knowles, R D (1996) Transport impacts of Greater Manchester's Metrolink light rail system, *Journal of Transport Geography*, **4** (1), pp 1–14, Exeter.

NAO (1998) Report into the first four PFI (UK version of PPP) highway schemes, National Audit Office, London.

PROFIT (2000) Private Operations and Financing of TEN's, Final Report – Public Private Partnerships; introductions handbook, recommendations and conclusions, NEI, Rotterdam; DG TREN, European Commission, Brussels.

SDG (1992) *Public Transport Funding: How does Britain compare?*, SDG, Richmond.

TRaC (1999) Survey of private sector investors in transport projects (unpublished – commercial confidentiality), University of North London, London.

CHAPTER 12

Funding an Integrated Transport Policy

'Integrated transport' may be defined as a cross analysis of different modes of transport (road: car, bus, tram; rail) and different investment options for providing solutions to the two main problems arising from the growth in car and truck usage:

1. congestion
2. pollution

There is a generally accepted view that the long term (30–40 years' time span) solution to the energy and pollution consequences of the motor car in Europe and the other oil using areas of the world (see Figure 12.1) must be the delivery of an integrated transport policy.

Most EU countries house an established pattern of spatial development, with clearly definable areas, namely:

- major urban areas;
- urban 'ribbon' development along valley floors;
- rural areas (affluent, often referred to as 'urban shadow');
- rural market towns;
- remote (often called 'deep rural') rural areas.

Each of these area types has particular transport needs. Future aspirations for transport service provision in each area type need to be explicitly stated so that a blueprint may be developed with appropriate targets for such provision by each transport mode.

There is a clear recognition that it is the urban journey to work movement where the most dramatic changes must occur. This does not mean that other aspects of policy, such as greater inclusivity with a focus on accessibility rather than simply mobility should not be vigorously pursued, in parallel. However, without addressing the journey to work problem, it is unlikely that other aspects will achieve or deliver overall aspirations.

The current policy requirements expressed by the European Commission, national governments and local authorities show the optimistic and realistic levels of investment. Integrated transport is the base of the solution – at a strategic and an operational level. Its rationale and elements are considered.

The use of the 4 I's (explained later in this chapter), and in particular investment, is fundamental to its achievement. However, the underlying questions remain – whether investment is at a sufficiently high level to influence modal split, and what the future sources of the funding are.

DEFINITION OF AN INTEGRATED TRANSPORT POLICY

In contemplating urban transport problems there is a fundamental policy decision between an *Integrated Transport Policy* which has one Policy Authority (Public); public investment and ownership; private investment and ownership; or a combination of public and private enterprise (using tendering?) (indeed which of these are compatible?) and *Free Market Competition* with policy determined by profit potential; private ownership; private control; and no integration or planning of policies between companies.

Considerable discussion has surrounded this policy but what does it mean? An integrated transport policy examines four relationships:

- Integration within and between different types of transport – better and easier interchange between car/bus/rail etc, with better information on services and availability of integrated tickets. Thus it is between public and private transport, between motorised and non-motorised (walking, cycling) transport within public transport.
- Integration with the environment – considering the effect of transport policies on the environment and selecting the most environmentally friendly solution whenever possible.
- Integration with land use planning – to reduce need for travel and to ensure new developments can be reached by public transport.
- Integration with policies on social welfare, education, health and wealth creation so that cross-cutting policies on issues such as social inclusion, school travel, cycling and walking, and the profitability of business work together rather than against each other.

The preferred structure to achieve such integration nationally, regionally or locally has three prerequisites:

- a single policy and budgetary authority at the strategic (geographic) level both national and regional;
- a single co-ordinating body for all modes of transport at the strategic (geographic) level both national and regional;
- operational level cooperating bodies to achieve seamless interchange between modes, within modes, and between modes and land uses/

human activities. This relates to physical interface and the provision of through ticketing.

While services in the third category may be provided by contractors, the first two should involve a single body.

Such a system exists in most member states of the European Union where high investment levels, with co-ordination policies of services, fares and infrastructure developments, may be found in major centres as well as in local areas. The regional councils of France have transport as a major policy issue with their responsibility covering local railway services (with SNCF) and for bus operations in the municipalities. In Sweden regional public transport bodies run local bus and rail services in a country with many rural areas, a small population (8 million) and a concentration of people in a small part of the total land area. The Netherlands has a national ticketing system for local public transport (the Nationale Strippenkaart) and a national railway service but with provinces being responsible for all bus, rail and train-taxi services and for stations. Track operations are retained by the state-owned Railned. In Austria, the *Land* (equivalent to the consortia areas) has responsibility within its areas for all local public transport and land use planning, linking into national policy for rail services. Joint ticketing exists on all services within the *Land*. The proposals for smaller, new member states equate in many ways to these, and would be taken further to the point where control and finance, policy and service provision, though not necessarily all operations, would be conducted by one national and a small number of regional bodies.

Elements

If the analysis is confined (for the moment) to the passenger transport then the elements may be integrated (with a trade-off on expenditure between them based on a single multi-modal evaluation technique). The elements are:

- road investment;
- rail investment (infrastructure/rolling stock);
- bus investment (terminals and vehicles);
- public transport interchanges;
- walking/cycling facilities investment;
- traffic management (physical and fiscal);
- public transport fares levels, public transport service level, and consequent contractual payments.

GOVERNANCE OF AN INTEGRATED TRANSPORT POLICY

With one financing authority, the use of the same investment criteria would be possible. These would be applied to fares (and thus achieve cross-price elasticity effects), improved service quality (with for example payments for maintenance of stations and train interiors), wage rates (to assist in achieving required staff levels) and capital investment in new trains, signalling, station refurbishment, and new track. These could be compared with the use of Government funds for new roads and road maintenance. The comparison should be on one basis, cost benefit analysis (with the inclusion of externalities such as environmental factors, urban development, journey times, congestion and comfort of passengers), and not cost revenue or profitability analysis, to provide a consistent approach to setting investment priorities.

The principle of current passengers paying for future facilities is also one which should be discontinued. Fares increases in an integrated market would reduce demand for public transport but the existence of a cross-price elasticity effect in the market would transfer passengers onto the roads. An integrated policy with a single basis of evaluation enables the rail and road solutions to be considered together.

Budgetary authority

There is no reason why this should be regarded as a drain on the public purse. An integrated system would provide better value for money since the most appropriate solution to any particular problem could be selected. At present the various highway and public transport authorities in any region can only consider solutions within their own statutory limits. There is no overall authority to decide whether a road or railway would be the optimum allocation of resources in that particular case.

The business approach?

Rail transport has in the past been operated as a business rather than having social and economic benefits as the objectives. This approach is partly historic in that the majority of the original operators were private companies and partly because the operators received funds from customers as well as Government and should therefore be seen as commercial enterprises.

The only effective way in which railways can be used to reduce congestion is to take an integrated approach to all modes and see them as part of the overall transport facility. This would provide best value for money, the most appropriate solution in cost benefit terms would be selected and all investment would be assessed on a common basis.

An integrated approach to funding

With one financing authority, the case for public funding to reduce fares, improve service quality or provide investment could be compared fairly with the use of Government funds for new roads and road maintenance. Clearly, however, such an authority requires adequate funding to make major improvements to the public transport system to cope with the projected demand from increased employment in the next decades and from the shift of car users to rail and bus.

APPLICATION OF AN INTEGRATED TRANSPORT POLICY

Rationale

The key objective of integrated transport is to provide for a split between accessible and affordable modes of travel which both are sustainable and become preferred modes of travel.

However, EU member states have different spatial characteristics ranging from densely populated urban areas through major towns and important rural centres to deep rural areas. The potential for transfer to public transport therefore varies between urban and rural areas. But even such a difference can be narrowed. However, improvements are required in the public transport system before car users can be persuaded to change and non-car owners are able to make reasonably timed and priced journeys.

The responsibilities of government must extend to road and rail transport, thus enabling it to balance investment between the best solutions to transport problems.

Local transport plans (LTP) of the form proposed by the UK government for the co-ordination of transport movements have a crucial role in promoting integrated and sustainable transport. They should be seen in the context of users and suppliers and backed by appropriate policies, powers and resources. The policies and proposals in the LTPs should relate and support unitary development plans (UDP) and be compatible in a regional context. An integrated transport policy is not anti-road nor pro-public transport; rather it seeks to optimise investment expenditure on a sustainable basis. It means getting best value for the investment made but bearing in mind the long term consequences that personal travel and movement of freight have on the environment, health and quality of life. It is not a low cost policy nor need it be unaffordable. A national/regional model offers benefits in terms of a framework for policies that are consistent in all areas of a country to fund and deliver public transport.

The provision for bottom-up decision making by county councils alone or in consortia will ensure that the distinctive need characteristics of urban and rural areas are provided for. Decisions on the rail network have to be made nationally or internationally; decisions on local bus and associated public transport (including taxis) have to be made regionally/locally, with the operations integrated into one total journey network.

To develop an integrated transport policy best suited to a country's needs, certain key functions have to be in place:

- a national rail network;
- the national road network;
- bus policy (regulation);
- regional public transport policies;
- local roads;
- land use planning;
- bus quality partnerships;
- traffic management.

The suggested structure will achieve all the requirements of an integrated transport policy, but the concerns that it will lead to a top-down approach from a central government, although understandable, can be overcome if the functions of the national and regional bodies are clearly set out.

Summary of responsibilities

To achieve an integrated transport policy, the following responsibilities, powers and functions are those which government and local authorities between them need the policy-making role for, and power to finance:

- road construction investment and maintenance;
- bus service frequencies, routes and subsidy/contract payment levels;
- investment incentives;
- rail investment;
- rail passenger service levels and contractual arrangements with TOCs;
- environmental issues;
- land use/development;
- current powers of the Traffic Commissioners;
- traffic reduction/traffic management policy and regulation;
- personal safety of pedestrians, cyclists and provision for those groups;
- mobility impaired people;
- liaison with Sustrans other cycling bodies;
- airport development and air service development and regulation (with appropriate private sector involvement);
- bus industry regulation;
- public transport policy generally;

- rail regulation (Rail Regulator) and user group representation;
- regulatory framework for taxis/private hire cars;
- port development and shipping services promotion;
- integration of road/rail freight operations.

It has been argued that the European Union needs to establish an integrated passenger transport policy and that it should learn the lessons from the mass transit policies pursued in the United States following federal legislation (United States Senate, 1991) requiring each State to determine a plan to reduce environmental pollution resulting from high traffic flows. Most have constructed urban mass transport system infrastructures of varying capacities (light rail, full metro, heavy rail) dependent on the size of the urban area, and in all cases the infrastructure was either new or underwent major upgrading and refurbishment. The policies indicate a realisation that private cars form the major proportion of traffic flows in urban areas and that an alternative mode at a competitive (if subsidised) price has to be provided before car users will consider a modal change. Such policies are essential if urban pollution resulting from car use is to be reduced.

The two primary issues which emerged from experience in the United States were:

- a common policy for all states in the Union
- a policy based on an integrated approach to evaluation of all modes of passenger transport with road, rail and waterway schemes being considered using the same multicriteria model.

The integrated approach is also fundamental to the provision of seamless interchange between the car and public transport (eg at park and ride interfaces) and between various forms of public transport (bus, light rail, river bus and train) while the evaluation techniques outlined have therefore to use common criteria. A range of measurement methods both monetary and non-monetary, quantitative as well as qualitative, have been used in various US states.

If a common policy throughout Europe is to be achieved for investment appraisal of new infrastructure then a common set of criteria is required. These criteria will need to take account of transportation factors and the specific issues which arise in peripheral areas of the European Union. The criteria would of course need to take into account the recently issued White Papers:

- Commission Communication on the future development of the Common Transport Policy (COM(92) 494, December 1992)
- The impact of transport on the environment – A Community Strategy for Sustainable Mobility (Green Paper) (COM(92) 48, February 1992)

- Towards fair and efficient pricing in transport – policy options for internalising the external costs of transport in the European Union (Green Paper COM(95) 691, December 1995)
- The Citizen's Network – fulfilling the potential of public passenger transport in Europe (Green Paper COM(96), 1996)
- A Strategy for revitalising the Community's Railways (COM(96) 421, July 1996).

THE 4 I's

In an English Tourism Council study (ETB, 1999; ETC, 2001; Cole, 2001) the following 4 I's were identified as the integration equation for passenger transport:

Information + Interchange + Investment = Integration

The absence of any of these elements will hinder or even prevent the development of an integrated passenger transport system.

Information

Visitors, particularly those coming from overseas, need to know more than simply how to undertake the first stage of their journey. They need to know how to travel beyond any given intermediate transfer point and on to their chosen destination – the Dutch refer to this as trip chain management through the Planner Plus information system. Each mode of transport can provide information about its services, such as the National Rail Enquiry Service, airport hotlines, as well as coach and bus timetables and route planners.

The drawback of single one-mode information systems is that planning more complex travel in advance is not well served. Additionally, they assume that all travellers are the same, and do not cater for differences in visitor types or specific markets such as people with disabilities.

Train and bus operators have low budgets (£20 million per annum on rail advertising, £6 million on Transport Direct/Traveline) available to promote these modes when compared with car manufacturers (£480 million per annum). The majority of the public may also perceive car travel costs as being petrol only and, subsequently, have little appreciation of the true costs of motoring, and the relative costs of train/bus options.

Currently, the pricing structure of rail tickets (where the cheapest fares can only be booked in advance) penalises both tourists making last-minute plans and also those not aware that tickets bought on the day of travel are more expensive. Greater information needs to be made available here with a simplified, easier to understand fare structure for the railways.

The ultimate goal should be the Planner Plus system provided by Netherlands Railways (NS), giving the travel information identified in a recent study (INIT, 2003) of information needs and improvements:

- Train, bus and coach times and taxi telephone numbers, and fares, as the primary needs (air/ferry information was also identified).
- Rail information is well provided for by the NRES telephone line but is difficult to find on the internet.
- Simplified fares structure is complex.
- Bus information available locally is usually good.
- Traveline provides a telephone service similar to Planner Plus for bus and rail services with online maps for the total journey.
- Timetables are difficult to read, and often not lit, at bus stops and railways/bus stations.
- Signage outside bus/rail stations is in general poor and at best average. Railway station on-platform information on buses, taxis, routes to telephone and village/town centre requires improvement.
- Connecting services bus/rail are often uncoordinated.
- There is a need for travellers to have their own pre-information on locations. More training in route geography for call centre staff was identified.
- Printed versions of through travel information as produced by Planner Plus in the Netherlands would be welcomed by travellers.
- Although not an information issue, a lack of left luggage facilities was criticised compared with other EU member states. The security issue was dismissed by most travellers.

Interchanges

High quality seamless interchange facilities are an essential requirement to match the convenience of private vehicles. Particular attention needs to be paid to the ease of ticketing arrangements, eg tickets that allow travel on different types of transport, and the physical environment of interchanges:

- Ticketing – the ability to purchase tickets for the entire journey, across all transport modes, needs to be improved, without introducing complex pricing structures that become a disincentive to travel. In addition, the case for issuing tickets allowing entry to certain attractions, as well as travel, needs to be considered.
- Physical environment – tourists, usually with luggage, require ease and comfort when changing between transport modes, as otherwise it will be difficult to persuade people of the benefits of using public transport. In order to make interchanges attractive and user-friendly, there is a need to provide for ease of movement; luggage storage facilities; secure parking for cycles, cars and motorcycles; undercover links; clear

signage and timetable displays; short walking distances; well maintained facilities; and personal safety and security.

Visitors are likely to be burdened down with luggage; they may well have young children with them or could be impaired in terms of their mobility due to age or physical disability. The ease with which they can change between modes from train to bus or taxi will be critical to determining their experience of public transport and whether they would wish to use it again.

Studies into traveller needs (DCMS, 1999; ETC, 2001; INIT, 2003) have suggested the following criteria for seamless interchanges:

- clear, comprehensive information on the interchange characteristics;
- ease of movement (particularly for those with heavy luggage or young children);
- secure parking for cycles, cars and motorcycles;
- undercover links between modes;
- clear directional signs, between modes and to local destinations (eg town centre, hotels);
- short walking distances;
- good timetable displays;
- well maintained infrastructure, clean toilets, etc;
- personal style;
- left luggage facilities;
- car hire provision.

Action has to be taken to implement these policies, so providing seamless interchange between train, bus and taxi. As with many policies, their success lies in the positive impact on traveller convenience.

Investment

On the strategic level, the achievement of travellers' requirements – the prerequisite to inducing modal change – is through funding and organisation of change.

There is a general recognition that changes in personal commitment are the real key to achieving more sustainable mobility. Changing personal behaviour is not easy particularly when motor car advertising is 24 times that of railway expenditure. Blaming the government is a familiar excuse, in that it might be argued that public awareness of the public transport options is its responsibility. Making the train or bus more attractive requires investment. Sometimes it needs to smarten up the image and the service quality. Often, because of long term underinvestment, a more radical and more expensive expenditure programme is needed.

The argument that as the transport industry is in the private sector then public funding should not be forthcoming is now recognised as unrealistic.

Public funding on a large scale is however the answer to improved quality and reliability, but recognising that private investors require a financial commitment over a longer term than provided by government treasuries.

The primary means of affecting modal split in the short term is through attracting more passengers out of their cars and on to public transport. The opportunities to reduce leisure journeys are few; some opportunities exist for some people to work from home on say one day a week but service providers and production workers, by the very nature of their jobs, are excluded.

QUESTIONS

The White Papers and reports on integrated transport produced throughout Europe are a reconciliation of the need for the best transport systems and the financial reality. Is the policy achievable? Will the investment be provided? What of rural areas? Road improvements will be vital for both public and private transport use. But will the car have to continue to be the most common means of travel and is any other alternative better in energy/pollution terms given the sparsity of the population? New GPS/GIS techniques for controlling and improving rural bus operations are in use in Gwynedd and in Carmarthenshire to assist in modal transfer. Tourist honeypots may benefit from small urban solutions because of high seasonal passenger flows.

The chapter returns to the issue of evaluation and funding in more detail later.

THE EUROPEAN UNION CONTEXT

There is currently an imbalance in the development of different modes of transport, with road investment being predominant. This leads to inefficiencies in the network in terms of social and environmental costs. Freight transport has expanded by 50 per cent in the last two decades and this may be expected to rise further with the enlarged European Union. Road freight has so far been the main beneficiary of this increase. Likewise passenger transport has increased rapidly, with private car use accounting for the majority of this increase.

The imbalance between modal split is also evident in transport infrastructure across the Union (EC, 1992). The peripheral regions (in Wales, Scotland, Spain, Portugal, Greece, Ireland and the 'new' (2004) member states) have seen underinvestment in infrastructure. This is addressed through the European regional development fund and the cohesion fund. The White Paper outlines a policy for enabling inter-modal operations to give more consumer choice, a more efficient network and one which assists in development particularly of more peripheral EU areas.

There is a lack of good methodological interrelationships between the member states of the European Community which have different technical specifications and operating practices, caused mainly by the fact that transport planning in the past has been geared towards a national perspective. This highlights the need for a trans-European transport network for each mode of transport, gradually integrating each to a multi-model, multicriteria approach. Particular emphasis has been put on developing the links between the peripheral regions of the community with its central core, the London-Paris-Brussels-Amsterdam-Cologne 'golden banana' (EC, 1992).

One way of tackling under-capacity in certain modes of transport and over-capacity in others is to charge full infrastructure and other costs to users, for example through road tolls, or by harmonising excise duties. The predominant use of the private car has led the European Commission to consider a 'Citizens' Network of public transport across Europe, for services which interconnect air, bus and rail systems to provide efficient alternatives to private car use (EC, 1995).

EUROPEAN UNION POLICY

In the policy documents referred to above there is a clear indication of a preference for an integrated transport policy.

The objective (set out in 'Towards Fair and Efficient Pricing in Transport') of internalising externalities is to ensure that the cost and benefits of transport facilities are paid for in full by the user rather than fall on others. Not all costs and benefits are received only by those who pay for them. The internal costs or private costs are borne by the persons engaged in the transport activity (eg time, vehicle fuel costs) and external costs which are paid for by others or by society. Thus if a user generates environmental costs they are included in social costs but not necessarily in the internal costs of the polluter.

The Citizens Network Green Paper (EC, 1995) makes it clear that to achieve a Europe-wide network, local link points are 'essential'. There is a need for local integrated transport policies at national, regional or municipal level and it is here that the development of integrated solutions to passenger transport problems should be dealt with first.

There are two levels of integration identified by the Commission. Firstly integrating individual modes (car, cycle and walking) and public transport is 'essential' through the construction of seamless interchange infrastructure (multi-modal terminals, park and ride facilities). Secondly, and in parallel, the establishment of an information and traffic management system which allows assessment of travel choices before and during the journey is required.

Travel from Great Britain to The Netherlands between two cities of similar size provides an example of good practice 'seamless' interchange.

Oxford–Delft

- Car to park and ride.
- Bus to Oxford Station.
- Train to Paddington.
- Heathrow Express to Heathrow Airport, T4. Travelator within T4.
- KLM/BA to Amsterdam Schiphol Airport.
- Seamless interchange to Nederlandse Spoorwegen Station – Schiphol.
- Cross platform interface at Rotterdam.
- 5-minite wait for train to Delft.
- Bus station/bicycle park adjacent to Delft station.

Integration is therefore necessary ('essential') through the co-ordination of bus, tram, metro and rail operators. This applies to the physical structures (eg terminals, stations) and to ticketing information systems and tariffs.

The Nationale Strippenkaart in the Netherlands is the national ticket usable on all trams, metro, and buses all over the country and on some commuter trains. This comes nearest to the concept of the fully integrated ticket.

Transport planning 'should be integrated between all modes' (EC, 1995) so that maximum benefit can be achieved from improvements and investment in any particular mode, with the use of inter-modal terminals, public transport priority measures (eg bus lanes) with techniques to increase the use of methods to encourage the use of public transport and discourage the use of private cars. Merely improving public transport will not attract car users (as the United States' experiences have shown); there also needs to be a mix of the type of measures with which this chapter began.

THE CONGESTION PROBLEM

It has long been suggested that London should have a strategic transport authority – in 1905, in 1925, in 1943, in 1980, in 1989 and in 1996 and in most years in between.

In March 1989 the Confederation of British Industry (CBI, 1989) became the latest in a long list of bodies who produced what they saw as solutions for London's transport congestion. It was almost the twenty-first anniversary of the 'Transport in London' White Paper (MOT, 1968) which proposed an overall transport planning authority for London with wide powers of control over London Transport, British Rail and highways. These powers would be held by the Greater London Council and the Minister of Transport.

Consider two separate statements:

First: 'London should be a transport priority zone under the authority of a government minister ... who would have sufficient powers to provide real and obvious cohesion between future rail, road, Underground and land developments to ensure that all modes of transport complement each other.'

Second: 'The cause of the London traffic problem, that is to say the want of proper adequate streets, is not primarily finance, nor the growth of London; it is the want through the centuries and at the present time of some controlling authority with comprehensive power such as has existed in Paris, Berlin and Vienna.'

It might at first be thought that both statements were made in the last few months. The second however was a statement of the underlying cause of congestion in London both on the roads and public transport identified by Sir Lyndon Macassey (1927), President of the Institute of Transport, in his Presidential address: 'The problem of London traffic'. He continued: 'A chief essential in providing comprehensively, in an area like Greater London, the maximum of travelling facilities at a minimum of cost is that each type of agency of transport whether railways, tubes, tramways or omnibuses shall be used for handling the kind of traffic for which it is technically and economically best fitted. There has been no public attempt whatever to secure such co-ordination of function. Perhaps the most striking illustration (of detrimental competition) is the competition between London General Omnibus Company's buses and the tramways of the London County Council. Illustrations could be multiplied almost indefinitely to show the unco-ordinated provision and uncorrelated growth of the means of transit and the absence of all co-ordination in their operation.'

Sir Lyndon was President of the Institute of Transport in 1924. There have been calls by the GLC in 1980, the CBI in its 1989 report, the source of the first statement (CBI, 1989), the last Government's policy document Transport – The Way Forward (DOT, 1996) and by planners and academics before and since.

Indeed it is made abundantly clear that transport has a major role to play in the country's environmental and congestion-solving strategy. Transport 'should play a positive role in saving our towns and cities. To ensure this the Government's aim is to civilise urban traffic – easing congestion, helping to improve the local environment and reducing air and noise pollution. Good transport management and effective alternatives to the car can also help.' In larger cities road congestion is caused mainly by local traffic. 'The Government believes that what is needed is a balanced traffic management policy ... improvements to traffic flow on strategic routes ... improved public transport ... greater priority for buses ... more positive use of parking controls (by local authorities) ... designation of the Red

Route network ... promote safe cycling ... develop a cycle network across London ... bypasses (to) redirect traffic to more suitable routes ... good public transport' (DOT, 1996).

This is further emphasised in recent reports from London Transport (LT, 1995, 1996) and from London First and from the Government Office for London (GOL, 1996, London Pride Partnership, 1996) which further indicate concerns about London's position as a world city and its role as a major financial centre from which many jobs and billions of pounds of foreign exchange earnings are derived.

A finer grouping of policy objectives one would be hard pressed to find. These are all contained in the Government's environmental strategy for Britain. However, few decisions have been made on major funding into rail metro, light rail or bus infrastructure, particularly since most of those operations are in the private sector and would require extensive negotiations prior to commencement it would have been expected that discussions on proposals would by now have been well advanced.

Causes of congestion

The causes of road congestion are insufficient capacity, greater demand and a low level of investment in new roads or road improvements. Congestion on public transport is caused by a significant increase in demand on a system which has suffered from decades of low investment.

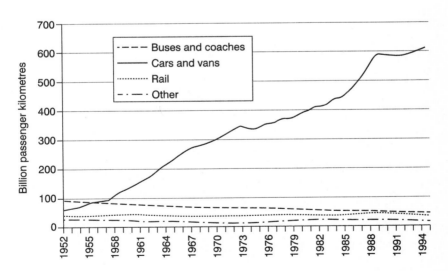

Figure 12.1 *Passenger travel by mode 1952–1995 Great Britain*
Sources: *Transport Statistics Great Britain*, HMSO, London (various editions to 1996)
Developing an Integrated Transport Policy, DETR, London 1997

The main reasons for this increased demand are the upsurge in economic activity, affordable cheap fare policies and a change in public awareness of mass transit, which can bring a major shift by commuters from car to rail.

Car ownership has increased by almost 10 times since the 1950s and doubled since 1970 in the UK and most of western Europe (see Figures 12.1 and 12.2). The forecasts show a similar rate of growth up to 2030 (see Figure 8.4). The accession of new states to the European Union is an indicator of the changes that have taken place in what was the Soviet Union. In countries such as Poland, Lithuania and the Czech Republic car ownership has risen from around 5 per cent of households in the 1980s to 30 per cent of households by 2003 as a consequence of middle-income growth. A second period of increased disposable income is predicted within the next 10 years, and levels of car ownership are expected to reach 50–60 per cent of households (Poland, Lithuania Ministries of Transport), with a consequent significant rise in energy consumption, congestion and pollution in these areas.

Road congestion

The London Assessment Studies commissioned by the Department of Transport in 1986 examined traffic problems in four main London Corridors. The South Circular Road study (DOT, 1989b) showed that private cars constituted on average over 80 per cent of total vehicles on that

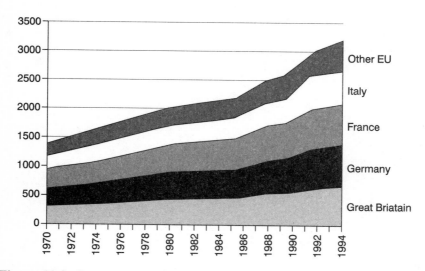

Figure 12.2 *Passenger traffic: cars in selected member states, 1970–1994*
Sources: European Union, *Transport in Figures*, Second Edition, Luxembourg (1997), Developing an Integrated Transport Policy, DETR, London (1997)

energy consumption per capita
Tonnes oil equivalent

toe per capita
0–1
1–2
2–3
3–4
> 4

Figure 12.3 *Who uses the energy?*
Source: British Petroleum (BP) plc

road, light vans used by delivery firms and repairers represent 12 per cent while heavy goods vehicles constituted only 2 per cent of the total (see Figure 12.4).

To achieve any major impact on road congestion therefore it is clear that reductions in car flows will play a key role. By coincidence passengers are also the customers for whom other alternative modes are available. Traffic speeds also need to be considered in parallel to modal split; car ownership has risen and those speeds have fallen to an average of 11.5 mph in the peak (CIT, 1992) and speeds on some main roads are little different from what they were in Sir Lyndon Macassey's day.

London's peak traffic problems may be divided into three types – commuter movements in the central business district (the City and the West End), orbital movements, and local work or school traffic. Added to this are the 'off peak' movements in the central area when even then, a minor incident can cause serious traffic jams.

MARKET FORCES AND AN INTEGRATED TRANSPORT POLICY

Is there a 'Single Market'?

The cheap fares policies of the GLC between 1980 and 1983 led to a change in public awareness of rail mass transit. There was a major shift by commuters from car to rail as a result of fares reductions, clearly

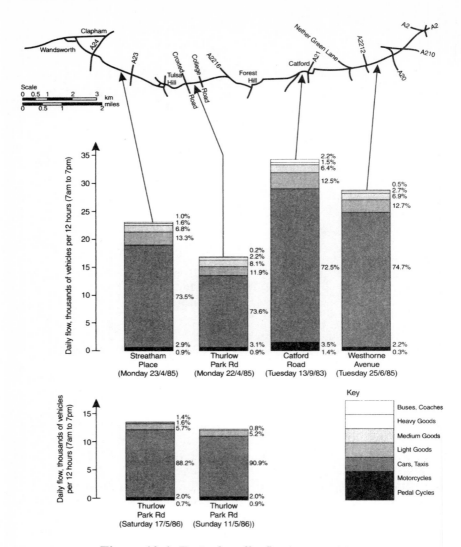

Figure 12.4 *Typical traffic flow composition*
Source: Department of Transport South Circular Road Assessment Study Stage 1 Report
Problems, Travers Morgan, London 1986 (TAS, 1986)

indicating that a single market existed for commuters rather than separate car and rail markets. This was paralleled by the introduction and development of the London Transport/BR Travelcard which made regular travel more convenient and the card's multi-ride facility led to additional trips during the day and for evening or weekend leisure travel which the cardholder perceived as 'free'. The growth in popularity of London as a tourist destination has also led to increased usage of the central sections of the Underground.

In the 1980–1985 period the lowering and raising of fares showed a cross price elasticity of demand over the total commuter market which indicated that the market was not separate segments – car, bus, tube, rail – but a single integrated market within which travellers would move from one mode to another as they responded to changing relative charges of each mode of transport.

The existence of cross-priced elasticity indicates a need to consider all the available transport modes in determining the most efficient solution. This applies to movements into Central London, orbital journeys, local journeys in the peaks and often throughout the day. Such consideration can only be achieved if there is a single authority responsible for all the strategic transport decisions for the whole of London and with control of all aspects of the strategic transport budget.

A Metropolitan Transport Authority responsible for roads and public transport (through a partnership) with financial and strategic planning powers was suggested 25 years ago (HOC, 1980).

A transport authority of this form would provide for a trade-off in transport expenditure between capital expenditure on new roads (eg urban motorways), traffic management schemes (for example through fewer parking spaces, greater resources spent on preventing illegal parking, road pricing – as a means of a parking restraint, and area control) and the use of public transport (through subsidies, investment, improved service quality and integrated ticketing).

Table 12.1 *Effects of LT fares charges on peak central area commuter traffic (% change)*

	Fare %	Underground %	Car %
1980–81	−38	+6	−6
1981–82	+82	−13	+14
1982–83	−27	+11	−9
1980 base figure (000's)		435	184

Source: London Regional Transport: The LT Fares Experience, 1984 (Economic Research Report 259 (LT, 1984; TfL, 2002a)

In the Stage 2 Assessment Study Reports (DOT, 1989b) the consultants presented options on road and rail solutions but the only Government commitment to rail investment with definite funding for network extensions has been for the Jubilee Line Extension to London Docklands and Stratford via South London, and the Docklands Light Railway extension to Beckton. The cheap fares policy of the GLC in the early 1980s showed that if mass transit fares were reduced then car travellers would transfer. Currently there is no passenger capacity for this transfer at peak times on certain parts of the Underground and heavy rail networks.

A lead has been set by Paris and Washington, DC on a large scale, Amsterdam and Manchester as major cities, and Bordeaux, Grenoble and Sheffield as cities of 300,000 inhabitants. Many countries have taken the lead in bus investment (Scandinavia, Germany). Many other cities still require that investment lead – Edinburgh and Dublin and many where investment is urgently required (Cardiff, Bristol).

EVALUATION AND FINANCING OF RAILWAY AND ROAD INVESTMENT WITHIN AN INTEGRATED TRANSPORT POLICY

Basis of evaluation

This brings the argument back to its most difficult point. The Central London Rail Study contained a development strategy for improving services to rail passengers, forecasts of demand, suggestions on improving existing resource utilisation, a list of strategic choices and packages of measures whose costs are justified in terms of revenue and external (to the railway) benefits. This is an integrated transport policy approach where the proposals consider congestion on railways and buses together with the options for attracting car users onto the network in a context of the total funding to be provided and the priorities for expenditure.

Integrated approach to priority evaluation

The evaluation technique used by governments to prioritise transport schemes will reflect their policies and the developments they would wish to see in the rail and road network and the public transport system within an integrated transport policy. The expenditure relates to capital infrastructure projects and not to revenue support payments (subsidy).

There are two primary characteristics within the overall evaluation process:

- establishing the policy and sustainability of individual projects;
- ranking the projects within a priority list.

Evaluation context

Any schemes put forward to a government for funding will have to meet its evaluation criteria. In the UK, these were based solely on COBA and the Environmental Import Analysis. The shortcomings of the two techniques, which were created separately, have now largely been overcome through the New Approach to Transport Appraisal (NATA, 1999) elements, which 'will enable the application of scarce resources to be most effective and enable investment discussions to be consistent with policy objectives' (NATA, 1999; NAfW, 2001; STAG, 2001; GOMMS, 2001).

Schemes may come individually or as 'packages', for example:

- new infrastructure schemes making a contribution to community regeneration;
- integrated transport packages (from companies, consortia or partnerships);
- safe Road to Schools Schemes; or
- road schemes.

There are five criteria. Each one represents a particular benefit from the scheme and is considered using a set of questions that will help the reader identify the underlying meaning of each criterion (GOMMS, 2001). The criteria are:

1. *Accessibility:*
   - access improvements to services;
   - wider regional, national British/EU accessibility or remove a serious constraint;
   - reduction in community severance.
2. *Safety:*
   - overall safety benefits/reduced accidents;
   - encouragement of healthy modes/lifestyles;
   - improve personal security.
3. *Environment:*
   - net improvement in noise environment;
   - localised air quality disbenefits;
   - impact on CO_2 emissions;
   - impact on landscape, townscape, special sites.
4. *Economy:*
   - benefit cost ratio;
   - benefits for sustainable development/job creation;
   - proposal complements/enhances similar benefits;
   - impact on congestion/added capacity.
5. *Integration:*
   - fit with other strategies/transport/land use policies;
   - assist intermodal interchange;
   - improve traveller confidence.

Criteria

An approach that clarifies the application of each criterion involves using questions to produce a score:

- *Accessibility:*
  Does the proposal contain feature(s) that significantly improve access to service (eg education, health, leisure) for the non-car owner/user or for the mobility impaired?
  Examples would be improved pedestrian entrance/pathway/bus stops/links to public transport/education/health centres, or in areas of low car ownership or of known social exclusion.
  Does the proposal contribute to wider accessibility at a regional, national or European level? (Does it remove a constraint for movement between regions or nations?)
  The strategic objectives of a scheme can be identified here and thus by implication will be beyond the journey to work, for example the provision of a missing section of an otherwise high quality piece of infrastructure, eg the provision of a bypass on a strategic road. This does not include journey time improvements, which are covered in criterion 4.
  Does the proposal reduce community severance?
  If a community is currently 'severed' by high traffic volumes or by a physical barrier (eg road, railway) then included would be a scheme to reduce or eliminate that. Localised links between communities or establishing new links between adjacent areas/settlements not previously joined would be included. An example might be a footbridge or cycleway, or improved means of crossing the railway where the settlement itself is currently severed by the railway. This is particularly the case with new infrastructure (motorway, Channel Tunnel Rail Link).
- *Safety:*
  Does the proposal provide overall safety benefits in terms of accidents?
  If a COBA analysis has been carried out effectively, results on cost savings can be included. If this data set is not available then a qualitative judgement on the likely reduction in accidents (pedestrian vehicle conflict) or potential accidents is required. Examples might be a main road through a settlement where a bypass would improve the situation.
  Does the proposal enhance opportunities for those modes that encourage healthy lifestyles, eg walking or cycling?
  Examples would include cycle priority measures or infrastructure links: Sustrans GB Cycle Network Bridges could characterise this. Further examples are secure cycle parking at bus/railway stations or walkways linking settlements/woodland/open space.
  Does the proposal include measures that will improve the personal security needs of travellers or others?

The 'personal security' (not personal safety) aspects relate to improvements to areas where fear of risk from attacks on people or property is present. Examples include redesign of bus/train waiting areas/buildings; rebuilding of such buildings; improved lighting; cameras; easier opportunity for police surveillance. These elements could be at park-and-ride, modal interchanges, public transport facilities and car parks (Cozens et al, 2002).

- *Environment:*

  Does the proposal have a net improvement in the noise environment of residential/noise sensitive properties (schools/hospitals)?

  Government guidelines should indicate that net noise changes should be considered in the context of noise mitigation measures (eg noise reducing surfaces) if these are included in the cost. If such an analysis is not available then changes in noise level should be estimated in terms of traffic flow changes. A calculation based on half the current flow (−3dbA) or double flow (+3dbA) might be applied to dwelling houses or other sensitive properties within 100 metres and direct line of sight to the source of noise.

  Are there localised air quality disbenefits at sensitive receptors?

  If the threshold for a detailed air quality assessment under DMRB is not exceeded then it is reasonable to ignore local used air quality disbenefits for road schemes (government guidelines). This also applies to rail schemes, eg freight sidings with extensive movements; tunnels; steep gradients; and sharp curves.

  Examples (both noise and air quality) relate to the impact of a scheme on 'residential' properties or schools, hospitals and possibly offices. Intermittent noise occurrences might also be considered if these are frequent, eg train services at a (say) 15-minute frequency. These are not definitive rules set down; judgement is therefore required on the extent of the impact.

  Does the proposal avoid an increase in or even reduce CO_2 emissions?

  This can normally be considered if there has been a measured assessment and if this indicates there has been no 'significant' rise in CO_2 emissions.

  A question to be asked in relation to a bus/rail scheme is whether a modal shift from the car has resulted. If there is a significant change (occurred or expected) then a high score results, and if only a slight change then 0 or +1 will be appropriate (see scoring range below).

  Examples might be a quality bus corridor (as in Dublin) where a significant reduction in car usage and increased bus usage resulted from reduced bus journey times (by as much as 40 per cent) and new buses on the routes.

  What is the effect on designated nature, landscape, townscape or heritage conservation sites, conservation areas or species protected by statute?

Examples are situations where an AONB/SSSI is likely to be affected by the scheme or where adverse conditions consequent upon heavy traffic can be reduced. A negative score would be achieved by an infrastructure scheme proposed to be built across wetlands (eg a new entrance into a coastal park). The disturbance of a heritage site or the reopening of a railway line where abandonment has resulted in special habitat conditions developing would also score badly, while reducing traffic through improved cycle or bus facilities in a national park would clearly be positive. There may be instances of small towns, eg Newquay or Tenby, where reduced car access coupled with electric bus services in the town (as in central Florence) will have a positive impact on townscape and historic buildings.

Other examples might be balancing the impact of the A55 construction in total against preserving the Conwy estuary (through a £100 million tunnel construction) or the historic walled town, and similarly in considering the positive and negative effects of bypasses on the surrounding countryside and on farming.

- *Economy:*

  These sections relate to the COBA analysis (journey time scoring and vehicle operating cost savings elements) evaluated in monetary terms. This technique applies in its primary form to roads analysis. However, COBA Plus, incorporating public transport investment, continues to use resource cost as the base and includes wider benefits, journey time savings (to public transport users and continuing road users), road vehicle operating costs net effect, crowding relief and additional rail/bus revenue.

  a) *What is the overall benefit to cost ratio (BCR) for the proposal (user benefits and public transport benefits)?*

    Proposals are to be ranked according to the BCR calculated using cost benefit analysis techniques (COBA or COBA Plus). A coarser analysis based on cost and benefits calculated between primary nodes and considering noticeable changes in journey time may be used. The particular variation used should be identified.

    Examples would be a bypass incorporating traffic flow as a result of avoiding narrow roads and junctions in an older settlement. Similarly bus priority measures or new vehicles or busways may be evaluated, as may a new rail proposal. Improved rail/bus frequencies, reliability and punctuality may be considered (see criterion 5, 'Integration – improve traveller confidence', to avoid double counting) where these impact on, for example, journey time or other cost benefit elements.

  b) *Does the proposal complement or enhance similar benefits or earlier proposals? (Cross refer to (c) below.)*

The schemes would include access to strategic economic sites/areas included in local authority/development agency plans. This relates in particular to schemes resulting in a reduced need to travel.

c) *Does the proposal provide benefits for sustainable development and/or job creation (eg tourism, designated regeneration areas, dependent development schemes)?*

Examples would be improved links between peripheral areas of the country (in European schemes the EU Interreg areas, eg southern Greece, Portugal, Italy, Ireland, Wales and Scotland) and primary markets in urban industrial areas of EU member states. Included might be road or rail infrastructure or vehicle improvement schemes where the impact on inward investment and thus job creation could be seen or even measured. However, it might also relate to public transport information system improvements which help encourage local leisure or work travel by more sustainable means.

d) *Does the proposal address a problem of congestion by providing additional capacity?*

This may be applied where sustainable economic activity is adversely affected by congestion and where CBA does not capture the full economic benefits. The benefits may not be included in (a) above because average traffic speed is too low (ie below the cut-off in the COBA speed flow curve).

Examples are where potential inward investors perceive congestion (possibly at a single 'bottleneck') and where the behavioural reaction affects their investment strategies. It may also divert drivers on to other roads. The additional capacity may be applied to a road scheme; alternatively the planned solution may be in enhanced public transport.

• *Integration:*

Does the proposal accord with other agendas (including health and community) and transport and land use policies of other authorities/ operators?

This assessment enables a transport scheme to be placed in the context of other strategic policies pursued by local authorities and government. It also enables considerations of conflicts with other strategic transport corridor objectives. Thus issues cutting across several strategic policies may be accounted for.

Examples include consideration of social exclusion or health access objectives. Within transport, examples might be the integration of different modes, links with land use planning and human activities, and evidence that all relevant players are involved in the scheme.

A decision to restructure bus services may show benefits to the socially excluded; they may provide for a large increase in services calling at the railway station, central business district and regional hospital. With improved modal interchange (rail/bus) and public transport facilities, new links might be introduced between the railway station, bus interchange improvements and better access to an edge of town site (hospital, recreation stadium, shopping centre, as for example in Sheffield).

Does the proposal assist the interchange between travel modes? Does it enhance wider modal freight movements?

Through ticketing proposals could also be included.

Examples of freight interchange facilities could be the extent to which a multimodal freight centre produces benefits (if any) for the region. What opportunities are there to use interchange facilities to change modal split? Are there cheaper intermodal exchange equipment/ techniques to attract major haulage operations, e. Freightliner, to move more traffic by rail rather than trans-ship to road at points remote from the region?

Does the proposal improve the confidence of travellers to complete the journey using public transport/private modes (eg car, cycle) on the overall transport network?

This would include the provision of improved information, eg timetables and routes, the dissemination of such information (INIT, 2003) and improvements to reliability (WTRC, 2003; Cole, 2004). The question is – can the traveller make a journey in the knowledge that waiting time is minimised because trains/buses are reliable, connections are made and a door to door trip can be achieved? A comparison lies between the Netherlands' Planner Plus information system on all modes – bus/rail/taxi – and Transport Direct or Traveline in Britain. Netherlands' railways have also returned to a 98 per cent on-time reliability.

Scoring levels

The scoring to determine priority of schemes is partly quantifiable but often qualitative/subjective. The scoring can be shown in an indicative form as follows:

Score	Impact
+2	Significant improvement
+1	Same/partial improvement
0	No change
−1	Worsening
−2	Significant disadvantages

Appraisal summary

An appraisal process such as this can be used to evaluate the options identified by those bidding for central government funds. Scores for individual schemes will vary and ought to if the process is to identify a priority list. The general picture that arises from such an analysis is that in reality individual rail schemes within an area are not going to have a major effect on reducing road congestion. As a knock-on effect of this, the environmental and safety scores of many schemes will be relatively low. The same applies to the economic opportunities perceived to result from specific schemes. Conversely a bypass might cause environmental problems along the route, but removing traffic from a town or village will assist in pushing up the score (eg Newbury).

As would be expected, nearly all rail schemes scored highly on integration, fitting in with transport strategies, assisting intermodal interchange and improving traveller confidence.

Note

This section is based on a priority evaluation methodology developed out of NATA by a team at the National Assembly for Wales Transport Directorate (2001), of which the author was a member.

COST BENEFIT/MULTICRITERIA EVALUATION

An integrated transport policy, in determining its funding priorities, requires an evaluation technique that enables a series of different road, rail, sea or air options to be evaluated using the same criteria. These techniques and their elements are either cost benefit or multicriteria techniques (see Chapter 9 for the elements involved). The analysis includes the traditional monetary elements (eg journey time, vehicle operating cost and accidents costs) and the externalities (eg environmental factors, employment and economic development). Chapter 10 contains a more detailed discussion of these techniques. The following illustrate this approach:

Time

Do they measure the benefit effectively?
Is there a minimum time period perceived by the user as meaningful?
Should time saving benefits only begin to be measured after, say, five minutes?

Accident costs

Are current values appropriate?
Are personal psychological effects fully costed?
Is the statistical base for assessing accident rates appropriate?

Interchanges (links and modal points)

What are the journey time savings?

Does the hub encourage inter-modal freight?

How seamless does passenger interchange have to be?

How is rail and water movement of freight between member states encouraged (in place of road)?

What is the optimum number of modal (or marshalling) points in freight trains in a domestic or international European rail network?

Are the same criteria applicable to urban rail systems as to high speed intercity services?

How does the evaluation of new rail infrastructure better recognise social and environmental benefits?

Peripheral regions

How are journey times affected?

What is the impact of the efficient movement of goods to/from peripheral areas?

What are the comparative effects of differing levels of investment in passenger and freight intercity services eg between France (Fournier, 1991; SNCF, 2003) and the United Kingdom?

Peripheral regions are at the extremities of Britain and of the Union. In general, they are characterised by low income per head levels, low densities of population and a poor rail network. Thus the rates of return on investment in financial terms are likely to be low or even negative. An essential question therefore is how the lower rates of return (in cost benefit or financial appraisal) are to be reconciled with an equating of needs of individuals in such areas which are likely to be similar to those in densely populated and heavily industrialised urban areas. In addition how are such rates of return equated to a policy of development in peripheral areas?

Transit countries/regions/areas

What are the potential effects of efficient rail networks on the environmental position?

How are the inter-state impacts measured?

How is the total efficiency of transportation within Great Britain and within the European Union to be included?

The analysis carried out for the Cross Rail Business Case (TfL, 2002) uses the New Approach to Transport Appraisal technique. The Department for Transport has specified the multimodal GOMMS approach for all road and public transport schemes, and its elements are contained in the Cross Rail analysis. The Appraisal Summary Table identifies how each element is measured or described (see Chapter 10).

Non-integrated approach to evaluation

The evaluation of new roads is carried out in some countries on a cost benefit basis where the benefits (or returns) are relief of congestion, reduced journey time, reduced vehicle operating costs and reduced accident costs. Railway investments on the other hand are evaluated on a cost revenue basis. Some railways in Britain receive no government grant based on the argument that these payments sustain the profitability of the privatised railway (OPRAF, 1996). In the 1980s and 1990s British Inter City services' rate of return objective was 5 per cent financial (cost revenue) on its assets.

In investment terms the primary financial criterion for the railway as a whole was that investment should yield a test discount rate of return of at least 7 per cent compared with the minimum cost alternative. In the subsidised sectors (eg London commuter rail network), the appraisal was conducted in relation to the cheapest way of keeping the existing service running rather than discontinuing it. Other grants (eg Section 56) would be set against the costs.

Funding levels

Further expenditure would be needed on London's commuter railway network – all of which is now operated by private companies through franchises issued by the Strategic Rail Authority. London Transport estimated (1996) a capital investment programme of £10 billion to achieve a 'decently modern metro'. London First, an organisation representing major companies, banks and City institutions, puts the figure at nearer £23 billion if additional metro, bus-related and outer suburban schemes to reduce traffic flow and pollution in those areas are also considered. Only such a level would compare favourably with the $1 billion per annum for the New York Subway and Commuter Rail System and the $12 billion spent (1984–92) building the Washington DC Metro. The amounts of money required are formidable and only likely to come from private capital sources if private financiers are given a risk allocation that is acceptable and the rate of return is attractive. Conversely they might not necessarily be keen to invest in the area of greatest need or with the highest cost-benefit based returns but a low financial rate of return. (Chapter 10 considers public private partnership investment.)

Funding of transport

In following this principle, several questions arise. How, for example, would the funding for different modal options be achieved? What levels of funding will be available and how will the evaluation and allocation of the funding be decided? A national transport partnership could also be seen within a supportive fiscal framework using various fuel taxes. A land use planning policy should be integrated with transport infrastructure through the county councils. Changes in the decision-making process inherent in the proposals outlined above, the setting of environmental targets promoting greener forms of transport, and landscape and countryside protection policy could then provide a sustainable integrated transport policy.

The current institutional, legislative and administrative structures in the UK do not aid the processes of integration of transport service provision. Indeed, transport provision in the UK is often not treated as a public service and hence a worthwhile cause for investment (capital and revenue) of public funds in the manner that has occurred in other EU countries. Research by the Commission for Integrated Transport (CfIT) has shown that the UK generally has suffered from massive underinvestment in transport for half a century resulting in greater dependence on the car.

Comparisons within Europe

In the immediate past, the UK has typically invested less than 1 per cent of its GDP in transport infrastructure. This is less than the EU average. For bus systems, the UK has provided the lowest level of support in the EU. For rail, the UK has provided higher levels of support but considerably lower investment in infrastructure than comparable EU countries (France and Germany). Consider the level of investment in cities in those countries

Table 12.2 *Comparisons of European cities – transport expenditure*

| | Expenditure in euros per capita | |
	Public transport **Capital and revenue support**	**Roads** **Capital and maintenance**
Stuttgart	341	228
Nantes	130	310
Bristol	17[1]	25[1]
Newcastle	13[1]	113[1]
Leeds	7[1]	34[1]
Cardiff[2]	37	86
Cardiff[3]	60	86
Cardiff[4]	235	269

Notes:
1. Estimate based on Local Transport Plan.
2. Excluding concessionary fares, based on 2002–03 Budget, Cardiff City Council.
3. Including concessionary fares based on 2002–03 Budget, Cardiff City Council.
4. Based on the expenditure of Stuttgart and Nantes (average of the two) and applied to Cardiff on a pro rata euro per capita basis, this is what Cardiff would/should receive to be comparable with the average of the two other cities.

compared with a sample of UK cities with similar sized public transport networks (CfIT, 2003).

The UK has amongst the highest public transport fares in the EU. Comparison of the cost of public and private transport per kilometre in a sample of European cities has suggested that using the car is cheaper in UK cities than elsewhere.

In the UK, public transport operators cover 75–95 per cent of their operating costs through commercial revenue. This compares with operators covering 35–65 per cent of operating costs in other EU countries (CfIT, 2003).

The public sector in other EU countries provides greater support to transport service provision than in the UK. However, in the area of concessionary fares for public transport the situation in Wales does bear favourable comparison with the remainder of the EU (Cole, 2002a). The conclusions of the CfIT research were that transport is underfunded in the UK, and remedies here to be found, and until recently there were flaws in the current appraisal process for transport schemes. The fundamental approach to economic appraisal had changed very little since its introduction in the 1960s. The benefit cost ratio in the economic assessment had dominated the decision-making process despite being regarded as a somewhat limited (excluding environmental factors, for example) representation of benefits. That may be the reason for an inconsistent lack of investment in transport schemes in the UK over the past five decades (CfIT, 2003). The new approach to transport appraisal (NATA, 1999) described in this chapter is intended to overcome these issues.

Table 12.3 *European cities' public transport – primary income sources*

	Commercial revenue %	Revenue support %
Stuttgart	46	54
Nantes	47	53
Bristol	82	18
Newcastle	86	14
Leeds	66	34
Edinburgh	80	20
Cardiff[2]	97	3
Cardiff[3]	66	34

Notes:
1. *Source:* Cardiff Bus/Cardiff City Council 2002–03 Budget.
2. Excluding concessionary fares.
3. Including concessionary fares.

Rail network strategy

Consider the recent debates on railway and bus funding where investment figures have been calculated, to see if Great Britain's investment programme fits the new (NATA) criteria.

The recent discussion on the SRA (2002) Strategic Plan provides an illustration of this dichotomy. Three separate public bodies have produced conclusions reflecting the needs: that 'despite an increase of the UK Government's share of rail investment to £33.5 bn, it is still dwarfed by the real cost of modernising Britain's railway network' (House of Commons Transport Committee, 2002). Specification for incremental outputs (RPC, 1999) and the guide for franchise bidders (NAfW, 2000) provide good examples of the basis for a smartened-up railway. The comparison in Tables 12.4 and 12.5 relate to Wales. It represents, however, many smaller, newer EU countries and the regions and semi-autonomous governments/ areas of larger states.

If the public/private partnership split in the UK government report 'Transport 2010' is taken, then about 50 per cent of the cost of the above programme would fall on the public sector. However, forms of finance other than PPPs, eg bonds, may alternatively be used.

Railways are only a part of the integrated equation. The roads programme in both urban and rural areas involves connections within a country, from and to the rest of Europe. Buses are the biggest carrier of passengers. Therefore, despite the more complex disaggregated nature of the operation, bus operator and county council activities require funding of sufficient bus priority routes, newer vehicles, higher quality waiting facilities, interchanges with other modes and much improved real time information for passengers.

Table 12.4 *Alternative expenditure levels*

New investment	Thoroughly modern European railway (reflection of the vision) £m	Smartened-up railway £m
South Wales ML	400	
Valley Lines	250	
North Wales ML	150	200
Other (including Wrexham, Manchester, Cambrian)	400	
Total cost	1200	200

Source: Agenda, Summer 1999; Swift; RNMS (2000); SRA (2002); various rail studies (1996–2001)

Table 12.5 *10-year investment programme*

	Vision £bn	Expected £bn
New investment	1.2	0.2
Renewals and maintenance	0.8	
Contractual payments (subsidy)	1.0	1.0
Total cost	3.0	1.2

Note:
Public and private expenditure on the railway system is in two parts: 1) new investment – enhancement of the service (through new/upgraded track, signals, stations and trains); 2) revenue support/contractual payments and renewal of the existing infrastructure.

Future sources of funding

- *Increased state funding.* The straightforward solution would be to request that central government increases its funding levels of transport to those occurring in comparable EU countries. Although the UK government is attempting to do that, it is not proven that the existing approach through PFI to PPP can deliver sufficient funds to meet current and future needs (see Chapter 11).
- *Congestion charging.* Experience from the September 2000 fuel crises and the Central London congestion scheme (2003) suggests that congestion charging (pain) will be a success (gain). Research during the fuel crisis (Chatterjee and Lyons, 2002) found that a third of commuters used public transport, cycled, walked or car-shared instead of driving. A quarter of parents walked or cycled their children to school instead of driving and one in seven car users shopped more locally than usual for groceries, going either by car, walking or cycling. The availability of fuel service elasticity or the cost of using the car (cross-price elasticity) illustrates how economic principles may be applied to travel patterns.
- *Value capture (development gain).* A convenient transport system is a significant factor in establishing land and property values. It is therefore reasonable that a share of the increase in value created as a result of the transport system is captured for investment in transport. As the capture of value has hitherto not been recognised as a potential source of funding, there are a few instances where private investors have promoted or taken equity in transport schemes. Timing is a key issue, and private investors need to be brought on board before routes/services have been finalised/announced. Involving interested parties could become standard practice, with a capital gains tax/levy on those who benefit substantially directly as a consequence of provision of transport services.

Note

This section draws on research carried out by the Commission for Integrated Transport, the English Tourism Council, the Wales Transport Strategy Group and the Wales Transport Research Centre. The author led the research in the last three.

CONCLUSION

In many States of the United States there is a clear belief that congestion and environmental benefits accrue from capital investment and operating payments to public transit (NYMTA, 1990). Certainly in the major cities, future movement demands through the automobile are not comparable with a sustainable transportation policy which takes full account of the environmental implications: and a highway system cannot provide sufficient capacity. But in the USA there is no naive belief that pricing Americans our of their cars will be easy. The belief in Washington DC and Los Angeles is that a new system must take the opportunity of being fast and comfortable and therefore by its very nature persuade drivers to leave their cars at home.

Transit systems don't always follow people's demand patterns. The growth of suburban dwellings and job decentralisation away from traditional centres has increased the number of orbital trips along the DC Beltway, and the M25. A radial system alone cannot provide the required service for those, so the need must be for both orbital and radial systems of high frequency trains with interchanges.

The answer therefore is an integrated policy of road investment, traffic management, public transport investment, pricing, and land use. This will attract some road users (in particular car users) away from their vehicles and onto the buses and trains, thus reducing congestion and pollution, and providing a freer flow for remaining users. The Los Angeles investment programme is expected to reduce road traffic flows by 10–15 per cent (LACTC, 1991). If European experiences (eg. South Yorkshire and London in the 1980s) is an indicator, this will be sufficient to provide significant benefits for road congestion. It parallels too the Central London Rail Study (DOT, 1989a) findings on the impact of transit investment on road congestion. But there the parallel ends. Los Angeles had a 30 year agreed plan (though as in Britain government support has reduced); Paris has a 15 year agreed Masterplan; New York is on its second year plan and Washington DC had a 12 year plan. Although some individual major schemes (eg. Crossrail in London) are being considered in Britain, these are few in number and mainly in London, and are not being considered as part of an integrated transport and environment policy. Indeed Government decisions with the PFI have prevented some schemes (eg Crossrail) beginning, delaying others (in the CTRL) and preventing co-ordination of development (LHR Express and Crossrail).

And, while in Britain the integrated bus/rail arrangements in Newcastle, Manchester and London are being broken up, in the United States, France, the Netherlands and Germany the trend is to build more, easier, interchanges and emulate the form of multiride ticketing there is, or was, in some British cities. The outcome of such a policy is a movement towards a sustainable transport policy. The investment costs of such improvements are high, but not so high as the cost of equivalent highway capacity. And given that they are in the main dependent on the electric traction the environmental effects of providing the extra capacity are considerably less in absolute terms and in spatial terms than the road alternative.

The policies within the European Union therefore differ: on one side there are governments set on a course based on market forces and supported in this by the Competition Directorate General (DG-COMP). Alternatively, government might well consider a more radical approach to regulating the privatised public transport (bus and rail) network. The remaining major industrial states (but in particular France, Germany and the Netherlands) are pursuing a policy of the form described in this paper and are supported by the Transport Directorate General (DG-TREN) in the Citizen's Network White Paper (EC, 1995). It is quite clear that the latter policies are those which will achieve a sustainable mobility basis for passenger transport in the future. Conversely free moving market forces (for example, the use of road pricing, ironically an element of market forces, which was seen as an infringement of the motorist's right to drive) make up a policy which will not solve the congestion or environmental pollution problems faced by major urban areas in the European Union.

REFERENCES

CBI (1989) *Traffic Congestion in London*, London.

CfIT (2003) *Comparison of Transport Policies in the UK and Other Member States*, Commission for Integrated Transport, London.

Chatterjee, K and Lyons, G (2002) Travel Behaviour of Car Users during the UK fuel crisis and insights into car dependence, in *Transport lessons from the fuel tax protests of 2000*, eds G Lyons and K Chatterjee, Ashgate Aldershot.

CIT (1992) *London's Transport – The Way Ahead*, Chartered Institute of Transport (Bames R, Cole S, Finney N, Niblett R, Smith R), CIT, London.

Cole, S (2001) Tourism from a transport perspective, Conference paper in Journey to Success, English Tourism Council, London.

Cole, S (2002) Transporting visions, *Agenda*, September 2002, Institute of Welsh Affairs, Cardiff.

Cole, S (2002a) Concessionary fares policies for bus services in the UK – the Welsh perspective, Conference proceedings, London, Centre for Transport Policy, Robert Gordon University, Aberdeen.

Cole, S (2004) Right tracks, *Agenda*, Institute of Welsh Affairs, Cardiff.

Cole, S, Watkins, S & Potter (2003) Provide and promote: transport in Wales 2040, Conference paper to Integrated Transport Delivered?, 3rd Wales Transport Conference, May, Cardiff.

Cozens, P, Hillier, D, Neale, R and Whitaker, J, (2002). Investigating perceptions of personal security on the Valley Lines rail network in South Wales (UK), World Transport Policy and Practice, Vol. 8.

DCMS (1999) *Tomorrow's Tourism*, Department for Culture, Media and Sport Tourism Division, London.

DETR (1998) Integrated Transport Policy White Paper, HMSO, London.

DfT (2002) Delivering Better Transport, Progress Report, Department for Transport.

DOT (1989a) Department of Transport, British Rail, London Regional Transport, London. Central London Rail Study.

DOT (1989b) Four Assessment Studies were commissioned – South London, East London, West London and South Circular Road. The Stage 1 reports were produced by Consultants in December 1986 identifying the problems and issues. In January 1989 Stage 2 reports included recommendations. The studies covered reducing congestion, lorry movements, road safety, the environment, and access.

DOT (1996) *Transport – The Way Forward* (CM 3234), Department of Transport, HMSO, London.

EC (1992) The future development of the common transport policy 'sustainable mobility', COM 92/494, European Commission, Bruxelles.

EC (1995) The Citizen's Network, COM(95)601 Green Paper, Brussels.

ETB (1999) English Tourist Board submission to Tomorrow's Tourism, Department for Culture, Media and Sport, London.

ETC (2001) *Journey to Success*, English Tourism Council, London.

Fournier (1991) The Railways in Europe SNCF today and tomorrow, Franco-British Chamber of Commerce (Additional data from J-P Loubinoux, Direction de L'Economie et finances, SNCF).

GOL (1996) *A Transport Strategy for London*, Government Office for London, HMSO.

GOMMS (2001) *Applying the Multi-modal New Approach to Appraisal of Highway Schemes*, Department for Transport, London.

HOC (1980) House of Commons Select Committee on Transport, Transport in London (HC 127 Session 1980–81).

INIT (2003) *Information Needs of the Independent Traveller*, Wales Transport Research Centre for the Welsh Assembly Government, Cardiff.

LACTC (1991) Los Angeles County Transportation Commission. Proposed 30–Year Integrated Transportation Plan, Los Angeles, CA.

London Pride Partnership (1996) London's Action Programme for Transport: 1996–2010.

LT (1987) The LT Fares Experience, Economic Research Report R259 1984: Report. 1991: Report.

LT (1995) *Planning London's Transport*, London Transport, London.

LT (1996) *To Win as a World City*, London Transport, London.

Macassey, Sir L (1927) The Problem of London Traffic, *Institute of Transport Journal* (November, pp 14–21), Inst of Transport, London.

MOT (1968) Transport in London, White Paper, Ministry of Transport, HMSO, London.

NafW (2000) A guide to bidders for the Wales and Borders (rail) franchise.

NafW (2001) Transport Grant – Assessment Criteria, TG Submissions, National Assembly for Wales, Cardiff.

NATA (1999) *Integrated Transport Economics Appraisal: New approach to transport appraisal*, Department for Transport, London.

NYMTA (1990) New York Metropolitan Transportation Authority Strategic Business Plan 1991–95, New York, NY; WMATA (Washington) (1968) Benefit/Cost Analysis of the Adopted Regional Transit System – DRA Consultants' report, Washington DC.

OPRAF (1996) Press release on Great Western Trains franchise; East Coast main line franchise; London.

RNMS (2000) Rail Network Management Statement, Railtrack plc, London.

RPC (1999) Incremental outputs.

SNCF (1990) Rapport d'Activité 1989, Paris.

SRA (2002) *Strategic Plan*, Strategic Rail Authority, London.

SRA (2004) *Franchise Replacement Process*, Strategic Rail Authority, London.

STAG (2001) *Scottish Transport Appraisal Guidance*, Scottish Executive, Edinburgh.

TfL (2002) Cross Rail Business Case, Transport for London, SRA, Cross London Rail Link, September 2003, London.

TfL (2002a) London Underground and Bus Demand Analysis.

Traffic Assessment Studies (1980) Four reports on transport options were prepared for East (including North) London, South London, West London and the South Circular Road, Department of Transport, London.PAGE383

United States Senate (1991) Intermodal Surface Transportation Act – ISTEA – Washington DC.

WTRC (2003) *Capitals United*, Wales Transport Research Centre, for the Institute of Welsh Affairs, Cardiff.

CHAPTER 13

Regulation or Competition?

INTRODUCTION

The operation of a dynamic market transport is dealt with in Part 1. The advantages of free competition can be seen through the existence of cross-price elasticity and service elasticity. Market segmentation and the use of pricing policies have also been effective in the bus, rail and air markets. Competition is the basis of sales of most goods and services under free market conditions, ie those found in 'Western' societies, and has been applied to all modes of transport.

However, there are drawbacks in the provision of services that are not financially viable, and interventions by public authorities became necessary to achieve an optimum social and economic (not to be confused with financial) position.

In the UK the Office of Fair Trading has seemed, until recently, to be unable to distinguish between competition that did not deliver passenger benefits but upon which it focused and the achievement of net economic benefits by non-competitive means.

The concept of supply-side competition (or franchising, as exists in London and on most rail operations – see below for detailed analysis) has not been acceptable to the OFT unless there is on-road competition. The evidence shows that supply-side competition delivers better services and better value for money. The OFT has changed its view (though UK law remains the same) in relation to travelcards and co-ordinating tickets but requires independently arrived-at fares. Ironically it is easier for bus companies to merge than to co-ordinate services, which many small operators might wish to do. The analysis of the effects of quality contracts outside London will provide the opportunity for students to test the merits of free competition against a co-ordinated franchised network.

This chapter puts the argument against pure free market competition but sets an alternative – the supply-side competitive model – to be considered. The model implies, in economic terms, the use of market forces to identify demand, the use of competitive tendering (widely used in the private sector) to minimise costs and the use of intervention by a public sector body to optimise socioeconomic benefits.

THE UK BUS MARKET

The Transport Act 1985 and subsequent legislation (TA, 2000) resulted in a fundamental change to the operation of bus services in Great Britain (except London) over the last 20 years (2004). The road service licence system was replaced by a system of registration of commercial services and tendering for supported services. An operator's licence holder may run a local bus service anywhere if this does not require a subsidy so long as it registers the service with the traffic commissioner. There is no time limit on the operation of the service and the service can be changed or stopped by giving 42 days' notice (56 days from 2000) to the commissioner. The only objections which can be made are those by local authorities on road safety or traffic congestion grounds (DOT 1985, CPT 1986). In London almost all services are operated on the basis of a London Transport bus agreement – in effect a tendered franchise from Transport for London (TfL) to operate one of its services. The financial viability of any service is likely to be affected by its non-membership of the TfL Travelcard scheme and thus its inability to receive TfL revenue. All TfL tendered services are restricted to pre-qualifying companies.

The decisions as to which services should be subsidised are made by shire and district councils in England, shire councils in Wales, regional and islands councils in Scotland, the Passenger Transport Executives and TfL. These supplement the commercial network. The subsidy system is one which can be operated on a full cost basis where the funding authority pays the operator and retains all the revenue, or on a net subsidy basis where the operator receives the revenue and a subsidy is paid to cover the remaining costs. The system of full cost contracts enables the council to control its spending by adjusting fare levels when necessary. And with no financial risk to the operator with net deficit contracts, operators tend to base their bids on an assumption that revenue will be minimal, thus avoiding financial risk and possibly inflating contract prices. Both types of contract require a check on service quality and reliability but the 'cost contract' also requires a check on revenue. The provision of student and old persons concessionary fares, the interchange of tickets and the provision of rover tickets for tourists all become internal transactions within the county council. This method is probably the nearest to the competitive franchising operation described below.

The White Paper 'Buses' (DOT, 1984) argued that co-ordination and planning of bus services on the pre–1986 scale was unnecessary and wasteful when a significant proportion of bus services could be provided commercially. The old form of network subsidy blunted competition and acted as a disincentive to operators to find new operating ideas and cut costs. There was little incentive to develop markets and operators were hampered by traffic commissioners' rules which required a new operator to prove the need for a service.

EFFECTS OF DEREGULATION

The deregulation of express bus services since 1980 showed that the industry was potentially dynamic and able to respond to new opportunities. Without restrictive regulation, fares could be reduced on many bus services while they remained profitable. The experience of long distance express coach services has been reduced fares, increased frequencies, new higher quality services such as 'Rapide' and new operators entering the market. The number of people travelling has gone up and new vehicles with greater comfort have entered the market. This saw National Express services increasing from 10 million passengers in 1980 to 15 million in 1985. However, by 1993, National Express demand had fallen to 10 million. The significant fares increases are the suggested reason (White, 2003) because coach services are price sensitive and have a high price elasticity (–1.0). When fares were subsequently cut, National Express passenger numbers rose to 13 million per year (2002).

The deregulation policy was justified by the success of the main corridor express services and in turn for the extension to local bus services.

The market element on long distance routes failed in that National Express remained the dominant operator because of its comprehensive service network, interconnecting services and a widely spread marketing and retail network. The vast majority of small companies took no action because of the high risk, a lack of entrepreneurial drive, the small size of the firm, the dangers in moving into new markets (Hibbs, 1986) or a pessimistic view of a competitive market. They decided to remain in contract and private hire operations. A second group introduced services and failed. Most of their operations were between London and a home base area. When several companies formed British Coachways in the late 1980s they could not compete with a well-established operator. They had limited experience in marketing such an operation and in general did not use bus stations as calling points. Even when National Express fares increased in the early 1990s no new major competitor emerged (White, 2003).

Consolidation of services followed the initial entries into the competitive market, as companies realised the limits to growth. This took the form of joint services and a concentration on corridors to and from London or along motorway corridors with very few cross-country routes developing.

The most significant effect of deregulation on private operators' service development has been commuter coach operation into big cities. National Express, the largest inter-city coach operator, reacted with lower fares in response to competition from local operators. The company also concentrated on direct inter-city services and many smaller settlements (eg below

20,000) have suffered from the withdrawal of services, so eroding travel opportunities. Cross elasticity on commuter services into London has been evident between train operating companies and coach operators where the railway has responded with discount ('saver') tickets in a price elastic market and improvements in service quality, with the deployment of newer, faster trains. But cross price elasticity resulted in a loss of passengers and revenue from the railways as a result of deregulation.

Consumers have gained in terms of fare levels and increased frequencies on main routes, especially to and from London. However while overall there is a net benefit, certain travellers have been adversely affected, such as those on secondary coach routes with reduced frequency or a withdrawn service (OECD, 1990). Rail users, too, have benefited through lower fares while maintenance of train frequencies, service quality and investment in the railways has only been achieved through government assisted investment.

Bus fares in general have not fallen in real terms. Local bus service demand is price inelastic (–0.4) in the short run while service elasticity (ie reliability) is +0.4. The fall in demand following deregulations is likely to have resulted from price changes, changes in rates and frequencies (instability) and confusion when in some other cities several bus companies began to compete. There was a fall in unit cost but this was largely the result of reduced wages.

More recently bus kilometres have increased in some cities with higher frequency, newer low floor vehicles, fares reductions in the off-peak and for specific groups (eg children during school holidays) and concessionary fares schemes.

Price competition has been introduced in cities following a new company entering the market. However, it has only been successful where there is high demand and high frequencies can be justified.

Two markets that have been identified as showing the benefits of deregulation are Oxford and Brighton.

The local bus companies, City of Oxford Motor Services Ltd (Go Ahead Group) and Stagecoach Oxford, have been in competition since the late 1980s. Two bus companies with extensive management experience of both bus operations and the Oxford area brought reduced fares, increased frequencies and an increase in bus patronage (one of the few instances of this outside London). It has been argued that this increase was partly due to low car ownership amongst students and tourists in the city and a framework of bus priority measures, park and ride schemes and expensive (£18 per day) car parking in Central Oxford introduced by Oxfordshire County Council and Oxford City Council. (See Chapter 2 for price and service elasticity factors.) The competition extended to Oxford–London Express services with lower rates in real terms and frequencies increased from hourly daytime operations to 15 minutes headway with hourly frequencies at night. The disbenefits are a lack of integration of services of both companies, the absence of inter-availability of tickets, and the congestion caused in central Oxford (particularly in the Cornmarket).

The existence in Oxford now of two major UK bus groups, Go Ahead and Stagecoach, will make it an interesting case study for students over the next ten years as it has been for the last ten years. Brighton has restrictive car parking, but the sole operator, Go Ahead, has adopted a positive approach to fares and service provision. Both components have a strong local image.

The deregulation proposals brought a short term reduction in fares on some services in urban areas as the benefits of increased competition were achieved. In rural areas there has been limited innovation by low cost operators using buses, minibuses and taxis to provide a more flexible and responsive pattern of services with the use of high technology such as GPS to monitor operations and provide real time customer information (WTRC, 2004). The expected effect is the introduction of greater choice into local public transport, with services more in tune with passenger requirements. The new tendering system will give the county councils a much clearer indication than previously of the cost of supporting a particular service, thus enabling them to weigh up clearly the cost and benefits of subsidy and give better value for money for the subsidies they provide.

Ironically, in an area where a bus company has a monopoly of commercial services and where tendered bus services are produced by several operators, this same principle may apply when a low cost competitor enters the market. (Chapters 2 and 4 describe the impact in the airline passenger market.)

CONCERNS ABOUT A DEREGULATION POLICY

A number of criticisms have been made of this policy and concerns expressed over the life of the policy by Parliamentary committees, consumer bodies and the passenger transport industry.

In Great Britain in general the use of public transport has been made more difficult following bus deregulation. While network benefits such as integrated timetables and ticketing have been imposed by regulatory frameworks on train operating companies, outside London no framework exists for the bus industry. Much of this lack of co-ordination has been forced on operators by competition rules making information difficult to obtain and journeys other than simple ones difficult. Under these conditions the main users of buses are those with no car available (UKRT, 1997).

For passenger transport, there are tensions between competition, which can increase efficiency on specific routes, and integration, which is critical for journeys involving transfers. Over recent years, deregulation of the bus industry and rail privatisation, together with reductions in local authority powers, have produced a more fragmented service and a lack of clear responsibility for ensuring that network benefits occur. Unless these problems are overcome, the potential benefits from increased competition may be more than outweighed by the disadvantages (HOC, 1984).

This is particularly the case as land use patterns and activities are no longer related to a simple radial route pattern and journeys have become increasingly complex. Interchange and seamless connections are essential if competitive bus operators are to bring reductions in congestion and pollution.

Instability

Instability in the market is the first of a number of concerns which have been expressed about bus deregulation. It is possible under the free market arrangements for companies to enter and leave the market relatively quickly. A period of notice is required but in the case of a company leaving the market because of low or no profit, it is unlikely to continue to operate at a loss and may either not operate at all or provide a much reduced level during the notice period. Even with a notice period, movements into and out of the market, especially in the early years when companies are testing market potential and profitability, will lead to instability.

What the passenger requires is a stable supply with continuity of service. Instability results when routes, services, operators, fares and timetables are subject to change at short notice. This instability may last for some considerable period of time before a new equilibrium is established. Destabilisation to the established pattern of train services is largely prevented by franchise contracts and the limited use of open access agreements as train operating companies respond to competition. The proposals overlook the effect which uncertainty and constant change in bus timetables can have on levels of patronage and although services, may be more responsive to local needs, the particular approach being adopted will introduce an unpredictability into local transport which did lower the usage of local public transport.

Co-ordination of services

The county councils in England and in Wales have a duty to co-ordinate public transport. But a deregulation policy would consider comprehensive planning inappropriate for those services which can be provided commercially. Bodies have reservations and believe the consumer should be afforded the advantages of the co-ordination services in terms of compatible service timings, co-ordinated timetable information, and through ticketing so far as this is possible (HOC, 2004). Another concern is that passengers would lose the benefits of co-ordinated services along a corridor; the intervals between services would become irregular, tickets would not be interchangeable, connections would be lost, and publicity fragmented or not provided (UKRT, 1997).

The lack of co-ordination is likely to be of particular inconvenience in tourist areas as information could not be kept up to date, and public confidence in the system would be lost. This would be likely to act against the objective of promoting the tourist industry. Many county councils are also in favour of retaining their present duty of co-ordination and not being a mere registration authority.

Others conclude that the proposals will 'dash all prospects of long term co-ordinated planning of services' and counties will be limited to reacting to the weaknesses of the free market which have been found unable to cope with the mobility requirements of the widely dispersed rural population found in rural Wales, the Scottish Highlands or East Anglia. The tendering system for loss making routes has advantages but co-ordination seems an effective basis for tendering. Rail operators have expressed concern for those passengers who begin or end their journeys by using local bus services. Local authorities and bus/rail operators, had (up to 1985) adopted a policy of encouraging the improvement of interchanges, including the development of bus stations at railway terminals. The resultant uncertainty reduced the opportunities for the development of bus/rail interchanges and integrated timetables providing for local feeder bus services, except where these were tendered services.

In the view of operators (Kreppel, 1997) and consumer groups (HOC, 2002, 2004), the advantages of reintroducing co-ordination (which emphasises passenger information and makes public transport more convenient for the passenger) outweighs the minor restrictions which co-ordinating puts on the operation of the free market (CPT, 1996). In practical terms it will ensure regular services, plan bus stops, prevent bunching and double parking of buses, and ensure that resources are being used in the best way.

Competition on subsidised routes

The majority of subsidised rural routes are either radical routes from a town centre extending beyond the urban area, or inter-urban routes which also service urban areas at both ends of the route. The highest revenue yield per bus mile is in the urban areas, consequently any competition with subsidised rural services will be met on these sections of the route. Free market competition will also be concentrated on high yield times of day (eg from 07.30 to 18.30 Monday to Friday).

The example in Figure 13.1 shows two commercial services, A and B, operating on the same corridor as the tendered subsidised service C. These competitors will abstract revenue from the subsidised rural service (C) with two possible options:

1. If the subsidised service (C) fares remain high then a cross elasticity factor will result in passengers waiting for the lower fare vehicle (operated by A or B).
2. If the subsidised service reduces its fares to compete on the urban section of the route, the internal cross subsidy within the route will be reduced as a result of reduced revenue from the urban sector.

Where services are operating on a purely commercial basis only the populated sections of such urban/rural routes will be served, so in this example operators A and C terminate their services at the end of the built-up area.

Any services into a town centre will be limited to those roads which are suitable for bus operation. It is likely, therefore, that subsidised and commercial services will operate along the same sections of road and both operators will pick up and set down along that road. The tendering operator for the subsidised service will find it relatively easy to forecast the costs of operation, but revenue will depend on the extent of the competition and this will be very difficult to predict, given the ease with which a new operator could enter the market.

A county council would therefore have to choose between the two fares policy options for subsidised services described above. In either case, this would result in the withdrawal of services considered socially necessary, or a new round of tendering with the possible increase in subsidy, unless the commercial operator considered that its return was insufficient (because the route did not yield enough revenue for several operators), and in the meantime gave notice of withdrawal. This is likely to result in a detrimental effect on the service which could not be alleviated by the introduction of new services or new types of vehicle, and protection for subsidised services may be justified.

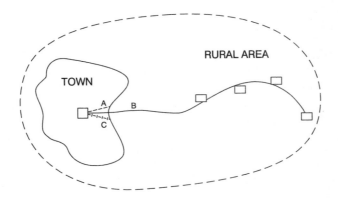

Figure 13.1 *Competition between commercial urban services and competitive tendering services along one corridor*

Cross subsidy

There was a tendency in the 'Buses' White Paper and in the consequent current (2004) legislation to regard cross subsidy as the subsidising of loss making routes with surpluses from profitable routes, while other forms of cross subsidy were not fully considered. Peak bus operations with a high yield per bus mile will subsidise off peak (10.00 to 15.00), evening and Sunday journeys particularly if there are low peak related costs. Profitable sections of routes support less used sections: for example, where rural sections of inter-urban services are subsidised by the urban sections at either end. Rural and suburban services running into large centres of population are cross subsidised by urban sections of the route; summer services support winter services in tourist areas; and peak journeys into a city centre such as Chester will support lesser used outbound journeys, although both services are operating in the peak.

The extent of cross subsidy and its importance in the financing of loss making bus services should not be underestimated. If we consider varying conditions of operation, the extent and use of cross subsidy will vary even between two urban centres as well as between rural and urban areas.

Cross subsidy can only be justified under free market conditions where it contributes to profitability. This may occur when the lesser used services are seen as feeder services contributing to the overall main network. A company may also wish to create a local image of providing all local services and not engaging in 'cherry picking' for which it may be criticised. For similar marketing reasons it may not want another company to enter the market (for example on Sundays) to gain experience of the area and begin to compete on its profitable weekday routes; it will also enable the company to improve its image. Under free market conditions, operators will therefore only choose to run services on routes and at times which are profitable but in some instances this profit may be used to cross subsidise loss making journeys. The advantage of removing cross subsidy is that a county council will know exactly how much it is paying for each service provided. It will be able to make better decisions about whether a journey or a route is worth keeping and to deal with need within a fully considered priority list. It would not then be the role of a bus operator to make these decisions on social grounds. Any decision on subsidy by the bus operator will then be made on the basis of operational or revenue criteria rather than need. The removal of commercial cross subsidy in industrial urban areas could lead to an increase in county council revenue support while in rural parts there would be little change in the subsidy requirements. Any reduction of revenue support under these circumstances is therefore likely to result in a reduction in rural, evening and Sunday services and in depot closures.

Alternative operators

The operators of competitive services and tendered social services will come from several possible sources although there are limits imposed by managerial and operational experience and vehicle type available. The primary operators after deregulation were not a variety of small operators as envisaged by the government of the day, but a concentration in the hands of a few groups. Table 13.1 shows that while there may be several niche operators (CPT 1996; HOC (Badgerline evidence) 1996) providing tendered bus services, rural services or specialist (eg student or hospital) services, they do not threaten the larger companies. However the actions taken by the Office of Fair Trading and the Monopolies and Mergers Commission against larger operators for predatory pricing and other activities indicate a belief that few towns can support two large profitable operators. In addition agreements not to compete might be made between companies who appear to be 'reluctant' to compete directly with one another. (HOC (OFT evidence) 1996).

In the case of existing operators, the commercial network will be operated on a profitable basis giving a satisfactory rate of return, while the county councils put out to tender the loss making journeys on a particular route, eg evening and Sunday services, as well as loss making suburban and rural services. However, long established stage carriage operators may withdraw from services which they had operated for many years because of the low rate of return and the uncertainty of future returns resulting from increased competition. Meanwhile, new entrants to the market have found

Table 13.1 *Ownership of the British bus industry 1985 and 2003*

Approximate percentage of total bus and coach industry turnover*			
1985	%	2003	%
National Bus Co	28	First	22.1
London Transport	13	Stagecoach	15.9
Scottish Bus Group	6	Arriva	14.5
PTEs (7)	18	Go Ahead	8.3
Municipals (50)	10	National Express	5.7
		Small groups	3.2
		Employee owned	0.3
		Management owned	8.6
Sub-total, public sector	75	Public (municipal)	6.5
		TfL	4.3
Private sector	25	Independent	10.6

Sources: Confederation of Passenger Transport (1996, 2004); HOC (1996); TAS Bus Industry Monitor (2004)

* Local and non-local companies.
Note: London operations are now provided by private companies in the TfL franchising system.

Table 13.2 *Local bus services: the shift from public to private sector*

	Vehicle kilometres		Passenger journeys	
	Public sector	Private sector	Public sector	Private sector
GB outside London				
1985/86	91%	9%	96%	4%
1988/89	41%	59%	58%	42%
1993/94	14%	86%	19%	81%

Source: Bus and Coach Statistics GB 1993/94, Table 9.1

that the costs of stage operation are considerably higher than those of coaching or road haulage, eg where a private company takes over tendered services from a large group (eg First, Stagecoach) subsidiary (Chapter 5).

The proposers of deregulation held the view that a new pattern of services would emerge from deregulation which would provide a better service for communities and outlying areas. It was clear however that there were not sufficient suitable alternative operators with adequate financial backing to replace existing operators. The supply of suitable buses will also be dependent on the financial arrangements for leasing new vehicles or the extent of disposal by bigger operators and leasing companies of second hand vehicles.

Establishing demand patterns

In a free market it is for the passengers to demonstrate what they want or for market research to identify needs and for operators to respond. A county council may be involved in collecting and making available market data, and some have taken a lead in this. Smaller companies, especially in the early years, will not have the resources or the expertise to carry out market analysis; the passenger will not be fully aware of what services are available, and there is no evidence to suggest that punctuality of services will improve. Under these conditions it will be difficult for passengers' demands to be made known and frequent changes resulting from an unstable range of services may lead them to seek alternative travel modes.

Conclusions on bus deregulation in the medium term

In assessing the success or otherwise of bus deregulation in Great Britain, when the objectives of the government of the day (Conservative in 1985) are compared with outcomes the policy does not achieve the primary objective of increased patronage though some of the outputs were achieved.

Table 13.3 *Summary of objectives and outputs*

Output	Objective	Actual
1. Reliability (after initial teething troubles	Increase	No change
2. Service structure	Very little change	Few major changes
3. Innovation	Lots of new ideas	Some very good ideas
4. Fares (real terms)	Fall in fares	Little change
5. Concessionary fares	Continued/extended	Extended
6. Patronage	Increases	Fall (some exceptions)
7. Public expenditure	Reductions	Increasing

The primary policy goal, as identified by government ministers, to stop the reduction in patronage has failed.

Bus deregulation in Great Britain. OECD (1990) Summary

Reasons

- Cross subsidy disadvantage to profitable routes.
- With competition – scope for increased efficiency.

Effects

- Overall growth in mileage.
- Savings in direct bus subsidies but increase in admin. and publicity costs.
- No significant fares changes.
- End of integrated ticketing (eg Travelcards, except Gwynedd Rover Tickets).
- Large fares increases in some PTE's.
- Early organisational problems largely overcome (eg Thames Transit).
- 60% of services from private operators compared with 8% before deregulation. (Many tendered but some registered.)
- Abuse of market power:
  - predatory pricing;
  - bus station usage.

Post-1998

Changes to governmental intervention policies in public transport since the late 1990s have put this analysis into a more difficult context than hitherto. Students should use this situation as a case study to consider the impact of a change in the bus-operating framework. The introduction of concessionary fares for example has increased demand in some areas

Table 13.4 *Local bus service passenger journeys million passenger journeys: GB*

	London	English Metropolitan areas	English other areas	Scotland	Wales	All outside London	Total Great Britain
1983	1,087	2,011	1,629	680	180	4,500	**5,587**
1993/94	1,117	1,334	1,268	526	130	3,258	**4,375**
2002/03	1,542	1,149	1,206	445	109	2910	4452
change							
1983–1995	+11%	−36%	−22%	−27%	−29%	−29%	**−22%**
1993–2003	+38%	−14%	−5%	−15%	−16%	−11%	+2%

Source: Bus and Coach Statistics GB 1995/96 (DfT, 1996, 2004) Table 2.1

(eg Wales) by 5 per cent. Other interventions such as long bus lanes (eg in Edinburgh) will also improve journey time and reliability and, through service elasticity effects, increase patronage.

A SUPPLY-SIDE COMPETITIVE FRANCHISING SYSTEM

The objective of the deregulatory policy is to increase competition, reduce costs, reduce fares and obtain value for money in public transport subsidy. There is already some evidence that costs and fares will be reduced and the total of buses operating will increase on busy routes at certain times of the day. It also appears that opportunities to reduce overall subsidy levels – especially in rural areas – may result. More suitable vehicles would also be introduced in areas where subsidy is currently high or where there is no public transport. The practical problems of the current proposals identified in this chapter are instability; lack of co-ordination, timetabling and information, with few published timetables, 'bunching' of buses at popular times, consumer uncertainty, lack of information and many different kinds of vehicles; competition on subsidised routes especially on profitable sections; and a difficulty in establishing demand patterns. The new environment assumes that there can be two networks – a commercial network and a social network – but for the reasons outlined this is not a workable option.

There is an alternative system the objectives of which would enable bus services to be provided in a competitive market, reduce operating costs and revenue support levels, make bus operations more demand sensitive, improve value for money and prevent large companies dominating the market. Such objectives could be achieved within a competitive framework and yet avoid the instability referred to above. The franchises would be issued by the local authority (who would also be the co-ordination and subsidy authority) for a route, group of routes, travel corridor or small area. It forms the basis of that used by TfL and which is closer to franchising than to deregulation. Its adoption suggests that there are variations between the two which could provide a better competitive framework than the one proposed.

Competitive franchising will prevent a return of the pre–1930s situation with many operators, constant changes in timetables, and passenger confusion. In the present state of the bus passenger market and given the presence of the car as an alternative (which was not so in the 1920s) many passengers are likely to changes modes. Its effect will be to take competition *off* the roads and instead establish pre-operational competition under the aegis of the franchising authority.

A form of competitive franchising can meet many of the operational and financial problems inherent in the present deregulatory position in Britain. It could:

- allow competition;
- provide a more secure market where restructuring has led to some dominant companies;
- prevent instability;
- enable the retention of the county councils' co-ordinating function, and the continuity of proper timetables and regular operations;
- provide value for money;
- take competition off the roads, but allow its full value to be achieved within a franchising system;
- enable a phased introduction of its proposals;
- allow alternative forms of competitive franchising to be pursued;
- allow for an integrated bus network;
- enable the subsidising authority to predict its subsidy expenditure more accurately;
- achieve efficiency without the existence of an unstable market.

Characteristics of a competitive franchising system

These might be as follows:

- Routes would be specified by the franchising authority and tenders invited from potential operators. Such routes might be profitable or unprofitable.
- The operator awarded the contract would not have to face subsequent competition on the routes specified during the contract period.
- The franchise would be granted on the basis of the lowest subsidy requirement for a specified group of services. An alternative is to allocate a specified amount of money for the service package and award the contract to the operator providing the highest service level.
- The subsidy would be awarded for the whole of the contract period.

- The contract period would be three to five years. The minimum period is determined by the operators' requirement to make a reasonable return on investment and the maximum period must allow for competitive re-advertising sufficiently frequently to encourage the contractor to provide a quality of service required by the passenger and the franchising authority.
- The right to develop subsidiary interests such as vehicle maintenance, advertising etc as profit making functions.
- An operational plan and financial forecasts should be provided at the application stage. Performance can then be monitored against this plan.
- Assets such as buses, garages and employees could be transferred from an operator losing a contract to the newly contracted operator at the end of the franchise period. This would provide further encouragement for a higher quality of capital equipment to be included in an operator's investment programme.
- All revenue and profit, together with the agreed subsidy figure, would be retained by the operator. Alternatively, a shire county franchising arrangement could be similar to the present LTB scheme where the authority receives all the fare revenue and the operator receives an agreed sum for running the service.
- The size of each franchised operation will be small enough to enable companies of varying size to compete.

Such a system of competitive franchising has features in common with that currently operated in London where it is a workable framework for competition and subsidy. In the competitive market it is a common form of selecting operators for hotels and food retailing outlets. It is this parallel with the highly competitive and profitable franchised operations used by familiar high street companies, such as fast food chains, which suggest its suitability for the competitive aspects of bus operations.

The adoption of a competitive tendering process for the free market and subsidised operations can be compatible through the concept of network franchising. Individual routes or sets of routes, whether profitable or loss making, would be grouped together and put out to tender on the basis of three-to-five-year contracts. It would achieve the benefits of competition while providing greater stability and co-ordination of services. Such a scheme has a wide support amongst a variety of organisations representing consumers and operators who accept the value of competition in public transport as a means of achieving better defined value for money from bus subsidies.

A franchising framework can work with a county council, a consortium of counties in a joint transport authority or a PTE. While reducing unit costs, encouraging innovation, maintaining the benefits of competition it can retain the good features – travelcards, marketing co-ordination of bus and rail – in a network that meets people's needs.

REFERENCES

CPT (1986) The route towards tomorrow's buses, Confederation of Passenger Transport UK (formerly BCC) London

CPT (1996) Local transport – meeting the challenge. Confederation of Passenger Transport UK, London.

DfT (1996, 2004) *Bus and Coach Statistics 1995/96*, 2003/04 (and earlier editions), Department of Transport, The Stationery Office, London.

DOT (1984) Buses White Paper, Department of Transport, HMSO, London.

DOT (1985) Preparing for Deregulation – Tomorrow's Buses, Department of Transport, London.

Hibbs, J (1986) *The Country Bus*, David and Charles, Newton Abbot.

HOC (1984) Public Transport in Wales, Select Committee on Welsh Affairs, House of Commons, London.

HOC (1996) The consequences of bus deregulation. Select Committee on Transport, House of Commons, HMSO, London.

HOC (2002) The Bus Industry, Report HC 828, Session 2001–02, House of Commons, London.

HOC (2004) Draft Transport (Wales) Bill, Report HC 759, Session 2003–04, House of Commons, London.

Kreppel A (1997) in Clarke, Rh. *Western Mail* (August), Caerdydd/Cardiff.

OECD (1990) Competition policy and deregulation of road transport, Organisation for Economic Co-operation and Development, Paris.

OFT (1990) Local Bus Services in Kingston-upon-Hull. Office of Fair Trading, London (an example of OFT reports).

TA (2000) Transport Act, House of Commons, London.

UKRT (1997) Making Connections. United Kingdom Round Table on Sustainable Development, Department of the Environment, London.

White, P (2003) Regulatory options for the bus industry, *Transport Economist*, **30** (1), London.

WTRC (2004) BWCABUS experiment in Carmarthenshire using Geographical Positioning Systems and a routeing model to divert demand responsive buses into a primary route.

Part 3: Transport and Development

CHAPTER 14

19th Century Britain

THE NEED FOR TRANSPORT

The development of an economic system has a number of prerequisites without which growth, or an increased rate of growth, cannot be achieved. There is a need for technology, skilled labour, adequate quantities of labour, natural elements (such as raw materials, water or climatic conditions), markets, and management skills to co-ordinate these factors. However, there is an uneven distribution of raw materials, labour, capital assets and markets throughout the world, so that the needs of modern societies must usually be satisfied from worldwide locations. To meet this demand, manufacturers need to transport raw materials to factories to produce the finished goods which in turn are transported to the markets.

In addition, workers must be transported. Travel-to-work patterns in large cities often reflect the higher wages and the lack of dwellings in the central business district compared with the suburbs; in small towns it often reflects the wage differential between the urban centre and its rural hinterland. For some specialised workers (such as those in City financial institutions) jobs are located only in the City of London and a long journey to work is a requirement. Travel to recreational facilities or as part of an annual holiday has become an accepted part of the activity, particularly with increased car ownership and a real terms reduction in flying costs.

It is possible to illustrate that transport increases development and vice versa. The development of the Metropolitan Railway led to the growth of suburbs in north-west London. The development of Milton Keynes New Town in Berkshire was concurrent with the building of new roads, yet its new railway station resulted from the growth of the town in much the same way as the growth of Telford New Town in Shropshire justified the construction of the M54 motorway.

In general, it is the rate of growth, rather than any growth at all, which is determined by the quality of the transport system. The examples in the following chapters illustrate that economic growth has been dependent upon transport in 19th century Britain, in the 20th century Third World and in the redevelopment of areas of high unemployment in the UK.

TRANSPORT AND THE DEVELOPMENT OF 19TH CENTURY LONDON

The tremendous economic expansion in Britain in the 19th century was based on a number of prerequisites to economic growth. The agrarian revolution in the 18th century had provided an agricultural sector with higher output levels and land productivity than elsewhere, which was able to feed the growing industrial population.

This increase in agricultural output did not cause the industrial take-off, but without it the industrial urban population would have either starved or more likely returned to the land, thus reducing the amount of industrial labour available, with the consequent constraint on the rate of growth. The financial system had also evolved, providing cheap and easy access to commercial credit and an easy system of payments. Despite the bank crashes of the early 19th century which showed how imperfect the system was, this availability of capital and a low interest rate made possible the construction of factories, mines and railways.

The initial take-off in Britain was due to the cotton-textile industry (Baines, 1835) which had a massive rate of growth from 1770 to 1830. In Rostow's (1960) view, this scale of industrial growth led to the development of urban areas, the demand for coal, iron, machinery, the need for working capital and 'ultimately the demand for cheap transport'. Transport, and in particular the railway, was probably the single most powerful force in economic take-off (Hamilton & Potter, 1985). It affected the rate of economic growth and provided a cheap, efficient means of transporting raw materials, finished goods and people; it was a source of demand for coal, iron and capital, and led to the vast increase in output in these sectors from 1830 onwards.

Horses and trams

London in 1750 was about the size of the present central business district – the City and the West End. The City had expanded considerably from Roman times when it was primarily a commercial and trading centre based on the area within the present City of London. In 1766, London's first bypass, the New Road (now Marylebone Road) marked the northern edge of the built-up area. The growth of the city was restricted to the journey-to-work area. Most people walked to work, while only the rich travelled by horse-drawn carriage. The size of the urban area was also restricted by the capacity of the transport infrastructure to distribute food to the urban population.

Within the urban area, in the first half of the 19th century, the vast majority of people still walked to work. They either worked in factories near their houses or commuted to their offices. Those who walked to the

City lived in Camden Town, Islington, Stepney, Camberwell or Southwark (which was reached by a toll bridge) as well as in overcrowded housing and tenements in the central area. The development of these inner 'suburbs' was possible so long as the distance between their homes and the banking and money houses in the City was less than two miles and involved a journey time of 30 minutes or so.

Horse buses carried a significant number of middle-class workers such as senior clerks, foremen and publicans. They were rich enough to afford the fares while the common labourer with a wage of 21 shillings (£1.05) a year and many of their better-paid fellow workers were forced to walk. The rich were able to live even further out when the first commuter railway opened to Greenwich. The train would move greater numbers of people at lower cost and with a substantially reduced journey time; but despite lower fares it was still expensive by most people's standards.

The horse tram network began in the 1870s and by 1874 extended to Archway, Finsbury Park, Stamford Hill, Hackney, Stratford, Poplar, New Cross, Camberwell, Brixton and Stockwell. Horse trams ran into the City, although they were banned from the West End. They were required as 'street railways' to provide cheap workmen's fares and, unlike the horse buses, operated early in the morning. The economics of their operation made them a possibility for workers' travel. They were easier to move than horse buses because they ran on flat rails rather than cobbles and a horse tram could carry twice as many passengers as a horse bus. The London Tramways Company could justifiably claim that they had taken the poor out to new suburbs in the late 19th century (LWT, 1983).

Table 14.1 *Commuter modal split 1854*

	No	%
Thames River steamers	15,000	5.2
Train	27,000	9.4
Horse bus	44,000	15.4
Walking (approx)	200,000	70.0
	286,000	100.0

Source: Charles Pearson, City of London Solicitor

Table 14.2 *Fares and journey times: London to Greenwich 1836*

Mode	Fare	Journey time
Stage coach	1/– (5p)	1 hour
Thames River Boat	9d (4p approx)	1.5 hours
London and Greenwich Railway	1/– (5p) inside	
(London Bridge to Deptford)	6d (2.5p) open truck	12 mins

Source: London Transport Museum

This urban growth was not restricted to London. The large northern municipalities such as Liverpool set up extensive tramway systems. These were often linked for through running, for example between Manchester, Salford, Bolton, Oldham and Stockport. In smaller towns and cities such as Chester, Reading and Cardiff, similar developments took place which enabled people to live further away from their work, in less crowded conditions.

The railway

The main line railways made little contribution to the development of the London urban area in the early 19th century. They were not generally interested in commuters and catered mainly for the wealthy long-distance passenger. The Great Western Railway (GWR) operating out of Paddington Station opened in 1838 but for many years its first station was Ealing. Even that did little for the development of what is, in 1998, a desirable suburb well within the built-up area. Ealing in 1852 was 'a place of no great size though being near the fashionable end of London had long been a favourite residence'. The village had been linked to London by main road, but the coming of the main line railway made it more attractive (LWT, 1983). The terminus itself, at Paddington, was not the choice of the railway directors, who had requested permission to terminate at West Brompton. But like the London and Birmingham Railway's plans, they were rejected by the rich and influential West End inhabitants, and both railway companies built outside the New Road. Paddington and North Kensington became a popular area for town houses for the Welsh gentry and West Country landowners, thus expanding the urban sprawl into a previously rural area. The Great Western, however, did begin to accelerate the urban development of Ealing, Southall, Uxbridge, Windsor and towns further west, such as Reading. The railways were required to charge no more than 1d (0.4p) per mile on certain workers' trains and soon through trains operated to the City along the Circle line via Paddington (Bishop's Road).

Even in 1861 the continuous urban area of London was still comparatively small. It developed west to Paddington and Old Brompton, north to the smart new middle-class suburbs of St John's Wood and Portland Town (whose development was followed in 1868 with the opening of the Baker Street to Swiss Cottage Railway), to Camden Town, Holloway and Hackney. The vast cattle market at Camden lay separate from the built-up area, and Holloway prison was in the countryside. The urban area extended eastwards to the Lea Valley, Stepney and Bromley by-Bow.

Some settlements developed on the main roads out of London. Ribbon development of housing grew along the Great Cambridge Road at Tottenham, Upper Edmonton and Waltham Cross and along the A1 (the Great North Road) at Holloway and Highgate, but these were largely for the wealthy or for agricultural workers. The wealthy moved to Enfield with the arrival of the Eastern Counties Railway and to East Barnet when the Great Northern Railway built its station. Chipping Barnet (now High Barnet) was a market centre on the St Albans road, but it also grew as an overnight stopping place for stage coaches being, at the start of the 19th century, one day's travel from London. All these settlements were small and outside London, but all were set for growth in 1861.

From the 1860s onwards a new era of railway building took place in London. The first sections of the Metropolitan Underground Railway opened between Paddington (Bishop's Road) and Farringdon to overcome the hopelessly congested roads which could no longer cope with the increasing numbers of commuters. The Great Western Railway Company began to realise the importance of the commuter, and from 1863 through trains were operated to the City (Peacock, 1978). This enabled many of the wealthier City commuters to travel in from as far away as Ealing with a reasonable journey time – which was a greater influence than the fare levels. The Hammersmith and City line was an extension of the Metropolitan Railway. The latter ran under the New Road while the extension to the village of Hammersmith in 1864 ran through open countryside and skirted the fashionable suburb of North Kensington 'where between 1810 and 1852 nearly a thousand acres of green fields have been covered with fine squares and noble spacious streets lined with detached villas' (Measom, 1852), following the development of Paddington station and the need for Belgravia-style houses not too far from the West End.

The street pattern to the south of the Great Western Line had been established before 1865, and there was no significant land use change until the railway arrived. The opening of Ladbroke Grove, Hammersmith and Shepherds Bush stations in 1864, followed by Westbourne Park in 1866 and Latimer Road in 1868, led to considerable housing development in the area. Two farms at Porto Bello and Netting Barn which appear on the 1861 map had vanished by 1871 and development, which was restricted to land south of the railway in 1869, had by 1871 completely surrounded it. By the late 1880s, the built-up area stretched up to half a mile beyond the railway and this was the edge of built-up London. Similar patterns of development took place in other parts of London as the railway system spread into rural areas. The new housing developments were limited to the distance that people were prepared to walk to their local station. Houses within half a mile of a station sold well. In many cases those more than a mile away did not sell at all until a new railway line was built or until the coming of improved local bus and tram services. The effect of the railways can still be seen in London housing patterns. The housing close to Victoria railway station is relatively densely developed compared with later housing further away.

The development of the deep level tube and its extension was also closely related to urban development. The West End had only horse buses

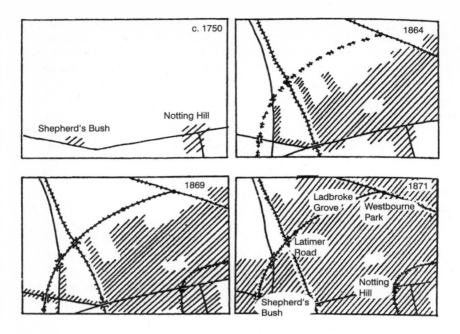

Figure 14.1 *Urban growth in west London – the role of the Metropolitan Railway*

until the construction of the Central London Railway tube line led to its growth as a shopping and commercial centre. The western curve of the Circle line was opened in 1868 and, like the Hammersmith and City line, had its effect on the Notting Hill Gate and High Street Kensington areas. The opening of the District line at Hammersmith in 1874 further assisted the development of that area and in 1879 it was extended to Ealing. That resulted in a regular rapid link to the City to augment the GWR service, and considerable housing development in Ealing. The areas in between these lines at West Acton and further west at Park Royal and Hanger Lane were not serviced by the underground railways nor by the main line GWR whose station at Greenford was too far away. The housing in this area is therefore mostly of the 1920s and 1940s periods when stations on the Central line extension were opened.

METROLAND

In any consideration of the relationship between railways and the spatial development of London, the effect of the Metropolitan Railway on the lands to the north-west of London has to be included. Many of London's suburbs now considered to be part of the conurbation were, before the railway arrived, 'in the middle of nowhere'. When Ruislip station was opened in 1903 it was described as being 'built for the future accommodation of the most picturesque residential neighbourhood near London' and many building sites were already in preparation (Edwards & Pigram, 1977).

At Rayners Lane, another side of the Metropolitan Railway was apparent; its land development activities. Had it not been for this the Metropolitan Railway would have been financially embarrassed. It paid its shareholders a dividend only twice during its existence and reflected the situation of many railway companies. Although Rayners Lane station was built in 1906, it was still remote in the 1920s. In 1928 a large tract of land was bought by Metropolitan Railway Country Estates and the Harrow Garden Village was laid out, with private developers building the houses. There was a variety of different styles of housing from neo-Tudor to typical 1930s, built around village greens and tree lined avenues. Eastcote and Ruislip Gardens developed as a joint venture between the Railway and T R Nash Limited who built a vast estate. Mass produced housing was being built in the 1930s but much of the local transport was by horse and cart, with bricks for the Manor Homes estate coming from the Metropolitan goods yard at Ruislip. As the 'underground' suburbs developed, however, the reconstruction of roads was a major task for local authorities and bus services were introduced to provide feeds into stations. Swakeleys Road, Ickenham, was widened to become a main arterial road in 1936 and was used to operate an early bus route between Uxbridge and Pinner in 1931. By the 1890s the Metropolitan Railway had built its 'main' line from Baker Street to Verney Junction via Amersham and Aylesbury. But here also large scale development did not take place until the 1930s. At Moor Park, for example, freehold houses were advertised in 1930 'at £2,275, detached, near a golf course and only 25 minutes from Baker Street' (Edwards & Pigram, 1983). By 1933 yet another change occurred with the arrival of Piccadilly line trains, following the takeover of the Metropolitan Railway by London Transport. This provided another route to the central business district.

These examples illustrate the close relationship between the growth of urban London and the opening of the railway lines. Other similar effects can be detected around London. The extension of the Northern line from Archway to High Barnet (1940) and Mill Hill East (1941) led to housing developments there, particularly from the late 1940s, and a similar relationship can be seen with the extension of the Central line services eastwards to Loughton. The earlier development of the line by Eastern Counties Railway had not been such a financial success and services had been suspended. The arrival of the railway in the 1860s did not bring the necessary commuters, since there were insufficient people with incomes high enough to pay the train fares. The coming of the railway therefore did

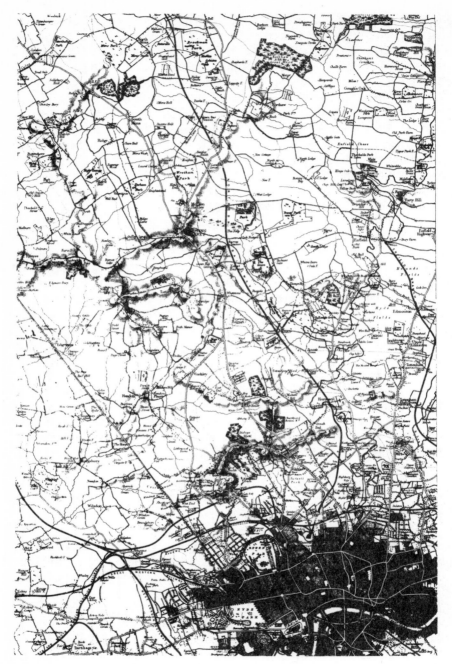

Figure 14.2 *The London area in 1861*
(reproduced from a map by Edward Weller)

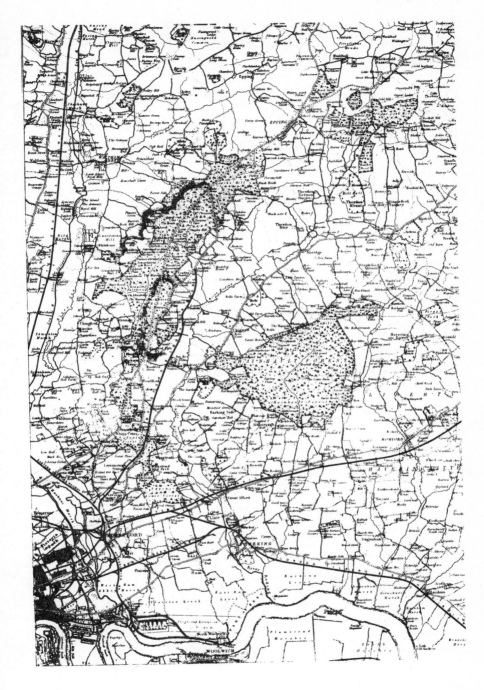

not always guarantee development and one of the best remaining examples is at Blake Hall on the Central line – closed in 1981 after over 30 years of serving hardly anyone.

ECONOMIC IMPACT OF THE RAILWAYS OUTSIDE LONDON

The towns and the railways were both part of the economic boom of the 19th century. The Industrial Revolution led to the development of towns as centres of industry, to the mass production of goods in factories, and necessitated the building of a railway network. The railways transported goods and people faster than the canals. They brought in raw materials and took out manufactured goods from the towns.

Railway stations and goods yards became a major focal point in provincial towns. The yards were distribution centres for food, coal and supplies of all kinds. Alongside the yards developed factories, workshops, warehouses, coal yards, timber merchants and breweries, all built near the main track so that from their sidings they could bring coal, grain, iron ore, cotton or malt – depending on their activities – and move out finished manufactured goods. The original McEwens brewery at Fountainbridge in Edinburgh had its own private sidings, and beer destined for London was taken by rail to Leith docks, and thence by ship to Princes Wharf on the Thames from where it was distributed by horse and wagon. Housing no longer needed to be built from local stone or brick, and use was made of cheaper or better bricks from other parts of the country.

The speed of the railways enabled them to form the basis of the distribution network of London newspapers. The middle classes in remote towns expected to receive their *Daily Mail* or *News Chronicle* by breakfast time. The 'national' morning newspapers had arrived, though their contents were usually more related to central London than to Aberystwyth or Penzance. Mail, too, was distributed faster and more cheaply than before, and special newspaper and mail trains were operated under contract.

The railways led to the development of railway towns such as Wolverton, Crewe and Swindon, which had previously been small villages. The GWR selected Swindon as a major engineering centre; it built the railway works, vast sidings and houses of varying sizes for men on different levels of seniority. Much of old Swindon still consists of railway housing, but in the late 20th century Swindon was affected again by transport. The introduction of InterCity 125 trains meant a journey of 52 minutes from Paddington, 70 minutes from the West End and 80 from the City, and the construction of the M4 motorway also made it a car commuting centre. New Swindon has become another London dormitory town, but before the 1960s its transport infrastructure was inadequate for such a role.

The railways themselves had a direct effect on the demand for coal, iron ore and mechanical engineering products. Coal was used for steam engines and for all industrial energy. From the 1840s, railway demand for iron and later, steel rails increased the demand for iron ore and coal for smelting. Collieries and railways often developed together (Symonds, 1979). One of the earliest private railways was the Carmarthenshire Railway, built in 1797 to carry coal, ironstone and limestone to the ironworks and the docks for export.

The quality of food available in towns improved considerably. Prior to the railways, cattle and sheep had been brought long distances along drovers' roads to the towns for slaughter and sale – the result was thin cattle and tough meat. The railways brought fresh meat, vegetables and milk and, for the first time in many inland towns, fish. Milk had been scarce because it was perishable but the railways ran early milk trains from rural areas to towns.

The railways also caused the depression of agricultural prices in 1879 when prices fell despite a bad harvest because alternative food sources could now be easily tapped. The development of steamships and railways in Britain and the USA made it easy and cheap to import prairie wheat from America. This caused many British and European farmers to change from wheat to pasture, dairy farming, fruit farming and market gardening, thus increasing the availability of such food in the newly expanded urban markets. Railways therefore enabled the growth of large towns by providing commuting services for city workers and making available sufficient food of edible quality. There were still cattle grazing within a mile of city centres at Ancoats (Manchester) and Paddington (London), but the railway extended the area of supply of foodstuffs to the whole country and with the coming of refrigeration in the 1870s extended it to most parts of the British Empire through railways and steamships.

The railway and the tram led to the development of large seaside resorts, linked to the industrial centres. Blackpool served Lancashire; Skegness and Great Yarmouth attracted travellers from the Midlands towns; Barri and Porthcawl received holidaymakers from the Welsh mining valleys; and towns such as Brighton, Bournemouth, Margate and Southend served the people of London. Spas such as Buxton, Cheltenham and Llandrindod were visited for the health characteristics of their waters. All of these places were now hours rather than days away from the industrial towns, where fares were affordable by many, and where people could be taken in large numbers so making financially viable the opening of hotels and boarding houses, parks, beach developments and entertainments.

The railways had a major impact on the financial world. They were major users of capital and provided much extra work for clerks in the

City's banking houses. Consequently, there was an increase in demand for railway transport to take these commuting clerks to work. The railway also affected retail distribution. Small shops emerged in any settlement which had a railway, since they could now obtain a variety of consumer goods. Chain stores developed particularly in food and clothing from the 1890s, and new multiple stores were built in large towns to serve a much wider urban area with customers travelling into town on the railway. Businesses like Selfridges, Harrods, and Whiteley's developed in London, G H Lee in Liverpool, and Lewis's and Kendal Milne in Manchester. Conversely, the small shops in the London suburbs lost some business as it was now cheap to travel to the central shopping area. However, as real disposable income increased so retailing expanded generally, although local fairs and markets declined and the travelling merchant was much reduced in economic importance. The influence of large cities increased and London became the real centre of power.

One of the most noticeable social effects of the railways was the standardisation of time. Local time was effectively removed and Greenwich Mean Time introduced throughout Britain.

CONCLUSION

Thus historically transport changes have had a marked effect on urban spatial characteristics and activities into the 21st century. This relationship has been continuous and interactive; while the transport system determines the shape and size of the city, previous growth of the city's layout (eg the Roman structure of central Chester) affects the road layout, the location of railways and canals and determines which transport modes are possible (Hill et al, 1997). Transport changes affect social and physical aspects of urban life. They influence accessibility which in turn affects location choice and the economic success of individuals and business, thus affecting prosperity and the location of housing in relation to work/leisure locations and land (eg agricultural land on the edge of the urban area) not influenced by the original transport change (eg the arrival of the railway). Thus the impact of transport on urban growth and on subsequent urban regeneration and the interaction of both is often far wider than may at first be supposed.

This is the first of four analyses illustrating the links between transport and economic growth. Transport does not cause growth, but allows it to take place, and a more efficient form of transport emerging in the second half of the 19th century – the railway – enabled greater volumes to be carried in less time and for significantly lower cost. This increased output, productivity and profits as well as accelerating the growth of urban centres of varying sizes.

REFERENCES

Baines E (1835) History of Cotton Manufacture. London.

Edwards D & Pigram R (1983) The Golden Years of Metropolitan Railway. Midas Books, Tunbridge Wells.

Edwards D (1977) & Pigram R, Metro Memories – A Pictorial History of Metroland. Midas Books, Tunbridge Wells.

(EW 1861) Edward Weller, Engraver, 34 Red lion Square, 1861 and onwards.

Hamilton K and Potter S (1985) Losing Track. Routledge & Kegan Paul, London.

Hill E, Wenban-Smith A, Simmonds D, Grant M, & Sidebotham J, (1997) Demonstrating the regeneration impacts of transport investment, European Transport Forum, Transportation Methods, Vol 1. PTRC London.

LWT (1983) The Making of Modern London: The Horse and the Railway. London Weekend Television.

Measom G (1852) The Illustrated Guide to the Great Western Railway. Marshall, London. (Reprinted by Berkshire County Library, 1983).

Peacock T (1978) Great Western London Suburb Services, Oakwood Press, Blandford.

Rostow W W (1960) The Stages of Economic Growth. Cambridge University Press, London.

Symonds M V (1979) Coal Mining in the Llanelli Area. Llanelli Borough Council Publishing.

CHAPTER 15

Transport and Economic Activity

DEFINITION

An area in need of economic regeneration can be best defined by reference to its economic features:

(a) a high level of unemployment;
(b) a low income per head;
(c) migration of population, especially younger members, out of the area in search of better paid jobs or indeed any job;
(d) the economic activities on which earlier prosperity was based are in decline, eg coal mining, heavy industry;
(e) an unattractive environment, possibly partly the result of earlier economic development, with industrial dereliction and an unsatisfactory choice of town centre shops and out of date housing.

OPTIONS FOR GROWTH

New types of industry

In such areas the basic need is to attract new economic activities. These could be light industrial factories producing electronic equipment, electrical domestic goods, clothing or food processing. New jobs have also been provided by office developments, and white collar jobs have risen from being 16 per cent of the working population in 1951 to over 42 per cent in 2003. An increasing number of companies are now moving head office departments from London to the regions, to Wales or to Scotland where office rents are considerably cheaper, and large government offices have been moved to areas of high unemployment, such as the Inland Revenue to Bradford; the Driver and Vehicle Licence Agency to Swansea; the Forestry Commission to Edinburgh; and Companies House to Cardiff.

Although some employees at such establishments are experts transferred from London, the majority of jobs are in clerical/computer areas which creates work for local people.

In many industrial areas, tourism is seen as having the greatest potential for the future. Towns in which, 30 years ago, the concept of tourism as an important employer would have been inconceivable are now using government capital grants and tourist board marketing to create jobs in the tourist industry. The Big Pit Museum at Blaenafon, Wales and the Cornish tin mines have provided full size 'working models' of industrial archaeology which are each year attracting large visitor numbers. Land which was once a scene of steel and coal industries has been cleared and recreated as tourist centres.

Jobs to people or people to jobs?

Should attempts be made to 'save' areas of high unemployment? Some would argue that it is better in the long term to encourage a percentage of the population to move to more prosperous areas and then to readjust the region at a lower level of economic activity.

Against such a view is the argument that the social infrastructure – schools, hospitals, roads – would be under-used in such circumstances but would have to be duplicated in the areas to which the people migrated.

Some industrial movement might be encouraged within a depressed area. Narrow valleys, while suitable for coal mining or even a long thin steel plant, may not be suitable for a modern car or electrical components factory. New jobs in these industries might be easier to attract to larger land areas or to green field sites. The contrast between the lack of industrial development in the Rhondda valley and the economic expansion in the areas around Bridgend and the Vale of Glamorgan, adjacent to the M4 motorway and the main railway line, illustrates this.

The development of housing along the route of railway services out of London remains a characteristic of land use change being affected by transport facilities (see Chapter 14).

FORMS OF STATE AID

Aid from national governments, EU structural funds or development banks (eg European Bank for Reconstruction and Development, World Bank) is geared to making low economic activity areas more attractive to the industrialist, so creating more job opportunities. Aid may take the form of:

- the provision of low rent factories, often in industrial estates;
- a grant towards the construction of premises or the installation of plant and equipment;
- a reduction in taxes or rates in the early years of a new industry to assist its cash flow position;
- grants to train labour or to pay a part of their wages;
- aid to industries/offices towards the cost of moving their location, and aid to workers involved in such moves (eg removal and furnishing costs);
- awarding government contracts to firms in redevelopment areas;

- the construction of 'new towns' to improve the image and living conditions of the region;
- the provision of infrastructure grants for new roads, railways or airports to improve movement of goods and people;
- grants towards the construction of a railway on a less efficient route (eg the decision to build the TGV Nord/Eurostar high speed line via Lille rather than Amiens on the London-Paris route.

GOVERNMENT POLICY IN BRITAIN AND IN IRELAND

The basis of government policy is to 'achieve sustainable development (DOE, 1994) through striking the right balance between securing economic development, protecting the environment and sustaining future quality of life'. The problems of increasing traffic cannot be solved solely through building more roads but also through improving existing roads (DfT, 2003). The policy document argues that motorways (including the M25) are often bypasses and limit the environmental disbenefits to existing corridors whilst providing arteries for trade. The Trans European Network is essential in facilitating trade and improving economic and social cohesion through improving existing routes and providing missing links – they are a 'high-quality' not necessarily a 'motorway' network.

The Scottish Executive sees the provision of transport and transport infrastructure as serving the diverse needs of the Scottish economy through:

- providing competitive and sustainable modes of transport to enable journeys which offer speed, reliability, safety and convenience
- taking into account the needs of deprived, remote and island communities
- enhancing the competitiveness of the economy within an environmentally sensitive framework.

Its 'comprehensive transport policy' has to be sustainable in environmental, economic and social terms but which meets the needs of Scotland in remaining economically competitive in world terms (SO, 1997). The Green Paper makes clear that improvements in the Scottish roads network over the last twenty years have accompanied the increasing strength of the Scottish economy with substantial reductions in journey times. That success indicates there may well be reduced prospects from similar investment but 'the network will remain a critical aspect of transport infrastructure'.

However the Green Paper also indicates that the current assessment methods do not examine amongst other things the impact of transport infrastructure on economic growth (see Chapter 10) and that the same relationship does not exist in all cases of inward investment; roads will not therefore always assist competitiveness (SO, 1997).

The assessment of road schemes has to be considered within an integrated transport policy (see Chapter 12) and aspects of the present cost-benefit appraisal could be extended to examine environmental and economic regeneration aspects (NATA, 1999; SACTRA, 1999). A national trunk road programme (NAfW, 2002) would seek to establish the priority aims for road investment to assist economic regeneration (bearing in mind financial and environmental constraints on new provision and the balance of the latter with personal mobility while most governments' objective in transport will be to provide better road rail and air links to bring business closer to major markets elsewhere in Europe together with a need for policies that will promote the regeneration of towns and villages in urban and rural areas.

The peripheral location of Wales and indeed Ireland with its associated economic and social problems are reflected in Objective 2 (industrial area) and Objective 5 (rural area) status and the Interreg position. These countries require good communications between them and the Trans-European Network, for example, and the southern (M4/A48/A40) corridor and northern (A55 Expressway) corridor are important to Ireland's links to the main European Union markets but consistent with the EU's objectives on sustainability. The aim of road and rail construction programme in economic development terms is to:

- provide effective and economic (competitive) access to the Single European Market
- provide a network of good quality strategic roads thereby reducing journey times and operating costs for commercial users
- assist in economic regeneration and promote tourism.

It is important to provide good road links with other European countries (EC, 1995; EC, 1997) as well as a good network of internal roads which link effectively into strategic European highways, in particular the upgrading of the two corridor routes to Ireland, thus improving access to ferry ports at Fishguard, Pembroke Dock, Swansea and Holyhead.

There is clearly considerable concern amongst governments in the peripheral areas of Europe exemplified by the greater emphasis on achieving high quality transport links by governments in Scotland, Wales, northern and south western England, Ireland, Greece, Hungary, Poland and the Baltic states compared with those authorities within the 'blue' banana of the European Union where economic activity is at its highest.

THE ATLANTIC ARC

The 'motorways of the seas' concept has a primary objective of transferring freight from the road sector to the short sea shipping lanes. The first
area under consideration by the European Commission under the Interreg
Programme is the Atlantic Arc, incorporating Portugal, Spain, France,
Ireland and the United Kingdom.

The globalisation of production and trade has an impact on consumption
and consequently on the increasing need for transport between producer
and consumer. A report by the Atlantic Transnational Network (ATN,
2005) identifies other effects of such a change in modal split:

- Through an analysis of the market determine how much freight will
  transfer to the sea route. The predominant criteria are cost and existing
  practice.
- The infrastructure improvements required to link the ports to the
  consumer market or the source of materials for export.
- The employment generative effect. This is not a factor in the
  commercial decision, but the public sector authorities see market intervention as a means of providing additional jobs.

In this chapter it is the extent to which the motorways of the seas will
generate new employment in these western peripheral areas that this
study will show. A study of port facility development and its effect on
regional GDP growth (Villaverde Castro and Coto-Millan, 1997) in
Santander (Basque country), northern Spain concluded that the contribution of the port was in line with other service industries. Other studies,
such as those on the effect of high speed train services or the construction
of an airport, conclude that development may bring new jobs but may
equally displace workers in another area (Tomkins *et al*, 1998) where
there is less well developed infrastructure. The STAG (2003) guidance
on evaluating benefits has an interesting approach – if the 'redistributive
impact was to an area of greater need then this would be seen as a
benefit'. However, a need to distinguish between overall growth and
redistribution of benefits following an investment is necessary to avoid
double-counting.

Location criteria – an overview

Industrialists wishing to locate a new factory and local authorities wishing
to attract them identified the following criteria used in making location
decisions:

- existing production facilities – care of labour force;
- labour availability, eg unemployment, female;
- labour relations;

- labour suitability – experience in similar industry, eg declining steel industry and replacement car industry;
- wages levels;
- site availability;
- transport infrastructure
  - roads (especially motorways)
  - rail siding – high speed intercity
  - siding facilities and grants for freight operations;
- government financial and other assistance;
- amenities – housing, sports, culture, leisure, shopping – particularly if key workers or executives are to be attracted to the area.

LOCATION CRITERIA – THE POSITION OF TRANSPORT

The transport criterion is one with which this chapter is concerned, the relative importance given to it by inward investors and the extent to which good quality transport infrastructure has an effect on economic growth.

A survey for Lloyd's Bank (2001) based on responses from 1000 companies in Great Britain asked which factors were considered the most important in determining the location of industrial or commercial premises. The transport element ranked at least fourth overall and has been the second most important factor. However it has to be seen in the context of all the other locational criteria including for example specific skills of the local workforce and government incentives. It was of even more importance to companies involved in distribution (including manufacturers), retailing and catering (Van de Vliet, 1997).

In the goods market transport can increase producer efficiency because it increases competition, as transport facilitates trade and commerce by widening the market area for goods. Overall within the European Union, international commercial theory suggests that free movement of goods and people results in higher productivity and increased purchasing power. Two arguments almost diametrically opposed are put forward. There is an argument that economies of scale, structural adjustment or a more widespread availability of new technologies are all made possible through a high quality transport network. However, the argument put forward elsewhere in this book (see Chapter 2) is that, under perfect competition, the producer will locate in the area of lowest cost. Thus the expansion eastwards of the European Union will, it is argued, see more manufacturing jobs located there than in the more 'western' states so long as wages in, for example, Poland or Latvia remain relatively low compared with France or the UK. This is one aspect of the competitive market. This is the two-way road concept on a large geographical scale. Thus 'in response to new competition from distant areas, for example, inefficient (or perhaps higher cost) local industries may be put out of business' (ECMT, 2001).

However, the effect of transport is not restricted to the infrastructure quality. There are also the efficiency issues linked to accessibility to domestic and international suppliers, knowledge and labour. The quality factors (see Chapter 1) such as distances, journey time, reliability and risk will affect employers, operations and investment decisions.

At High Wycombe, Buckinghamshire, the location of a 'mega'-brewery by Courage plc to replace three smaller breweries located in the London urban area was determined by the ease of access to the motorway network of southeast England via the M25; but the employment gain in rural Buckinghamshire was at the expense of closures and job losses in the East End of London.

These may also be affected by geographical accessibility (real or perceived) and congestion (McQuiad and Greig, 2002). Associated commuting and other journeys also affect costs.

The role of transport

The argument that good transport infrastructure leads to economic growth or development is not proven. Indeed there have been many instances where the building of a new airport has not brought in large numbers of tourists or where a new road or railway has not led to new inward investment. There is some evidence at a regional level that road infrastructure improvements are positively associated with levels of new foreign direct investment (Hill and Munday, 1994).

That the whole area requires good access if economic targets are to be met is often heard from those responsible for generating new jobs. However, it may be that the absence of such infrastructure has prevented or constrained economic growth (BRF, 1994) or economic regeneration – that good transport infrastructure is a necessary, but not sufficient, condition for economic growth and development. The conclusion can only be that good transport links for countries such as Wales, Ireland, Portugal or Greece (sometimes perceived as on the periphery of Europe) are a prerequisite, if employment is to grow through economic regeneration. This is reinforced by an analysis of the economic circumstances of the world's fastest growing regional economies (IWA, 2002).

Manufacturing industry in particular requires regular and predictable delivery on a day-to-day basis – although labour-intensive private sector services also require regularity and predictability in the journey times of commuters and customers. Inward tourism, a major employer in many areas, has to be competitive in accessibility terms. Ironically those who demand high levels of accessibility also come to Wales to enjoy the peace and quiet and beautiful scenery, unhindered by the congestion and pollution (much of it caused by the motor car) of their urban lives (see for example Valuing the Environment, 2002). Transport should therefore be a driver of, not a response to, economic development.

The view of the freight industry

Freight transport touches every aspect of society and the economy; even everyday 'shopping is for consumer goods that were at some point freight' (FTA, 2004). An efficient supply chain brings the consumer all the year round product availability, up to the minute fashions and a rapid response to consumer demand. The European Union is one of the world's two biggest economies and is sustained by 'global freight routes which supply its needs competitively, at the right price, time, condition and quantity' (FTA, 2004).

Road freight accounts for over 80 per cent of EU inland freight movements, despite a rise in rail movements. This the road haulage industry suggests is due to:

- direct access to/from the collection points (door to door);
- flexibility for the manufacturer or logistics company to match capacity and demand;
- ability to operate 'just in time' delivery systems;
- lower unit costs.

The Rail Freight group would argue that the road freight industry is not responsible on its own for the infrastructure costs and that there is not a level playing field (Berkeley, 2004). In the analysis of transfers from road to rail, two Interreg studies (ATN, 2005; Arc Atlantique, 2004) identified cost as a major determinant of change and the role of cross-price elasticity (see Chapter 2) in the decision.

The companies' view

Major companies represented by the CBI consider transport to be essential to modern economic and social life in that it provides the facilities for goods and services to reach suppliers and customers and for employees to get to work and meet customers. The CBI (2003) sees Britain as on the periphery of Europe, and one common view is that only high quality domestic and international transport and reliable and short journey times support the more efficient production and supply techniques (such as JIT, 'just in time') which many firms use to maintain competitiveness.

However the CBI also views the pressures imposed by transport intensity (the level of usage of infrastructure) resulting from economic growth as an element to be considered within the environmental impact framework and that users should face appropriate prices which reflect the environmental cost. This might be achieved by reducing particular types of vehicle flow (eg motor cars) or by better design of new roads.

Nevertheless the CBI indicates that business satisfaction with the road and rail network in Britain falls below that of our major competitors within the European Union (CBI, 1995).

A study (EY, 1996) for the UK Department of Transport showed that transport can be an important element of a company's operating costs and congestion or unreliability add to costs particularly for trips involving urban distribution. Companies also usually regard nearness to the trunk road network as a major location criterion, although many are less than clear about the impact of new transport infrastructure on business costs and over 60 per cent in the survey reported benefits derived from particular transport infrastructure improvements. New areas for development may also be opened up by new infrastructure, for example estuarial crossings, but they may be more important in deciding the final location rather than reducing costs. Indeed it may not be altogether advantageous for an area if a new road or bridge provides ease of access. A company may be able to decide, for example, between Cardiff and Bristol as locations for a south of Wales/west of England regional office following the building of the Severn Crossing whereas previously they would have had two offices and more study.

Rural areas

A study (Atkins, 1997) identified several key points raised by companies considering relocation to a rural area:

- transport costs are higher than in other areas
- discomfort and inconvenience of road links is the main problem
- companies often find it difficult to persuade customers that the remoteness will not prevent deadlines being met (despite firms in the DBRW area being expert at compensating action)
- the perception by senior management that regular journeys along rural roads will be inconvenient – these people make the location decisions
- despite the problems of poor infrastructure, massive road improvements were not acceptable despite journey time benefits because of the high value put on environmental and quality of life factors by companies in the area.

DO ROADS REALLY BRING ECONOMIC SUCCESS?

Many companies and local authorities have argued this case but others have cast doubts for several reasons.

Transport infrastructure – an essential prerequisite to economic growth?

There is a body of opinion that argues that the availability and reliability of transport links are seen by business as important in achieving high levels of efficiency. Transport infrastructure can play an important part in attracting investment, serving more peripheral areas and encouraging economic regeneration (DOT, 1996). However, there is a potential conflict between business concerns for increasing the capacity of the road network, and environmental interests that have taken an opposing view. Indeed, the pollution and environmental consequences of new road (or rail) construction, or enhanced use of either mode, at particular locations can act as a disincentive to economic activity, eg tourism.

The view supporting investment, however, points to the effects of good quality transport links on competitiveness, on how transport (and congestion) affects costs and the extent to which new infrastructure has reduced operating costs (CBI, 2003). The relative weight that companies put on the level of transport costs and the predictability of transport times and schedules will determine how new infrastructure affects business investment and location decisions and thus the link between traffic growth, transport investment and economic growth.

How important a good transport system is to inward investors can be seen in a recent survey for Lloyds Bank based on responses from 1000 companies in Great Britain asking which factors were considered the most important in determining the location of industrial or commercial premises. The transport element ranked fourth overall. However, it has to be seen in the context of all the locational criteria including for example specific skills of the local workforce and government incentives. It is of even more importance to companies involved in distribution (including manufacturers), retailing and catering. For inward investment projects the site size and the state aid package remain major criteria but transport often still ranks third (Van de Vliet, 1997).

Table 15.1 indicates that transport is not the major criterion, and a recent study of the impact of the Channel Tunnel found very little positive benefit in Kent (ESRC Urban and Regional Seminar Series, Preston, 2002).

'Transport – the route to economic development' (FEDA, 2002) highlighted the need for an economic development strategy to include not only urban area considerations but also rural development, social inclusion policy, integrated transport policy and a business case approach. All are relevant in the context of peripheral areas of the European Union and other major economic units (eg North America, China, India).

Table 15.1 *Order of importance of relocation factors*

Factor	
Availability of quality workforce	6.7
Cost and availability of business/property	5.4
Overheads, e.g. rates, wages	5.2
Transport network	**4.9**
Overall business environment	4.2
Quality of personal life	3.9
Government incentive	3.0
Quality of potential local clients	2.9

8 – most important, 1 – least important
Source: Business and Market Research for Lloyds Bank, 2001

Transport infrastructure is not linked to economic growth

A number of studies however have demonstrated 'a lack of a convincing association between road investment and economic gains' (Greenpeace, 1994). The importance of transport as *the* location determinant has been questioned by European governments who concluded that transport is a 'secondary consideration in company strategy when deciding where to locate their activities'. Other costs, particularly labour, are more of an influence, because transport only accounts for 3–5 per cent of total costs. In 12 countries surveyed by the European Commission (EC Advisory Committee on Transport, 1979) an improved road link between a developed area and a relatively underdeveloped location improved the traffic flow in both directions. However, it contained the risk of investment resources being transferred from the less developed area towards the economically stronger region.

These effects can be identified in Wales in the impacts of the A55 expressway in the north and the M4 corridor in the south. Both roads were developed to enhance inward investment and attract tourists, but they also reduce travel time (for work or shopping and for road haulage) to cities outside the area. This is the so-called 'two-way road' effect (Cole, 2004; Blank, 1979), providing new opportunities for competitive firms and individuals within the region but also opening up that region to new competition from outside.

The recent Standing Advisory Committee on Trunk Road Assessment (SACTRA) report on Transport and the Economy (1999) was not definitive. Its review of available evidence led it to conclude that only modest economic enhancements as a result of road infrastructure improvements would occur *in a developed industrial economy* such as is found in western Europe. This is despite suggestions that good quality roads lead to high rates of return (using economic growth and productivity increases as measures).

SACTRA found that there was only limited statistical and case study evidence on the type and size of effect resulting from changes in transport costs. The report indicated a strong theoretical expectation that all or part of a successfully achieved transport cost reduction may subsequently be converted into a range of different wider economic impacts. This, in principle, provides for the possibility of improved economic performance. Empirical evidence of the scale and significance of such linkages is, however, both weak and disputed, and the report concluded that, while the theoretical effects listed can exist in reality, none of them are guaranteed (SACTRA, 1999: 17).

The links between infrastructure quality and economic growth have been found to be weak or non-existent, highly conditional and dependent on precise policy implementation. The reverse effects on economic growth have been evidenced. One issue is the decentralisation of economic activity into green field sites on the edge of urban areas which are difficult to serve by public transport and generate high levels of car usage.

In general therefore the conclusion has been that local conditions very much determine the effect of transport facilities on economic activity levels. Built infrastructure 'including transport is a necessary but not sufficient condition for improving economic performance' and it is most effective where rapid economic expansion is being held back by 'bottlenecks'. In particular, where 'existing infrastructure was underdeveloped, investing in transport capital schemes in conditions of low economic growth where the capacity was already in place was unlikely to boost economic activity' (EEDA, 2000).

A further study (OECD, 2002) into the impact of transport infrastructure on regional development found that greater social inclusion was unlikely to be achieved through improved accessibility and transport alone, but also required parallel initiatives including work skills, housing and social policy. There have also been indications of a weak link between transport investment and regeneration because of a lack of co-ordination between the two policy areas (Lawless and Dabinett, 1995).

The Greenpeace report is very critical of a British Road Federation report that presented the case for economic benefits of road investment through reduced congestion, operating costs and journey times. Greenpeace argues that assumptions based on additional road capacity freeing up road space and leading to these efficiencies are negated by academic and SACTRA evidence that new road capacity generates new traffic. However, Greenpeace does not dismiss the role of transport in economic development; it merely restricts the discussion to roads. The complexities of the transport industry operating through a 'variety of policies (including road, rail, combined transport and public transport) in relation to land use will reduce congestion in the location involved'. All have a role to play in economic development as 'firms need high quality infrastructure to enable them to compete in international markets and high quality local transport facilities to enable staff to make journeys to work easily using a variety of modes'.

There is therefore a considerable degree of divergence of views in the effectiveness of good transport links in assisting economic development and growth.

Roads and land use planning – the wrong development?

The development of new road schemes is often planned separately from land use change proposals. Local authorities have been unable to influence trunk road plans in their area and attempts to revitalise towns and cities have failed because 'trunk roads have attracted development to greenfield sites making town centre regeneration more difficult and often in opposition to local authority policies' (Transport 2000, 1997). Thus while roads have led to economic developments and new job opportunities, these may not necessarily be the most appropriate. The use of route or corridor action plans (of the Scottish Executive type) examines corridors as a whole including road and rail transport options, the problems, the community needs and the economic impact.

POLICY IN OTHER EU MEMBER STATES

The policies in Great Britain have to be related to those policies in its nearest neighbours – France, Germany and the Netherlands (Blank, 1979).

The Netherlands

The economy is dependent on the distribution sector with the port of Rotterdam and Schipol Airport being major international hubs which require efficient freight and passenger links to other parts of the European market in order to maintain their market leadership. However growth has to be achieved through a sustainable policy. The road network is not the solution to most problems and the use of rail for the new major freight link from Rotterdam to other major European cities and a link between modal split and land use are examples of the policies being pursued.

France

The creation of a Master Plan for roads and the evolution of the TGV high speed train network are seen by the French Government as essential in improving regional accessibility for the western parts of France. The development of the Atlantic and Mediterranean seaboards will require high quality road and rail links as a prerequisite though not a guarantee of rivalling the London-Frankfurt-Milan 'golden banana' of economic growth and enabling all parts of France to be directly linked to other areas of the European Union (UIC, 1992).

The investment appraisal techniques for new TGV train services in France (see Chapter 9) incorporate employment impacts. However an ECMT (1991) report indicates that infrastructure does not automatically have positive effects on local development and anyway those events are themselves affected by local influences. The Paris-Lyon TGV service begun in 1983 produced considerable journey time savings but did not affect the pattern of economic activity. While some firms in Lyon were able to penetrate the Paris market, Paris industrial and commercial organisations began seeing Lyons as a remote suburb, so that 'the two areas merge and increase further the peripheral status of the Lyon region'.

Germany

The objective of transport infrastructure development (the Federal Transport Infrastructure Plan – BVWP – 1992) is to provide the mobility needed to make Germany a location of economic activity. This however will be achieved through integration of different transport modes for both freight (especially the use of combined modes) and a shift of domestic air traffic from air to high speed rail. The particular needs of the eastern part of Germany in achieving good links to other EU states requires high levels of expenditure to upgrade the infrastructure (ECMT, 1991).

CONCLUSION

Transport and economic development policy

A strong economy, a sustainable environment and an inclusive society are three sound transport policies. They all influence development (some by requiring development, others by protecting areas from development), and they all influence movement patterns.

The 19th and 20th centuries have seen an explosion in the variety of jobs, the variety of education and training opportunities and the variety of leisure and social activities that development projects are designed to facilitate. The range of locations being made available for those activities encourages travel.

As national output per head grows, so does the range of human activities, both for society as a whole and for the individual lifestyle. Thus every development proposal has to be examined not only for its economic, environmental and social impact but also for its transport implications.

Efficient transport is fundamental to the efficiency of any economy. The ability to move materials is an integral part of all sectors – supplies for manufacturing plants; animal feed supplies for farms; retail goods. The ability of visitors to get to and from tourist areas and to travel within those areas is also important for the tourism industry. The costs of transport in terms of direct costs and costs caused by delays are important influences on business competitiveness and contribute to investment decisions. As a result, transport networks can help to make regions of Wales more competitive, especially for inward investors that are widely believed to be particularly sensitive to transport links in reaching decisions on location. Local transport links also shape the availability of labour to existing and prospective employers.

In any strategy there has to be an awareness of the 'two-way road'. It may attract new jobs but it can also lead to centralisation of production and distribution nearer to the markets.

It may also have social impacts such as house price increases and in some areas it can lead and has led to cultural change as a result of insensitive incomers (eg rural Wales, Cornwall and southern France) or cultural conflict in countries where European visitors may be insensitive to the modesty of dress codes.

All modes of transport are important to supporting economic prosperity. New and improved roads have an important role in opening up development but they do not create jobs on their own. Investment in roads needs to be part of a wider strategy to promote economic development at national, regional and local level. Equal consideration needs to be given to the potential of rail, sea and air transport to support economic growth.

But sustainability and integrated transport are seen as being in the vanguard of public policy. Accessibility by appropriate non-car modes and reducing the need for travel have become key principles in our land use planning. To be successful, however, two catalysts emerge – changes in public behaviour and attitudes and increased investment. As a part of this, current thinking is changing and more consideration is being given to an assessment of the transport (not traffic) impact of new land uses, green travel plans and the use of planning conditions to minimise the adverse effects of economic regeneration.

In the UK, these reverse a long period marked by competition within and between modes rather than by co-ordination and integration. Government objectives are typically to promote accessibility and choice at the same time as reducing damage to the environment and risks to health and safety (TFW, 2001).

The impact of transport

The overall conclusion is that an efficient transport network is a necessary pre-condition for economic growth with two reservations:

1. it does not guarantee economic growth
2. it is not sufficient on its own to encourage economic growth but is inter-dependent on a series of factors which determine the location and expansion of economic activity.

There was a clear link from the 1970s in the minds of most inward investors that transport costs and the total quality of transport (including journey time predictability) are important considerations in business location (Hart, 1993). This view is still generally held; there has to be a sufficiently large amount of infrastructure to provide a stimulus to other factors; transportation acts as a catalyst for growth and productivity change (Gillen, 1996).

An improved transport policy can unlock unfulfilled economic potential in an area; it can save transport costs; it can increase the level of accessibility particularly for those industries where it is of great importance – manufacturing, distribution and tourism; it can change the perceptions of an area, and where the latter inhibits growth it can encourage economic activity.

However above all it is a complementary factor and represents only one element of a package of improvements designed to revive economic activity, to increase employment levels, and to attract new investment or expand existing industries (Cole, 1984, Atkins, 1997).

Two final points to consider are firstly whether the jobs 'created' by new transport infrastructure and other factors are new or are displaced from elsewhere thus providing no overall economic benefit. The European Commission in a recent internal report (LTT, 1997) suggested that the benefits of the Trans-European Road Network (TERN) may have been over-estimated because the assumption was of no overcapacity in the economy and that euroute construction would not merely move investment. A study of the relative costs of manufacture and transport (Granada, 1997) indicated that low cost transport made it financially attractive for companies to produce a pair of trousers in Portugal and in Lithuania for sale in the high income countries of the European Union. The saving in labour costs outweighed considerably the transport costs in the final unit cost per garment.

Secondly transport may be a less effective form of public investment than other forms of expenditure used to boost economic activity.

REFERENCES

Arc Atlantique (2004) The promotion of short sea shipping in the Atlantic Arc report (Interreg IIIB).

Atkins (1997) Transport investment in rural areas, Report for the Development Board for Rural Wales; Submission to SACTRA, W S Atkins, Epsom, Surrey.

ATN (2005) Ports and hinterlands report, Atlantic Transnational Network (Interreg IIIB)/National Assembly for Wales.

Berkeley, T (2004) Rail Freight Group, *Hansard*, House of Lords, London.

Blonk, WAG (Ed) (1979) *Transport and Regional Development*, Gower, Aldershot, England.

Bray, J (1995) Spend, Spend, Spend – How the Department of Transport wastes money and manages the roads programme.

BRF (1994) Roads and Jobs: the economic impact of different levels of expenditure in the roads programme, British Road Federation, London.

BVWP (1992) German Federal Ministry of Transport, Berlin.

CBI (1995a) Moving forward, a business strategy for transport. Confederation of British Industry, London.

CBI (1995b) Missing links: settling national transport priorities, Confederation of British Industry, London.

CBI (2003) *The UK as a place to do business: Is Transport Holding the UK Back?*, Confederation of British Industry, London.

Cole, S (1984) Alternative locations for a Nissan Car Manufacturing Plant, Alwyd County Council, Yr Wyddgng, Wales.

Cole, S (2004) Transport Strategy for the North of Wales, Liverpool Research Group in Macroeconomics Business Prospect vol 2 (1).

DfT (2003) *Trunk Roads in England: Review*, Department for Transport, HMSO, London.

DfT (2002) *Valuing the Environment*, Department for Transport, London.

DOE (1994) *Sustainable Development, The UK Strategy*, Department of the Environment *et al*, HMSO, London.

DOT (1996) *Transport: The Way Forward*, Department of Transport, London.

EC (1995) The Trans-European Transport Network, European Commission, DGVII, Brussels.

EC (1997) PACT: a user's guide, European Commission DGVII, Brussels.

ECMT (1991) Transport and the spatial distribution of activities, European Conference of Ministers of Transport No. 85 (Plassord, F), OECD, Paris.

ECMT (2001) Transport and economic development, Conclusions of Round Table 119, European Conference of Ministers of Transport, Brussels.

EEDA (2000) Infrastructure benchmarking study, SDG report to East of England Development Agency, Cambridge.

EY (1996) Ernst and Young: Survey of 250 companies and consultants report for the Department of Transport, London.

FEDA (2002) Transport, economic development, inward investment and tourism, Workshop at the Federation of Economic Development Authorities (FEDA) Conference, York. The author was the facilitator.

FTA (2004) *Trade Routes*, Freight Transport Association, Leamington Spa.

Gillen, D & Waters, WG (1996) Transport infrastructure, investment and economic development, *Logistics and Transportation Review*, vol 32 (1), London.

Granada (1997) Research on transport/labour costs in Europe for World in Action.

Greenpeace (1994) (J Whitelegg) *Roads, Jobs and the Economy*, Greenpeace, London.

Hart, T (1993) Transport investment in disadvantaged regions (quoting Logan, 1971), *Urban Studies*, vol 30/2, Pergamon Press, Oxford.

Hill, S and Munday M (1994) The UK regional distribution of FDI, Macmillan, London.

IWA (2002) *Competing with the World: A study of the economic development strategies of the world's richest nations*, Institute of Welsh Affairs, Cardiff.

Lawless, P and Dabinett, G (1995) Urban regeneration and transport investment: a research agenda, in Environment and Planning 27(7) July 1995.

LTT (1997) Roads and economic progress (24 April), *Local Transport Today*, London.

McQuiad, R W and Greig, M (2002) A model of the commuting range of unemployed job seekers, in *Transport Planning, Logistics and Social Mismatch*, ed D Pitfield, Pion, London.

NAfW (2002) Trunk Road Forward Programme/Blaenraglen Cefnffyrdd, National Assembly for Wales, Cardiff.

NATA (1999) *Integrated Transport Economics Appraisal: New approach to transport appraisal*, Department for Transport, London.

OECD (2002) *Impact of Transport Infrastructure on Regional Development*, OECD, Paris.

SACTRA (1999) Transport and the Economy, HMSO, London.

Scottish Transport Appraisal Guidelines, Scottish Executive, Edinburgh.

SO (1997) Keeping Scotland Moving, Scotland Office, Edinburgh.

STAG (2003) Scottish Transport Appraisal Guidelines, Scottish Executive, Edinburgh.

TFW (2001) *Transport Framework for Wales*, National Assembly for Wales, Cardiff.

Tomkins, J *et al* (1998) Noise versus access: the impact of an airport in an urban property market, *Urban Studies*, 35.

Transport 2000 (1997) Roads 21, a roads policy for the next century, London.

UIC (1992) European Infrastructure Master Plan, Union Internationale des Chemins de fer, Paris.

Valuing the Environment (2002) Department for Transport, London.

Van de Vliet, A (1997) Urban pulling power, *Management Today*, September 1997.

Villaverde Castro, J and Coto-Millan, P (1997) Economic impact analysis of Santander port on its hinterland, *International Journal of Transport Economics*, 24.

Whitelegg, J (1994) Roads, jobs and the economy, Greenpeace, London.

Index